DATABASE AND APPLICATION SECURITY XV

IFIP - The International Federation for Information Processing

IFIP was founded in 1960 under the auspices of UNESCO, following the First World Computer Congress held in Paris the previous year. An umbrella organization for societies working in information processing, IFIP's aim is two-fold: to support information processing within its member countries and to encourage technology transfer to developing nations. As its mission statement clearly states,

IFIP's mission is to be the leading, truly international, apolitical organization which encourages and assists in the development, exploitation and application of information technology for the benefit of all people.

IFIP is a non-profitmaking organization, run almost solely by 2500 volunteers. It operates through a number of technical committees, which organize events and publications. IFIP's events range from an international congress to local seminars, but the most important are:

- The IFIP World Computer Congress, held every second year;
- open conferences;
- working conferences.

The flagship event is the IFIP World Computer Congress, at which both invited and contributed papers are presented. Contributed papers are rigorously refereed and the rejection rate is high.

As with the Congress, participation in the open conferences is open to all and papers may be invited or submitted. Again, submitted papers are stringently refereed.

The working conferences are structured differently. They are usually run by a working group and attendance is small and by invitation only. Their purpose is to create an atmosphere conducive to innovation and development. Refereeing is less rigorous and papers are subjected to extensive group discussion.

Publications arising from IFIP events vary. The papers presented at the IFIP World Computer Congress and at open conferences are published as conference proceedings, while the results of the working conferences are often published as collections of selected and edited papers.

Any national society whose primary activity is in information may apply to become a full member of IFIP, although full membership is restricted to one society per country. Full members are entitled to vote at the annual General Assembly, National societies preferring a less committed involvement may apply for associate or corresponding membership. Associate members enjoy the same benefits as full members, but without voting rights. Corresponding members are not represented in IFIP bodies. Affiliated membership is open to non-national societies, and individual and honorary membership schemes are also offered.

DATABASE AND APPLICATION SECURITY XV

IFIP TC11 / WG11.3
Fifteenth Annual Working Conference on
Database and Application Security
July 15–18, 2001, Niagara on the Lake, Ontario, Canada

Edited by

Martin S. Olivier
Rand Afrikaans University
South Africa

David L. Spooner
Rensselaer Polytechnic Institute
USA

KLUWER ACADEMIC PUBLISHERS
BOSTON / DORDRECHT / LONDON

Distributors for North, Central and South America:
Kluwer Academic Publishers
101 Philip Drive
Assinippi Park
Norwell, Massachusetts 02061 USA
Telephone (781) 871-6600
Fax (781) 681-9045
E-Mail <kluwer@wkap.com>

Distributors for all other countries:
Kluwer Academic Publishers Group
Post Office Box 322
3300 AH Dordrecht, THE NETHERLANDS
Telephone 31 786 576 000
Fax 31 786 576 474
E-Mail <services@wkap.nl>

Electronic Services <http://www.wkap.nl>

Library of Congress Cataloging-in-Publication Data

IFIP TC11/WG11.3 Working Conference on Database and Application Security (15th : 2001: Niagara-on-the-Lake, Ont.)
Database and application security XV : IFIP TC11/WG11.3 Fifteenth Annual Working Conference on Database and Application Security, July 15-18, 2001, Niagara-on-the-Lake, Ontario, Canada / edited by Martin S. Olivier, David L. Spooner.
p. cm. — (International Federation for Information Processing ; 87)
Includes bibliographical references and index.
ISBN 1-4020-7041-1
1. Database security—Congresses. I. Olivier, Martin S. II. Spooner, David L. III. Title. IV. International Federation for Information Processing (Series) ; 87.

QA76.9.D314 I33 2001
005.8—dc21 2002016211

Printed on acid-free paper.

Printed in Great Britain by IBT Global, London.

Contents

Part VIII New Application Areas

Part IX Panel and discussion

Preface

This volume contains the edited papers from the Fifteenth Annual IFIP WG 11.3 Working Conference on Database and Applications Security, held July 15–18, 2001 in Niagara on the Lake, Ontario, Canada. Preliminary versions of the papers were distributed at the conference. Following the conference, authors had the opportunity to revise their papers for publication here. In addition, we include a summary of the discussions that took place during the conference sessions. As a result, this book captures the important research issues in database and application security today and documents recent progress in addressing them.

We would like to thank the many people involved in making the conference a success. In particular, we would like to thank Sylvia Osborn, the general chair of the conference, for a great job hosting the conference, doing all the local arrangements, and organizing the panel. We also thank those who submitted papers, reviewed papers, and attended the conference, some but not all of whom are listed below and throughout this book. We also thank Pierangela Samarati, chair of IFIP WG 11.3, who handled the coordination of the conference with IFIP and Sujeet Shenoi who once again arranged travel funds to enable many people to attend the conference. Finally, we thank the Office of Naval Research, the IBM Centre for Advanced Studies, and The University of Western Ontario for their financial support of the conference.

Listed below are many of the people who helped organise the conference.

General chair: Sylvia Osborn, The University of Western Ontario

Program chairs:

- Martin S. Olivier, Rand Afrikaans University
- David L. Spooner, Rensselaer Polytechnic Institute

IFIP WG 11.3 chair: Pierangela Samarati, University of Milan

Reviewers:

- Vijay Atluri, Rutgers University

- Elisa Bertino, University of Milan
- Jerome Carerre, ONERA Centre de Toulouse
- Sabrina de Capitani di Vimercati, Universita di Brescia
- Steven A. Demurjian, The University of Connecticut
- Lucas Dreyer, Rand Afrikaans University and Arivia.kom
- Wolfgang Eÿmayr, Software Competence Center Hagenberg
- Don Faatz, MITRE Corporation
- Eduardo B. Fernandez, Florida Atlantic University
- Michael Gertz, University of California, Davis
- Dieter Gollmann, Microsoft Research
- Ehud Gudes, Ben-Gurion University
- Thomas H. Hinke, National Aeronautics and Space Administration
- Tom Johnsten, Western Illinois University
- Carl Landwehr, Mitretek Systems
- T. Y. Lin, SJSU
- J. Bret Michael, Naval Postgraduate School
- Marta Oliva, University of Lleida
- Sylvia Osborn, The University of Western Ontario
- Brajendra Panda, University of North Dakota
- George Pangalos, Aristotelean University of Thessaloniki
- Joon S. Park, US Naval Research Lab / ITT Industries
- Günther Pernul, University of Essen
- Charles E. Phillips, Jr. (Chip), University of Connecticut
- Pierangela Samarati, University of Milan
- Indrajit Ray, University of Michigan-Dearborn
- Indrakshi Ray, University of Michigan-Dearborn
- Adrian Spalka, Univ of Bonn, Germany
- Sujeet Shenoi, University of Tulsa
- Roshan Thomas, NAI Labs at Network Associates
- Dan Thomsen, Secure Computing Corporation
- Reind P. van de Riet, Vrije Universiteit
- Marianne Winslett, University of Illinois
- Simon Wiseman, Defence Evaluation and Research Agency

DAVID L SPOONER AND MARTIN S OLIVIER

I

KEYNOTE ADDRESS

RECENT ADVANCES IN ACCESS CONTROL MODELS

Sushil Jajodia
Center for Secure Information Systems
George Mason University, Fairfax VA 22030-4444, USA
jajodia@gmu.edu

Duminda Wijesekera
Center for Secure Information Systems
George Mason University, Fairfax VA 22030-4444, USA
dwijesek@gmu.edu

Abstract Advances in application areas bring new dimensions to access control needs. This paper discusses several access control models that have been recently proposed to address these emerging needs including models that provide policy-neutral flexible access control and their efficient implementations; models that incorporate richer semantics for access control in emerging Internet applications, such as adding provisions; and models for XML documents. We also discuss the recent work on policy algebras and subject identity issues in secure federations.

Keywords: Access control, security, security policy

1. INTRODUCTION

Traditionally, access control plays an integral part in overall system security. Over the years, many different access control models have been developed, and discretionary and mandatory access control models have received considerable attention. Discretionary access control is based on having subjects, objects, and operations as primitives and policies that grant access permissions of the form (o, s, a), where subject o is allowed to execute operation a on object o. Mandatory access control is based on having clearance levels for subjects and classification labels for objects as primitives and policies that grant accesses to subjects whose clearance levels are higher than those of the objects they access. These models have been used in the commercial and military domains, and implemented in operating systems, database management systems and object-oriented systems.

Advances in application areas bring new dimensions to access control models. The needs to support multiple access control policies in one security domain, Internet-based transactions, cooperating coalitions, and workflow systems have brought new challenges to access control. In response, new access control models are being proposed to address these emerging needs.

Section 2 addresses problems posed by and solutions proposed to solve the problems in the area of multiple access control policies in one security domain. Section 3 discusses the concept of *provisional authorizations* that was introduced to meet the needs in the area of Internet commerce. In response to a user request, these applications requires decisions that go beyond the traditional *yes/no* answers. Section 4 addresses problems faced in merging multiple security policies of collaborating organizations. Section 5 addresses issues related to managing identities of subjects in such cases. Section 6 discusses role-based access control(RBAC), access control problems posed by extensible markup language (XML) documents, and workflow systems. Finally, Section 7 concludes the paper.

2. NEED FOR FLEXIBLE ACCESS CONTROL MODELS

Large numbers of access control models proposed over the years [Dobson and McDermid, 1989] have been developed with a number of pre-defined policies in mind and thereby have introduced a sense of *inflexibility*. Two alternatives accommodate more than one access control model simultaneously. The first is to have more than one access control mechanism running at the same time, one for each policy. The second is to make access control an application responsibility. The first alternative calls for every application to be closely bound to its access control module, which decreases their portability. The second alternative requires all applications to enforce a consistent access control. Additionally, the responsibility of enforcing access control is vested in applications; it will not impose the same rigorous standards of verification and testing imposed on system code.

Consequently, both alternatives are undesirable. This can be seen by considering a number of access control policies that have been used over the years [Castano et al., 1994]. A popular policy is the *closed world* policy, where accesses that cannot be derived from thoses explicitly authorized are prohibited. A rarely used alternative is the *open world* policy, where accesses that are not explicitly denied are permitted. Some policies include explicit prohibitions in terms of negative authorizations. This, coupled with generalizations, specializations of these policies to structures such as subject and object hierarchies [Bruggemann,

1992, Rabitti et al., 1991] yield numerous combinations. Hence, custom creation of policy enforcement mechanisms or passing of these complications to applications is practically infeasible.

One of the solutions for this problem has been to develop flexible authorization models [Jajodia et al., 1997, Jajodia et al., 2001b], where the flexibility comes from having an access control model that does not depend on any policies or meta policies, but is capable of imposing any of them specifiable in their syntax. One of the main advantages of this approach is that access control can now reside within the system, but yet be able to impose application specific policies. Given that there is a need for flexible access control models, the following requirements would be desirable:

Expressability: It must be possible to model existing policies, such as *denials take precedence*, and be able to model policies of emerging applications, such as provisions and obligations (to be discussed shortly).

Decoupling Policies from Mechanisms: The primary need for flexibility is to obtain policy-independent frameworks. Hence, policies expressible in such frameworks must be enforceable using generic enforcement mechanisms.

Conflict Resolution: Having a flexible framework may invite conflicting policies and, consequently, the framework must be able to facilitate their resolution.

Efficiency: Due to the high frequency of requests coming to access control systems, their processing must be fast. Thus, efficient and simple mechanisms to allow or deny access requests are crucial.

Next we describe one such flexible framework for access control and show how it meets these requirements.

2.1. FAF - A Flexible Authorization Framework

The Flexible Authorization Framework (FAF) [Jajodia et al., 2001b], is a logic-based framework to specify authorizations as rules in a stratified rule base. The FAF architecture has four modules as shown in Figure 1.

The *propagation module* contains basic structures such as authorization subjects and object hierarchies (for example, directory structures) and a finite set of rules is used to derive authorizations stemming from structural properties, referred to as *propagation policies*. Propagation policies specify how access permissions are to be propagated through subject and object hierarchies, and FAF allows the system security officer (SSO) to write them. This freedom may result in overspecification, implying that the system must allow and deny the same access request simultaneously. Therefore, the *conflict resolution module* implements *conflict resolution policies* to eliminate such inconsistencies and these policies are specifiable by the SSO. By applying decision policies, which is again a set of rules written by the SSO, a decision will be made either to grant or deny every authorization request. This stage has a meta-policy denying all permissions that cannot be specifically derived using the given set of rules. The last stage consists of checking for integrity constraints, where all authorizations that violate integrity constraints will be denied. This component lives outside the scope of the rule base and is an external module used by FAF.

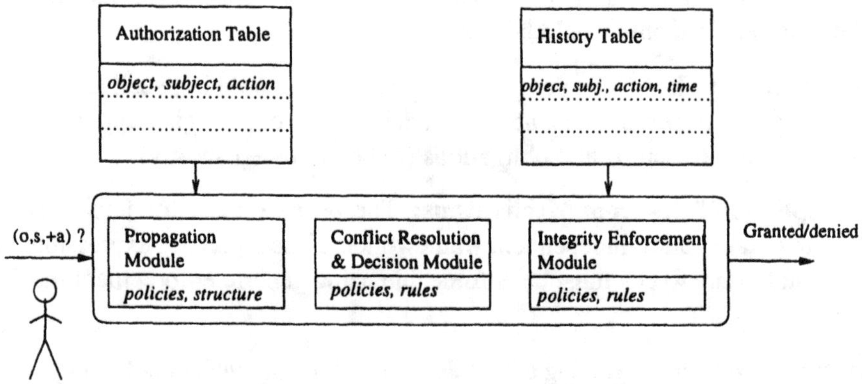

Figure 1. FAF System Architecture

FAF rules are written using a number of predicates, such as `cando`, do, and `dercando`. Their semantics are as follows:

1 A ternary predicate `cando(o,s,a)`, representing grantable or deniable requests (depending on the sign associated with the action), where o, s, and a are object, subject, and a signed action term, respectively.

2 A ternary predicate `dercando(o,s,a)`, with the same arguments as `cando`. The predicate `dercando` represents authorizations derived by the system using logical rules of inference (modus ponens plus rules for stratified negation [Apt et al., 1988]).

3 A ternary predicate do, with the same arguments as `cando`, representing the access control decisions made by FAF.

4 A 5-ary predicate `done(o, s, r, a, t)`, meaning subject `s` with role `r` active has executed action `a` on object `o` at time `t`.

5 Two 4-ary predicate symbols $\texttt{over}_{AO}$ and $\texttt{over}_{AS}$. $\texttt{over}_{AO}$ takes as arguments two object terms, a subject term and a signed action term. $\texttt{over}_{AS}$ takes as arguments a subject term, an object term, another subject

term, and a signed action term. They are needed in the definition of some of the overriding policies.

6 A propositional symbol `error` indicating violation of an integrity constraint. It is a rule with an `error` head that must not have a body that is satisfiable.

An example policy governing the electronic trading is given by the following FAF rules:

$$\begin{array}{rcl}
\texttt{cando}(item, s, +buy) & \leftarrow & \texttt{in}(item, Goods, ASH), \\
& & \texttt{in}(s, Buyers, ASH). \\
\texttt{cando}(item, s, +sell) & \leftarrow & \texttt{in}(item, Goods, ASH), \\
& & \texttt{in}(s, Sellers, ASH). \\
\texttt{dercando}(item, s, +a) & \leftarrow & \texttt{cando}(item, s, +a). \\
\texttt{do}(item, s, +a) & \leftarrow & \texttt{dercando}(item, s, +a) \\
\texttt{do}(item, s, -a) & \leftarrow & \neg\texttt{do}(item, s, +a). \\
\texttt{error} & \leftarrow & \texttt{do}(item, s, +buy), \texttt{do}(item, s, +sell)
\end{array}$$

The predicate `in(x, y, hierarchy name)` is used to specify properties of subject and object hierarchies AOH and ASH, respectively. ASH consist of two directories, `Buyers` and `Sellers`. The object hierarchy AOH has one class, `Goods`. Rules whose heads are $\texttt{dercando}(o, s, a)$ literals are derivations of authorizations. Thus, the first two rules state that a subject `s` is allowed to buy or sell if it is in the appropriate directory. The next stage in the sequence is conflict resolution and ensuring the completeness of access control decisions, and they are stated in two rules with $\texttt{do}(o, s, a)$ heads. Hence, all derived positive permissions are allowed, and all actions for which positive permissions cannot be derived are denied. The last step is *integrity checking* and is given by rules with an `error` head. The integrity rule says that no subject is allowed to buy and sell the same item.

With respect to our requirements, logically, expressability of FAF is limited to that of stratified logic programs, but many policies, such as closed world and open world policies, denials-take-precedence policy, and Chinese Wall policy, are expressable in FAF [Jajodia et al., 2001b]. In addition, to capture the evolving nature of policies and, consequently, their impact on access control, FAF has been enhanced to add and remove rules [Jajodia et al., 2001b], and to remove already granted access permissions [Wijesekera et al., 2001]. What would be interesting is to find ways to incorporate error-handling capabilities into the logical framework of FAF so that constraints specified by important classes of application-level policies such those used in role-based policies [Ahn and Sandhu, 2000] can be resolved inside the FAF rule enforcement engine.

For the decoupling of policies from their enforcement mechanisms, FAF has no built-in policies except for the meta-policy of refusing access that cannot be derived by any combination of rules. Notice that first it is necessary, as otherwise the system would be incomplete, and second, the stance taken by this meta-policy is arbitrary and can be changed to an open meta-policy by changing the rule about $\neg\mathrm{do}(s, o, -a)$. Conflict resolution in FAF is totally left to the SSO and hence is satisfactorily modularized.

Finally, the efficiency of FAF depends upon the execution of the stratified rule base. But FAF [Jajodia et al., 2001b] materializes rules and authorization tables, enhancing its efficiency.

3. PROVISIONAL AUTHORIZATIONS

Traditional access control uses the model that *a user makes an access request of a system in some context, and the system either authorizes the access request or denies it.* Models vary in what types of accesses are being considered (e.g., read, write, query, execute a function), who makes the request (e.g., user, member of a group of individuals), what objects are being accessed (e.g., file, directory), and what constitutes the context of the request (e.g., role). However, today's rapidly expanding environments, such as electronic commerce, make such models that authorize or deny a request overly simplistic and less accommodative. In practice, it is not unusual that decisions regarding accesses depend on specific actions to be performed before the decision is taken and on the guarantee that certain other actions will be taken after the access. Since the two sets of actions are conceptually different and require different management techniques, we distinguish the first and second set of actions as *provisions* and *obligations*, respectively.

An example is electronically purchasing goods for credit. The purchaser will be able to purchase an item online subject to the proviso that she enters her credit card, she is found to be *credit worthy*, and she agrees to pay back the loan. Notice that the original access decision is based on three provisions: entering the credit card, finding the purchaser to be credit worthy, and signing the purchase agreement. Once the provisions are satisfied and the purchase is completed, the purchaser is obligated to pay back the loan according to the credit agreement (notice that a credit card user's signature attests to this at the time of purchasing). To capture such applications, *provisional* authorization models have been proposed [Jajodia et al., 2001a, Kudo and Hada, 2000]. Two example systems that provide provisional authorizations are as follows.

3.1. Extending FAF with Provisions

Figure 2 shows the architecture of the provisional authorization system proposed in [Jajodia et al., 2001a]. When users submit an authorization request,

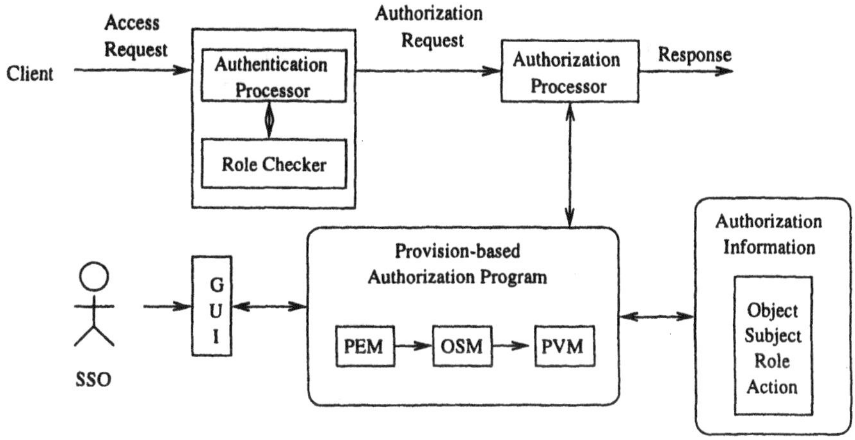

Figure 2. Provision-based Authorization Architecture

the system invokes its authentication and role-checking modules that verify if the user is who she claims to be and whether she is allowed to assume requested roles. Then, the access request is passed on to the provision evaluation module to find the *weakest* conditions under which the requested access can be honored. Then, the weakest condition under which the access may be granted is passed to an *order specification* module that yields a set of ordering constraints on the actions involved. For instance, the ordering constraints may require that the name and address be filled in before the social security number. Then, the ordering constraints are handed off to a *provision verification module* to check if any conditions were previously fulfilled by the requester and, if so, simplifies the condition (and ordering constraints) and waits for reduced conditions to be fulfilled by the requester before final authorization. Formally referred to as $\mathsf{pASL}_{\mathcal{L}}$, the syntax is enhanced to be of the following form (where $Head \leftarrow Body$ is a FAF rule and ϕ is a predicate external to FAF):

$$\phi : Head \leftarrow Body$$

The following set of rules models a $\mathsf{pASL}_{\mathcal{L}}$ specification for provisional accesses. An online store allows its customer to purchase by registering and further allows the customer to upgrade her registration to a *preferred customer*. These two policies are stated in the first two rules. Next two rules state that the purchase price of an item is \$100 for a non-preferred cutomer and \$80 for a preferred customer. Thus, a customer has the choice of remaining in the non-preferred category and paying \$100 or registering as a preferred customer and paying \$80 per item. Further suppose there is a one-time cost of \$10 to register as a non-preferred customer and to pay a \$20 fee for upgrading. Then it is preferable to buy as a non-preferred customer for a one-time-only purchase, but to become a preferred customer for multiple purchases. This is so because the cost of the one-time purchase is $80 after paying a one-time fee of $30, as opposed to paying $100 after paying a registration fee of $10. pASL$_{\mathcal{L}}$ provides this computation for its customers.

```
register(s, customer): cando(item, s, +buy) ←
                           in(contract, Contracts).
upGrade(s, prefCust):  dercando(item, s, +buy) ←
                           cando(item, s, +buy).
payFees(s, $100):      do(item, s, +buy) ←
                           cando(item, s, +buy).
payFees(s, $80):       do(item, s, +buy) ←
                           dercando(item, s, +buy).
```

3.2. Provisional Authorizations for XML

Provisional authorizations have been used in XML [Bray, 1998] documents [Kudo and Hada, 2000]. Specifically, the work of Kudo et al. tailors the general idea of provisions to XML documents as described below:

- Limits objects to those given by `XPath` [XPathP, 1999] expressions.
- Ensures that provisions require the system to transcode XML documents, carried out by a *transcoding* module. Provisions are specified as actions to this module and are limited to `logging` (requests), `verifying`(digital signatures of requestors), `encrypting` (contents to be given to requestor), `transforming` (the contents of documents to fit release constraints stated by the access control module), and `read`, `write`, `create`, and `delete` new data structures to fit the request.
- Limits the access propagation policy in XML documents to propagating permissions upwards and downwards, and preventing propagation along hierarchies [Jajodia et al., 2001b].
- Limits conflict resolution policies to denials take precedence, permissions take precedence, and nothing takes precedence [Jajodia et al., 2001b].
- Provides a syntax referred to as XACL.

It is noteworthy that from the access requestor's perpective, the security transcoding *filters* the fields of the object according to the policies applicable within the access control system, without the requestor's knowledge, to those occurring in subject-switching algorithms proposed in [Yang et al., 2001].

4. ALGEBRA OF POLICIES

Another area that has advanced in recent years is that of policy algebras for access control [Bonatti et al., 2000, Wijesekera and Jajodia, 2001]. Due to mergers and aquisitions in the commercial sector and joint missions in the military sector, many security-sensitive organizations need to merge their security policies. Such policies exist, but they are based on different irreconcilable models and implemented in incompatible languages. Consequently, an algebra of policies goes a long way in providing conceptual coherence among these policies at a higher abstract level, thereby providing a basis for comparison and determining areas of contrast. Details of two recent approaches are given in Sections 4.1 and 4.2.

4.1. The Modular Approach of Bonatti et al.

Bonatti et al. [Bonatti et al., 2000] develop a comprehensive framework for composing access control policies, where an access control policy is a set of ground terms over an alphabet for (subject, object, action) terms. Thus, it is a set-based approach influenced by logic programming. BNF definitions of policies are given below, where **id** is a terminal and T is a template. Here, C consists of arithmatic constraints constructed from $<, \leq, =, \geq$, and $>$ signs. R represents the recursive closure under a set of Horn clauses:

$$p := \mathbf{id}, \mid p + p \mid p \& p \mid p - p \mid p^C \mid o(p, p, p) \mid p * R \mid T(p) \mid (p)$$

$+$ and $\&$ are, respectively, union and intersection operators, permitting accesses that are allowed under either or both components, respectively. The difference operator ($-$) allows accesses permitted under the first component but not under the second. p^C restricts the scope of policy p to those accesses satisfying the constraint C, and $p * R$ represents recursive closure of policy p under the rule set R. $o(p_1, p_2, p_3)$ is syntactic sugar for $(p_1 - p_2) + (p_1 \& p_2)$ and represents policy overriding. T is a template and $T(p)$ represents its instantiation with p.

The paper further shows how to translate policy expressions into logic programs by creating a labeling mechanism for the syntax tree of the expression, which is referred to as the *canonical translation*. Although the modular approach does not explicitly support negative authorizations, the paper shows how to model a policy such as denials take precedence as $p^+ - p^-$, where p^+ and p^- contain positive and negative authorization terms of p, respectively.

4.2. Propositional Policy Algebra

The algebra proposed in [Wijesekera and Jajodia, 2001] is a propositional version consisting of a syntax to view policies as abstract symbols and their semantics as authorization state transformers. Here, an authorization state is a collection of (subject, object, access set) triples and a set of propositions satisfied by them. BNF definitions of policy expressions of [Wijesekera and Jajodia, 2001] are given below, where p is a non-terminal, p_a is a terminal taken from a countable collection $\{p_i : i \geq 1\}$ atomic policies, and ϕ is a propositional symbol:

$$p := p_a \mid p \cup p \mid p \cap p \mid p - p \mid p;p \neg p \mid \odot p \mid p^* \mid (\phi p) \mid (p \| \phi) \mid \max(p) \mid \min(p)$$

The disjunction operator ($\cup$) permits accesses that are allowed under either of its components, while conjunction operator ($\cap$) allows only those that are permitted by both components. The difference operator ($-$) permits accesses that are allowed under the first component, but not under the second. The sequence operator (;) permits accesses that are allowed as a consequence of its second component after the first is applied. The negation operator ($\neg$) changes all positive authorizations to negative ones and vice versa. Applying the invalidate operator ($\odot$) to a policy removes all authorizations granted under that policy. The closure operator (*) allows accesses permitted under repeated application of policies and is an extension of the composition operator. The reason for recursion is to allow accesses that are permitted by some rules in a rule base. Provisions (:) are as described in Section 3. The scoping operator ($\|$) allows only those authorizations that meet the scoping restrictions. In case both positive and negative permissions are granted, `max` and `min` operators resolve conflicts by selecting the positive and negative permissions, respectively.

Semantically, policies allow specified subjects to execute desired actions over given objects. Accordingly, policies are interpreted as abstract transformers of (subject, object, action set) triples. The paper also provides some syntactic rules to simplify policy expressions and indicates how they can be used to determine completeness, consistency, unambiguity, and semantic equivalence of merged policies.

5. SUBJECT IDENTITY IN SECURE FEDERATIONS

Consider the problem of providing authorized accesses to a secure coalition such as one launched by allied forces against Afghanistan, Iraq, or Bosnia. Federated databases and systems are suitable in providing support for such federations, where each participant wants to contribute to the common mission but maintain a high degree of security and operational autonomy. In providing access control to such systems, there are two alternatives. One is to create individual subjects in each cooperating system. The other alternative is to allow every participant *anonymous* access to some data. None of these alternatives are completely satisfactory, as the former places extra burden on the users because they have to manage many accounts and are responsible for interpreting, translating, and collecting information that they may not have the knowledge to manage. The second alternative is infeasible as this is an *all-or-nothing* solution that limits fine-grained access control offered by components.

A viable alternative to this problem is *subject switching*, where a federated layer interprets data supplied by the components and switches the identity of the subjects to those of subjects in participating components. The advantage of this approach is that the federated subject then has a lesser burden in using the system with a finer grain of access control, and the disadvantage of the system is that federated users may not get exactly what they request, as these may be limited by agreements and policies existing between the components and the federation. An access control model and algorithms to do the best under a given set of policies are discussed in [Yang et al., 2001].

6. OTHER RECENT ADVANCES

Role-based access control (RBAC) is an active area in access control, where the accesses to objects are dependent on the roles played by the subjects at the time the accesses are granted. It is an alternative to discretionary and mandatory access control, and has several advantages, such as in organizations with a stable structure, but a dynamic workforce accesses can remain relatively static and bound only to roles. Prevention of fraud and misuse are also enforceable by imposing *separation of duty* constraints. Recent advances in this area have been a proposal for standards [Ferraiolo et al., 2001], role constraint languages RCL [Ahn and Sandhu, 2000], applying RBAC to the World Wide Web [Sandhu, 1996], and applying RBAC to workflow systems [Bertino et al., 1999].

Another topic of recent interest has been in the area of securing XML documents [Damiani et al., 2000]. Their security depends on three aspects: authenticity, integrity, and confidentiality. Confidentiality depends on access control policies and mechanisms. Some issues that are being addressed in access control of XML are specifications that take the structure of XML documents into account, fine-grained access control of document components and fields, and access control based on credentials.

Workflow systems also continue to pose considerable challenges for access control [Atluri, 2001], where accesses must synchronize with workflows. Several recent attempts apply RBAC to workflows [Atluri et al., 2001, Bertino et al., 1999], where constraints posed by workflows need to be reconciled with those of RBAC models.

7. GOOD NEWS

In recent years, researchers and developers have devoted a great deal of energy on topics such as firewalls, incorporation of encryption on communication protocols, and intrusion detection systems. However, there is a growing realization that while these are critical to building secure systems, they do not provide all the answers and, consequently, the focus is shifting toward host and application security. We need to accelerate our research and work with vendors to develop the practical uses of our solutions.

Acknowledgement

This work was partially supported by the National Science Foundation under the grant CCR-0113515.

References

[Ahn and Sandhu, 2000] Ahn, G.-J. and Sandhu, R. (2000). Role-based authorization constraints specification. *ACM Transactions on Information and Systems Security*, 3(4).

[Apt et al., 1988] Apt, K., Blair, H., and Walker, A. (1988). Towards a theory of declarative knowledge. In Minker, J., editor, *Foundations of Deductive Databases and Logic Programming*. Morgan Kaufmann, San Mateo.

[Atluri, 2001] Atluri, V. (2001). Security for workflow systems. *Information Security Technical Report*, 6(2):59–68.

[Atluri et al., 2001] Atluri, V., Chun, S., and Mazzoleni, P. (2001). A chinese wall security model for workflow systems. In *ACM Conference on Computer and Communications Security*.

[Bertino et al., 1999] Bertino, E., Ferrari, E., and Atluri, V. (1999). An approach for the specification and enforcement of authorization constraints in workflow management systems. *ACM Transactions on Information and Systems Security*.

[Bonatti et al., 2000] Bonatti, P., di Vimercati, S. D. C., and Samarati, P. (2000). A modular approach to composing access control policies. In *Proc. 7th ACM Conf. on Communications and Security*, pages 164–173.

[Bray, 1998] Bray, T. (1998). *Extensible Markup Language (XML) 1.0*. World Wide Web Consortium (W3C), http://www.w3.org/TR/REC-xml, 1.0 edition.

[Bruggemann, 1992] Bruggemann, H. (1992). Rights in an object-oreinted environment. In Landwehr, C. and Jajodia, S., editors, *Database Security V: Status and Prospects*, pages 99–115. North Holland.

[Castano et al., 1994] Castano, S., Fugini, M., and Samarati, P. (1994). *Database Security*. Addison-Wesley.

[Damiani et al., 2000] Damiani, E., di Vimercati, S. D. C., Paraboschi, S., and Samarati, P. (2000). Design and implementation of an access control processor for xml documents. *Computer Networks, vol. 33, no. 1-6, 2000, pp. 59-75*, 33(1-6):59–75.

[Dobson and McDermid, 1989] Dobson, J. and McDermid, J. (1989). A framework for expressing models of security policy. In *Proceedings of IEEE Symposium on Security and Privacy*, pages 229–239.

[Ferraiolo et al., 2001] Ferraiolo, D. F., Sandhu, R., Gavrilla, S., Kuhn, D. R., and Chandramouli, R. (2001). A proposed standard for role-based access control. *ACM Transactions on Information and Systems Security*, 4(3).

[Jajodia et al., 2001a] Jajodia, S., Kudo, M., and Subrahmanian, V. S. (2001a). Provisional authorizations. In Gosh, A., editor, *E-Commerce Security and Privacy*, pages 133–159. Kluwer Academic Press, Boston.

[Jajodia et al., 2001b] Jajodia, S., Samarati, P., Sapino, M. L., and Subrahmanian, V. S. (2001b). Flexible support for multiple access control policies. *ACM Transactions on Database Systems*, 26(2):214–260.

[Jajodia et al., 1997] Jajodia, S., Samarati, P., and Subrahmanian, V. (1997). A logical language for expressing authorizations. In *Proceedings of IEEE Symposium on Security and Privacy*, pages 31–42, Oakland, CA.

[Kudo and Hada, 2000] Kudo, M. and Hada, S. (2000). Xml document security based on provisional authorizations. In *Proceedings of the 7th ACM Conference on Computer and Communications Security*, pages 87–96.

[Rabitti et al., 1991] Rabitti, F., Bertino, E., Kim, W., and Woelk, W. (1991). A model of authorization for next-generation database systems. *ACM Transactions on Database Systems*, 16(1):89–131.

[Sandhu, 1996] Sandhu, R. (1996). Role hierarchies and constraints for lattice-based access control. In *Proceedings of the Europeon Symposium on Research in Computer Security*, pages 65–79.

[Wijesekera and Jajodia, 2001] Wijesekera, D. and Jajodia, S. (2001). Policy algebras for access control - the propositional case. In *Proceedings of the Eighth ACM Conference on Computer and Communications Security*. to appear.

[Wijesekera et al., 2001] Wijesekera, D., Jajodia, S., Parisi-Presicce, F., and Hagestrom, A. (2001). Removing permissions in the flexible authorization framework. Submitted for publication.

[XPathP, 1999] XPathP (1999). *XML Path Language (XPath)*. World Wide Web Consortium (W3C), http://www.w3.org/TR/PR-xpath19991008, 1.0 edition.

[Yang et al., 2001] Yang, J., Wijesekera, J., and Jajodia, S. (2001). Subject switching algorithms for access control in federated databases. In *Proceedings of the Fifteenth Annual IFIP WG 11.3 Working Conference on Database and Applications Security*.

II

ROLE AND CONSTRAINT-BASED ACCESS CONTROL

ROLE-BASED ACCESS CONTROL ON THE WEB USING LDAP

Joon S. Park
Information and Software Engineering Department
George Mason University
jpark@itd.nrl.navy.mil

Gail-Joon Ahn
College of Information Technology
University of North Carolina at Charlotte
gahn@uncc.edu

Ravi Sandhu
Information and Software Engineering Department
George Mason University
sandhu@gmu.edu

Abstract This paper gives a framework for how to leverage Lightweight Directory Access Protocol (LDAP) to implement Role-based Access Control (RBAC) on the Web in the *server-pull* architecture. LDAP-based directory services have recently received much attention because they can support object-oriented hierarchies of entries in which we can easily search and modify attributes over TCP/IP. To implement RBAC on the Web, we use an LDAP directory server as a role server that contains users' role information. The role information in the role server is referred to by Web servers for access control purposes through LDAP in a secure manner (over SSL). We provide a comparison of this work to our previous work, RBAC on the Web in the *user-pull* architecture.

Keywords: Access Control, LDAP, RBAC, Web Security

1. INTRODUCTION

The emergence of Web technology has changed life styles and the world economy. It enables us to access various information regardless of the distance between service providers and requesters. Web technology has continued its rapid evolution, most recently towards increasingly secure transactions on enterprise-wide infrastructure. However, information security problems have become more important as the world uses more information systems, since the security of information systems directly or indirectly affect organizations, which rely on information technology. An organization's enterprise intranet security depends on largely on access control management. RBAC (Role-based Access Control [SCFY96]) has been accepted as a proven technology for strong and efficient access control. As the vehicle of access control management, RBAC can be used to provide the services that focus on how users' role information can be used instead of users' identities.

Park and Sandhu identified two different approaches for obtaining user's attributes* on the Web: *user-pull* and *server-pull* architectures [PS99]. They classified the architectures based on "Who pulls the user's attributes?" In the user-pull architecture, the user pulls her attributes from the attribute server and then presents them to the Web servers, which use those attributes for their purposes. In the server-pull architecture, each Web server pulls user's attributes from the attribute server as needed and uses them for their purposes. To show the feasibility of those approaches, RBAC (as one example of secure attribute services) on the Web has been implemented in the user-pull architecture and described in our previous papers [PS99b, PSG99, ASKP00]. In this paper, we describe how we implement RBAC on the Web in the server-pull architecture using commercial off-the-shelf (COTS) technologies, such as LDAP (Lightweight Directory Access Protocol [HSG99]) and SSL (Secure Socket Layer [WS96, DA99]). Furthermore, we compare this work with our previous work, based-on our hands-on experiences.

This paper is organized as follows. Section 2 briefly introduces RBAC and the existing technologies that we use for our server-pull implementation in this paper. In Section 3, we describe two different operational architectures of RBAC on the Web. Section 4 describes how we implement RBAC on the Web in the server-pull architecture using existing well-known Web technologies. Section 5 compares the server-pull and user-pull RBAC architectures based on our hands-on experiences. Finally, Section 6 concludes this paper.

2. RELATED TECHNOLOGIES

2.1. Role-based Access Control (RBAC)

Role-based Access Control (RBAC [SCFY96]) has rapidly emerged in the 1990s as a technology for managing and enforcing security in large-scale enterprise-wide systems. The basic notion of RBAC is that permissions are

* An attribute is a particular property of an entity, such as a role, access identity, group, or clearance.

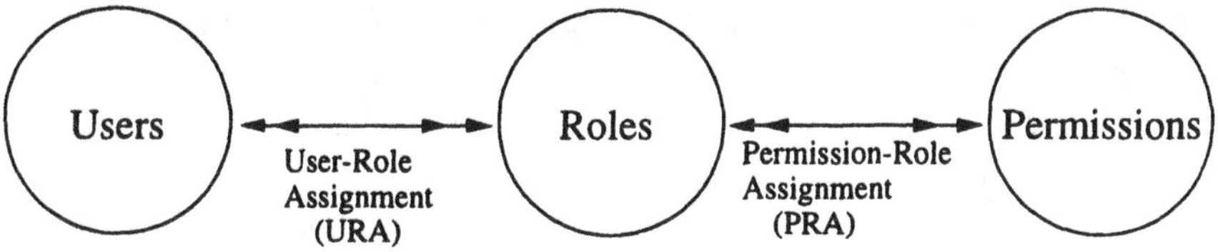

Figure 1. A Simplified RBAC Model

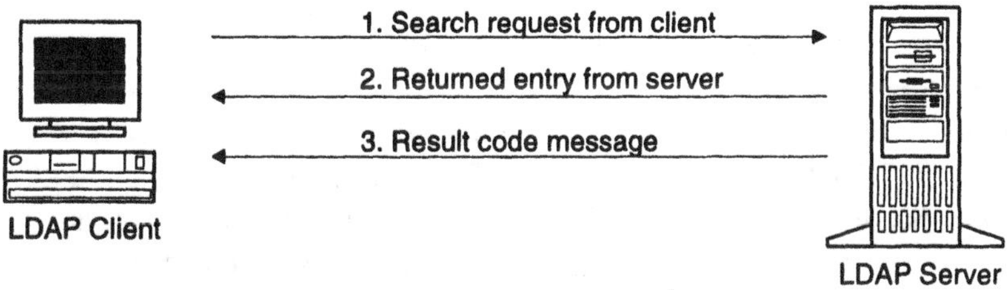

Figure 2. LDAP Operation

associated with roles, and users are assigned to appropriate roles. Figure 1 shows a simplified RBAC model. RBAC ensures that only authorized users are given access to certain data or resources. This simplifies security management. Intuitively, a user is a human being or an autonomous agent, a role is a job function or job title within the organization with some associated semantics regarding the authority and responsibility conferred on a member of the role. Permissions are simply treated as abstract token. A user can be a member of many roles and a role can have many users (denoted by double arrows in Figure 1). Similarly, a role can have many permissions and the same permissions can be assigned to many roles.

System administrators can create roles, grant permissions to those roles, and then assign users to the roles on the basis of their specific job responsibilities and policy. Therefore, role-permission relationships can be predefined, making it simple to assign users to the corresponding permissions through the roles. Without RBAC, it is difficult (especially, in a large enterprise system) to determine and change what permissions have been authorized for what users.

2.2. Lightweight Directory Access Protocol (LDAP)

User information is often fragmented across the enterprise, leading to data that is redundant, inconsistent, and expensive to manage. Directories are being viewed as one of the best mechanisms to make enterprise information available to multiple different systems within an organization. Directories also make it possible for organizations to access information over the Internet. The most common information stored in a directory service is information about users on a network; this can include user id, passwords, assigned groups, or network access rights. In order to retrieve the information, a directory access protocol is used to convey the entries from directory-oriented server. The trend towards directories has been accelerated by the recent growth of LDAP (Lightweight Directory Access Protocol [HSG99]).

LDAP is a protocol that enables X.500 based directories to be read through Internet clients. It was developed by the University of Michigan and the Internet Engineering Task Force (IETF) as a set of network services to provide object management and access over TCP/IP networks. LDAP is also a message-oriented protocol. When an LDAP client needs a specific entry in an LDAP server, the LDAP client generates an LDAP message containing a request and sends this message to the LDAP server. The server retrieves the entry from its database and sends it to the client in an LDAP message. It also returns a result code to the client in a separate LDAP message to terminate the session. Figure 2 shows this interaction between the LDAP server and client. With this feature of directory services, we use an LDAP server and client for our server-pull RBAC implementation.

Although we use LDAP between Web servers and role server for RBAC in the server-pull architecture, it is also possible to use LDAP for the user-pull architecture, where clients can retrieve their roles from the role server via LDAP and present them to the Web servers.

2.3. Secure Socket Layer (SSL)

SSL [WS96, DA99] was introduced with the Netscape Navigator browser in 1994, and rapidly became the predominant security protocol on the Web. Since the protocol operates at the transport layer, any program that uses TCP (Transmission Control Protocol) is ready to use SSL connections. The SSL protocol provides a secure means for establishing an encrypted communication between Web servers and browsers. SSL also supports the authentication service between Web servers and browsers.

SSL uses X.509 certificates. Server certificates provide a way for users to authenticate the identity of a Web server. The Web browser uses the server's public key to negotiate a secure TCP connection with the Web server. Optionally, the Web server can authenticate users by verifying the contents of the client certificates.

Even though SSL provides secure communications between Web servers and browsers on the Web, it cannot protect against end-system threats. For instance, after a user, Alice, receives her attributes from a Web server over SSL, it does not mean that the attributes are still safe. In other words, once the user receives

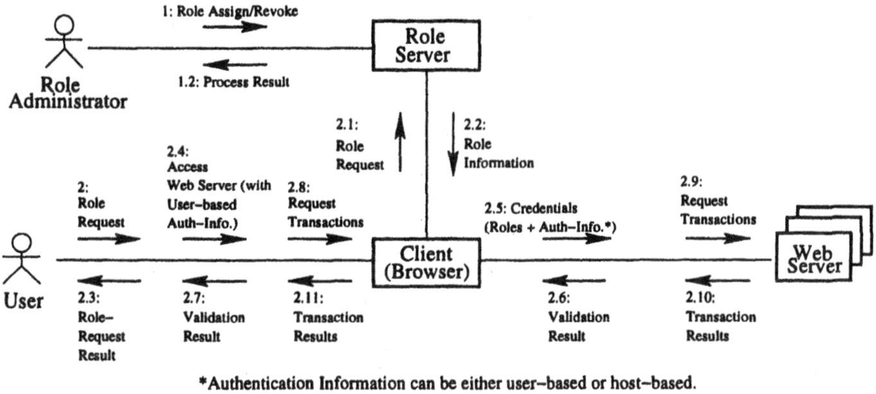

Figure 3. A Collaborational Diagram for the User-Pull Architecture

some attributes from the server over SSL, an attacker is able to change the attributes in the user's machine, because SSL does not support security in the user's end system. However, as we will see later in this paper, SSL can be used as part of our implementation to protect information on the Web.

3. OPERATIONAL ARCHITECTURES

Park and Sandhu identified two different approaches for obtaining a user's attributes on the Web, especially with respect to the user-pull and server-pull architectures, in which each architecture has user-based and host-based modes [PS99]. In this section, we embody those general approaches for RBAC on the Web with specific components and relationships. Basically, there are three components in both architectures: client, Web server, and role server. These components are already being used on the Web. Clients connect to Web servers via HTTP using browsers. The role server is maintained by an administrator and assigns users to the roles in the domain [SP98]. Detailed technologies (such as authentication, role transfer and protection, and verification) to support these architectures depend on the applications that are used.

3.1. RBAC in User-Pull Architecture

In the user-pull architecture, a user, say Alice, pulls her roles from the role server and then presents them to the Web servers, as depicted in a UML (Unified Modeling Language [BJR98]) collaborational diagram in Figure 3. We call this a user-pull architecture, since the user pulls her roles from the role server, in which roles are assigned to the users in the domain. HTTP is used for the user-server interactions with standard Web browsers and Web servers.

In the user-pull-host-based mode, the user needs to download her roles from the role server and store them in her machine, which has her host-based authentication information, such as IP numbers†. Later, when the user wants to access the Web server, which requires proper authentication information and roles, her machine presents that information to the Web server. After client authentication and role verification, the Web server uses the roles for RBAC. However, since this mode is host-based, it cannot support high user mobility, while it may support more convenient services than the user-based mode, which requires user's cooperation (e.g., typing in passwords).

On the other hand, the user-pull-user-based mode supports high user mobility. The user can download her roles to her current machine from the role server. Then, she presents those roles to the Web server along with her user-based authentication information, such as her passwords. After user authentication and role verification, the Web server uses the roles for RBAC. In this mode, the user can use any machines, which support HTTP, as long as she has right user-based authentication information (e.g., passwords).

In this user-pull architecture, we must support the binding of roles and identification for each user. For instance, if Alice presents Bob's roles with her authentication information to the Web server, she must be rejected. General approaches for binding user attributes and their identities are discussed by Park and Sandhu in [PS00].

3.2. RBAC in Server-Pull Architecture

In the server-pull architecture, each Web server pulls the user's roles from the role server as needed and uses them for RBAC as depicted in a UML collaborational diagram in Figure 4. We call this a server-pull architecture, since the server pulls the user's roles from the role server. HTTP is used for the user-server interactions with standard Web browsers and Web servers. If the role server provides users' roles securely, the Web server can trust those roles and uses them for RBAC.

In this architecture, the user does not need access to her roles. Instead, she needs only her authentication information. In the server-pull-host-based mode, she presents her host-based authentication information (e.g., IP numbers) to the Web server. Role obtaining mechanism is transparent to the user, while limiting the portability. However, in the server-pull-user-based mode, Alice presents her

† Address-based authentication is a convenient authentication mechanism because the authentication process is transparent to users, but such a method is not always desirable. For example, if the user's IP address is dynamically assigned to her computer whenever she connects to the Internet, or the user's domain uses a proxy server, which provides the same IP numbers to the users in the domain, this is not a proper authentication technique. In addition, we cannot avoid IP spoofing, which is a technique for gaining unauthorized access by sending messages to a computer with a trusted IP address.

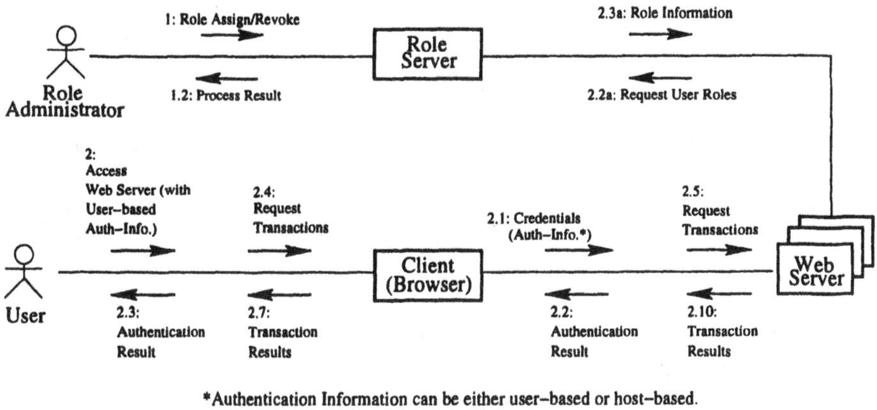

Figure 4. A Collaborational Diagram for the Server-Pull Architecture

user-based authentication information (e.g., passwords) to the Web server. This supports high portability, while it requires the user's cooperation (e.g., typing in passwords). After user authentication, the Web server downloads the user's roles from the role server and uses them for RBAC.

We describe an implementation of this architecture in both user and host-based modes in Section 4. A detailed comparison of the user-pull and server-pull architectures is discussed in Section 5.

4. IMPLEMENTING RBAC ON THE WEB IN THE SERVER-PULL ARCHITECTURE

We use LDAP to communicate between the directory-oriented role server and Web servers. In our implementation, we use Netscape Directory Server as an LDAP-supporting role server and use its group objects as users' role attributes. This directory-oriented role server contains users' role information to be used for access control by Web servers.

The basic scenario of our implementation is that a client presents her authentication information to a Web server and then, after a successful authentication process, the Web server gets the client's role information from the role server via LDAP to use those roles for RBAC services in the Web server.

For this purpose, we set up a computing environment based on the server-pull architecture (see Section 3.2) as shown in Figure 4. Figure 5 shows the transaction procedures of our experiment. We have three major components: Web server, role server, and client. The role server keeps URA (User-Role Assignment) information. The Web server contains resources, which require particular roles to be accessed. The Web server also contains a PRA (Permission-Role Assignment) table, which specifies the required roles for particular resources

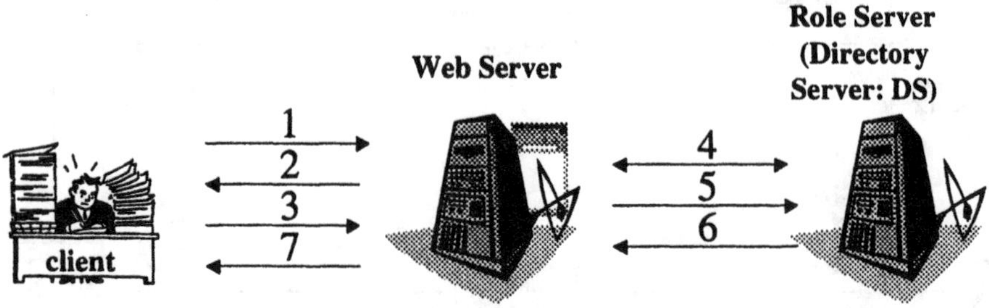

1 Authenticate client (using password or client certificate)
2 Display the initial page
3 Request resources by clicking a link
4 Establish SSL between DS and Web server
5 LDAP over SSL; Request client 's role information to DS
6 LDAP over SSL; Return client 's role information to Web server
7 Display appropriate resources after authorization check based on client 's roles

Figure 5. Transaction Procedures for RBAC in Server-Pull Architecture

in the Web server. This table is referenced to check if the user has proper roles to access particular resources in the Web server. Clients use Web browsers to connect Web servers over HTTP or HTTPS.

The detailed transaction procedures are as follows. A client presents her authentication information to a Web server. We can use username/passwords, IP numbers, client certificates‡, or other authentication techniques for this purpose. The Web server authenticates the user using proper authentication mechanism. Once a user is authenticated by the Web server successfully (otherwise, the user gets an error message), the Web server triggers the CGI (Common Gateway Interface) scripts that call an LDAP client software. This LDAP client software sends a search query to the LDAP server, which retrieves the user's roles from the directory server through SSL. The retrieved roles are sent back to the LDAP client in the Web server during the same SSL session. When the user requests an access to the resources, which requires particular roles to be accessed, by clicking the corresponding link in the initial page, the Web server compares the user's roles (that it pulled from the role server) with the ones in its PRA table.

‡To use client certificates, which is an optional operation of SSL, we need to configure the Web server to accept and understand particular client certificates. Note that this SSL channel is optional and independent from the SSL connection between Web servers and the role server.

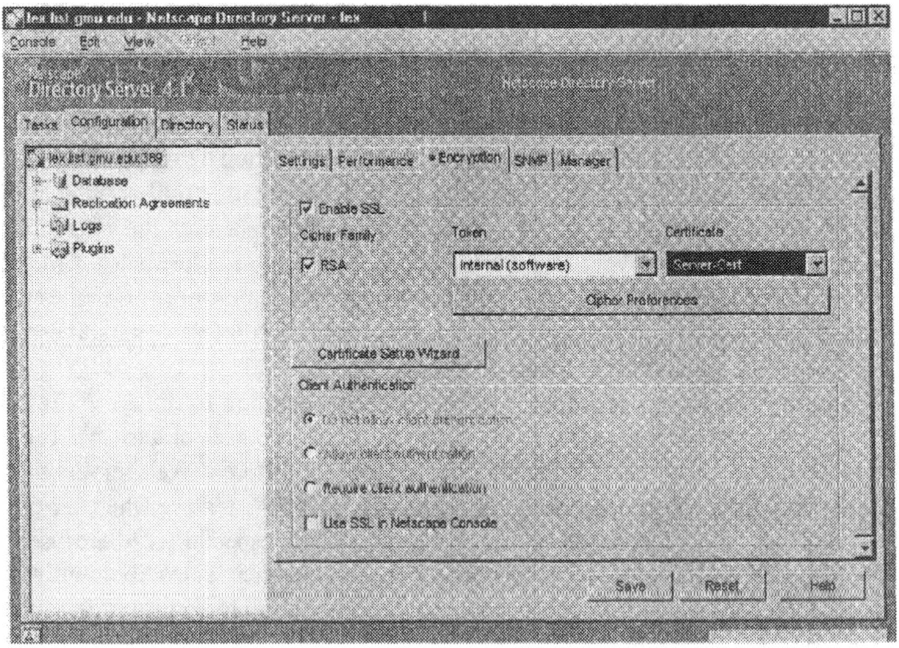

Figure 6. Directory Server: Enabling SSL

If the user has corresponding roles in the table, the Web server allows the user to access the resources.

Figure 6 is a snapshot showing the directory server (role server in our case) configuration. This directory server is running a process called *slapd* (LDAP server daemon) to allow requests from LDAP clients. We configure this server to have two network ports: one is for regular port and the other is for secure communications. For the secure communications, we need to enable SSL establishment between the LDAP client (installed in the Web server in our implementation) and directory server, more specifically the LDAP server.

5. DISCUSSION

In this section, based on our hands-on experiences, we discuss the tradeoffs between the user-pull (implemented and described in [PS99b, PSG99, ASKP00]) and the server-pull (implemented and described in Section 4) architectures using different technologies for RBAC on the Web. In the user-pull architecture, the user pulls her roles from the role server, and then presents the role information to the Web servers along with her authentication information. In the server-pull architecture, the user presents her authentication information to the Web servers, which pulls the user's role information from the role server for RBAC after a successful authentication.

The user-pull architecture requires a user's cooperation to obtain her roles, but it enhances the Web server performance. Once the user obtains her roles, she can use them in many different sessions even in different Web servers until the roles expire. This increases the reusability. By this feature, the user-pull architecture is a good solution for the applications, especially, where users' convenience is required for maintaining and using their roles frequently in diverse Web sites, such as pay-per-access. However, the longevity of the roles decreases the freshness of the roles. For instance, if the user already pulled her roles, the updated version in the role server would not become effective instantly. Namely, an additional synchronization process is required. Thus, when the dynamic role update is critical, the role server should push the status change of users' roles, such as role revocation, to the Web servers for updated information.

The server-pull architecture requires the Web server's cooperation for obtaining the user's role information - which decreases the Web server performance - from the role server. In this architecture, the Web server retrieves the user's role information from the role server for each session. This increases the freshness of the roles, so the information update (e.g., role revocation) is more efficient than the user-pull architecture, because all the roles are stored in the role server and pulled by the Web servers on demand. By this feature, the server-pull architecture is a good solution for the applications, especially, where dynamic

Table 1. A Comparison of User-Pull and Server-Pull Architectures

	User-Pull Architecture	Server-Pull Architecture
User's Convenience	Low	High
Performance	High	Low
Reusability	High	Low
Role Freshness	Low	High
Single-Point Failure	Low	High

role update is critical, such as stop-payment in electronic transactions. However, it decreases reusability and increases the single-point failure vulnerability because every session requires an access to the role server. We summarize the comparison of the user-pull and server pull architectures in Table 1.

6. CONCLUSION

We have developed the system architectures and mechanisms for achieving RBAC on the Web. We have also described several proof-of-concept implementations to demonstrate the feasibility of our approaches. After we had practical experiences in both the user-pull and server-pull architectures of RBAC on the Web, we compared the tradeoffs of both approaches. A comprehensive description and analysis for RBAC on the Web using different technologies in different architectures is available in [PSA01]. We believe that our work can be an important step towards offering strong and efficient security management based on users' roles on the Web.

References

[ASKP00] Gail-Joon Ahn, Ravi Sandhu, Myong Kang, and Joon Park. Injecting RBAC to Secure a Web-based Workflow System. In *Proceedings of 5th ACM Workshop on Role-based Access Control*, pages 1–10, Berlin, Germany, July 2000.

[BJR98] Grady Booch, Ivar Jacobson, and James Rumbaugh. *The Unified Modeling Language User Guide*. Addison-Wesley, 1998.

[DA99] T. Dierks and C. Allen. *The TLS (Transport Layer Security) Protocol*. RFC 246, January 1999.

[HSG99] Timoth Howes, Mark Smith, and Gordon Good. *Understanding and Deploying LDAP Directory Services*. Macmillan Technical Publishing, 1999.

[Neu94] B. Clifford Neuman. Using Kerberos for Authentication on Computer Networks. *IEEE Communications*, 32(9), 1994.

[Net99] Netscape Communications Corporation. Netscape Directory Server 4.1 Deployment Guide. *http://developer.netscape.com/docs/manuals/directory/dir40/de/contents.htm*, 1999.

[PS00] Joon S. Park and Ravi Sandhu. Binding Identities and Attributes Using Digitally Signed Certificates. In *Proceedings of 16th Annual Computer Security Applications Conference (ACSAC)*, New Orleans, Louisiana, December 2000.

[PS00b] Joon S. Park and Ravi Sandhu. Secure Cookies on the Web. *IEEE Internet Computing*, 4(4), 36-44, July-August 2000.

[PS99] Joon S. Park and Ravi Sandhu. Smart Certificates: Extending X.509 for Secure Attribute Services on the Web. In *Proceedings of 22nd National Information Systems Security Conference (NISSC)*, Crystal City, Virginia, October 1999.

[PS99b] Joon S. Park and Ravi Sandhu. RBAC on the Web by Smart Certificates. In *Proceedings of 4th ACM Workshop on Role-based Access Control*, pages 1–9, Fairfax, Virginia, October 1999.

[PSA01] Joon S. Park, Ravi Sandhu, and Gail-Joon Ahn. RBAC on the Web. *ACM Transactions on Information and Systems Security*, 4(1), February 2001.

[PSG99] Joon S. Park, Ravi Sandhu, and SreeLatha Ghanta. RBAC on the Web by Secure Cookies. In *Proceedings of 13th Annual IFIP 11.3 Conference on Database Security*, Seattle, Washington, July 1999.

[SCFY96] Ravi S. Sandhu, Edward J. Coyne, Hal L. Feinstein, and Charles E. Youman. Role-based Access Control Models. *IEEE Computer*, 29(2):38–47, February 1996.

[SP98] Ravi Sandhu and Joon S. Park. Decentralized User-Role Assignment for Web-based Intranets. In *Proceedings of 3rd ACM Workshop on Role-based Access Control*, pages 1–12, Fairfax, Virginia, October 1998.

[WS96] D. Wagner and B. Schneier. Analysis of the SSL 3.0 Protocol. In *Proceedings of 2nd USENIX Workshop on Electronic Commerce*, Oakland, California, November 1996.

[YLS96] Nicholas Yialelis, Emil Lupu, and Morris Sloman. Role-based Security for Distributed Object Systems. In *Proceedings of IEEE Fifth Workshops on Enabling Technology: Infrastructure for Collaborative Enterprise*. 1996.

CONSTRAINTS-BASED ACCESS CONTROL

Wee Yeh Tan
School of Computing
National University of Singapore
Building S-16, Level 5, Room 05/08
3 Science Drive 2, Singapore 117543
Tel: +65 874 8850
Fax: +65 779 4580 *
tanwy@comp.nus.edu.sg

Abstract The most important aspect of security in a database after establishing the authenticity of the user is its access control mechanism. The ability of this access control mechanism to express the security policy can make or break the system.

This paper introduces constraints-based access control (CBAC) – an access control mechanism that general associations between users and permissions are specified by the rules (or constraints) governing the access rights of each user. This association is not restricted to static events but can include dynamic factors as well.

One of the many advantages of CBAC is that even a static CBAC is a generalisation of most of the access control mechanism in use today. We demonstrate how CBAC can efficiently simulate role-based access control (RBAC) and access control list (ACL). In fact, CBAC allows the introduction of any abstract concepts as one would do roles in RBAC. On top of that, CBAC also allows the users to specify interactions between these concepts.

Any flexibile access control method usually raises concerns over its time efficiency. We advocate the use of partial solutions to the access control constraints to improve the efficiency of CBAC.

Keywords: constraints, access control, security

1. INTRODUCTION

The security services does not stop after establishing the authenticity of a user. A secured system still has to determine if each user has access rights to the various resources within the system. The access control subsystem is, hence,

* Partial funding provided by a Strategic Research Programme on Computer Security funded by NSTB/MOE

tasked with limiting the activities of the authenticated user. While establishing the user's authenticity prevents unauthorized users from entering the system, the access control mechanism in the system prevents authenticated users from accessing unauthorized services or resources. This provides a finer grain of control over the use of the system.

The main issues surrounding the design of access control mechanism are its **efficiency** and **effectiveness**. For a mechanism to be effective, it need to be sufficiently expressive and at the same time help (not complicate) the management of permissions. While more advanced data structures and algorithms can be devised to improve efficiency, the question of effectiveness is better approached with a higher level specification language for programming the access control mechanism.

Several advances have been made to the area of access control specification and policies have been devised to narrow the gap between what the security adminstrators want and what the access control system can provide. The most common approaches are the **Discretionary Access Control (DAC)**, the **Lattice-based Access Control (LBAC)** and the **Role-based Access Control (RBAC)** [Sandhu and Samarati,].

DAC controls access by explicitly specifying the authorization for each user to each resource in the system. Implementations of DAC can be found in a variety of systems, from Unix's file access control, to ACL. While DAC is extremely flexible, management of access control permissions can be a pain due to the flat structure. DAC does not provide real assurance on the flow of information in a system. For example, there is no guarding against a user with the correct access rights leaking classified information to an unauthorized user.

LBAC, also known as Mandatory Access Control, enforces a direction in the flow of information in a lattice of security labels. In this approach, each user and resource is assigned a security clearance. A user can only read a resource of lower security clearance and the user can only write to a resource with a higher security clearance. While the write restriction may seem counter intuitive at first, this restriction is necessary to guarrantee that information only flows upwards in security clearance. This approach is not well accepted outside of the military due to its lack of flexibility.

The third approach, RBAC [Sandhu et al., 1996, Sandhu, 1996], models access control after the roles of the individuals in the organization. In this model, users are assigned the various roles they play in the organization and permissions are granted so that the roles can fulfill their task. Roles can be taken more broadly to include abstractions of users and permissions are to be granted to these abstractions. In [Sandhu, 1996], RBAC is shown to subsume LBAC. RBAC is widely adopted by several major databases like Oracle and Informix.

More recent development of web-based applications, Enterprise Resource Planning systems and other large scale systems that depends on a database backend requires a richer set of access control policy than is available today. Application developers are writing their own codes to provide the access control policies they wish to enforce where the access control mechanism provided by the database falls short. A typical web-application will include both codes to authenticate its users as well as codes that implements some access control policies before accessing the database on behalf of the user. More recent research like [Bertino et al., 1998] also confirms the need for a more expressive access control language.

This paper introduces Constraints based Access Control (CBAC), our approach to extensible access control. Constraints are used to specify general associations between the users and their authorizations. Further constraints may be placed between the environmental factors, e.g. time of day, and these factors can affect the outcome of the authorization.

The following section will introduce CBAC formally and explain the rational behind a constraints based approach. We will then explore the expressiveness of CBAC by simulating both ACL and RBAC, further explore the use of the rich syntax of CBAC, and introduce a flexible grant/revoke semantics supported directly by CBAC. Section 4 discusses implementation issues and presents an implementation model for developing the CBAC mechanism and the database server seperately. A list of future work is presented before we conclude the paper.

We conclude this introduction with a motivating example. In CBAC Inc, a pay clerk can access the pay table but only within working hours, and the access must be within an hour of the clearance given by the database adminstrator. The following constraints is imposed to the access of the said table:

- The user must play the role of the pay clerk
- The time of day must be within the working hours
- DBADM has given the clearance
- Clearance is within 1 hour.

2. CONSTRAINTS-BASED ACCESS CONTROL

Constraint programming is a declarative form of programming where the programmer specifies the problem in terms of constraints and an automatic solver finds solutions to the problem within the specified constraints [Marriott and Stuckey, 1998]. The mathematical nature of constraints allows the automatic solver to prune the search space by ensuring consistency between the available solutions. This feature also allows the solver to detect contradictions in constraints without iterating through potential assignments. Several systems have been developed from Constraints Programming research and a handful, like iLog, has been successfully deployed in the industry.

There are several reasons constraints are a natural choice for specifying access control policy:

- Constraints can be used directly to specify relationships between entities, events and authorizations.
- Constraints has a strong theoretical foundation and has been applied to program verification. The same principles can likely be applied directly to policy verification.
- Constraint programming languages are turing-complete.
- Advances in the field of automatic constraint solving will have a direct and beneficial impact on this application.
- Techniques like constraint simplification can help weed out redundant rules. The simplified rules are likely to be easier to analyse.
- With the recent interest in Constraint Databases, a constraint based approach to access control like CBAC's matches exactly the tuple generating rules in CDB.

Direct specification of all access control policies in CBAC leads to better consistency in the final authorization with respect to the security policy. In essence, the security adminstrator will specify the policy as a set of constraints and the access control system, in this case the constraint solver, ensures that all accesses complies with the specified constraints. When a user attempts to access a resource, the constraint solver is invoked to check his permissions against the specified constraints.

Definition 1 *We define CBAC as follows:*

- *U, O, and P (users, resources and permissions respectively)*
- $auth : U \times O \times P \rightarrow \{yes, no, partial\}$, *a function that answers if the user is given some permission for a particular resource. 'partial' represents a partial solution when the system cannot determine at the said time whether the user should be allowed to access the resource. I.e. further information that is not available at the time of check is required to give an final answer.*

For purpose of presentation, we use a CLP based system [Jaffar and Lassez, 1987] and syntax to demonstrate the constraints in CBAC *. An authorization constraint, is a predicate in the form

```
auth(User, Resource, Permission) :- C_1, C_2, ... , C_n.
```

where `C_i` is some generic constraints. This predicate is invoked with the necessary parameters when an authorization is required.

The following are some examples of the use of CBAC/CLP.

- User 'adminstrator' is allowed access to every resource.

```
auth(adminstrator, _, _).
```

- All users are allowed all permissions to the tables they own.

```
auth(User, Resource, _) :-
   is_dbtable(Resource), own(User, Resource).
```

- A user can only read from or write to a row that contains his username from table 'particulars'.

```
auth(User, Tuple, [read, write]) :-
  Tuple = particulars(User, ... ),
```

- A pay clerk can access the pay table but only within working hours, and the access must be within an hour of the clearance given by the database adminstrator.

```
auth (User, Object, _) :-
   role(User, pay_clerk),
   date_time(Time), in_working_hour(Time),
   clearance(dbadm, Clearance),
   time_of_clearance(Clearance, T_Clear),
   time_diff(Time, T_Clear, T_Diff), T_Diff <= 60.
```

- List all resources that can be read by User `judge_dred`.

```
auth (judge_dred, Resource, read).
```

3. EXPRESSIVENESS OF CBAC

This section discusses the expressiveness of CBAC. In sections 3.1 and 3.2, we shall show that CBAC subsumes both ACL and RBAC by simulation. We also describe in these sections how the simulations can be done efficiently. Lastly, we shall discuss how CBAC can be used to handle policies like control flow and how GRANT/REVOKE can be supported natively by CBAC.

---

*CBAC does not limit the use of constraint solver to CLP

3.1. A CBAC simulation of ACL

ACL, or access control list, is a list bound to each resource in the system. The list indicates, for the particular resource, the access rights of each users.

Definition 2 *ACL can be viewed as a function defined formally as follows*

- *U, O, and P (users, resource, and permission respectively)*
- $ACL : O \times U \rightarrow P$*, a function mapping the resource O and user U to his access authorizations P.*

A user is allowed to access the resource O if the permission P returned by ACL is equivalent to or dominates† the authorization required for his current actions. In actual implementation, the ACL might be a list attached to the resource. Upon access, the access control system retrieves this list and looks up the user's permission in the list. This is matched against the action the user is trying to perform to determine if the access is to be granted.

Given that ACL is a list that is optimised for searching, a direct simulation will have the same semantics but will not enjoy the same optimization. Instead, we introduce a rule as follows:

```
auth(U, O, P) :-  /* User, Resource and Permission */
  auth_acl(O, U, P).
```

The term `auth_acl` is introduced so we can store the authorization list as a constraint fact with Resource O, User U and Permission P as the first, second and last term of the fact respectively. This is to take advantage of the indexing of facts and rules that is normally done on CLP systems. The abstraction is also allows us to introduce more authorization constraints that applies across the access control system.

We can include terms in the ACL in CBAC using constraint facts as follows:

$\forall ACL(O, U, P)$, `assert(auth_acl(O, U, P))`.

The execution sequence of the CBAC program proceeds as follows in resolving the read authorization for User `judge_dred` on Resource `pilot_table`:

1 `auth(judge_dred, pilot_table, read)` resolves to

2 `auth_acl(pilot_table, judge_dred, read)`.

This term is looked up in both the rules as well as the facts database and the system returns *yes* if there is a solution to this binding and *no* otherwise.

† In the case of a hirerachy of permissions

3.2. A CBAC simulation of RBAC

Role-Based Access Control works by associating permissions to roles and roles to users. This design models the security policies of organizations with the assumptions the roles sufficiently determines the access authorization of the users. RBAC is recently adopted by several well known databases like Oracle, Sybase and Informix. Due to the varying definitions of RBAC, we took the definition off [Sandhu, 1996].

Definition 3 *The $RBAC_0$ model consists of the following components:*

- *U, R, P, and S (users, roles, permissions and sessions respectively)*
- *$PA \subseteq P \times R$, a many-to-many permission to role assignment relation,*
- *$UA \subseteq U \times R$, a many-to-many user to role assignment relation*
- *$user : S \rightarrow U$, a function mapping each session s_i to the single $user(s_i)$ (constant for the session's lifetime), and*
- *$roles : S \rightarrow 2^R$, a function mapping each session s_i to a set of roles $roles(s_i) \subseteq$ $\{r|(user(s_i), r) \in UA\}$ (user's role may change with session) and session s_i has the permissions $\cup_{r \in roles(s_i)}\{p|(p, r) \in PA\}$.*

For this simulation, we define the following predicates:

- `ua(U, R)`, UA binding as defined above,
- `pa(R, O, P)`, binding between roles, resource and permission,
- `user(S, U)`, mapping from session S to user U. Fails if user has no current session.
- `roles(S, R)`, roles R that are active for session S.

The authorization function `auth` is defined as:

```
auth(U, O, P) :- auth_rbac(U, O, P).
auth_rbac(U, O, P) :-
  user(S, U), roles(S, R), /* R = active roles of user U */
  pa(R, O, P).             /* Get P for O,R */
```

Once again, we abstract `auth_rbac` from `auth` to enable introduction of further constraints at that level. We also assume that role-assignment is consulted prior to the role activation. In other words, the user is not allowed to activate an unauthorized role so there is no need to do a check after retrieving the activated role.

Given the same indexing method for facts described in section 3.1, the worst case analysis is

$$O(\Sigma_R|\texttt{pa(R, O, P)}|).$$

3.3. Beyond the Simulations

Consider organization CBAC Inc again. The leave clerk should be authorized to access the leave table of all employees in order to accomplish his job. The above is perfectly captured in RBAC model, "Any user with the role of a leave clerk should be allowed to modify the leave table". However, we may want to exert a little more control over the access to the leave table. We might want to say that this authorization to modify the leave table should be given only when the employee has taken leave. This workflow is not captured in RBAC. On the other hand, it is not difficult to see how CBAC can naturally model this workflow step by checking for an assertion of some employee taking leave before allowing the leave clerk through.

```
auth(U, O, P) :-
   in_dbtable(O, leave),        /* O is from leave table */
   O = leave(Employee, ...),    /* break up leave tuple */
   leave_applied(Employee),  /* Employee applied for leave */
   auth_rbac(U, O, P),       /* RBAC authorization */
```

Next, we might chose to employ different kinds of access control mechanism for different kinds of tables. CBAC captures them within the same syntax. E.g. we may want to have an rbac-based control from some tables but acl based control for others. The above can be handled with the disjunction of constraints.

```
auth(U, O, P) :-
   acl_controlled(O),
   auth_acl(O, U, P).

auth(U, O, P) :-
   rbac_controlled(O),
   auth_rbac(O, U, P).
```

The above examples are aimed at demonstrating how expressive CBAC can be. In fact, CBAC/CLP provides the full expressive power of the underlying CLP language which is Turing-Complete.

3.4. Grant and Revoke Semantics

The GRANT/REVOKE semantics is a heavily debated issue in implementing any access control mechanism. The question usually revolves around what happens to the access rights of a user whose right is granted by another user when the latter's rights are revoked. In a nutshell, any of the following scenarios may be the answer, depending on the system.

1 *Revoke the rights of all the users down the pipeline.* This gives rise to a cascading REVOKE where a right granted may be revoked if the grantor's rights are removed. Removing the access rights of a user implicitly means

removal of access rights granted by this user. It is easy to see how this model gives rise to better control over the access rights.

2 *Revoke the rights of only the users specified, leaving the implicated users alone.* Here, we honour any rights that has been granted and requires explicit removal of any rights. This model is more flexible than the former but requires more work in tracking down the rights that needs removal. This is the approach taken by today's implementation of SQL.

In [Rosenthal and Sciore, 2000], Rosenthal et. al. proposed to extend the SQL grant/revoke model to allow grantors to impose limitations on use of granted rights as well as a flexible revocation scheme. The approach falls between the two scenarios described above. It gives the adminstrators control over the revocation of access priviledges via revoke with limitation predicates, as well as extends the grantor control via predicated grants. This is not unlike the use of constraint rules in describing authorization except that CBAC allows the description of more complex relationship beyond simple predicates.

Use of constraint rules in CBAC should reduce the need to delegate GRANT priviledges to users. Where necessarily, the adminstrators can in fact provide rules that asserts authorisation constraints. Such rules can be as straight forward as an SQL GRANT or support cascading revocation as described in the first senario, or even a predicated GRANT as proposed in Rosenthal et. al. Revocation of user rights can be done through similiar interfaces provided by the adminstrator.

The following example shows how the predicated grant and flexible revocation can be acheived in CBAC.

```
auth(U, O, P) :-
  granted(U, O, P, Grantor),
  not revoked(U, O, P, Grantor),
  auth(Grantor, O, P).
```

Authorisation is given if granted permission is not revoked and grantor still has rights to the resource. The grantors can be allowed free play in asserting their own granted and revoked rules thereby acheiving predicated grants and flexible revocation. Grants and Revokes by different grantors are independent of each other so a grantor cannot revoke the rights granted by another.

4. CBAC: IMPLEMENTATION ISSUES

Efficiency and effectiveness are the 2 main considerations surrounding the design of access control mechanism. We have explore how CBAC can help management of permissions as well as demonstrated the expressiveness of CBAC in the previous sections. The concern about efficiency will be addressed in the sections that follows.

First, the bad news. CBAC allows access if there exists an assignment of variables such that `auth(...)` is realized. The general problem is thus to find an assignment to a problem that is subjected to some constraints, in our case, access control constraints. This is a constraint satisfaction problem (CSP) that is NP-Complete in general [Tsang, 1993]. In other words, a huge system of access control constraints might run into an search that is potentially very expensive. An access control system running on exponential time[‡] will be unusable since it will take too long to respond with the appropriate access authorization.

4.1. Efficiency Considerations

While the general CSP may be NP-Complete, our access control check need not be. In reality, the access control requires only very small constraint programs without deep searches. The typical use of CBAC would be to compute fairly straight forward access authorizations which can be done very efficiently. As we have demonstrated in the section 3, CBAC indeed works efficiently for simple authorization. Complex authorizations would have to come at a cost anyway. Only very few special authorization would need more computation.

The consistency checking mechanism in most constraint solvers are important to ensuring the performance when applying constraints to access control. Constradictions, defined as constraints that will yield no solutions, can be identified by the consistency checking algorithm before further search is invoked. The same consistency checking algorithm will help prune the search space of wrong solutions. Automatic constraint solvers have been known to perform better with a more streamlined set of rules than a larger set of more explicit rules. The former translates to a smaller set of access control rules that facilitates checking and encourages a more unified set of access control policies than patching.

We do not attempt to conclude that CBAC would be optimal for all complex authorizations but its use of a constraint engine that can generate partial solutions can in fact help even in speeding up the database search.

Partial solutions generated by constraint solvers when it cannot give a definite answer may be useful in limiting SQL searches. In a typical system, normal users may be allowed to access only their own record. This check is usually done through a frontend that accesses the database on the user's behalf. A smarter application programmer would realise that in this senario, the `username` can be used to limit the SQL search. For example, if user 'NormalUser' tries to access the system to retrieve his payroll statement, the SQL query formulated by the application can be:

```
select * from payroll where employee='NormalUser';
```

In CBAC, the access control will be written as:

[‡]Until we can prove that $P = NP$

```
auth(U, O, P) :- O = payroll(U, ...).
```

Since `payroll(U, ...)` is a non-entailing but linear constraint, the constraints system will return it as the partial solution. This partial solution can be passed on the database backend as an additional condition yielding the same effect as the smart programmer. In fact, we can do this for any number of linear constraints.

The advantage of CBAC stands out when there are many such applications.

4.2. Implementation Model

This section discusses a priliminary implementation model for CBAC on existing databases. The model is designed so that the CBAC layer can be developed independently from the database server. This philosophy will allow us to use existing databases as well as existing constraint solvers. The assumptions for the model area as follows:

- The database backend need not have constraint solving capabilities
- All connections to the database has to pass through the CBAC layer
- Existing access control system may continue to be in place

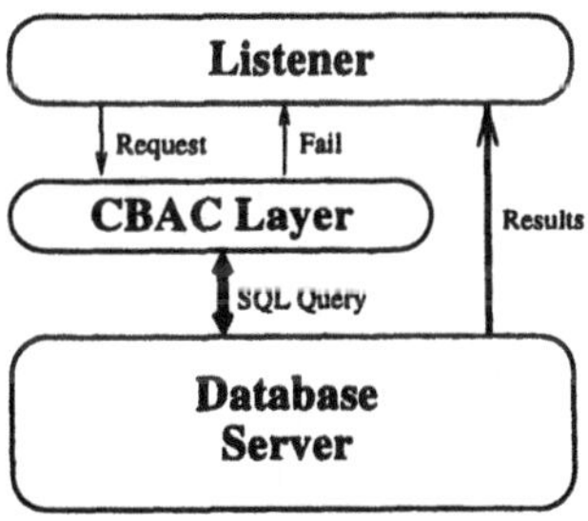

Figure 1. Incorporating CBAC into existing databases

Our proposed model seperates the system into 3 layers as shown in figure 1.

- **Listener**. The listener listens for incoming connection and does the authentication as required by the database server.
- **CBAC layer**. The CBAC layer will store all the access control constraints and apply them on incoming queries before passing the queries to the database.
- **Database Server**. This is the existing database server.

In this model, all queries will pass thru the CBAC layer. Queries may be modified by the CBAC layer to the security specifications before being passed to the database backend. There are also mechanisms that will allow the CBAC layer to "check" with the database backend so that proper access control status can be determined.

Results from the database server is sent directly to the frontend.

The CBAC layer works as follows:

- Any queries that can be cleared directly is passed unchanged to the database backend.
- Queries that fail the security specifications are dropped and CBAC will return an "Access Violation" to the frontend.
- The use of constraint based specification allows for queries that can only be cleared pending some conditions. If these conditions can be answered by the database backend, e.g. linear constraints, the partial solution is added as extra conditions to the original query and the modified query is passed to the backend as cleared.
- Otherwise, the CBAC layer may need to formulate its own queries to the database until any of the above conditions prevails.

The CBAC layer will be compatible with whatever access control strategies the existing database server employs since the SQL queries still need to pass through the existing access control mechanism of the database. In fact, if the existing database server uses RBAC, the CBAC layer may pass the RBAC checks to the database instead.

5. FUTURE WORK

This paper presents a fresh approach to specifying access control directed at database systems. Several issues are yet to be smoothened out.

- *Further implications of applying CBAC to databases.* Most access control mechanism build on top of SQL which is familiar to most database adminstrator but CBAC introduces a rule-based language which may not be familiar to most users.
- *Further implications of the GRANT/REVOKE mechanism.* While we paint a rosy picture about the GRANT/REVOKE mechanism and are comfortable about that CBAC can support predicated grants and conditional revocation, the impact of loose use of GRANT is yet to be known. One of the problems that are not addressed is forming of infinite loops through the grant semantics – the grantor grants himself. The flexible

grant/revoke mechanism discussed in section 3.4 introduced an additional level of search that will have an impact on the efficiency of the entire system if loosely used.

- *Customising the constraint solver for CBAC.* Most constraint solvers are built to be general engines and will remain as such. Some work can be done to customise constraint solvers to speed up the evaluation of constraints that are frequently used by CBAC.

- *CBAC dependency on the database when unresolved authorization constraints are non-linear is not clear.* We are certain this can happen due when complex constraints are involved but are not sure the communication costs for the resolution.

- *A tighter integration with existing databases.* The layered approach will only serve as a demonstration of how the CBAC engine and the database server can be seperately developed. A tighter integration is required to reduce the communication cost between the two systems.

- *Use of validation libraries on CBAC rules.* The expressiveness of CBAC allows users to write authorization rules without introducing another frontend check. This permits us to compute a closure of the access control of the system without having to worry about any further access mechanism at work outside of CBAC. There are validation tools that work with constraint solvers and they may be applied to validate the access control constraints.

6. CONCLUSION

In this paper, we have presented CBAC, a radically different approach to database access control that is still work-in-progress. This constraints based approach allows the users the full flexibility of the constraints language.

Specifying access control policies using a constraints based language has many advantages. Most of the time, access control policies are specified in rules that can be translated directly into constraint rules. The expressiveness of the constraints language removes the reliance on access proxies. This greatly simplifies the job of access control analysis since all information is available at a single point instead of being spread across several programs and possibly different languages. The use of constraint rules also help the analysis.

We showed how CBAC can simulate both ACL and RBAC and went further to demonstrate CBAC with a workflow example. We also discussed the grant/revoke semantics that can be acheived within CBAC. The database adminstrator now can specify exactly how grant/revoke is used with the same language that authorizes the user-rights of his database.

· CBAC casts the access control graph into a CSP problem which is NP-Complete. However, as demonstrated by the examples, the use of CBAC would typically be restricted to fairly straight forward computations that will not result in deep searches. Partial solutions generated by the constraint solvers can be added to the final SQL query to limit the database search.

An implementation model that keeps the development of CBAC and the database server seperate is also presented.

In summary, CBAC presents a rich syntax for describing access control policies. It is important to note that CBAC still needs a lot of work to deployment as we have highlighted in section 5. Despite the followups required, we believe that CBAC deserves attention, not only from the database developers, but also from developers of massive systems where access control policies are important.

References

[Bertino et al., 1998] Bertino, E., Bettini, C., Ferrari, E., and Samarati, P. (1998). An access control model supporting periodicity constraints and temporal reasoning. In *ACM Transactions on Database Systems*, volume 23, pages 231–285.

[Bertino et al., 1993] Bertino, E., Samarati, P., and Jajodia, S. (1993). Authorizations in relational database management systems. In *1st ACM Conference on Computer and Communications Security*, pages 130–139.

[Castano et al., 1994] Castano, S., Fugini, M., Martella, G., and Samarati, P. (1994). *Database Security*. Addison Wesley.

[Jaffar and Lassez, 1987] Jaffar, J. and Lassez, J.-L. (1987). Constraint logic programming. In *Principles of Programming Languages*.

[Marriott and Stuckey, 1998] Marriott, K. and Stuckey, P. J. (1998). *Programming with Constraints*. The MIT Press.

[Rosenthal and Sciore, 2000] Rosenthal, A. and Sciore, E. (2000). Extending sql grant and revoke operations to limit and reactive privileges. In *IFIP Working Conference on Database Security*.

[Sandhu, 1996] Sandhu, R. S. (1996). Role-based access control. Technical report, Laboratory for Information Security Technology, Geore Mason University.

[Sandhu et al., 1996] Sandhu, R. S., Coyne, E. J., Feinstein, H. L., and Youman, C. E. (1996). Role-based access control models. *IEEE Computer*, 29(2):38–47.

[Sandhu and Samarati,] Sandhu, R. S. and Samarati, P. Access control: Principles and practice. www.isse.gmu.edu/faculty/sandhu.

[Tsang, 1993] Tsang, E. (1993). *Foundations of Constraint Satisfaction*. Academic Press.

SECURE ROLE-BASED WORKFLOW MODELS

Savith Kandala and Ravi Sandhu

Savith Kandala
CygnaCom Solutions.

Ravi Sandhu
SingleSignOn.Net and George Mason University

Abstract: In this paper we introduce a series of reference models for Secure Role-Based Workflow systems. We build our models over the well-known RBAC96 framework. The RBAC96 model supports the notion of abstract permissions. The nature of permissions is highly dependent upon the implementation details of the system, so we interpret the permissions for a Workflow system in terms of its components such as tasks, instances of the tasks and operations on them like execute, commit, abort etc. With this interpretation, we show that most of the components of RBAC96 still remain intact. The only components that change are the nature of permissions and their assignment to roles. The models are developed using the recently introduced four-layer OM-AM framework (comprising objective, model, architecture and mechanism layers). In this paper, we focus on the top two layers of OM-AM. We systematically describe our security objectives and construct our models to address these objectives. We also formally describe the models in terms of their components and their interactions. The main purpose for proposing these models is to articulate requirements for building Secure Role-Based Workflow Systems.

Key words: Access control, Role-Based workflows, workflow authorizations, and RBAC

1. INTRODUCTION

Workflow Management Systems (WFMS) are used to coordinate and streamline business process in an enterprise. A workflow defines various activities of an enterprise in terms of certain well-defined tasks. Users according to organizational rules carry out these tasks. Quite often, roles represent organizational agents intended to perform certain job functions within the organization. Users in turn are assigned appropriate roles based on their qualifications and responsibilities. [2]

RBAC96 [7] is a general model for role-based access control (RBAC). It treats permissions as un-interpreted symbols. The nature of permissions in the RBAC96 model is highly dependent upon the implementation details of a system and the general kind of system that it is. For example, an operating system protects files, directories, devices, ports, etc., with operations such as read, write, execute, etc., a relational database management system on the other hand protects relations, tuples, attributes, views, etc., with operations such as SELECT, UPDATE, DELETE, INSERT, etc. More generally, RBAC96 allows for abstract permissions specific to applications such as CREDIT and DEBIT in an accounting application. The nature of permissions in a WFMS can also be interpreted similarly, as a WFMS should control access to the tasks and instances of these tasks in the system with operations such as execute, commit, abort etc.

Preliminary ideas for Secure Role-Based Workflow models were presented in Transaction Control Expressions (TCEs) [6]. The TCE model is very natural and intuitive, and in fact reflects the world of forms and books in a Computer-Based System. However, TCEs were proposed much before RBAC96 was conceptualized and as such does not have all the components and specifications of RBAC96. The Task-Based Authorization Control (TBAC) [12] model was introduced to provide the notion of just-in-time permissions. It enables the granting, usage tracking and revoking of permissions to be automated and coordinated with the progression of various tasks. From a conceptual standpoint, TBAC focuses on the processing states and life cycle of authorizations and therefore cannot be directly compared to RBAC96. Bertino, Ferrari and Atluri (BFA) [2] have recently proposed a model for specifying and enforcing authorization constraints for WFMS. The model emphasizes on constraint specification and enforcement and as such does not encompass all the concepts of RBAC96.

The main contribution of this paper is that it shows, by aptly defining the nature of permissions RBAC96 can be extended to model Secure Role-Based Workflows. A consequential contribution is that it shows the OM-AM framework is a useful tool for modeling secure systems. The main purpose for proposing these models is to articulate the requirements for building secure role-based workflow systems.

The rest of the paper is organized as follows. Section 2 of the paper briefly describes the OM-AM framework, which was used to construct our Secure Role-Based Workflow models. Section 3 of the paper describes the RBAC96 model. Section 4 of the paper introduces our first model for Secure Role-Based Workflows with very simple security objectives. Section 5, Section 6, Section 7 introduce the models for Secure Role-Based Workflows with progressively complex security objectives. Section 8 of the paper gives the future work to be done and the conclusion.

2. THE OM-AM FRAMEWORK FOR SECUIRTY ENGINEERING

In this section we briefly describe the four-layer OM-AM framework for security engineering, a detailed description can be found in [9]. The four layers are objective, model, architecture and mechanism surrounded by a sea of assurance, which permeates all layers (as shown in Figure 1). Objective and model are concerned with articulating what the security objectives and attendant trade-offs are, while architecture and mechanism address how to meet these requirements. In this paper we use the top two layers of this framework to formulate the security objectives and build our models.

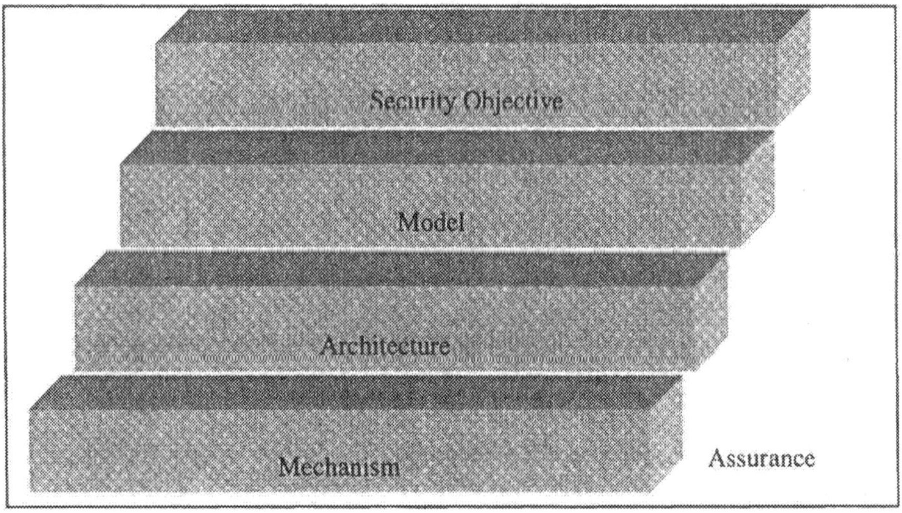

Figure 1 The OM-AM Framework for Security Engineering

3. THE RBAC96 MODEL

In this section we give a brief description of the RBAC96 model. This model has become a widely cited authoritative reference and is the basis of a standard currently under development by the National Institute of Standards and Technology. The main components of the RBAC96 model are users, sessions[1], roles, role hierarchy, permissions, user-assignment relationship, permission-assignment relationship and constraints. Figure 2 illustrates the RBAC96 model.

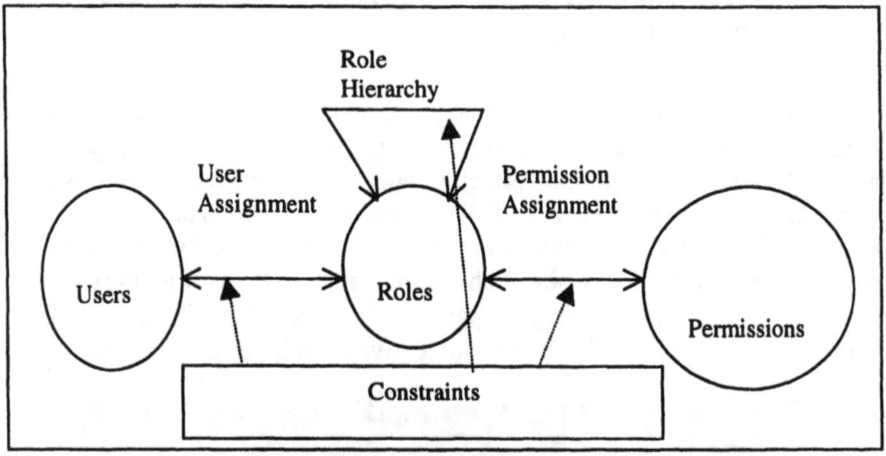

Figure 2 The RBAC96 Model

We now describe the RBAC96 model in terms of the OM-AM framework as described in section 2 of this paper.

Security Objective: The basic objective of RBAC is to simplify access control administration. It also provides ease of support for important security principles, particularly (1) least privilege, (2) separation of duties, (3) abstract permissions and (4) separation of administration and access.

Model: The RBAC96 model has the following components:

U – set of users, R – set of roles, P – set of permissions

$UA \subseteq U \times R$ (User Assignment)

$RH \subseteq R \times R$ is a partial order on R also called the role hierarchy or Role dominance relation written as $\leq$

$PA \subseteq R \times P$ (Permission Assignment)

permissions: $R \rightarrow 2^P$, a function mapping each role r to a set of permissions.

permissions:* $R \rightarrow 2^P$ extends permissions in presence of a role-hierarchy.

permissions$(r_i) = \{ p \in P \mid (p, r_i) \in PA\}$

*permissions**$(r_i) = \{ p \in P \mid (\exists r \leq r_i)[(p, r) \in PA]\}$

Constraints are predicates, which applied to various components, determine if its value is acceptable or not.

[1] To simply our discussion we omit this component since it does not impact the results of this paper.

4. SECURE ROLE-BASED WORKFLOW MODEL$_0$

In this section we describe our first model for Secure Role-Based Workflows. We start by describing the various components of a Workflow System. A *task* in this model can be a program, a process or a procedure that is stored in the schema of the Workflow System. A *task instance*[2] is an instance of the task, or in other words it is a copy of the task that is made to run an instance of it. We also define an *Instance Mapping* that maps each task to its instances and is defined as follows.

Definition 1: Instance Mapping
Let TT be a set of tasks and TI a set of task instances, the Instance Mapping $\mathfrak{I}: TT \rightarrow 2^{TI}$ *is a mapping that maps each task to its various instances, such that* $\mathfrak{I}(a) \cap \mathfrak{I}(b) = \phi$ *if* $a \neq b$ *and* $a, b \in TT$

We interpret *permission* in this model to be an authorization to *execute* a task. We further refine our interpretation by specifying that the permission to execute a task implies the permission to execute any instance of the task.

In order to model our interpretation of permissions, we define *Explicit Permissions* (EP) to be a cross product between the set of operations and the set of tasks. These Explicit Permissions are assigned to roles. We call this permission assignment relation as *Explicit Permission Assignment* (EPA).

We call permissions on task instances as *Implicit Permissions* (IP), and define them as a cross product between the set of operations and the set of task instances. For the moment we introduce a single operation on a task instance, called *execute* which authorizes execution of the task. Subsequent models will introduce additional operations. The permissions on task instances (IP) are assigned to roles based on EPA. If a task is assigned to a role then all instances of the task are also assigned to the same role. We call this assignment relation as Implicit Permission Assignment (IPA).

The crux of our Secure Role-Based Workflow models lies in these two relations EPA and IPA. Figure 3 below illustrates the model completely.

We now describe our model in terms of the OM-AM framework as described in section 2 of this paper.

Security Objective: Permissions in a Workflow System are interpreted as the authorization to execute tasks. Permission to execute a task implies permission to execute any instance of the task.

Model: U, R, RH, UA are unchanged from RBAC96

[2] We consider the details like how these task instances are created, or how these task instances come into existence to be outside the scope of this paper. We leave these details to the Workflow Management System.

OP = {execute} (singleton set which contains the execute operation)
TT – set of tasks, TI – set of task instances
$\Im$ – An instance mapping that maps each task to its instances
$\Im : TT \rightarrow 2^{TI}$ such that $\Im(a) \cap \Im(b) = \phi$ if $a \neq b$ and $a, b \in TT$
EP (set of EXPLICIT PERMISSIONS) = OP × TT
IP (set of IMPLICIT PERMISSIONS) = OP × TI
P (set of permissions) = EP ∪ IP
EPA (set of explicitly assigned permissions) ⊆ R × EP
IPA (set of implicitly assigned permissions derived from EPA)
$IPA = \{(r_i, \text{execute}, t_i) \mid [\exists (r_i, \text{execute}, t) \in EPA] \wedge t_i \in \Im(t)\}$
PA (Permission Assignment) = EPA ∪ IPA
permissions: $R \rightarrow 2^{IP}$, a function mapping each role *r* to a set of permissions.
permissions:* $R \rightarrow 2^{IP}$ extends permissions in presence of a role-hierarchy.
$permissions(r_i) = \{(\text{execute}, t_i) \mid (\exists [(r_i, \text{execute}, t) \in EPA] \wedge t_i \in \Im(t)\}$
$permissions^*(r_i) = \{(\text{execute}, t_i) \mid (\exists r \leq r_i)[(r, \text{execute}, t) \in EPA] \wedge t_i \in \Im(t)\}$

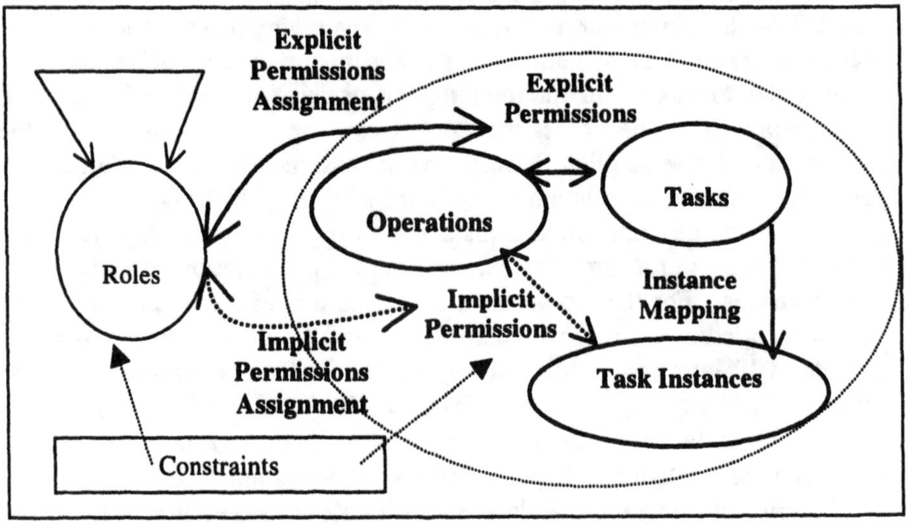

Figure 3 Secure Role Based Workflow Model $_0$

A proof-of-concept implementation to demonstrate the practical feasibility of this model is described in [1]. The system implemented ensures that users belonging to a specific role can execute the task instances. This model was not formally described in [1] we have described it formally here. The paper [1], describes an experiment to inject RBAC into an existing web-based workflow system using commercial-of-the-shelf (COTS) technology with minimal changes to the existing system.

5. SECURE ROLE-BASED WORKFLOW MODEL$_1$

In this section we describe our second model for Secure Role-Based Workflow systems. An obvious shortcoming of the previous model is that there is no notion of the task instances being completed. Therefore, there is no restriction on how many times a task instance can be repeatedly executed. We introduce the notion of states in tasks, and constrain the state transitions and the operations possible in each state in this model to improve upon the previous model.

For the purpose of this paper, we only consider transactional tasks. We believe that non-transactional tasks as well as two-phase commit tasks can also be modeled in a similar way. Figure 4 below, illustrates the states and the state transitions for some task structures.

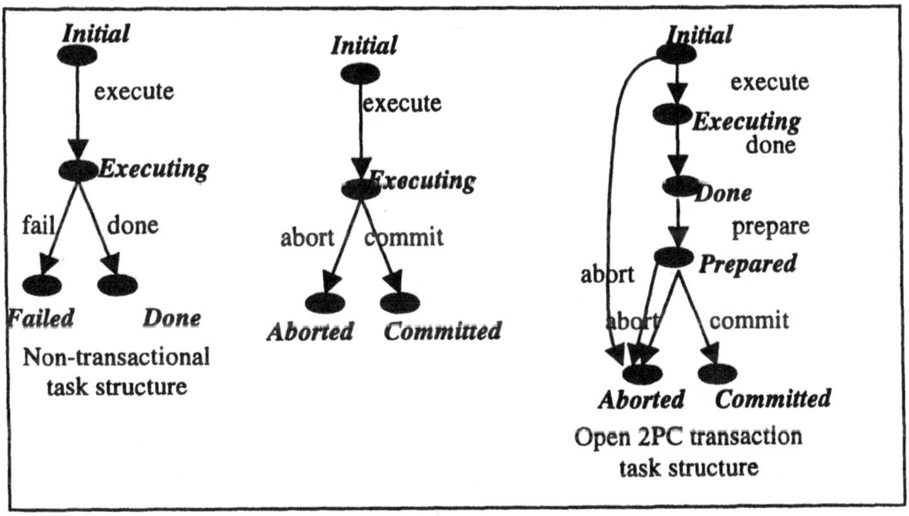

Figure 4 Some Task Structures

Consider the transactional task structure; the task is in the *Initial* state. The *execute* operation transitions the task instance to the *Executing* state. From this state there are two operations that are possible, *commit* and *abort*. The *commit* operation transitions the task instance to the *Committed* state and the *abort* operation transitions the task instance to the *Aborted* state. Although, we do not emphasize this in figure 3 below, from the *Aborted* state task instances are put back in the *Initial* state, so that they could be tried again for successful execution.

It should be noted that this task structure does not determine the means of execution or the functionality of the task, but only a high-level description of the (visible) state transitions.

We further restrict the permissions on task instances by stating that if a task instance is in the *Initial* state then the only possible operation on it should be *execute*. Similarly, if the task instance is in *Executing* state, then the possible operations should be *commit* or *abort*. By further restricting the assignment of implicit permissions we ensure that only those task instances that are in the proper state are assigned to roles. In order, to get the current state of a task instance and list possible operations of a task instance we define two functions *CurrentState* and *PossibleOperations*.

Definition 2: CurrentState determines the current state of the task.
Let TI be the set of task instances and S the set of states.
CurrentState: TI → S maps each task instance to its state.
CurrentState(ti) = { s | s ∈ S and s is the current state of ti}

Definition 3: PossibleOperations determines the operations possible in a given state.
Let S the set of states and OP the set of operations
PossibleOperations ⊆ S X OP specifies the operations possible in each state. (For transactional tasks we consider PossibleOperations = {(Initial, execute), (Executing, commit), (Executing, abort)})

As mentioned earlier, the crux of our Secure Role-Based Workflow models lies in the two relations EPA and IPA. The definitions for EP, IP and EPA remain unchanged from our previous model. The definition IPA is changed to include its dependency on EPA and the state of the task instance.

In order for the model to be complete we should consider the following constraints. First, either all permissions ((execute, t), (commit, t), (abort, t)) on the task t are assigned to a role or none of them are assigned. Second, the user who invokes the operation *execute* on the task instance, should also invoke either *commit* or *abort* operation on the same task instance. We list these constraints informally in the model.

We now describe our model in terms of the OM-AM framework as described in section 2 of this paper.

Security Objective: Security Objective for Role-Based Workflow Model $_0$ + Tasks have states (Initial, Executing, Committed, Aborted) and only certain operations (execute, commit, abort) can be performed in each state.

Model: U, R, RH, UA, TT, TI, EP, IP are unchanged from $RBWM_0$
OP (set of operations) = {execute, commit, abort}
S (set of states) = {Initial, Executing, Committed, Aborted}
T (set of state transitions) = {(Initial, execute, Executing), (Executing, commit, Committed), (Executing, abort, Aborted)}
CurrentState(ti) = { s | s ∈ S and s is the current state of ti}

PossibleOperations = {(Initial, execute), (Executing, commit), (Executing, abort)}

$P = EP \cup IP$

$EPA \subseteq R \times EP$ (Set of explicitly assigned permissions)

$$IPA = \{(r_i, op, t_i) \mid [\exists (r_i, op, t) \in EPA] \wedge [t_i \in \Im(t)] \wedge [(CurrentState(t_i), op) \in PossibleOperations]\}$$

$PA = EPA \cup IPA$

permissions: $R \rightarrow 2^{IP}$, a function mapping each role *r* to a set of permissions.

permissions:* $R \rightarrow 2^{IP}$ extends permissions in presence of a role-hierarchy.

$$permissions(r_i) = \{(op, t_i) \mid [\exists (r_i, op, t) \in EPA] \wedge [t_i \in \Im(t)] \wedge [(CurrentState(t_i), op) \in PossibleOperations]\}$$

$$permissions^*(r_i) = \{(op, t_i) \mid (\exists r \leq r_i)[(r, op, t) \in EPA] \wedge [t_i \in \Im(t)] \wedge [(CurrentState(t_i), op) \in PossibleOperations]\}$$

Constraints: Either all permissions ((execute, t), (commit, t), (abort, t)) on the task t are assigned to a role or none of them are assigned.

The user who invokes the operation *execute* on the task instance, also is the only one who can invoke either *commit* or *abort* operation on the same task instance[3].

6. SECURE ROLE-BASED WORKFLOW MODEL$_2$

In this section we describe our third model for Secure Role-Based Workflows. Wc introduce the notion of task ordering at this stage. A workflow is considered to be a set of task types and their order of execution. Intertask dependencies determine how tasks in the workflow are coordinated for execution. The general type of dependency that is of interest is the *state dependency*. We use the Workflow Specification Language (WSFL) described in [4] to describe the workflow and the intertask dependencies. We focus on how the tasks can be placed together in a workflow with the use of state dependencies. The details of the language are not discussed in this paper, but can be found in [4].

A state dependency specifies how a transition of a task depends on the current states of other tasks. A state dependency is specified as a rule consisting *<left hand side> evaluator <right hand side>*. The state dependencies are expressed using the evaluator $\Rightarrow$, such that the left-hand side includes a predicate over task states and the right-hand side refers to a transition. For example, the following dependency specifies that if T1 is in a Committed state then T2 must transition to Initial state.

[3] The identity of the user who performs the operations should be recorded to enforce this constraint. This is a mechanism issue, which belongs at the bottom layer of OM-AM. As such it is out of scope for this paper where our focus is on the top two layers of OM-AM.

(T1, Committed) $\Rightarrow$ (T2, Initial);

Definition 5: (Workflow)
A workflow is defined as a compound task that is composed of a set of tasks and a set of intertask dependencies associated with it, which specifies the order of task execution. The intertask dependencies are specified in terms of state dependencies.

We discuss an example to demonstrate some of the specification features. The example has three tasks Initial Review, Correct Errors, and Process Application, and their order of execution is illustrated in figure 5 below.

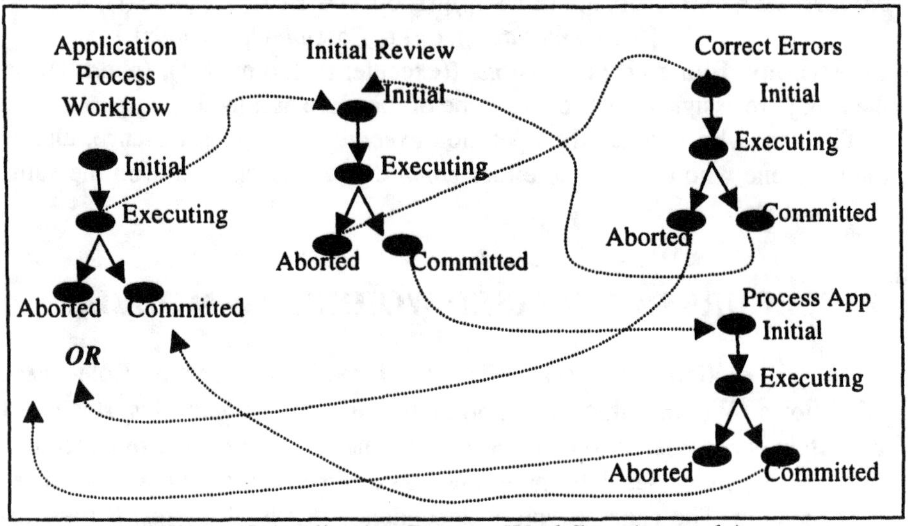

Figure 5 Application Process Workflow (example).

In terms of the above definition for Workflow we can write the intertask dependencies as follows:
Application Process Workflow = {Initial Review, Correct Errors, Process Application}
Intertask Dependencies:
(Application Process Workflow, Executing) $\Rightarrow$ (Initial Review, Initial);
(Initial Review, Aborted) $\Rightarrow$ (Correct Errors, Initial);
(Correct Errors, Committed) $\Rightarrow$ (Initial Review, Initial);
(Initial Review, Committed) $\Rightarrow$ (Process Application, Initial);
(Process Application, Committed)$\Rightarrow$(Application Process Workflow, Committed);
(Process Application, Aborted) $\Rightarrow$ (Application Process Workflow, Aborted);
(Correct Errors, Aborted) $\Rightarrow$ (Application Process Workflow, Aborted);

Intuitively, the intertask dependencies specified are consistent if and only if every path (with the exception of loops) from the Workflow *Initial* state terminates in the Workflow *Aborted* state or Workflow *Committed* state. Notice that the following scenario can occur Task *Initial Review* moves to aborted, Task *Correct Errors* is started and then committed, then Task *Initial Review* is moved to Initial, and so on. We assume that the loops eventually terminate and then the workflow terminates in either an aborted or committed state. We also consider formally specifying consistency checking of intertask dependencies to be outside of the scope of this paper and therefore do not specify them here. The *StartCondition Function* evaluates the intertask dependencies for the task instance and returns a boolean value TRUE or FALSE.

Definition 6: StartCondition Function evaluates the intertask dependencies for the task instance and returns a boolean value TRUE or FALSE.
Let TI be the set of task instances.
StartCondition: $TI \rightarrow \{TRUE, FALSE\}$.

As mentioned earlier, the crux of our Secure Role-Based Workflow models lies in the two relations EPA and IPA. The definitions of EP, IP and EPA remain unchanged from our previous model. The definition IPA is changed to include its dependency on EPA, the state of the task instance and the start condition of the task instance.

Definition 7: IPA – Implicit Permission Assignment.
$IPA = \{(r_i, op, t_i) \mid [\exists (r_i, op, t) \in EPA] \wedge [t_i \in \Im(t)] \wedge$
$[(CurrentState(t_i), op) \in PossibleOperations] \wedge$
$[(StartCondition(t_i) = TRUE] \}$

We now describe our model in terms of the OM-AM framework as described in section 2 of this paper.
Security Objective: Security Objective for Role-Based Workflow Model$_1$ + Tasks are executed according to the specified intertask dependencies.
Model: U, R, RH, UA, TT, TI, OP, T, S, EP, IP, EPA, CurrentState, PossibleOperations, are unchanged from RBWM$_1$
StartCondition: $TI \rightarrow \{TRUE, FALSE\}$
P (set of permissions) = $EP \cup IP$
EPA (set of explicitly assigned permissions) $\subseteq R \times EP$
IPA (set of implicit permissions) =
$\{(r_i, op, t_i) \mid [\exists (r_i, op, t) \in EPA] \wedge [t_i \in \Im(t)] \wedge$
$[(CurrentState(t_i), op) \in PossibleOperations] \wedge$

$[(StartCondition(t_i) = \text{TRUE}]\ \}$
$PA = EPA \cup IPA$
permissions: $R \rightarrow 2^{IP}$, function mapping each role r to a set of permissions.
permissions:* $R \rightarrow 2^{IP}$ extends permissions in presence of a role-hierarchy.

$$permissions(r_i) = \{(op, t_i) \mid [\exists\ (r_i, op, t) \in EPA] \wedge [t_i \in \Im(t)] \wedge [(CurrentState(t_i), op) \in PossibleOperations] \wedge [(StartCondition(t_i) = \text{TRUE}]\ \}$$

$$permissions^*(r_i) = \{(op, t_i) \mid (\exists\ r \leq r_i\ )[\ (r, op, t) \in EPA] \wedge [t_i \in \Im(t)] \wedge [(CurrentState(t_i), op) \in PossibleOperations] \wedge [(StartCondition(t_i) = \text{TRUE}]\ \}$$

Constraints: Same as the constraints for Role-Based Workflow Model_1

7. SECURE ROLE-BASED WORKFLOW MODEL$_3$

In this section we describe our fourth and final model for Secure Role-Based Workflows. We introduce notion of specifying authorization constraints on tasks at this stage. We mainly focus on the Separation of Duties (SOD) constraints. We use the syntax specified in Transaction Control Expressions (TCEs) [6] to model these constraints. Extensions beyond this fourth model may be possible but are beyond the scope of this paper. In other words we are not claiming that this is the last word on this topic. We now briefly describe the syntax proposed in TCEs for expressing SOD constraints by an example. The details of the syntax are not discussed here, but can be found in [6]. Consider the workflow example Process Checks with three tasks Prepare, Approve, Issue. If all the three tasks are to be performed by different users, we do not associate any symbols with the tasks and simply write them as

(Prepare,), (Approve,), (Issue,)

If any user can perform task Approve, and the task Prepare and task Issue have to be performed by different users we write them as follows

(Prepare,), (Approve, ↑), (Issue,)

If the tasks Prepare and Issue have to be performed by same user and task Approve has to be performed by a different user we write them as follows

(Prepare, ↓x), (Approve,), (Issue, ↓x)

(Note: The token "x" is for relating multiple anchors. For instance we can use the symbol ↓ with a token "y" to identify another set of tasks that need to be performed by the same user.)

Definition 5: (Workflow)

A workflow is defined as a compound task that is composed of a set of tasks, a set of intertask dependencies associated with it, which specify the

order of task execution and a set of TCE constraints. Each element in the set of TCE constraints is a two tuple (t, symbol) where t ∈ set of tasks and symbol is ↑ or ↓ (with token).

In order to enforce these constraints, the identity of the user who performs each task should be recorded. The TCE constraints can be viewed as constraints on the *Permissions* component of RBAC96. We are basically checking if the user attempting to perform an operation on a task instance satisfies the TCE constraints for the workflow instance.

We now describe our model in terms of the OM-AM framework as described in section 2 of this paper.

Security Objective: Security Objective for Role-Based Workflow $Model_2$ + Separation of Duty and related Constraints

Model: The model is unchanged from Role-Based Workflow $Model_2$, except for the additional constraint on Implicit Permissions.

Constraints: Same as the constraints for Role-Based Workflow $Model_2$ + The user attempting to execute Implicit Permission should satisfy the TCE constraints.

8. CONCLUSION AND FUTURE WORK

We have presented a series of Secure Role-Based Workflow models, which systematically span the spectrum from very simple at one end to quite complex at the other. We started with a simple security objective and formulated our first Secure Role-Based Workflow model. For each subsequent model we added more complexity to the security objective and formulated our models by building on earlier ones. In this paper, we have shown that RBAC96 can be extended to model Secure Role-Based Workflows. The models were formulated following the OM-AM framework, thus demonstrating the effectiveness of the framework. The models developed realize the promise of RBAC96, which is a policy neutral, flexible, easy-to-customize framework for articulating and enforcing access control policies. Each of the models proposed can be implemented, depending upon the requirements of the system. For example, we have given a reference to the implementation of $Model_0$ [1], where the requirement was to just ensure that a user belonging to a specific role could execute a task.

The work presented in this paper can be extended along several directions. One such possible direction could be moving further down the OM-AM framework in terms of Architecture and Mechanisms to implement the models. Another possible direction could be extending these models for distributed and heterogeneous workflow systems. Yet another possible research direction could be to investigate the possibility of fitting our models into an existing Workflow System. Finally, incorporating issues related to delegation and controlled overriding of constraints into these models is also a challenging research goal.

ACKNOWLEDGEMENT

This work is partially supported by the National Science Foundation at George Mason University.

REFERENCES

[1] Ahn G, Sandhu R, Myong H K, Park J. (2000) Injecting RBAC to Secure a Web-based Workflow System. Fifth ACM Workshop on RBAC, pp 1 – 10

[2] Bertino, E., Ferrari, E. and Atluri, V. (1997). A flexible model for the specification and enforcement of authorization constraints in workflow management system. Proceedings of the Second ACM Workshop on Role-Based Access Control.

[3] Clark, D.D. and Wilson, D.R. (1987). A comparison of commercial and military security policies. Proceedings of IEEE Symposium on Security and Privacy, pp. 184-194.

[4] Narayanan K, Sheth A, (1995) Managing Heterogeneous Multi-system Tasks to Support Enterprise-wide Operation. Distributed and Parallel Databases vol 3 number 2 April 1995 pp 155 - 186 [5] Nash, M.J. and Poland, K.R. (1987). Some conundrums concerning separation of duty. Proceedings of IEEE Symposium on Security and Privacy, pp. 201-207.

[6] Sandhu, R. (1988). Transaction control expressions for separation of duties. Proceedings of the Fourth Aerospace Computer Security Applications Conference, pp. 282-286.

[7] Sandhu, R., Coyne, E.J., Feinstein, H.L. and Youman, C.E. (1996). Role-based access control models. IEEE Computer, 29(2), pp. 38-47.

[8] Sandhu, R. (1990). Separation of duties in computerized information systems. Proceedings of the IFIP WG 11.3 Workshop on Database Security.

[9] Sandhu, R, (2000) Engineering Authority and Trust in Cyberspace: The OM-AM and RBAC Way. Fifth ACM Workshop on RBAC, pp 111 – 119

[10] Sandhu R, Ferraiolo D, Kuhn R, (2000) The NIST Model for Role-based Access Control: Towards a Unified Standard, Fifth ACM Workshop on RBAC, pp 47-64

[11] Simon, R.T. and Zurko, M.E. (1997). Separation of duty in role-based environments. Proceedings of Computer Foundations Workshop X.

[12] Thomas, R.K. and Sandhu R. (1997). Task-based authorization controls (TBAC) Proceedings of the IFIP WG 11.3 Workshop on Database Security.

[13] Ullman, J (1989) Principles of Database and Knowledge-Base Systems (2nd volume). Computer Science Press, New York.

III

DISTRIBUTED SYSTEMS

SUBJECT SWITCHING ALGORITHMS FOR ACCESS CONTROL IN FEDERATED DATABASES

Jacqueline Yang, Duminda Wijesekera, Sushil Jajodia
Center for Secure Information Systems, George Mason University, Fairfax, VA 22033-4444

Abstract: Authentication in federated database systems present difficulties because the autonomously operated components may not know the identity of federation users. One proposed solution is subject switching, where the federation translates the federated users identity to that of an agreed upon component subject. This translation may be problematic, due to not having component subjects with the same accesses requested by federation users. Therefore, we propose using proximity measures between requested and provided accesses and present two policy neutral algorithms to find proximity minimizing matches between a federation subject and a collection of component subjects.

Key words: federated database, access control, database security

1. INTRODUCTION

Demand for seamless information sharing has inspired many computing resources to be interconnected in numerous ways into large-scale information systems. Federated databases can provide integrated yet autonomously controlled services for permanent logical data storage. A federated database is a set of autonomous and possibly heterogeneous databases that participate in a collective enterprise without centralized control. Consequently, any component database of a federated system could participate in more than one federation and could be a federated database system itself. Implied autonomy of component databases in federated databases facilitates heterogeneity in data models, query languages, concurrency control, transaction management and access control.

Authentication of federation users presents problems in federated database systems because a user's identity may not be known to all component databases. One possible approach to deal with this problem is to permit federation users to assume the identity of the federation. This approach has the drawback that every federation user obtains all the access rights of the federation, unless the user accesses are restricted using some mechanism by the federation.

Another possible approach is to change the identity of the user to other federation subjects based on prior agreement between the federation and the components. This method, commonly refereed to as subject switching [JONS94], is the topic of this paper. In order to map a federation-wide subject to a component database, it is necessary to find a component subject with the same privileges, which may not be always possible. In this case, we propose two alternatives, called least under permissive and least over permissive. The former gives approximately the same privileges without giving more permissions than requested, while the latter gives the least amount over the requested permissions.

The organization of the remainder of this paper is as follows. Section 2 introduces the basic concepts, overall architecture and autonomy in access control of federated database systems, with a description of degrees of component autonomy. Section 3 presents the concept of and algorithms for subject switching. It further shows why subject switching is not always possible. As a remedy, Section 4 presents some metrics that can be used to approximately match access requirements of a federated subject to a collection of component subjects and provides some algorithms. Section 5 contains our concluding comments.

2. FEDERATED DATABASE SYSTEMS

A federated database system [HEIM85] consists of number of autonomous component database systems that control their interactions with other members in the federation in order to provide a substantial degree of information sharing. The DBMS of a component database system could be a centralized, distributed or another federated DBMS. Also any component database system can participate in more than one federation. In a federated database system, the components have control over the data they manage and their operations and determine the data that it wishes to share with other components. Federated database systems are categorized as loosely coupled or tightly coupled. Loosely coupled systems gives users freedom to join or leave a federation, and doe not provide federated schemas to be used at the federated level. Tightly coupled systems provide one interface at the federation level for federated services and provide federated schemas for users. This paper considers tightly coupled systems.

Autonomy is important for components in a federated database system. Veijalainen and Popescu-Zeletin [VEIJ88] identifies three dimensions of autonomies: *design*, *communication* and *execution*, and Sheth and Larson [SHET90] proposed an additional dimension, *association* autonomy, which is the freedom for a component database to join or leave the federation at will. Jonscher and Dittrich [JONS94] proposed another dimension of autonomy, *authorization autonomy*, which is the ability for component databases to autonomously control their access control decisions.

One major issue related to access control in tightly coupled systems is that if access to federated schemas are to be protected and the components are to retain their own access control decisions, then the identity and authentication of federation users have to be shared between components and the federation management [DeCa97]. Depending on the level of component participation in the identity and authorization of federated users, authorization autonomy can be further classified as (1) full authorization autonomy, (2) medium authorization autonomy and (3) low authorization autonomy [JONS94]. In full authorization autonomy, every federation user has to be known to each component, and has to be authenticated in order to access data. In medium authorization autonomy, the federation authenticates itself to components, and submits the federation user's identity and the request to the component. In low authorization autonomy, the federation authenticates itself and uses its own identity to access data. One of the major disadvantages of this arrangement is that unless controlled by other means, components databases now allow such a user to obtain all access rights of the federation, which is not an ideal situation. Even in the case of medium authorization autonomy, because component databases do not authenticate federated users, as suggested by Jonscher and Dittrich [JONS94], their identity can be changed in agreement between the federation and the components. This method is commonly referred to as subject switching.

In federations with full authorization autonomy, component databases share the identifiers and, consequently, there is no issue in mapping their identity to subjects known to components. If either medium or low authorization autonomy is preserved, subject identities need to be verified by the federation management only, as component databases trust the federation to validate the identity of its subjects. We assume that the federation management maintains mapping each federated (subject, component) pair to components pairs of the same type. This way, the federation need not apply for local access permissions for each federated user.

3. SUBJECT MAPPING ALGORITHMS

In order to map a federation wide subject to a component database, it is necessary to find a component subject with the same set of privileges, which may not be always possible. In that case, we propose an approximate matching algorithm where the local subject may have approximately the same privileges as the federated subject. Our algorithm is based on the federation management maintaining an access control list for each federated subject and federated and component subjects have a set of permissions and prohibitions (i.e., positive and negative permissions) per object. We also assume that the federation management maintains a list of subject IDs in every component database with their corresponding capabilities (i.e., combinations of access rights and prohibitions). In order to discuss our algorithms we need some definitions and measures of permission disparities between (subject, object) pairs.

3.1 Motivating Example

We motivate our work with a running example of a clinical trial, (such as testing a potential treatment regiment) which is carried out in a federation of two hospitals, and coordinated by a research center that must maintain an extensive database of outcomes of the trial. Independent of this study, all hospitals are required to maintain their autonomous databases, but will cooperate in carrying out the study. Thus, individual hospitals will be the components, and the research center will be the federated database. As there are different types of hospitals (such as teaching hospitals, regional trauma centers and rural hospitals), they may have different subject hierarchies. For example, teaching hospitals have medical residents of different seniorities, professors, and non-clinical researchers. We assume that all individuals who have a primary affiliation with a medical facility have local accesses assigned to them by their home institution, but in order to participate in the study they need to become a federation user. In addition, there are other federation users (such as members of regulatory bodies and state medical-ethics boards) that may need access to the study, but have no affiliations with participating hospitals. The researchers will be given different privileges to access the local data, depending on the requirements of the research. We assume there are two hospitals A and B having the same export schemas, *Patient, Treatment, Lab_Result* and *Complaint*. Hospital A in our example is a research hospital, and consequently, has a deeply nested hierarchy of database users for fine grain control of information. Hospital B is an affiliated rural hospital. Each of these hospitals created their local users with a set of assigned privileges as given below.

Hospital A: Large Teaching Hospital
{Staff_Physician: Patient:r, Treatment:rw, Lab_Result:r, Complaint:r}
{Medical_Resident: Patient:r, Treatment:rw, Lab_Result:r}
{Nurse: Patient:r, Treatment:r}
{Case_Worker: Patient:rw, Complaint:rw}
{Lab_Technician: Lab_Result:rw}
{Non_Clinical_Researcher: Patient:r, Treatment:r, Lab_Result:r}

Hospital B: Affiliated Rural Hospital
{Physician: Patient:r, Treatment:rw, Lab_Result:r, Complaint:r}
{Nurse: Patient:rw, Lab_Result:rw}
{Case_Worker: Patient:r, Complaint:rw}

Federation: Experimental Treatment Management
{Physician: Patient:r, Treatment:rw, Complaint:r}
{Researcher: Patient:r, Treatment:r, Lab_Result:r}
{Nurse: Patient:rw, Complaint:r}
{Regulatory_Supervisor: Patient:r, Treatment:r, Lab_Result:r, Complaint:r}
{Medical_Ethics_Supervisor: Patient:r, Complaint:r}

3.2 Access Compatibility Measures and Algorithms

Definition 1(Compatibility of Permissions and their Disparity Measures)
Let L be a collection of access requests, i.e. L = $\{(o_j, -a_j) : j < J\}$ where o_j, a_j are objects and actions.

1. We say subject S_1 is a *negative cover* of subject S_2 with respect to L if or every object, prohibition pair (o, -a) of L, if S_2 has prohibition (o, -a) then S_1 also has (o, -a).
2. If S_1 is negative cover of S_2, then the cardinality of $\{(o, -a)$ of $S_1\} - \{(o, -a)$ of $S_2\}$ is the *negative disparity* measure between S_1 and S_2.
3. We say subject S_1 is a *positive cover* of subject S_2 if for every object, permission pair (o, +a) of L if S_2 has permission (o, +a) then S_1 also has (o, +a).
4. We say that S_1 is a cover of S_2 with respect to L if S_1 a positive cover of S_2 and S_1 is a negative cover of S_2 with respect to L.
5. If S_1 is positive cover of S_2, then the cardinality of $\{(o, +a)$ of $S_1\} - \{(o, +a)$ of $S_2\}$ is the *positive disparity* measure between S_1 and S_2.
6. We say that the pair *(positive disparity, negative disparity)* is the disparity measure between S_1 and S_2.

[]

Intuitively, S_1 is a positive cover of S_2 if (positive) permissions on an access request list L allowed for S_2 are also allowed for S_1. The number of permissions that are additionally allowed for S_1 is the positive disparity measure of S_1 over S_2. Hence a positive cover of a subject dominates the subject with its permissions, while a negative cover of a subject dominates the subject with prohibitions. The pair (positive disparity, negative disparity) measures the collective permissions and prohibitions that a covering subject has over a covered object. The objective of our mapping algorithms is to minimize the disparity measure between requested permission for federated subjects and component subjects that they are mapped to.

If a perfect match (i.e., collection of component subjects with exactly the kind of prohibitions and permissions that are required by a federation subject) exits, then it can be found by searching. Failing a perfect match, we look for an approximate match. Appropriateness of the approximate match depends upon the security policy enforced. There are two alternatives: the first is to give the best possible permissions, and nothing more than requested and the other is to give the least amount over the requested permissions, named *least under permissive* and *least over permissive* algorithms respectively. In order to consider these notions, we first clarify our notion of a perfect match in the following definition.

Definition 2 (Perfect Match) Let S be a federated subject with an access request list L, and each component subject S_i in component database C_i has the access list $L_i = \{(o_j, a_j) : j < M_i\}$ for some integer. Let $L = U \{ L_i : 1 =< i =< n\}$. We say that component subject list $(S_1,\ldots,S_n)$ provides a perfect match for federation subject S if S_i is a cover with respect to L_i for every i.[]

Definition 2 exemplifies one of the basic simplifying assumptions of our work. That is, any federated subject S provides its request list L in terms of component requests, and any collection of component subjects $(S_1,\ldots,S_n)$ are considered to be providing all of them if subject S_i can provide its share L_i of L. Next two algorithms compute perfect matches for a given federated subject S with an access request list L. Section 4 proposes possible remedies in terms of best possible matches, when a perfect match fails to be found.

Algorithm 1 (Least Under Permitting Algorithm) Let S be a federated subject to be mapped to a collection of component databases C_i for $i < N$.

For each $i < N$:

Let N[i,j] for $j < N_i$ for some integer N_i be the sequence of all negative covers of S in C_i, arranged in increasing order of their negative disparity.

1. If the sequence N[i,j] is empty for some i, then subject S cannot be matched to the component database C_i.
2. Else (i.e., N[i,j] is nonempty), choose the least integer $j < N_i$ such that N[i,j] has the least positive disparity with respect to S_i. Then map S to subject N[i,j] of the component database C_i. If none of the N[i,j'] for $j' < N_i$ is a positive cover, then there is no subject that can provide accesses that are requested by the federation subject. []

Example 1 Consider the federation users and the local users for Hospital A and Hospital B. By applying Algorithm 1, we have the following mappings for Hospital A, but no match exists for Hospital B.
(Federation.Physician, Hospital_A.Nurse)
(Federation.Researcher, Hospital_A.Non_Clinical_Researcher)
(Federation.Regulatory_Supervisor, Hospital_A.Non_Clinical_Researcher)

Algorithm 2 (Least Over Permitting Algorithm) Let S be a federated subject to be mapped to a collection of component database C_i for $i < N$.

For each $i < N$:
Let $N[i,j]$ for $j < N_i$ for some integer N_i be the sequence of all positive covers of S in C_i, arranged in increasing order of positive disparity.

1. If the sequence $N[i,j]$ is empty for some i, then subject S cannot be matched to the component database C_i.
2. Else (i.e., $N[i,j]$ is nonempty), choose the least integer $j < N_i$ such that $N[i,j]$ has the least negative disparity with respect to S_i. Then map S to subject $N[i,j]$ of the component database C_i. If none of the $N[i,j']$ for $j' < N_i$ is a negative cover, then there is no subject that can provide accesses that are requested by the federation subject.[]

Example 2 By applying Algorithm 2, we have the following mappings for both Hospital A and Hospital B.
(Federation.Physician, Hospital_A.Staff_Physician)
(Federation.Researcher, Hospital_A.Non_Clinical_Researcher)
(Federation.Nurse, Hospital_A.Case_Worker)
(Federation.Regulatory_Supervisor, Hospital_A.Staff_Physician)
(Federation.Medical_Ethics_Supervisor, Hospital_A.Case_Worker)
(Federation.Physician, Hospital_B.Physician)
(Federation.Researcher, Hospital_B.Physician)
(Federation.Regulatory_Supervisor, Hospital_B.Physician)
(Federation.Medical_Ethics_Supervisor, Hospital_B.Case_Worker)

As stated, Algorithms 1 and 2 may not find a perfect match for the given federated subject and access request list. Theorem 1 shows that these algorithms find them if they exist.

Theorem 1 Suppose S is a federated subject with an access request list $L = \cup L_i$, where $L_i = \{(o_j, a_j) : j < M_i\}$ be the collection of objects in component database C_i for some integer M_i. Algorithms 1 and 2 will find a perfect match for S with respect to L if and only if it exists. Furthermore:
1. The least under permitting algorithms will find a perfect match that minimizes the negative disparity measure.
2. The least over permitting algorithms will find a perfect match that minimizes the positive disparity measure.

Proof: Suppose there is a perfect match $(S_1,\dots,S_n)$. Then, each S_i is a cover for S with respect to L_i. Therefore, N[i,j] found in step 1 of Algorithms 1 and 2, are non-empty for each i. Furthermore, in step 2:

1. Algorithm 1 finds the component subject with the least negative disparity because N[i,j] is ordered in the increasing order of negative disparity.
2. Algorithm 2 finds the component subject with the least positive disparity because N[i,j] is ordered in the increasing order of positive disparity.

Conversely, if either Algorithm 1 or 2 finds a set $(S_1,\dots,S_n)$, then each element S_i is the least j that is a positive/negative cover of S in N[i,j] with respect to L_i. Accordingly, $(S_1,\dots,S_n)$ is a cover for S with respect to $(L_1,\dots,L_n)$.[]

4. APPROXIMATIONS: METRICS AND MAPPINGS

The previous section showed that finding a component subject with a given list of authorization requirements is not always possible. Consequently, we propose to find the *best possible approximations* that can be provided by respective component databases. Approximate matching requires a metric to measure the proximity of the provided accesses to those requested, and algorithms to find the optimal among the class of possibilities. We propose these in the current section.

4.1 Metrics

In the absence of a perfect match, in mapping a set of access requirements, an attempt must be made to make the *best possible alternative* under the given circumstances. In doing so, we consider four differences. They are the permissions and prohibitions required by the federation subject, but cannot be matched, and the permissions and prohibitions provided by the component, but were not required by the federation subject. We propose the *access disparity metric* given in Definition 3 to quantify these differences.

Definition 3 (Access Disparity Measures for Approximate Mappings)

1. Suppose $\langle(o_i, a_i): i < k\rangle$ is a vector of possible signed accesses in the given security domain. We assume that a_i has positive (+) sign for permissions, negative (-) sign for prohibitions and a 0 when neither is specified. We call such an access list a *complete access list* for a subject.
2. Let S, S' be two subjects with access lists $L = \{(o_i, a_i) : i < k\}$, and $L' = \{(o_i, a'_i) : i < k\}$. Then, let the vector difference between $\langle(o_i, a_i) : i < k\rangle$, $\langle(o_i, a'_i) : i < k\rangle$ be constructed as follows:

Under Prohibition = |{ i : a_i is a prohibition, L has (o_i, a_i) but not L' }|
Over Prohibition = |{ i : a_i is a prohibition, L' has (o_i, a_i) but not L}|
Under Permission = |{ i : a_i is a permission, L has (o_i, a_i) but not L' }|
Over Permission = |{ i : a_i is a permission, L' has (o_i, a_i) but not L }|
Disparity Measure = (under prohibition, over prohibition, under permission, over permission)[]

As will be shown shortly, Definition 3 is a generalization of Definition 1, and applies to any pair of subjects and not only to pairs where the second subject is a positive or negative cover of the first. One of the advantages of this metric is that it accurately reflects the nature of approximation in subject mapping. Details captured in this metric also make it more difficult to use.

Thus, we present a simpler, yet intuitive metric that can numerically quantify access differences between two subjects in Definition 4. The main differences between Definition 3 and Definition 4 are that the latter provides an aggregate over the former, and consequently makes no difference between permissions and prohibitions. This relationship between matrices of Definitions 3 and 4 are stated and proved in Theorem 2.

Definition 4 (Numerical Disparity Measure)

1. Suppose S is a subject, and {(o_i, a_i) : i < k} is its complete access list. Let {(o_i, n_i) : i < k} be constructed from {(o_i, a_i) : i < k} by replacing:
   - $+a_i$ with +1.
   - $-a_i$ with –1.
   - Neither permission with 0.

   We call such a list the *numerical analog* of {(o_i, a_i) : i < k}.
2. Let S, S' be two subjects with complete access lists {(o_i, a_i) : i < k}, {(o_i, a'_i) : i < k} and their numerical analogs {(o_i, n_i) : i < k}, {(o_i, n'_i) : i < k}. Then we say Σ { | n_i - n'_i | : i =< k}the *numerical access disparity* between S and S'.[]

Numerical access disparity measure does not take any policy-based information nor assign any weights to the four types of differences existing between desired and provided permissions. For the relationship between metrics, Theorems 2 and 3 prove that Definition 3 is a generalization of Definition 1.

Theorem 2 (Comparing Disparity Measures to Approximate Measures)
Suppose S and S' are subjects with complete access lists {(o_i, a_i) : i < k} and {(o_i, a'_i) : i < k}. Then the following hold:

1. If S' is a positive cover of S, then under permissions of (S, S') is zero, and over permissions of (S, S') is the positive disparity measure defined in Definition 1.

2. If S' is a negative cover of S, then under prohibitions of (S, S') is zero, and over prohibitions of (S, S') is the negative disparity measure given in Definition 1.
3. If S' is a cover of S, then under permissions and under prohibitions of (S, S') are zero and over permissions and over prohibitions are positive disparity measures and negative disparity measures given in Definition 1.

Proof:
1. Suppose S' is a positive cover of S. Then according to Definition 1, for every object o, permission +a, if (o, +a) is on the access list of S, then it is on the access list of S'. Consequently, according to Definition 3 under permissions for (S, S') is 0. Furthermore, over permission for (S, S') is $|\{ i :$ $+a'_i$ is a permission and $+a_i$ is not a permission for $S\}|$, which is the positive disparity according to Definition 1.
2. Similar argument proves this fact.
3. Follows from combining cases 1 and 2 above.[]

Theorem 3 (Comparing Approximate Disparity Measures)
Numerical disparity measures defined in Definition 4 relate to disparity measures defined in Definition 3 as given by the following inequalities:
1. *Under Permission + Over Permission =< Permission Difference.*
2. *Under Prohibition + Over Prohibition =< Prohibition Difference.*

Proof:
Suppose the disparity measures for under permission, over permission, under prohibitions, over prohibition are respectively *Uper*, *Oper*, *Upro* and *Opro* for the subject pair (S, S') as defined in Definition 4. Suppose that these values are computed from complete access lists $L=\{(o_i, a_i) : i < k\}$ and $L'=\{(o_i, a'_i) : i < k\}$ for S and S' respectively.
Suppose that (o_i, a_i) is a permission that is not in the complete access list L' of S'. Then, in the computation of under permission *Uper* a_i contributes 1 to the count in Definition 3, but because a'_i could be either prohibition or 0, this a_i contributes either a 1 or a zero to the permission difference of Definition 4. Since the indices i for objects contributing to under permissions and over permissions are disjoint, we get the relationship *Under Permission + Over Permission =< Permission difference*. A similar argument applies for prohibitions.[]

4.2 Approximate Mapping Algorithms

In the absence of a perfect match for a given access request set and the policy that all prohibitions have to be enforced, Algorithm 1 can be changed to grant a subset of permissions that have been requested.

Algorithm 3 (Approximate Under Permitting Algorithm)
Let S be a federated subject to be mapped to a set of component databases $\{C_i : i < N\}$. Let $L_i = L^+_i \cup L^-_i$ be the prohibitions and the permissions required by S from the component database C_i, where $L^-_i = \{(o_j, -a_j): j < N^-_i\}$ and $L^+_i = \{(o'_k, +b_k) : k < N^+_i\}$.
<u>Stage 1:</u> *(Search for the component subject with minimal prohibitions)*
For each $j'=N^-_i$ down to 0:
For every subset M[i,j'] of size j' from objects $\{(o_j, -a_j) : j < N^-_i\}$:
Let N[i,j'] be the collection of negative covers of S with respect to objects in M[i,j'] arranged in increasing order of negative disparity of Definition 1.
Case 1: If N[i,j'] is empty then j'=j'-1.
Case 2: If N[i,j'] is non-empty, then choose S' from N[i,j'] such that it has the least positive disparity with respect to S and subjects in N[i,j'] according to Definition 1.
<u>Stage 2:</u> *(Search for component subjects with maximal permissions)*
For each $k'=N^+_i$ down to 0:
Let M[i,k'] be a subset of size k' from objects $\{(o_k, +a_k) : k < N^+_i\}$ and N[i,k'] be the collection of positive covers of S with respect to objects in M[i,k'] arranged in increasing order of positive disparity of Definition 1.
Case 1: If N[i,k'] is empty then j'=j'-1.
Case 2: If N[i,k'] is non-empty. Then, choose S' from N[i,k'] such that it has the least number of prohibitions for objects in $\{(o_k, -a_k) : k < N^-_i\}$.
<u>Stage 3:</u> *(Search for a subject with minimum numerical deviation)*
Let T(i,1), ..., T(i, n_i) be a list of all subjects in component C_i, arranged in an increasing order of numerical disparity with S. Then choose T(i,1) as the subject in component C_i.[]

Example 3 By applying Algorithm 3, we have the following mappings for both Hospital A and Hospital B. Comparing with Example 1, we have found the best approximate matches for each federation user.
(Federation.Physician, Hospital_A.Nurse)
(Federation.Researcher, Hospital_A.Non_Clinical_Researcher)
(Federation.Nurse, Hospital_A.Case_Worker)
(Federation.Regulatory_Supervisor, Hospital_A.Non_Clinical_Researcher)
(Federation.Medical_Ethics_Supervisor, Hospital_A.Nurse)
(Federation.Physician, Hospital_B.Physician)
(Federation.Researcher, Hospital_B.Physician)
(Federation.Nurse, Hospital_B.Case_Worker)
(Federation.Regulatory_Supervisor, Hospital_B.Physician)
(Federation.Medical_Ethics_Supervisor, Hospital_B.Case_Worker)

The difference between Algorithms 1 and 3 is that the former may not halt in case a perfect match cannot be found, whereas the latter always halts, doing the best approximate matching under the given circumstances. In

Algorithm 3, we first search for a match with as many number of prohibitions as requested by S, and if such subjects exist, we search for the one with the largest number of permissions requested. These two searches constitute steps 1 and 2 of Algorithm 3. If our search does not succeed, that implies that there is no subject in the corresponding component that does have either the required prohibitions or the required permissions. Then, we look for a component subject that has the least numerical disparity. This search constitutes Step 3 of our algorithm. The choice of the last alternative is somewhat arbitrary, and we are exploring better options for this case.

We can reverse steps 1 and 2 of Algorithm 3 and thereby obtaining the best approximate over permitting algorithm, as given below. Consequently, above explanation of Algorithm 3 applies to Algorithm 4 with the order of searching for permissions and prohibitions reversed.

Algorithm 4 (Approximate Over Permitting Algorithm) Let S be a federated subject to be mapped to a collection of component database C_i for i < N. Let $L_i = L^+_i \cup L^-_i$ be the prohibitions and the permissions required by S from the component database C_i, where $L^+_i = \{(o_j, -a_j) : j < N^-_i\}$ and $L^-_i = \{(o'_k, +b_k) : j < N^+_i\}$.

<u>Stage 1:</u> *(Search for component subjects with minimal permissions)*
For each $j'=N^+_i$ down to 0:
For each subset M[i,j'] of size j' from objects $\{(o_j, +a_j) : j < N^+_i\}$:
Let N[i,j'] be the collection of positive covers of S with respect to objects in M[i,j'] arranged in increasing order of positive disparity of Definition 1.
Case 1: If N[i,j'] is empty then j'=j'-1.
Case 2: If N[i,j'] is non-empty, then choose S' from N[i,j'] such that it has the least number of prohibitions for objects in $\{(o_j, -a_j) : j < N^-_i\}$.
<u>Stage 2:</u> *(Search for component subjects with maximal prohibitions)*
For each $k'=N^+_i$ down to 0:
Let M[i,k'] be a subset of size k' from objects $\{(o_k, -a_k) : k < N^-_i\}$ and N[i,k'] be the collection of negative covers of S with respect to objects in M[i,k'] arranged in increasing order of negative disparity of Definition 1.
Case 1: If N[i,k'] is empty then k'=k'-1.
Case 2: If N[i,k'] is non-empty. Then, choose S' from N[i,k'] such that it has the least positive disparity with respect to S and subjects in N[i,k'] according to Definition 1.
<u>Stage 3:</u> *(Search for a subject with minimal numerical deviations)*
Let T(i,1), …, T(i, n_i) be a list of all subjects in component C_i, arranged in an increasing order of numerical disparity with S. Then choose T(i,1) as the subject in component C_i.[]

Example 4 By applying Algorithm 4, we have the following mappings for both Hospital A and Hospital B. Comparing with Example 2, we have found the best approximate matches for each federation user.
(Federation.Physician, Hospital_A.Staff_Physician)
(Federation.Researcher, Hospital_A.Non_Clinical_Researcher)
(Federation.Nurse, Hospital_A.Case_Worker)
(Federation.Regulatory_Supervisor, Hospital_A.Staff_Physician)
(Federation.Medical_Ethics_Supervisor, Hospital_A.Case_Worker)
(Federation.Physician, Hospital_B.Physician)
(Federation.Researcher, Hospital_B.Physician)
(Federation.Nurse, Hospital_B.Case_Worker)
(Federation.Regulatory_Supervisor, Hospital_B.Physician)
(Federation.Medical_Ethics_Supervisor, Hospital_B.Case_Worker)

Similarly to Algorithm 3, Algorithm 4 may not halt in case a perfect match cannot be found. Instead, it will continue to search for a match with a smaller set of permissions requested. If it still fails, it will search for the one with minimal numerical disparity. Therefore, it will always find an approximate match for a federation user.

Theorem 4 (Properties of Algorithms 3 and Algorithm 4)
1. For any given federated subject S, Algorithms 3 and 4 terminate and provide a candidate for each component C_i.
2. If there are any candidates in some component C_i that are covers for S with respect to its access requests within C_i, then Algorithm 3 finds the one with the least minimum negative disparity, and Algorithm 4 finds the candidate with the least positive disparity.
3. If any component database C_i does not have a cover for S with respect to its access requirements, then both Algorithms 3 and 4 finds the candidate that has the least numerical disparity.

Proof:
1. Termination: In Algorithm 3, at the first stage, the component C_i is searched for a candidate subject S_i that has the smallest negative disparity with respect to the required accesses from C_i. In failing so, secondly C_i is searched for a candidate subject S_i that has the smallest positive disparity with respect to the required accesses from C_i. Failing to find any candidate at this stage, we get the candidate with the least numerical disparity. Hence the algorithm terminates. A similar argument applies to Algorithm 4.
2. Suppose component C_i has a cover for S with respect to the given access list L. Algorithm 3 uses Algorithm 1 as its first stage. Consequent to the

proof of Algorithm 1 at this stage, Algorithm 3 finds a candidate with the least negative disparity. A similar argument applies for Algorithm 4.
3. Suppose that there is no cover for S in component C_i. Then, Algorithms 3 and 4 shifts to Stage 3, where the component with the least numerical disparity is chosen.[]

5. CONCLUSIONS

We investigate the problem of mapping a federation user to a collection of component users in a tightly coupled federated database. Given a set of component subjects with their access capabilities and an access request list for a federation subject, it may not be always possible to map the latter to a collection of the former as required by subject switching. As a remedy, we suggest two algorithms, the least over permitting, and least under permitting algorithms. We have presented metrics to quantify the degree of disparity between the requested accesses and those that are possible to be granted. We presented two mapping algorithms that minimize these disparities.

ACKNOWLEDGEMENTS

This work was partially supported by National Science Foundation grant CCS-01113515.

REFERENCES

[DeCa97] De Capitani di Vimercati, S. and Samarati, P., *Authorization Specification and Enforcement in Federated Database System,* Journal of Computer Security, Vol.5, No.2, Pages. 155-188, 1997.

[HEIM85] Heimbigner, D., McLeod, D., *A Federated Architecture for Information Management,* ACM Trans. Off. Inf. Syst. 3,3, July 1985.

[JAJO01] Jajodia, S., Samarati, P., Sapino, M. L. and Subrahmanian, V. S. *Flexible Support for Multiple Access Control Policies* in Transactions of Database Systems, June 2001, To appear.

[JONS94] Jonscher, D., Dittrich, K.R., *An Approach For Building Secure Database Federations,* Proceedings of the 20th VLDB Conference, Santiago, Chile, 1994.

[SHET90] Sheth, A.P., Larson, J.A., *Federated Database Systems for Mansaging Distributed, Heterogeneous, and Autonomous Database,* ACM Computing Surveys, Vol.22, No.3, September 1990.

[VEIJ88] Veijalainen, J., and Popescu-Zeletin, R., *Multi-database Systems in ISO/OSI* in Standards in Information Technology and Industrial Control, Malagardis, N., and Williams, T., Eds North-Holland Pages 83-97, 1988.

EFFICIENT DAMAGE ASSESSMENT AND REPAIR IN RESILIENT DISTRIBUTED DATABASE SYSTEMS

Peng Liu and Xu Hao

Abstract Preventive measures sometimes fail to defect malicious attacks. With cyber attacks on data-intensive applications becoming an ever more serious threat, intrusion tolerant database systems are a significant concern. The main objective of intrusion tolerant database systems is to detect attacks, and to assess and repair the damage caused by the attacks in a timely manner such that the database will not be damaged to such a degree that is unacceptable or useless. This paper focuses on efficient damage assessment and repair in resilient distributed database systems. The complexity of distributed database systems caused by data partition, distributed transaction processing, and failures makes damage assessment and repair much more challenging than in centralized database systems. This paper identifies the key challenges and presents an efficient algorithm for distributed damage assessment and repair.

1. INTRODUCTION

Recently, people have seen more and more successful attacks on data-intensive applications, especially web-based e-business and e-government applications. Expanding cyber attacks pressure database management systems to not only prevent unauthorized access, but also tolerate intrusions. However, traditional database security techniques such as authorization [8, 9], inference control [1], multilevel secure databases [19], and multilevel secure transaction processing [4], are very limited to handle successful attacks, or *intrusions*. This indicates that *intrusion tolerant* database systems that can detect intrusions, isolate attacks, contain, assess, and repair the damage caused by intrusions can become a significant concern.

The focus of this paper is on a critical aspect of intrusion tolerant database systems, namely, damage assessment and repair. The primary goal of the attacks on a database, in most cases, is to damage the data stored in the database (in an undetectable way) and use the damaged data to mislead people to make wrong decisions. Compared with the attack of completely shutting down a database system, damaging a set of data items (or objects) can be much more dangerous, not only because they are more difficult to detect, but also because the damage can *spread* seriously in a database through benign operations. In particular, any benign transaction that reads a corrupted data item can help spread the damage accidentally. The main objective of an intrusion tolerant database system is to guarantee that damage spreading is (dynamically) controlled in such a way that the database will not be damaged to a degree that is unacceptable or useless. Being a key technique to control damage spreading, damage assessment and repair is a significant concern.

One key technique for building intrusion tolerant database systems is intrusion detection, which has attracted many researchers [14, 17]. Effective damage assessment and repair cannot be achieved without effective intrusion detection because intrusion detection can tell which users or operations can cause damage, however, intrusion detection makes the system attack-aware but not attack-resilient, that is, intrusion detection itself cannot maintain the integrity and availability of the database in face of attacks.

This paper focuses on the techniques to assess and repair the damage caused in a *distributed* database. Distributed databases are widely used in a variety of real world data intensive applications, and we need efficient damage assessment and repair algorithms to make them resilient to attacks. Several algorithms are developed to assess and repair the damage caused in a centralized database [3, 18, 11], however, the complexity of distributed database systems caused by data partition, distributed transaction processing, and failures suggests that they cannot be used in distributed database systems and new distributed damage assessment and repair algorithms are needed. First, since data are partitioned and stored on multiple *sites*, damage assessment and repair must be performed at multiple sites. Second, since one distributed transaction may access data stored at multiple sites, damage assessment, which is now based on the affecting relationships among distributed transactions, needs to coordinate and synthesize the affecting relationships among the subtransactions at each site. Third, distributed damage assessment and repair need to tolerate not only site failures but also communication failures.

Finally, it should be noticed that although our approach focuses on surviving attacks by malicious transactions, database intrusion tolerance can also be enforced at some lower levels such as *OS level*. However, although *transaction level* methods cannot handle OS level attacks, it is shown that in many applications where attacks are enforced mainly through *malicious* transactions transaction level methods can tolerate intrusions in a much more effective and efficient way. Moreover, it is shown that OS level intrusion tolerance techniques such as those proposed in [14, 13, 15, 5], can be directly integrated into a transaction level intrusion tolerance framework to complement it with the ability to tolerate OS level attacks.

1.1 Prior Work

Database recovery mechanisms are not designed to deal with malicious attacks. Undo and redo operations can only be performed on uncommitted or *active* transactions, and the durability property ensures that traditional recovery mechanisms never undo committed transactions [6]. However, the fact that a transaction commits does not guarantee that its effects are desirable. Specifically, a committed transaction may reflect malicious activity.

Although our assessment and repair model is related to the notion of *cascading abort* [6], cascading aborts only capture the *read-from* relation between active transactions, and in standard recovery approaches cascading aborts are avoided by requiring transactions to read only committed data [10].

1.2 Our Approach and Contribution

In this paper, we extend centralized damage assessment and repair techniques to distributed systems, in particular, we present an efficient on-the-fly transaction-oriented algorithm to assess and repair the damage caused in a distributed database. The algorithm has the following properties: (1) It is completely distributed, thus it has no single point of failures and it can tolerate malicious attacks on end systems and communication links. (2) It is on-the-fly. New transactions are continuously executed during the damage assessment and repair process. (3) It is efficient. Damage assessment and repair are performed, in parallel, at each participating site. (4) It works seamlessly with a commercial DDBMS, thus it can be directly applied to build resilient distributed database applications. (5) It provides transparent damage assessment and repair.

The rest of the paper is organized as follows. In Section 2, we present the model for distributed damage assessment and repair. We present the damage assessment and repair algorithm in Section 3. In Section 4, we address some performance issues of the algorithm. We conclude the paper in Section 5.

2. THE MODEL

2.1. Distributed Database Model

A distributed database is a set of data *items* (or objects) stored across a set of *sites* connected by a network. Each data item is stored at one and only site. A distributed transaction is a partial order of *read* and *write* operations on these data items that either *commits* or *aborts*. Two operations *conflict* if one is write. Two transactions *conflict* if they have conflicting operations. The execution of a set of distributed transactions is modeled by a (distributed) *history*. The model of a distributed transaction execution is such that there is one process, called the *coordinator*, that is connected to the user application and a set of other processes, called the *subordinates*. Transactions are assumed to have globally unique identifiers. The processes are assumed to have globally unique identifiers, which also indicate the sites (or locations) of the corresponding processes. For simplicity, we assume that each site participating in a distributed transaction has only one process of that transaction.

We assume the distributed database system supports transaction serializability and uses the two-phase locking (2PL) protocol. We assume the two-phase commit (2PC) protocol is used to guarantee the atomicity of distributed transactions, despite intermittent site or communication link failures. We assume the standard 2PC protocol is used here [6]. To save space, the details about how 2PC handles the log are not reviewed. It should be noticed that although our damage assessment and repair algorithm is specified based on the way log records are maintained, our algorithm can be easily extended to support other 2PC protocols such as presumed abort (PA) and presumed commit (PC) [16].

2.2. Damage Assessment and Repair Model

Our idea of damage assessment and repair is that only the malicious transactions and the innocent transactions affected by a malicious transaction, directly or indirectly, can cause damage and should be repaired. In order to make this idea more tangible, we first formally define the affecting relationship among transactions. Since damage can only be caused by committed transactions, our definitions care about only committed transactions. We denote the set of committed malicious transactions in a history by $\mathbf{B} = \{B_1, B_2, ..., B_m\}$. We denote the set of committed innocent transactions by $\mathbf{G} = \{G_1, G_2, ..., G_n\}$.

Definition 1 At a site, a committed subtransaction T_{jk} is *dependent upon* committed subtransaction T_{il} if there exists a data item x stored at the site such that T_{jk} reads x after T_{il} has updated x, and no other committed subtransactions update x between the time T_{il} updates x and T_{jk} reads x.

Definition 2 A committed distributed transaction T_j is *dependent upon* committed distributed transaction T_i in a history if one of T_j's subtransactions is dependent upon one of T_i's subtransactions.

Definition 3 In a history, a committed distributed transaction T_i *affects* committed distributed transaction T_j if the ordered pair $(T_j,\ T_i)$ is in the transitive closure of the *dependent upon* relation.

It is clear that the notation "affect" captures both direct and indirect affecting relationships. To illustrate, consider the following history over (B_1, G_1, G_2), which are assumed to be executed on two sites. Here r means a read, w means a write, and c means a commit.

At site A: $H_A = r_{B_{1A}}[x]w_{B_{1A}}[x]c_{B_{1A}}r_{G_{1A}}[x]r_{G_{1A}}[y]w_{G_{1A}}[y]c_{G_{1A}}r_{G_{2A}}[z]w_{G_{2A}}[z]c_{G_{2A}}$
At site B: $H_B = r_{B_{1B}}[u]w_{B_{1B}}[u]c_{B_{1B}}r_{G_{1B}}[v]w_{G_{1B}}[v]c_{G_{1B}}r_{G_{2B}}[v]r_{G_{2B}}[w]w_{G_{2B}}[w]c_{G_{2B}}$

Based on H_A, we find that G_{1A} is dependent upon B_{1A}, so G_1 is affected by B_1, and x and y are damaged. We find that G_{2A} is neither dependent upon B_{1A} nor G_{1A}. However, this does not ensure that G_2 will not be affected by B_1. Based on H_B, we find that G_{2B} is dependent upon G_{1B} (although G_{2B} is not dependent upon B_{1B}), so G_2 is dependent upon G_1. Since G_1 is dependent upon B_1, so (G_2, B_1) is in the transitive closure of the dependent upon relation. Therefore, G_2 is actually affected by B_1 and w is damaged.

3. THE ALGORITHM

We use two types of processes to do distributed damage assessment and repair (DAR): a *Local DAR Manager* on each site, and a *Local DAR Executor* on each site. The idea is to do distributed damage assessment and repair through local operations. At a site, the Local DAR Executor is responsible for scanning the local log to (a) identify the subtransactions that are affected by a malicious transaction and (b) compose the corresponding cleaning subtransactions for these subtransactions; the Local DAR Manager is responsible for coordinating the DAR process of (only) the distributed transactions that had their coordinators at the site and are affected by a malicious transaction. In particular, for each such transaction T_i, the Local DAR Manager will create the coordinator for T_i's cleaning transaction, and instruct (only) the Local DAR Executors at the sites where T_i's subordinates were located to assess the damage spread by T_i and to repair T_i. Cleaning transactions are executed just like an normal transaction.

The example described in Section 2 shows that in order to capture every transaction affected by a malicious transaction, global coordination among sites is necessary, since a transaction affected by a malicious transaction may be found unaffected at some of its subordinates' sites if only local information is used. Our algorithm does global coordination by making the Local DAR Managers and Executors collaborating with each other. In particular, after **B** is identified, it will be first sent, in parallel, to the Local DAR Managers at the sites where **B**'s coordinators were located. These Local DAR Managers then send an *ASSESS* message to ask each of the Local DAR Executors at the sites where **B**'s subordinates are located to assess the damage caused by **B** on their local data. The identifier of each affected (sub)transaction found by the Local DAR Executors then will be sent, in parallel, to the Local DAR Managers at the sites where the coordinators of these affected transactions were located, which will then send an *ASSESS* message to ask each of the Local DAR Executors at the sites where the other subordinates of these affected transactions were located to assess the damage indirectly caused by **B**. This kind of interaction between Local DAR managers and Executors will be *continuously* performed until all the damage is located.

The repair process is relatively simpler. The damage caused by each malicious or affected distributed transaction is repaired by a distributed cleaning transaction. The Local DAR Managers are responsible for creating the coordinators for these cleaning transactions. The Local DAR Executors are responsible for composing the cleaning subtransactions that comprise each cleaning transaction. It should be noticed that it is not guaranteed that a cleaning subtransaction will really clean each item it *wants* to clean. Sometimes, an item can be really cleaned after several cleaning subtransactions have updated the item. The reason is that cleaning subtransactions are composed only based on local information, which may not be complete.

```
CIT: array[ItemID] of record /* Cleaned Item Table */
    cLSN;
        /* the LSN of the record that records the write that damages the item */
    eLSN;
        /* the LSN of the end record of the log when the item is cleaned */
end;
LF: persistent array[LSN] of record /* Stable Log File */
    LogRecType: (read, write, abort, commit, prepare, end);
    LogRecContents: array of char;
    AppID: integer;
    TransID: integer;
    CoordinatorID: integer;
    [For commit/abort records] Subordinates: array of integer;
end;
```

Figure 1. Major Data Structures

3.1. Data Structures

Our algorithm is based on the transaction log maintained on each site. We assume every *read* (operation) is recorded in a log. Although this is not the case for most commercial distributed database systems, [3] shows that (a) in addition to logging reads there are several other ways to collect reads such as extracting read sets from transaction profiles, and (b) the algorithms based on in-log reads can be easily extended to use the reads maintained outside the logs. We assume each log has six types of records, namely, *read*, *write*, *abort*, *commit*, *prepare*, and *end* records. The other possible types of records such as *savepoints* and *checkpoints* are not considered here because they are irrelevant. We assume the log records at each site contain the type (*read*, *prepare*, *commit*, etc.) of the record, the identifier of the application, the identifier of the transaction, the identifier of the coordinator, the identities of the subordinates in the case of the *commit/abort* records written by the coordinator [16].

In addition to logs, our algorithm uses the following data structure:

- an *Cleaned Item Table* (CIT) at each site that contains the items that have been 'cleaned' at the site. Each item in this table is tagged with two numbers: $cLSN$, which indicates when the item is damaged, and $eLSN$, which indicates when the item is cleaned.

These data structures are described in Figure 1. Here $ItemID$ means the identifier of a data item. LSN, means log serial number, a unique number associated with each log record. LSN becomes larger as the log grows.

3.2. Damage Assessment and Repair Under Normal Operation

First, we describe the algorithm without considering failures. The algorithm is as follows. Note that here for clarity we assume during the DAR process no new malicious transactions will be added to **B**, although the algorithm can be easily extended to support newly identified malicious transactions.

Algorithm 1 Distributed On-the-fly Damage Assessment and Repair Algorithm
Input: **B**, the logs
Output: when the DAR process terminates, any prefix H_p of the history including the point where the process terminates results in the state that would have been produced by H'_p, where H'_p is H_p with all the transactions in **B** or affected by **B** removed
Initialization:
- make P, a pointer, pointed to the header of the log, which is before any log records;
- $assess\_list := \{\}$, $to\_assess := \{\}$, $undo\_list := \{\}$, $tmp\_undo\_list := \{\}$, $dirty\_item\_set := \{\}$, $tmp\_item\_set := \{\}$, $submitted\_item\_set := \{\}$; **/* See comment A */**

At the Local DAR Manager:
while TRUE
    if an *ASSESS* message arrives
        if the transaction (indicated by the message) is in the $assess\_list$
            do nothing;
        if the transaction is not in the $assess\_list$
            add the identifier of the transaction to the $assess\_list$;
            create a coordinator (process) for the cleaning transaction of the transaction, and inform the coordinator the set of subordinates of the transaction;
            if the *ASSESS* message is not sent out by a Local DAR Executor
                send an *ASSESS* message, which contains the identifier of the coordinator process and the transaction identifier, in parallel, to (only) the Local DAR Executors at the sites where the transaction had a subordinate;
            otherwise the *ASSESS* message is sent out by a Local DAR Executor, denoted E_i
                send an *ASSESS* message, which contains the identifier of the coordinator process and the transaction identifier, in parallel, to (only) the Local DAR Executors, except for E_i, at the sites where the transaction had a subordinate;
                send a *CLEAN COORDINATOR* message, which contains the identifier of the coordinator process and the transaction identifier, to E_i; **/* See comment B */**
end while

At the Local DAR Executor:
while TRUE
    if a *CLEAN COORDINATOR* message arrives
        associate the identifier of the coordinator with the transaction kept in the $undo\_list$;
    if an *SUCCESS* message (sent from a coordinator of a cleaning transaction) arrives

```
    move each item x that has been cleaned from the dirty_item_set to the CIT table, and
      associate x with the LSN of the current end of the log (namely x.eLSN);
    remove x from the submitted_item_set;
if an ASSESS message arrives
    if this is the first ASSESS message
        make P pointed to the first log record of the transaction;
    elseif the transaction is not in the undo_list /* See comment C */
        add the transaction (indicated by the message), together with the coordinator identifier, to
          to_assess;
        if the first log record of the transaction is before the record pointed by P /* See comment D */
            if the transaction is not in the tmp_undo_list
                make P pointed to the first log record of the transaction;
            else remove the transaction from the tmp_undo_list, and move the items that are written
              by the transaction from the tmp_item_set to the dirty_item_set /* See comment E */
if P points to a record and the termination conditions do not hold /* See comment F */
    Scan the log entry pointed by P:
        if the entry is for a cleaning transaction
            skip it;
        elseif the entry is for a transaction T_i in to_assess
            if the entry is a write record [T_i, x, v_1, v_2]
                if x is not in the CIT table
                    add x, together with the LSN of the write record (denoted x.cLSN), to
                    the dirty_item_set;
                elseif x.eLSN < w.LSN or w.LSN < x.cLSN /* See comment G */
                    add (x, x.cLSN) to the dirty_item_set;
            elseif the entry is a commit record [T_i, commit]
                compose the cleaning subtransaction for T_i; /* See comment H */
                send the composed cleaning subtransaction to its coordinator (the identifier of
                the coordinator can be found in to_assess);
            elseif the entry is of other types
                skip it;
        else
            case the entry is a write record [T_i, x, v_1, v_2]
                if x is not in the CIT table
                    add (x, x.cLSN) to the tmp_item_set;
                elseif x.eLSN < w.LSN or w.LSN < x.cLSN
                    add (x, x.cLSN) to the tmp_item_set;
            case the entry is a read record [T_i, x]
                if x is in the dirty_item_set and r.LSN > x.cLSN /* See comment I */
                    add T_i to the tmp_undo_list;
                elseif x is in the CIT table and r.LSN < x.eLSN /* See comment J */
                    add T_i to the tmp_undo_list;
            case the entry is an abort record [T_i, abort]
                delete all the data items of T_i from the tmp_item_set;
                if T_i is in the tmp_undo_list, remove it;
            case the entry is a commit record [T_i, commit]
                if T_i is in the tmp_undo_list
                    move all the items of T_i from the tmp_item_set to the dirty_item_set;
                    move T_i from the tmp_undo_list to the undo_list;
                    send an ASSESS message, which contains the identifier of the transaction, to the
                        Local DAR Manager at the site where the coordinator of T_i was located;
                    compose the cleaning subtransaction for T_i;
                    send the composed cleaning subtransaction to its coordinator (the identifier of
                    the coordinator can be found in the undo_list);
                else delete all the items of T_i from the tmp_item_set;
            case the entry is of other types
                skip it;
```

```
            P = P + 1;
end while

At a Cleaning Transaction Coordinator:
while TRUE
    if a cleaning subtransaction arrives
        if the cleaning subtransaction is not empty
            send the cleaning subtransaction to its (corresponding) subordinate for execution;
        else
            do nothing;
    if all the cleaning subtransactions have arrived /* See comment K */
            exit;
end while
run the 2PC protocol to commit the cleaning transaction;
when the cleaning transaction commits, send a SUCCESS message to each Local DAR Executor
that submits an un-empty cleaning subtransaction;
```

Comments

A. Inside a Local DAR Manager, the *assess_list* contains (the identifiers of) the transactions that have been reported to the Local DAR Manager. Inside a Local DAR Executor, the *submitted_item_set* contains the items that are being cleaned but still not cleaned. The *to_assess* contains the set of transactions in **B** that has a subordinate at the site, and the set of innocent transactions that had a subordinate at the site, are affected by **B** but are not identified by the Local DAR Executor. The *undo_list* contains the transactions affected by **B** and identified by the Local DAR Executor. The *tmp_undo_list* contains the transactions that are found affected but may abort later on. The *dirty_item_set* contains the damaged items. The *tmp_item_set* contains the items that could have been damaged. When a Local DAR Executor scans an innocent transaction, it does not know whether or not the transaction will commit later on. Even if the transaction reads a damaged item, it will cause no damage if it aborts later on. Therefore, we use the *tmp_item_set* and the *tmp_undo_list* to contain the information about which transactions may have caused damage, and which items may have been damaged. In this way, we need not to re-collect this information when a transaction commits.

B. Although E_i does not need the *ASSESS* message, E_i still needs the identifier of the coordinator process to repair the damage caused by T_i at E_i's site.

C. If the transaction T is in the *undo_list*, it is already found affected at the site, and an *ASSESS* message M has already been sent to a Local DAR Manager. The reason that this site still receives an *ASSESS* message for T is because the Local DAR Manager receives another *ASSESS* message for T before M.

D. Given the transaction is not in the *undo_list*, if it is not in the *tmp_undo_list*, it is still not found affected at the site. Hence if its first log record is before P, then the Local DAR Executor had not assessed the damage caused by the transaction when it was scanned, so we need to rescan the transaction and its following transactions.

E. Although the transaction is in the *tmp_undo_list*, since the transaction is already added to *to_assess*, the items of the transaction kept in the *tmp_item_set* will no longer be handled. Hence we need to move them now to the *dirty_item_set*.

F. Since the algorithm allows users to continuously execute new transactions as the damaged items are identified and cleaned, new transactions can spread damage if they read a damaged but still unidentified item. So we face two critical questions: (1) Will the DAR process terminate? (2) If the DAR process terminates, can we detect the termination?

Fortunately, [3] has answered these two questions in the context of centralized intrusion tolerant database systems. Here we give similar answers for distributed systems. First, when the damage spreading speed is quicker than the damage repair speed, the DAR process may never terminate. When the damage repair speed is quicker, the DAR process will terminate. Second, under the following conditions we can ensure that the DAR process terminates: (1) the cleaning transaction for every (reported) malicious transaction has been committed; (2) at each site, $dirty\_item\_set = \emptyset$; (3) at each site, $tmp\_undo\_list = \emptyset$, and $\forall x \in CIT$, $x.eLSN < l.LSN$. Here, $l.LSN$ denotes the LSN of the next log record for the Local DAR Executor to scan. (4) At each site, the Local DAR Manager has no *ASSESS* message to send, and the Local DAR Executor has no *ASSESS* message to respond. Condition 1 ensures that no malicious transaction is needed to repair. Condition 2 ensures that every identified damaged item is cleaned. Conditions 3 and 4 ensure that further scans will not identify any new damage. Please refer to [3] for more details about termination detection.

G. $w.LSN$ denotes the LSN of the write record. If $w.LSN > x.eLSN$, x is cleaned before the write operation, therefore, the write damages x again. If $w.LSN < x.cLSN$, this write is before the write that has been cleaned, so this write damages x before the cleaned write. So x is not really cleaned (by previous cleaning transactions).

H. The composing algorithm works as follows: for each item x written by T_i,

- **if** x is in the CIT table or the $submitted\_item\_set$, and $x.cLSN$ is larger than both the $cLSN$ value of x kept in the $clean\_item\_set$ (if any) and the $cLSN$ value of x kept in the $submitted\_item\_set$ (if any), then add no cleaning operation of x to the cleaning subtransaction of T_i (because x is already or to be 'better' cleaned);
- **otherwise**, add a write operation, which restores x to its previous value (before the write), to the cleaning subtransaction of T_i, and add $(x, x.cLSN)$ to the $submitted\_item\_set$.

It should be noticed that under some situations, for example, when T_i at the site is read-only, or when all the items written by T_i have been 'better' cleaned, an empty cleaning subtransaction may be composed.

I. $r.LSN$ denotes the LSN of the read record. If $r.LSN > x.cLSN$, x is read after x is damaged.

J. If $r.LSN < x.eLSN$, x is still not cleaned when x is read.

K. Since the coordinator was informed by its Local DAR Manager the list of subordinates of the transaction to clean, it knows the sites from which a cleaning subtransaction is expected.

3.2.1 Analysis of the Algorithm

Our algorithm has the following characteristics:

Claim 1. An ASSESS *message for transaction* T *is sent out by a Local Executor only if* T *is affected by a malicious transaction.*

Claim 2. For each innocent transaction affected by a malicious transaction (in **B***), the Local DAR Executor at every site where the transaction had a subordinate will assess and repair the damage caused by the transaction.*

Claim 3. When the DAR process terminates, every item that is updated by a transaction in **B** *or affected by* **B** *will be restored to the value before the item is damaged.*

Claim 4. If the DAR process terminates, the algorithm can detect the termination.

Based on these characteristics, the correctness of our algorithm can be specified as follows.

Theorem 1 Algorithm 1 is correct in the sense that (a) if the DAR process terminates, the algorithm can detect the termination and stop scanning the logs, and (b) when the DAR process terminates, any prefix H_p of the history including the point where the DAR process terminates results in the state that would have been produced by H'_p, where H'_p is H_p with all the transactions in **B** or affected by **B** removed.

3.3. Damage Assessment and Repair Under Failures and System Attacks

Let us now consider site and communication *failures*. We not only consider the failures caused by accidental *errors*, but also consider the failures caused by intentional attacks. In particular, during a DAR process, we assume a site can *crash* due to errors, we also assume a site can be attacked to crash. We assume due to errors or attacks, a message can be corrupted, lost (or dropped), faked, or replayed. We also assume a communication link can be broken for a while due to errors or attacks. We finally assume all failed sites ultimately recover, and all broken communication links are ultimately reconnected.

The impact of failures is two folds: First, corrupted, lost, faked, or replayed messages among the DAR Managers, the DAR Executors, and the cleaning transaction coordinators can cause a transaction to be assessed and repaired multiple times, can cause an innocent unaffected transaction to be "repaired" (rolled back), and can cause some malicious or affected transactions to stay at large. Second, crashed sites or broken communication links can disable some message interactions among the DAR Managers, the DAR Executors, and the cleaning transaction coordinators. In particular, when a site is unreachable during a period of time, its DAR Manager cannot receive (send) *ASSESS* messages from (to) DAR Executors at other sites; its DAR Executor cannot send *ASSESS* messages to DAR Managers at other sites; and its cleaning transaction coordinators cannot execute cleaning transactions at other sites. As a result, some information about affected transactions (generated at one site) cannot be distributed to other relevant sites in a timely manner, and some damaged items at one site can only be identified (and repaired) after another site becomes reachable.

The algorithm proposed in Section 3.2 can be easily extended to tolerate failures. First, our discussion in next section, namely Section 4, indicates that standard secure communication techniques such as IPSEC can be used to ensure that the messages between a Local DAR Manager and a Local DAR Executor or between a Local DAR Executor and a cleaning transaction coordinator will not be changed, dropped, faked, or replayed. Second, in order to tolerate failed sites and broken communication links, we assume that at each active site a *recovery process* exists and that it processes all messages from recovery processes at other sites and handles all the recovery tasks assigned by the Local DAR Manager and the Local DAR Executor. We assume that cleaning transaction coordinators (at each site) use standard distributed database fault tolerance services to execute cleaning transactions.

At an active site, when the Local DAR Manager or the Local DAR Executor find that a message cannot be sent out, they will forward the message, together with the information about who should receive the message, to the local recovery process, then "forget" the message and continue working. It is the responsibility of the recovery process to resend these unsuccessful messages when they can be sent out. When a site recovers, its recovery process will broadcast (or multicast) a *RESTART* message to all the other recovery processes, which will then send out all the messages for the recovered site.

Since a site may crash at any point of time, we need to periodically keep state information for the DAR components so that they need not restart the DAR process from the very beginning when a site recovers. In particular, at each site we assume a message log is kept for each DAR component, including the Local DAR Manager, the Local DAR Executor, the local recovery process, and the local cleaning transaction coordinators. Whenever a DAR component receives a message, the message will be first logged. In addition, we assume each DAR component periodically takes a checkpoint of its current state. When a message for a DAR component is logged, the message is tagged with the latest checkpoint taken by the component. In this way, when a site recovers, each DAR component, starting from its latest checkpoint, knows exactly which messages should be reprocessed. Moreover, when a message for the Executor is logged, it will also be tagged with the LSN of the log record that is currently scanned. In this way, the Executor can synchronize messages and scan operations.

The above method can ensure that every message will be processed, but it can neither ensure that every message will be received only once nor ensure that messages will be received in their original (sending-out) orders. Fortunately, we can use the message log kept for each DAR component to filter off the messages that had been received. Moreover, our algorithm can tolerate misordered messages. For each cleaning transaction coordinator, the arriving order of cleaning subtransactions does not matter. For each DAR Manager, if two *ASSESS* messages do not arrive in the original order, they will be processed in the wrong order. As a result, at a site even if T_i is dependent upon T_j, the Local DAR Executor could receive the *ASSESS* message for T_i before that for T_j (Note that this can happen even if each Local DAR Manager and Local DAR Executor receives *ASSESS* messages in their original orders). Fortunately, the correctness of our Executor algorithm, which is based on the (absolute) time order indicated by log records, is not affected by the order of arriving messages.

Since our DAR system is basically *nondeterministic* (See that a Local DAR Executor could do different things after receiving an *ASSESS* message and before receiving another *ASSESS* message), distributed fault tolerance techniques for deterministic systems such as message logging cannot be directly used [7, 20, 2]. Our approach, which can be viewed as a *pessimistic* message logging approach tailored based on the semantics of DAR processes, is simple, does not need global coordination, and can tolerate nondeterministic events.

4. PERFORMANCE ISSUES

Providing intrusion tolerance usually will affect the system performance. Therefore, a tradeoff between performance and intrusion tolerance should be (and has to be) made in most intrusion tolerant systems. Fortunately, our algorithm typically has very little impact on the performance of distributed transaction processing. The DAR components are completely separated from transaction processing components. In most cases when only few transactions are malicious the number of transactions affected by a malicious transaction is very small compared with the total number of transactions. We have done some performance study in centralized intrusion tolerant database systems using simulated data [12], the results show that on average only 2.72% transactions are affected by a malicious transaction. Although executing cleaning transactions makes the system busier, the number of cleaning transactions is typically very small compared with the total number of user transactions, and the Damage Confinement Manager can help prevent cleaning transactions from conflicting with user transactions. Our performance study in centralized intrusion tolerant database systems shows that on average only 0.32% items are damaged [12]. Although the DAR messages make the network busier, the number of DAR messages is typically very small compared with the number of transaction processing messages.

5. CONCLUSION

We have analyzed the problem of and proposed an efficient completely-distributed algorithm for damage assessment and repair in secure and resilient distributed database systems. We believe we have accomplished an important step towards providing "data integrity" guarantees to arbitrary distributed database applications in face of attacks.

Acknowledgments

Liu was supported by the Defense Advanced Research Projects Agency (DARPA) and Air Force Research Laboratory, Air Force Material Command, USAF, under agreement number F30602-00-2-0575.

References

[1] M. R. Adam. Security-Control Methods for Statistical Database: A Comparative Study. *ACM Computing Surveys*, 21(4), 1989.

[2] L. Alvisi and K. Marzullo. Message logging: Pessimistic, optimistic, causal and optimal. *IEEE Transactions on Software Engineering*, 24(2):149–159, 1998.

[3] P. Ammann, S. Jajodia, and P. Liu. Recovery from malicious transactions. *IEEE Transactions on Knowledge and Data Engineering*, 2001. To appear.

[4] V. Atluri, S. Jajodia, and B. George. *Multilevel Secure Transaction Processing*. Kluwer Academic Publishers, 1999.

[5] D. Barbara, R. Goel, and S. Jajodia. Using checksums to detect data corruption. In *Proceedings of the 2000 International Conference on Extending Data Base Technology*, Mar 2000.

[6] P. A. Bernstein, V. Hadzilacos, and N. Goodman. *Concurrency Control and Recovery in Database Systems*. Addison-Wesley, Reading, MA, 1987.

[7] A. Borg, J. Baumbach, and S. Glazer. A message system supporting fault tolerance. *Operating System Review*, 17(5):90–99, October 1983.

[8] P. P. Griffiths and B. W. Wade. An Authorization Mechanism for a Relational Database System. *ACM Transactions on Database Systems*, 1(3):242–255, September 1976.

[9] S. Jajodia, P. Samarati, V. S. Subrahmanian, and E. Bertino. A unified framework for enforcing multiple access control policies. In *Proceedings of ACM SIGMOD International Conference on Management of Data*, pages 474–485, May 1997.

[10] H.F. Korth, E. Levy, and A. Silberschatz. A formal approach to recovery by compensating transactions. In *Proceedings of the International Conference on Very Large Databases*, pages 95–106, Brisbane, Australia, 1990.

[11] P. Liu, P. Ammann, and S. Jajodia. Rewriting histories: Recovery from malicious transactions. *Distributed and Parallel Databases*, 8(1):7–40, 2000.

[12] P. Luenam and P. Liu. Odam: An on-the-fly damage assessment and repair system for commercial database applications. In *Proc. 15th IFIP WG11.3 Working Conference on Database and Application Security*, 2001.

[13] Teresa Lunt and Catherine McCollum. Intrusion detection and response research at DARPA. Technical report, The MITRE Corporation, McLean, VA, 1998.

[14] T.F. Lunt. A Survey of Intrusion Detection Techniques. *Computers & Security*, 12(4):405–418, June 1993.

[15] J. McDermott and D. Goldschlag. Towards a model of storage jamming. In *Proceedings of the IEEE Computer Security Foundations Workshop*, pages 176–185, Kenmare, Ireland, June 1996.

[16] C. Mohan, B. Lindsay, and R. Obermarck. Transaction management in the r* distributed database management system. *ACM Transaction on Database Systems*, 11(4):378–396, 1986.

[17] B. Mukherjee, L. T. Heberlein, and K.N. Levitt. Network intrusion detection. *IEEE Network*, pages 26–41, June 1994.

[18] B. Panda and J. Giordano. Reconstructing the database after electronic attacks. In *Proceedings of the 12th IFIP 11.3 Working Conference on Database Security*, Greece, Italy, July 1998.

[19] R. Sandhu and F. Chen. The multilevel relational (mlr) data model. *ACM Transactions on Information and Systems Security*, 1(1), 1998.

[20] R. E. Strom and S. Yemini. Optimistic recovery in distributed systems. *ACM Transaction on Computer System*, 3(3):204–226, August 1985.

ADMINISTERING PERMISSIONS FOR DISTRIBUTED DATA:
Factoring and Automated Inference

Arnon Rosenthal and Edward Sciore
The MITRE Corporation: Boston College and The MITRE Corporation

Abstract: We extend SQL's grant/revoke model to handle all administration of permissions in a distributed database. The key idea is to "factor" permissions into simpler decisions that can be administered separately, and for which we can devise sound inference rules. The model enables us to simplify administration via separation of concerns (between technical DBAs and domain experts), and to justify fully automated inference for some permission factors. We show how this approach would coexist with current practices based on SQL permissions.

Key words: Access permissions, derived data, view, federation, warehouse

1. INTRODUCTION

We believe that security can be greatly improved if data access permissions are appropriately consistent across systems, and are at appropriate granularity. Today's enterprise and multi-enterprise systems rarely meet that goal. There is little connection between privileges on data available from multiple databases. Also, while finer grained protections provide better security, most organizations reduce administrative costs by using coarse granules (e.g., entire tables) [Mai01]. A grand challenge for data security is to make large-scale administration easy enough that *ordinary* organizations will do it well. There are two main difficulties:

Size: There are many object types (i.e. tables and columns) to administer. SQL grants apply to a single physical table, so each copy or derived interface is administered separately. This complexity also makes it harder for planners to determine whether their users have enough permissions to get their jobs done.

Consistency: Permissions on derived products should, intuitively, be consistent with the sources, but the nature of the desired consistency is elusive (as discussed below). With the current model, there is little hope of giving clear guidance to data administrators.

We believe that the current security model should be extended so that:

- An administrator at a site should be able to infer permissions on derived information based on permissions granted on sources, wherever those sources reside. Moreover, the system should automate this inference and maintain consistency.
- The permission-granting ability should be split among various experts (e.g., domain experts, DBAs, and security experts), to take advantage of their different expertise.

In the subsections below, we argue that these capabilities are more than amenities. They are crucial.

1.1 The problems with automating permission inference

Many organizations have set the goal of capturing each fact just once (no redundant "fat-fingering") and making it available where needed. They must then provide the same fact as part of multiple interfaces, i.e., through multiple views, often materialized for performance, availability, and isolation. The goal is to have one steward responsible for each fact, who grants access permissions on it.

But how do these locally defined permissions affect derived tables elsewhere in the system? For example, who grants access permissions on federation (or warehouse) tables? The current situation is to assume that the federation administrator is trusted enough and knowledgeable enough to make the appropriate grants. Automated permission inference would be helpful in three ways:

- Permissions would be defined once and inferred where needed, eliminating the need for redundant grant specifications.
- The system would be able to assist administrators with understanding how their grants affect the entire system.
- Administrators of derived data would not need to be as trusted or knowledgeable.

However, automated permission is not easily done. Consider the following example. A system consists of two databases. One database contains a source table T, and the other contains a derived table T', which is simply a copy of T. Should T' have all the permissions of T? More? Fewer? The answer depends on the circumstances shown in the following cases:

a) T holds non-sensitive information telling nations' capitals and national holidays. But T resides on a sensitive financial or military system, whereas T' resides on a public server. T' should have more permissions.
b) T holds the same information as above, on a public web site. T' makes it available with a much better user interface and other amenities, but requires a subscription fee. T' should have fewer permissions.
c) T contains genetic sequences, on a biochemist's workstation, which has limited power and bandwidth. Gene publishers are allowed to access her data weekly to download changes to table T'. Table T is accessible only to local users plus the selected publishers; T' is public.
d) T is part of an order-entry system that handles millions of small transactions. T' is in a data warehouse, used for large data-mining analyses that absorb the CPU and hold long-duration locks. Clerks are given permission on T, and Analysts on T'.

The proper behavior differs drastically in the above situations. So at first glance, it seems that even the most trivial cases may require human review.

[Cap97, Cas97, Gud98] proposed the (optional) inference rule that be "if you have privileges on information used to derive a view, you get privileges on the view". The administrator could be asked to specify whether such inference should be allowed, i.e., to say whether privileges on T should also apply to derived products. This intuition that privileges should *sometimes* propagate is a step in the right direction, but needs significant extensions:

First, their formulation states that either all permissions propagate, or none do. For example, one cannot say "Employees' privileges propagate to the data warehouse, but Customers' privileges do not". Second, perhaps to keep the extra work modest, their proposal was just for *federated* architectures, not for views within a DBMS, or a data warehouse. Finally, their proposal asks administrators for an abstract decision about inference between two systems; there is no guidance on how to make the decision, e.g., by comparing *specific* risks and needs.

1.2 Problems with monolithic permissions

An administrator must consider multiple factors to decide whether a permission should be granted, e.g., whether the user is allowed to see the data, and whether the user is allowed to access the data from a particular computer. Each factor requires a very different expertise: the former requires business domain knowledge, to determine tradeoffs between the benefits and risk of greater accessibility; the latter requires technical judgements about systems issues such as performance and intrusion vulnerability.

Unfortunately, current permission specifications intertwine the various factors, without making them explicit. Often all the factors are hidden within a single decision; when the decision is changed, all must be reviewed. Other decisions are hidden from the database permission system, e.g., as permissions to logon to a platform or to connect to a DBMS.

The example of Section 1.1 illustrated this intertwining. Viewed according to their information content, the two tables T and T' should have the same permissions; however, other factors (hacker risk, performance, etc.) also had an impact. Therefore, the ultimate permissions could not be inferred automatically. However, by treating each factor separately, a much clearer picture can arise. Information content is global in nature – if information in T is releasable, the information in copyOf(T) is the same. On the other hand, physical platform concerns are local – permission to execute an operation on your machine does not necessarily imply permission on mine.

Current DBAs are required to have several kinds of understanding, which has exacerbated the shortage of skilled personnel. By splitting a permission specification into its factors, it is possible for people with different expertise (business experts, security experts, and system administrators) to each contribute their portion to permission administration.

1.3 Roadmap of the Paper

Our theory explicitly provides for permissions to be split into two kinds of factors – *information permissions* and *execution permissions.* Section 2 introduces permission factors and their inference rules. We discuss how permission factors should be specified, who should specify them, and provide inference rules.

Section 3 considers how one might implement a multiple-factor permission system, without discarding today's DBMSs. It outlines required capabilities and algorithms for a separate Permission Manager (*PM*) that contains most of the intelligence for managing factored permissions. The PM communicates with DBMSs that may not support factoring. We also discuss how new factors are introduced.

For simplicity, we assume that all databases are relational. Until Section 2.5 and 2.6 respectively, we assume that view logic requires no execution permissions to execute, and the code is public. Finally, we consider only policies for data access, not policies for delegating administrative authority [San99], i.e., SQL's *grant option.*

2. SPLITTING PERMISSIONS INTO FACTORS

2.1 Permissions on Operations

Each database request is submitted under the rights of some *subject.* The subject may be an individual, a process, or a role. (We expect the roles to be most common form of subjects in distributed systems [San99]). Issues such as how one authenticates users, assigns users to roles, and manages the role hierarchy (especially across organizations) are outside our scope. Increasingly, they are also out of the DBMS's scope, and performed in middleware security servers and directories.

A subject submits *requests* to the system. A request is expressed as in SQL, and may be a query, update, or stored procedure invocation. An *operation* is an abstract action at a particular granularity; example operations at table granularity might be Read(T) and DeleteFrom(T). A *full permission* authorizes an operation. Full permissions may be explicitly granted, or may be inferred from other permissions. The full permission (s,θ) denotes that subject s is authorized for operation θ.

Explicit permissions can be granted as individual pairs (s,θ), or in bulk (by a predicate on the operation description, e.g., all read-only operations on warehouse database DW_1, or all operations marked as inexpensive on operational data store ODS_2). While support for such predicates can be an implementation burden for vendors, many authors have recognized the desirability of capturing knowledge wholesale.

A request is implemented as some native code plus calls to additional operations, each of which requires a permission. Suppose that request R determines operations $\{\theta_1,\ldots,\theta_n\}$. Then subject s is *allowed* to execute the request R if each full permission (s,θ_i) exists.

For example, consider the two relations EMP(<u>E#</u>, EName, D#) and DEPT(<u>D#</u>, DName). The operation set associated with the request:

delete from DEPT where DName='sales'

would likely be {Delete(DEPT), Read(DEPT), Update(EMP)}, assuming that the related EMP records will be reassigned to a default department.

SQL, and hence our model, supports permissions on view operations by subjects who lack permissions on the base table. This is equivalent to defining several stored procedures, one for each action on the view (Read, Insert, etc.), and granting execute permission on these procedures. (If there are several interpretations of view update, each is treated as a separate stored procedure; resolution occurs before the security system is invoked.)

2.2 Permission Factors

The existence of a full permission (s, θ) allows s to execute θ on demand. As discussed in Section 1, it is not always easy to specify, propagate, and administer permissions in a large database. The question "should this user have full permission" requires that a judgement be made, based on a range of issues. This paper's main thesis is that it is better to treat a full permission as the conjunction of several independent, specialized permission factors. Compared to the full permission, each permission factor typically

- *Presents a simpler problem to the administrator.* The question posed by each permission factor is more concrete. The answer typically depends on a narrow slice of technical or domain knowledge.
- *Possesses an explicit definition of "consistency"* that is amenable to automated maintenance.

We assume that the system has a set of *factor types* $\{f_1,\ldots,f_n\}$. A *permission factor* is a triple (s, θ, f_i), which specifies that subject s is allowed to execute θ with respect to f_i. Permission factors are related to full permissions by the definition $(s, \theta) \equiv (s, \theta, f_1) \wedge \ldots \wedge (s, \theta, f_n)$

That is, s is allowed to execute θ iff s has a permission factor for θ with respect to every factor type. We do not need a new model for administrative authority – permission factors (like conventional full permissions) are managed by Grant and Revoke.

Factor types are partitioned into *information factor types* and *execution factor types*. Information factor types are concerned with "what is the result", i.e., what information is to be released or altered. Execution factor types are concerned with how the result is obtained – more specifically, with "which machine does which operation?" The following subsections give examples of several factor types.

The change from full permissions to permission factors increases the amount that administrators specify explicitly, but not the amount that they must consider. We contend that it can actually reduce the specification effort. The explicit split simplifies each decision, lets some decisions be handled very coarsely (e.g., on a per system basis), and reduces maintenance effort and errors by letting a single permission factor be modified without revisiting the others. It also makes it more likely that every factor type will indeed be considered. Meanwhile, storage is cheap and permission factors can usually be combined at Grant time rather than for each user request.

2.2.1 Information Factor Types

The information content of the database consists of a single copy of each fact (e.g., a patient's drug prescription). That fact may be physically replicated, and may be available through multiple interfaces. Information factor types enable permissions to be granted only on information content.

An information-factor Read permission says the data may be released to a subject. An information-factor Update permission authorizes an update that will (eventually) affect all physical copies. These permissions are technology independent – unaffected by how many systems have the information, or which system first receives the request. If we reorganize from centralized to distributed servers, no changes are needed. Administrators of information factor permissions are business experts, concerned with the business value of data sharing and data protection. They do not need to be technology experts.

We have identified two useful information factor types – *ordinary* and *overriding*. They differ in usage, rather than in semantics. Ordinary permissions are generally fine grained, and the right to grant them may be widely delegated to business experts. The union of all administrators' ordinary grants will constitute the ordinary information permissions for the entire system.

A danger in any administration system, but especially a large one, is that administrators lost in the weeds will grant permissions that violate organizational policies. Overriding-policy permissions may be used by a high level, security conscious administrator to unilaterally limit the effect of ordinary permissions granted by others. We anticipate very coarse-grained administration for overriding permissions. (An organization that does not wish to differentiate can ignore them by adopting the default of *Public* for all overriding privileges).

As an illustration, suppose that there exist only two factor types: ordinary and overriding. By definition, s may execute θ if and only if, both factors (s, θ, ordinary) and (s, θ, overriding) are granted. Suppose administrator x grants ordinary permissions on θ to subjects s1 and s2, and administrator y grants ordinary permissions on θ to s3. The permission factors granted are {(s1, θ, ordinary), (s2, θ, ordinary), (s3, θ, ordinary)}.

Now suppose administrator z grants the overriding policy permission factor (s1, θ, overriding). The net result is that only s1 can execute θ because it was granted both factor types.

Overriding-policy factor types can thus be used as a simple negative permission facility [Ber99] (but without the power and potential confusion of multiple levels of strength). Negative permissions are too broad brush – they limit permissions even from unrelated grantors. In [Ros00b] we explored a more fine-grained approach in which one limited permissions granted to a particular user (who might be an onward grantor). This enables any grantor to limit their own grants (and grants derived from theirs), without violating the rights of other grantors.

2.2.2 Execution Factor Types

Execution factor types concern whether it is appropriate to execute an operation at a particular server (site, machine, DBMS, middleware server, etc.). These permissions are the result of autonomous, local decisions – the fact that compensation analysts can read employee salaries on a budgeting machine says nothing about them having rights on the payroll machine. An organization can apply consistency constraints among the servers it controls, but these are organization-specific and outside our model.

We have identified several execution factor types. These correspond to physical-access limitations such as allowing only paid subscribers, keeping potential hackers off the machine, and controlling workload. A DBA or security officer might administer a "hacker risk" factor type. A DBA who tunes database performance might administer a "small transaction" factor type (where predicates only allow operations certified as not being resource hogs). A DBA and sales manager might negotiate the permissions associated with a "paid subscriber" factor type. Finally, we again want an *overriding* factor to act as a catchall for other types of restrictions.

For updates, the required permissions depend on the mechanism. If a user's update transaction updates all source and materialized derived products, the updating subject needs execution permission on all the objects. However, if a replication process provides the synchronization, then the updater needs execution permission on one source object, and the Replication Manager needs it on the others. In each case, the permission is given to whoever runs code on a machine.

Systems sometimes achieve the effect of execution permissions by imposing controls external to the DBMS, e.g., in an operating system or middleware server. In such cases, both the external system and our permission manager would keep a copy; changes in either environment would create changes to the other (in local syntax). In this way, a permission manager can present an administrator with an integrated, unified interface, so the answers to questions like "who can access table T?" will take all factor types into account.

2.3 Inference Rules

Our first inference rule is structural, stating that users have a permission factor for a request if they have the corresponding permission factors on the actions made by the request:

Inference Rule 1: Suppose request R is defined by actions $\{\theta_1,\ldots,\theta_n\}$, and that for each i, (s, θ_i, f) is a permission factor. Then we can infer the permission factor (s, execute(R), f).

This rule can be used, for example, to infer a permission factor on a view, based on appropriate permission factors on the underlying tables in the view's definition.

Our second inference rule applies only to information factor types. We say that two requests are *information-equivalent* if, for every population instance of the database, they produce the same result (i.e., queries return the same data, and updates produce the same changes). A user who has an information-factor permission for a request should therefore also be allowed to perform any information-equivalent request:

Inference Rule 2: Suppose requests R_1 and R_2 are information-equivalent requests. Then (s, execute(R_2), f) if and only if (s, execute(R_1), f)

The theory of information-equivalence is mature, and widely used in query optimization. We explicitly decline to extend the theory as part of a security system – extensions have wider and better-funded applicability in query optimization. Security facilities should be modular, and not require changes as functions are added to the query language.

Information equivalence is often determined by query rewrite, and can include expanding a view reference by its definition (as in rule 1), rewriting a query in terms of views, or performing query simplification based on constraints [Ros99, Ros00a].

Inference is used in two ways. First, one can *Infer Permissibility of a Request*: Given a request and a set of permissions granted, infer whether the permissions are sufficient to do the request. Second, one can *Infer Permissions on Object*: Given an object, infer the set of permissions on it. One uses this information to establish permissions to be imposed on a data warehouse, and to compare available permissions with business needs.

2.4 Some Examples

We revisit the four cases of Section 1.1, showing permission factors that capture each case. Here, *limited* will denote a role narrower than *public*.

a) *Sensitive server:* (public, Read(T), info); (employee, Read(T), execution); (employee, Read(T'), execution).
b) *Free versus subscription service* (public, Read(T), info); (subscriber, Read(T'), execution); (limited, Read(T), execution).
c) *Biologist* who wants to publish only via community servers: same as case a).
d) *Warehouse,* short and long transactions: (employee, Read(T), info); (clerk, Read(T), execution); (analyst, Read(T'), execution).

We now present an example taken from [Ber99]. Suppose a federation supplies a view, to be used only by employees. Actual permissions on the view, however, are determined by the underlying source databases.

To handle this case, we need not change the model; instead, we augment the representation of each federation operation by an explicit operation θ_{run_fed} that represents running code on the federation server. Now to execute a query θ that references T_1, and T_2, one needs full permissions for Read(T_1), Read(T_2), and θ_{run_fed}. The desired effect is obtained by using whatever permissions exist on the T_i plus (EMP, full, θ_{run_fed}). Any EMP who has access to the underlying data can access it through the federation.

2.5 Soundness and Completeness

We now examine the relevance of theoretical criteria of completeness and soundness. Incompleteness is tolerable – even weak inference is better than what we have today. It is also inevitable. Inference algorithms are difficult, and some problems are undecideable. Equally bad, they rely on declarations of constraint and operator identities, which incompletely describe the real situation.

Soundness (that the witness is equivalent to the original) is more crucial, since violations can lead to improper approvals. If the inference mechanism is untrustworthy, then a subject can choose to manually submit the witness for processing, in place of the original request. If the replacement was malicious, it will be able to misuse the subject's privileges, but no others.

Information equivalence cannot be trusted if an attacker can declare constraints. For example, if an attacker has permission (s, Read(T_1), info) and declares the false constraint T_1=T_2, the system will incorrectly infer (s, Read(T_2), info). One can frustrate such attacks by ensuring that only subjects possessing read and update access can declare new constraints. Most systems restrict constraint creation even more tightly, e.g., to table owners.

2.6 Controlling Use of View Definitions

Inference rule 2 stated that when two requests are information-equivalent, a subject who lacked permission for the first request could run the other. To do this substitution, however, the subject (or some process) must be able to read the view definitions.

When the view's source text is protected, generation of information-equivalent expressions can use only the subject's allowable knowledge of the view query. Several levels of information hiding are likely. The worst case is a black box where we cannot predict what tables are in the From list, i.e., what operations are invoked. Even rule 2 (implementation) rewrites are impossible. The next level allows a subject to know the view's inputs, (i.e., to know it is of the form f(T_1, ..., T_m)), but gives no insight into f. Next, one might see the query text, but some functions called from the query are opaque (e.g., secret constants can be opaque functions). The final level makes the entire query text is available for query simplification and rewrite.

3. THE PERMISSION MANAGER

We now suggest an approach to creating systems that support factored permissions. Section 3.1 discusses requirements, and argues that the best first step is creation of a *permission manager*. We sketch the interfaces and responsibilities of this manager, and how it interacts with a (possibly distributed) DBMS. The bulk of this section tells how permissions might be administered with this manager. Section 3.2 briefly presents some ways to support administrators who issue factored permissions. Section 3.3 addresses coexistence with unfactored (or less factored) permission sets.

3.1 Responsibilities of the Permission Manager

Commercial database systems will not soon be extended to handle factored permissions. Thus, we are led to an approach based on metadata management tools. We envision a management tool, called the *permission manager (PM)*, to be added to a system management framework. The permission manager would work with other security-related modules, such as an authentication manager and a directory server.

The PM has access to metadata of each local DBMS (schemas, view definitions, and grants), and performs the following functions:

- It receives grant commands (of both full and factored permissions), either directly from administrators, or indirectly, replicated from permissions that were granted within a DBMS.
- It performs inference and installs inferred full permissions into each local DBMS. Inference has two modes: "is a given request allowed?" and "what are all the requests that should be allowed on table T?"
- It allows administrators to add new factor types, and supports the retrofitting of legacy full permissions to the new factor type.
- It provides reports on who can do what operations. This lets administrators see if the permissions protect data sufficiently, and yet enable users' work to proceed.

Permissions are maintained in a single logical PM (which may be physically distributed and replicated). Administrators have the same Grant-option privileges as they do in the DBMS(s). Table names are assumed unique (concatenated with schema names), so a request can reference either source-system tables or derived tables (which may be materialized or virtual). The metadata manager is aware of database boundaries, so it can offer the options to establish execution permissions at database granularity.

Although the PM takes responsibility for permission inference and maintaining global consistency, each local DBMS retains the main responsibility for enforcement on run-time transactions, for several reasons. First, we do not want to tamper with code that is already running satisfactorily. Also, a DBMS checks *all* the interfaces to data (query, update, call level interfaces, usage of indexes, and so forth). It also uses tricks to improve efficiency, such as early binding of permission checks into object code modules. This coverage and efficiency would be costly to duplicate.

When the DBMS denies a request, the user can ask the permission manager to suggest possible alternative equivalent requests. The PM can be shown the rejected query, and invited to find a rewrite that uses other resources. In [Ros99], we gave several examples where either the user's query did not really need all the sources, or could be rewritten to use a view that had additional permissions. (A view that is just a carrier of security metadata need not be visible in the query-formulation interface.)

Some local systems may be file systems, with more primitive (non-granular) security. In such cases, one might wish to enforce some permissions within the distributed query processor. We assume that if the distributed query processor considers alternative tables as data sources (e.g., based on cost), then it is smart enough to look only at copies where the request has permission to execute.

3.2 Administering Permission Factors

Suppose that the permission factor p = (s, θ, f) has just been granted, where f is an information factor type. The permission manager should check:

- *whether p conflicts with any overriding-policy (negative) permissions.* If so, the grantor of p should be warned that the grant is ineffectual.
- *whether appropriate execution permissions exist.* If not, then the grantor should again be warned. The issue is whether the grantor intended p to mean "θ does not need to be protected for s", or "θ should be available to s". If the latter is intended, then the grantor must negotiate with DBAs to get execution permission for s.

When a new permission of any factor type is granted, the PM should:

- *check to see what other permissions are implied by the addition of p.* This information should be made available to the grantor.
- *provide a convenient way to give the info-grantee permission on other factor types*, to generate the full permission. If other factor types are handled by a different administrator, add the task to that administrator's In-Box.

It seems important not to impose restrictions on the order for administering permissions. For example, when a new role is defined, one might next negotiate machine access or else identify detailed information permissions, depending on personnel availability.

3.3 Aggregated and Split Permissions

The permission manager is responsible for dealing with legacy permissions. Whenever a factor is split into subfactors or new factor is introduced, we cannot instantly change existing permissions to use the factor. In fact, users may prefer not to change, but to use their old factors for quite a while.

We assume there is a tree of factor types, where the root node represents full permissions, the next level splits into *info* and *execution,* and each of these may be further refined. The following inference rule extends the definition of Section 2.2 to include a tree of factor types:

Inference Rule 3: Suppose factor type f is partitioned into $f_1,\ldots,f_m$. Then for all s, θ: $(s, \theta, f) \equiv (s, \theta, f_1) \wedge \ldots \wedge (s, \theta, f_n)$. That is, from (s, θ, f) one can infer all subsidiary (s, θ, f_j), and vice versa.

The permission manager tracks the explicit permission factors, and uses the inferred ones as needed. (We do not discuss implementation issues such as caching of inference results.) The following observation shows that by splitting a factor into subfactors, one does not lose expressive power:

Observation: Suppose instead of granting a permission factor for f, one issues explicit grants for each child factor f_j. Then any set of permissions granted on f can be simulated by permissions on the f_j.

There are actually several ways in which one can perform the above simulation. Let (s, θ, f) be the permission factor to be simulated. One simulation is to grant (s, θ, f_1), together with $(\text{PUBLIC}, \theta, f_i)$ for all $i>1$. Alternatively, one could grant (s, θ, f_i) for all i.

We do not try to guess which is "right". One might give a human a convenient interface for choosing among likely ways to elaborate (s, θ, f), but guesswork seems likely to give more error than benefit.

4. SUMMARY

Our goal is to reduce the labor and skill needed to administer access permissions, especially in enterprise and cross-enterprise databases. We explore the ramifications of a simple idea – to separate concerns and ask administrators to provide smaller decisions, each of which requires less broad expertise. Change becomes easier because one can revisit just one factor. Because information permissions are separate, we can exploit their more powerful inference theory. In all cases, inference is fully automated.

Execution permissions can simulate the cases handled in [Ber99], but permit decisions to be as fine (or as coarse) as administrators wish – not just one decision for each database. The techniques also apply to view tables in a single DBMS, and to tables in a warehouse. If the DBMS administrators do not trust the mechanism, the user can (at her own risk) perform it herself.

We then described how the theory could be implemented in a permission manager. When an administrator provides one factor's permission, we consider what is needed to further elicit the administrator's intent. For example, when one says certain information is readable by Public, does that just mean it need not be protected, or that we want to take steps to make it actually available? We also considered how to represent full permissions as factors, both to assimilate full permissions that a DBMS already has, and to support users who are uninterested in changing.

We deliberately stated our inference rules at a high level. Properties of this inference system, and (especially) efficient evaluation algorithms remain an open research question.

The outstanding pragmatic challenge is to implement tools to support our approach and make it attractive to administrators. Another challenge is to find ways to exploit the rewrite capabilities of query processors.

REFERENCES

[Ber99] E. Bertino, S. Jajodia, P. Samarati, "A Flexible Authorization Mechanism for Relational Data Management Systems," *ACM Trans. Information Systems*, Vol. 17, No. 2, April 1999, pp. 101-140.

[Cap97] S. De Capitani di Vimercati, P. Samarati, Authorization Specification and Enforcement in Federated Database Systems, *Journal of Computer Security*, vol. 5, n. 2, 1997, pp. 155-188.

[Cas97] S. Castano, S. De Capitani di Vimercati, M.G. Fugini, Automated Derivation of Global Authorizations for Database Federations, *Journal of Computer Security*, vol. 5, n. 4, 1997, pp. 271-301.

[Gud98] Ehud Gudes, Martin S. Olivier: Security Policies in Replicated and Autonomous Databases. DBSec 1998: 93-107

[Mai01] W. Maimone, VP, Oracle Corporation (personal communication)

[Ros99] A. Rosenthal, E. Sciore, V. Doshi, "Security Administration for Federations, Warehouses, and other Derived Data", *IFIP 11.3 Working Conference on Database Security*, Seattle 1999. (Kluwer, 2000). (Rosenthal papers are available at my homepage)

[Ros00a] A. Rosenthal, E. Sciore, "View Security as the Basis for Data Warehouse Security ", *CAiSE Workshop on Design and Management of Data Warehouses*, Stockholm, 2000.

[Ros00b] A. Rosenthal, E. Sciore, "Extending SQL's Grant Operation to Limit Privileges", *IFIP Workshop on Database Security*, Amsterdam, August 2000

[San99] R. Sandhu, V. Bhamidipati, Q. Munawer, "The ARBAC97 Model for Role-Based Administration of Roles", *ACM Trans. Information and System Security*, Feb. '99.

STATE-DEPENDENT SECURITY DECISIONS FOR DISTRIBUTED OBJECT-SYSTEMS

Joachim Biskup
University of Dortmund
44221 Dortmund
Germany
biskup@ls6.cs.uni-dortmund.de

Thomas Leineweber*
University of Dortmund
44221 Dortmund
Germany
Thomas.Leineweber@udo.edu

Abstract Distributed systems consist of many different objects, participating in distributed activity sequences. We present a system for state-dependent security decisions (SDSD), which can be used to specify and to enforce sets of allowed activity sequences. A specification is expressed as a protocol, which defines such a set as a regular language. The protocol is transformed into a finite automaton. Instantiated copies of the automaton are deployed by the actually participating objects, each of which has been wrapped by the SDSD-system with a security object. Knowing the automaton and based on additional control messages, the security objects can locally decide, whether a requested action is allowed or not. A running prototype implementing the SDSD-system is described, and its full integration into CORBA is outlined.

Keywords: security, distributed system, object system, state-dependent, dynamic access rights, enforcement, wrapping security objects, CORBA

---

*The work of Thomas Leineweber is supported by the Research Alliance Data Security North Rhine-Westphalia, http://www.datensicherheit.nrw.de/

1. INTRODUCTION

In distributed systems there are many entities, participating in distributed activity sequences consisting of possibly many actions. In order to control the execution of these sequences of actions, special access rights are needed. These access rights could be assigned on a static basis by giving all eventually needed rights at the beginning of an activity sequence. However, this policy does not consider the fact, that the activity sequences may not be fully predetermined and that the participants may be granted more rights than needed during the whole lifespan of the sequence.

Therefore, a policy with dynamic rights is needed, which stepwise assigns the access rights only for the specific action which has to be executed next. Moreover, the set of the allowed actions at one point of time should depend on the sequence of actions executed in the past. Such dynamic rights can also be called context-aware. This context-awareness is for example found in Workflow Management Systems [Georgakopoulos et al., 1995, Vossen and Weske, 1999].

These requirements have been treated in previous theoretical work on specifying and securely enforcing allowed sequences of activities, which are to be executed in a distributed environment. Conceptually, enforcement is achieved by a finite automaton a copy of which is passed to all actually participating objects which exploit the automaton in turn with a specialized security procedure. On completion of an activity, the security procedure uses offer-, get-, put- and invoke-messages to and from other objects for initializing the next activity and for setting the automaton into the next state. Based on the given information, the objects can locally and autonomously check, which activity they are allowed to perform. A central authority is only needed to start an automaton and to resolve questions whether an object has not obeyed to the rules how to change the state of the automaton.

This paper aims at presenting and discussing a prototypical implementation of this approach. The implemented *System for State-Dependent Security Decisions*, SDSD-system for short, uses standard object technologies like JAVA and CORBA.

The remainder of this paper is organized as follows. In Section 2 we give a short introduction to the specification of the protocols and the automatons the SDSD-system is based on. Section 3 describes our JAVA-prototype. Security considerations are sketched in section 4. Section 5 compares our approach with other approaches for distributed rights management. And Section 6 concludes with directions for further research and development.

2. STATE-DEPENDENT SECURITY DECISIONS (SDSD)

The theoretical foundation of our SDSD-system has been previously presented in [Biskup and Eckert, 1994, Eckert, 1997]. In order to turn the conceptual approach into practice, we have to consider at least four kinds of phases: *object preparation phases, specification phases, instantiation phases* and *enforcement phases.*

2.1. Object Preparation Phases

The SDSD-system has been designed as an additional security layer to be used on top of a functional layer. The functional layer is assumed to be a distributed object system based on message passing. The functional layer may already exist before, independently of the security layer. In object-preparation-phases, the SDSD-system wraps existing or newly created objects of the underlying functional layer with additional encapsulating security objects. Whenever in the functional layer new objects are created, they have to be immediately wrapped too. Any interaction with functional objects, including interactions with a human user, are monitored by the wrapping security objects. In particular, as shown by the example given below, some of the functional objects can be understood as formal representatives of human users, and accordingly such objects act on behalf of the represented users.

2.2. Specification Phases

In a specification-phase, a security administrator specifies a set of allowed sequences of activities. The specification of one set of allowed sequences of

protocol	→	PROTOCOL ident; PARTICIPANTS formal_participants; BEGIN activity END;	
formal_participants	→	formal_participant; formal_participants	
	→	formal_participant	
formal_participant	→	*ident*: $ident_{classname}$	
activity	→	step	
	→	activity; activity	sequence
	→	activity | activity	alternative
	→	activity*	repetition
	→	(activity)	
step	→	$ident_{activator}$ $ident_{executor}$ $ident_{action}$	

Figure 1. Definition of the language for protocols. Words of this language describe allowed sets of activity sequences

activites is done with a so-called *protocol*. The definition of the language for protocols is outlined in figure 1. Each protocol, as defined by the language, has a regular expression as a core, built from triplets (*activator*, *executor*, *action*), named *steps*. Such a step specifies that an *activator* (object) is allowed to initiate the execution of an *action* at the *executor* (object) – but only in the contexts given by the occurence of the step within the regular expression. This regular core of a protocol is embedded into additional features, which basically declare the *formal participants* in the activity sequences specified within the core.

The SDSD-system transforms a specified protocol into a finite automaton, the alphabet of which consists of the steps occuring in the protocol and which accepts exactly all specified activity sequences. An example for a protocol specification and the resulting automaton is given in figure 2.

The example-protocol has four formal participants: a *Representative* of the type *Agent*, two participants of the type *Employee*, namely *Decider* and *Bookkeeper*, and a fourth formal participant *Data* of the type *ContractData*. These four participants work cooperatively to establish a new insurance contract. After the Representative has inserted the contract in the Data, the Decider has to read the Data in order to decide, whether the insurance company wants to agree with the contract. If not, the contract is removed from the Data. Otherwise, the Bookkeeper waits for the payment receipt. If the contract is paid, the Data is correspondingly updated. Otherwise, the contract is removed.

2.3. Instantiation Phases

In an instantiation-phase an already specified automaton is instantiated. The instantiation consists of three parts. First, a new instance of the automaton

```
PROTOCOL insurance;
PARTICIPANTS
   Representative: Agent;
   Decider: Employee;
   Bookkeeper: Employee;
   Data: ContractData;
BEGIN
   Representative Data insertContract;
   Decider Data readContract;
   (
     Decider Data confirmContract;
     (
       Bookkeeper Data setContractPaid
     |
       Bookkeeper Data deleteContract
     )
   )
   |
   Decider Data deleteContract
END;
```

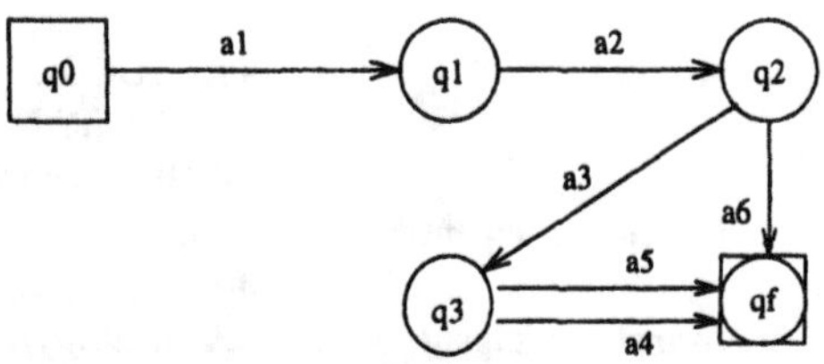

a1 = Representative Data insertContract
a2 = Decider Data readContract
a3 = Decider Data confirmContract
a4 = Bookkeeper Data setContractPaid
a5 = Bookkeeper Data deleteContract
a6 = Decider Data deleteContract

Figure 2. A specification for a protocol, defining a simplified set of activity sequences done in an insurance company while taking out a new insurance, and the resulting automaton.

is uniquely named, and second, the formal participants of the automaton are bound to some appropriate actual objects. These objects must be selected out of the collection of objects wrapped in preceding object-preparation-phases. The binding must respect all declarations, especially concerning the types. It also enforces the constraint, that different formal participants are bound to different objects. Third, a copy of the instantiated automaton (including the information of the actually bound objects) is sent to all objects which were bound. Upon reception of the copy of the intantiated automaton, the objects know, that they participate in the corresponding protocol instantiation and which other objects are participating.

2.4. Enforcement Phases

To every instantiation-phase, an enforcement-phase is assigned to. In an enforcement-phase, an actual activity sequence takes place. The objects bound to an instantiated automaton communicate with each other with offer-, get-, put- and invoke-messages for initializing any activity. In particular, as far as necessary, they get informed about the current state of the instantiated automaton. Using these messages the (wrapping security) objects can locally and autonomously check, whether the (wrapped) objects are allowed to perform a specific activity or not.

The state transition is organized as follows:

1 The actual participant that acted as the last executor sends an *offer*-message to all thc participants, which are allowed to act as the next activator according to the instantiated automaton.

2 If a recipient of an offer-message agrees to act as activator, it replies with a *get*-message.

3 The last executor chooses one of the recipients that returned a get-message as the actual next activator and sends him a *put*-message. The put-message authorizes the chosen participient – and only him – to be the next activator within the activity sequence.

4 The activator sends an *invoke*-message to the associated executor. This executor is now allowed to execute the associated action. After that, the executor changes the state of the automaton to the next state according to the executed step, more precisely, the information about the new state will be encoded in the forthcoming messages.

The messages provide all information needed to locally verify, whether the instantiated automaton may change into its next state, and they are cryptographically signed. Every message includes the identification of an instantiated automaton and its current state, the identifications of the sender and the receiver, the sequence number of the current state transition, and the signature of the last received message for this automaton. This signature is used as a link between the messages concerning the instantiated automaton, so that on demand, for instance in case of a detected security violation, a third party can reconstruct a continous flow of messages. The offer-, get- and put-messages additionally include the identification of the planned executor and the planned action, the invoke-message includes the complete associated put-message.

The verification whether an invoke-message conforms to the instantiated automaton can be sketched as given below. Such a verification has to be performed by any security object after having received a message requiring to execute an action on the wrapped functional object. The received message should contain all information needed in addition to the instantiated automaton, in particular n gives how many state transitions have been made with this automaton up to now. q is the state before doing the actual step, e_l is the last executor, a_c is the activator and e_c is the (intended) executor in the current state transition.

1 With help of the message's signature, it is verified whether the message really originates from the actual participant given in the message.

2 The signature of the included put-message is verified.

3 The *state-control* checks, whether e_l which sended the corresponding offer- and put-messages was really able to change the state of the instantiated automaton to the current state. This is possible, if there exists a step in the instantiated automaton where e_l is executor and the next state of the automaton is the current state.

4 The *transition control* additionally checks, whether it is possible for e_l to have performed the nth activity in a sequence complying with the instantiated automaton thereby reaching the current state. This is possible, if an appropriate path can be found.

5 Now, after having recognized the current state as a (presumably)* correct one and also all other relevant parameters to be correct, the *state-based access control* finally checks, whether according to the instantiated automaton the present state allows the execution of the requested action.

*As discussed in [Biskup and Eckert, 1994, Eckert, 1997], for a full proof of correctness additional data is required. We do no treat this extension here.

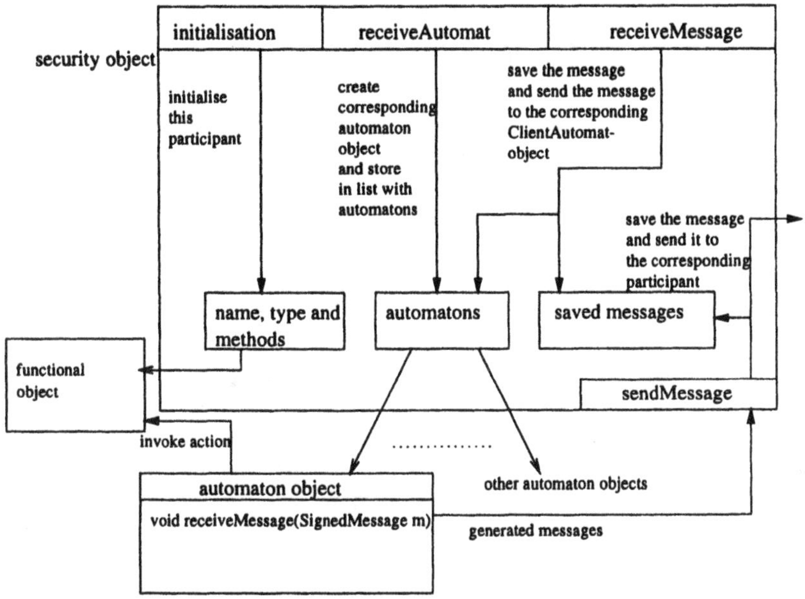

Figure 3. Structure of an object within SDSD, consisting of the security object, the functional object and the automaton objects.

3. THE PROTOTYPE

We implemented a JAVA-prototype for SDSD. The structure of an SDSD-object is shown in figure 3. It consists of a *functional object*, which conforms to the underlying functional layer, the wrapping *security object* and one *automaton object* per instantiated automaton the SDSD-object is participating in.

The *functional object* provides the actions that the SDSD-object can execute. This functional object is encapsulated in the *security object*. Only this security object holds a reference on the functional object, and, therefore, only it itself is able to invoke any actions on the functional object. When the security object and (possibly) the functional object (if it has not existed before) are created (object-preparation-phase), an identification, consisting of a unique *name*, the formal *type* of the functional object and (the identifiers or references for) its *methods*, are stored in the security object.

If an object wants to initiate a protocol (instantiation-phase) it can query such identifications. Having got this information, the object can decide on its selection which objects are to be bound to which formal participants of the protocol. Afterwards, the SDSD-system sends the instantiated automaton to the security objects of all actual participants. Each of them creates a new *automaton object* in order to persistently store the received instantiated automaton. Moreover, this

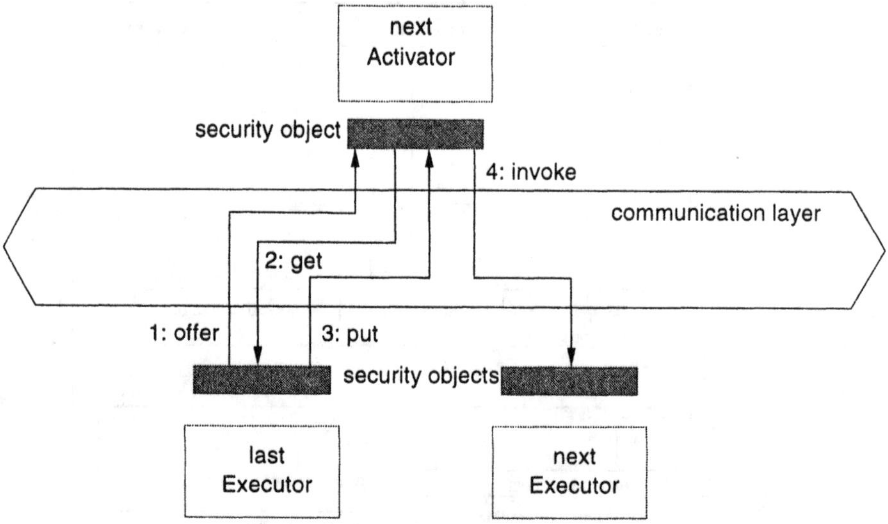

Figure 4. Message passing in CORBA

automaton object is responsible for the processing of those incoming messages which pertain to the stored instantiated automaton. It is also responsible for the generation of the responding messages. This can include possible human user interaction. The *automatons* block of the security object forwards incoming messages to the respective automaton objects.

The prototype performs communications among objects with the Common Object Request Broker Architecture (CORBA) [Object Management Group, b]. We use the ORB-Implementation delivered with the JDK1.3 from SUN. The initiator (object) of an activity sequence can load references to every available object, as offered by the preceding object-preparation-phases, with the use of a nameserver.

The messages between the security objects are sent using CORBA. They are implemented as CORBA valuetypes, so that they are passed to the receiver by value, not by reference, and can be queried locally without contacting the sender of the message. The methods of the security object are accessible from CORBA and handle the security decisions without interaction with the functional object but with help from the responsible automaton object.

4. SECURITY CONSIDERATIONS

Our conceptual approach requires that a functional object is not accessible without calling the wrapping security object, which shall not be bypassed. Given this property, a security proof for the conceptual approach has to demonstrate that nobody in the sequence of activities can successfully cheat without being detected.

As described in [Biskup and Eckert, 1994], there are essentially four different attacks on the automaton itself:

1 The actual executor generates a wrong successor state for the automaton.

2 The actual activator changes the state of the automaton.

3 Another SDSD-object tries to play the role of the last executor, although it is not.

4 Another SDSD-object tries to play the role of the acutal activator, although it is not.

These four attacks can be detected indeed under the following additional assumptions: the signatures are unforgeable, the actions are only executed if the tests described above are successfully completed, and all participants securely log all sent and received messages. Whereas the first assumption refers to the available quality of digital signature systems, the latter assumptions basically refer to a correct implementation of the SDSD-system.

In addition to these conceptual attacks there exist further attacks on the implementation of our prototype. Apparently, the main attack tries to get a reference on a functional object, so that its methods can be called without involving the wrapping security object. Therefore, no other object than the security object shall get a reference on the functional object. This requirement is (hopefully) achieved by the claimed properties of JAVA. More generally, we have to rely on appropriate properties of the programming system used for the implementation.

Another scenario is an attempt for a denial of service attack. In this scenario, one or more malicious SDSD-objects send a lot of false messages to other SDSD-objects. This behaviour could possibly overload both the communication layer and the targeted objects. Concerning the latter situation, the targeted objects can alliviate the attack by arranging the checks such that the most easily detectable false parameters are considered first in order to generate a quick rejecting result. Such checks include for example

- whether the targeted object is itself a participant in the instantiated automaton specified in the message, or
- whether the sequence number of the state transition is higher than the sequence number seen when the instantiated automaton has involved this object the last time.

Further considerations about denial of service attacks lead to the implementation of additional messages used as informational messages for the SDSD-objects participating in an instantiated automaton. An *end*-message is sent to all participating SDSD-objects of an instantiated automaton, when the automaton reaches its halting state and therefore the activity sequence is finished. With this message the SDSD-objects know, that they can discard all messages concerning this automaton from now on. The authenticity of the end-messages is secured by checking, whether the originator of the end-message is an SDSD-object that can act as executor in the instantiated automaton and the sequence number of the last state transition is possible.

A second additional message is the *revokeOffer*-message. This message is sent in parallel with the put-message to all recipients of the corresponding offer-message which are not chosen as the executor. The revokeOffer-message informs the recipients, that they are not chosen and that they can ignore other messages contradicting this message. The revokeOffer-message must have the complete same data as the corresponding offer-message, otherwise it is ignored.

5. COMPARISONS

There exist many different concepts for a distributed management of access rights. An early overview of the inclusion of access control models in workflow-management systems is given in [Ellmer et al., 1994]. It gives proposals, how to integrate Discretionary or Mandatory Access Control into workflow-management systems and notes the integration of transactional systems. In [Hale et al., 2000] a system is described that is based on a simple object model with components consisting of a message handler, information repositories, a set of methods and a set of subobjects. These components reflect the notion of our security object, which knows the possible actions of the functional objects, receives and sends messages and holds type-information of the functional object. In their model the components have individual access control lists, denoting the so-called *tokens* needed to be allowed to invoke actions.

In [Bertino et al., 1997], a model for the assignment of both users and roles to tasks is presented, and both static and dynamic separation of duties is considered. This model is comparable to the binding of actual objects to formal participants in the SDSD-system, which also provides a separation of duties. A dynamic separation will be possible in our system with a dynamic binding of the participants. This is necessary for workflow management systems that are able to change the workflow definition during the execution of the workflow and therefore can not bind all participants at the beginning of a workflow instance [Vossen and Weske, 1999].

[Thomas, 1997] shows with Team-based Access Control a way to distinguish between the permission assignment and a context-based permission activation. At the beginning of a task, permissions are assigned to the roles. These permissions are activated and deactivated during the execution of a workflow. A drawback is the fact, that the activation and deactivation has to be done explicitely, for example by trapping the calls on the objects and determining which permissions shall be active. Another proposal for the integration of static and dynamic access control is given in [Oh and Park, 2000]. It combines the static RBAC model [Sandhu et al., 1996] with the dynamic models given above, enabling the system to deal with workflow and non-workflow oriented tasks. It links the access not directly to the roles but uses the intermediary concept of tasks. These tasks have time constraints and and activation conditions for the access rights.

An integration of multilevel security into workflow-management systems is given in [Atluri et al., 2000]. It makes use of dependencies in the control flow between the different activities of the workflow-management system and specializes on the integration of multilevel security. It uses centralized components during the execution of the activity sequence, and it gives rights according to previous actions, based on the information on which security levels these actions were performed.

Table 1 compares the above mentioned security architectures with the SDSD-system. It is shown whether it is possible to specify allowed activity sequences, whether the rights are dependent on the previous activities, whether these rights are automatically activated and deactivated, whether a separation of duties is possible, and whether the access decision is locally done at the distributed objects without a central repository for access rights.

6. FURTHER WORK AND CONCLUSIONS

It will be necessary to lift the restriction which inhibits the system from specifiying explicit parallelism for the activity sequences. This could be weakly simulated within the current language for the protocols, but only at the price of blowing up the size of the protocols and without achieving real parallelism. Therefore, an appropriate extension of the language has to be found, and ways for dealing with real parallelism in the automatons have to be investigated.

Another field for further research is to enhance the SDSD-system to deal with delayed binding of the objects to the automaton and dynamic reorganisation of the protocol, respectively the automaton. With this enhancement, the SDSD-

Table 1. Comparison of different security architectures for distributed object systems

system	*set of allowed activity sequences*	*rights dependent on previous activities*	*automatic rights management*	*separation of duties enforced*	*local access decision*
Ellmer et al., 1994				X	X
Bertino et al., 1997		X		X	
Thomas, 1997		X		X	X
Hale et al., 2000				X	X
Oh and Park, 2000	X	X	X	X	possible
Atluri et al., 2000	X	X	X		
SDSD	X	X	X	X	X

system can be integrated into workflow-management systems offering these concepts like e. g. WASA2 [Vossen and Weske, 1999].

Further considerations have to be made on the problem, how to choose the actual activator from the SDSD-objects that responded with a get-message to the offer-message. This can be done in different ways:

- A local human user chooses for the security object, which SDSD-object will be the next activator.

- Every SDSD-object gets information for the handling of the incoming get-messages. This can include a decision on a first-come-first-served-basis or on a priority basis after a given time of waiting has elapsed. These information can be given central for the object upon creation or the protocol can specify, how the SDSD-objects have to decide. These specification can even be different for different SDSD-objects.

- In the definition of the activity sequence itself the alternatives are annotated with a specification how this actual alternative shall be handled. This specification can be again on a first-come-first-serve-basis or on a priority basis.

The CORBA Security Service [Object Management Group, a] provides a framework for the integration of security services into CORBA. We want to integrate the SDSD-system into the security service. A high-level view onto a possible integration is shown in figure 5. Compared with figure 4, where the security objects are outside of the communication layer, the security objects are now embedded in the communication layer in a way such that calls to the functional objects can not circumvent the security objects (as before with the explicit security objects in the current implementation).

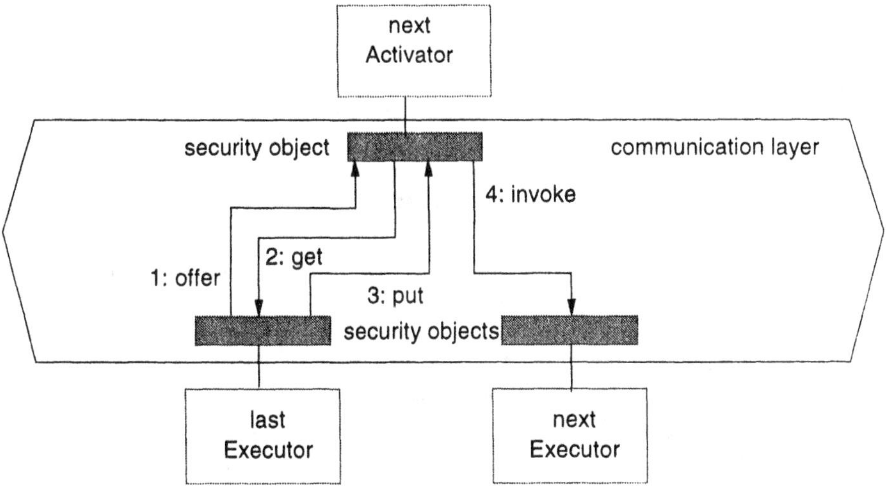

Figure 5. Possible integration into the CORBA security specification, moving the security object into the CORBA-communication layer (cf. figure 4).

These and similar extension would further enhance the achievements reached so far. The presented prototyp of the SDSD-system already allows for the dynamic, context-aware assignment of access rights, i.e. stepwise and based on previously executed actions. The running prototype is implemented in JAVA and CORBA, and thus it is portable for hopefully many applications.

References

[Atluri et al., 2000] Atluri, V., Huang, W.-K., and Bertino, E. (2000). A semantic-based execution model for multilevel secure workflows. *Journal of Computer Security*, 8:3–41.

[Bertino et al., 1997] Bertino, E., Ferrari, E., and Atluri, V. (1997). A Flexible Model Supporting the Specification and Enforcement of Role-based Authorizations in Workflow Management Systems. In *Proceedings of the Second ACM Role-Based Access Control Workshop*, pages 1–12.

[Biskup and Eckert, 1994] Biskup, J. and Eckert, C. (1994). About the enforcement of state dependent security specifications. *Database Security*, VII:3–17.

[Eckert, 1997] Eckert, C. (1997). *Zustandsabhängige Sicherheitsspezifikationen und ihre Durchsetzung*. Berichte aus der Informatik. Shaker Verlag.

[Ellmer et al., 1994] Ellmer, E., Pernul, G., and Quirchmayr, G. (1994). Security for Workflow Management. In *Proceedings of Sixth IASTED/ISMM International Conference on Parallel and Distributed Computing and Systems.*

[Georgakopoulos et al., 1995] Georgakopoulos, D., Hornick, M., and Sheth, A. (1995). An Overview of Workflow Management: From Process Modeling to Workflow Automation Infrastructure. In *Distributed and Parallel Databases*, volume 3, pages 119–153.

[Hale et al., 2000] Hale, J., Threet, J., and Shenoi, S. (2000). A ticket-based access control architecture for object systems. *Journal of Computer Security*, 8:43–65.

[Object Management Group, a] Object Management Group. CORBA Security Services Specification. `http://www.omg.org/technology/documents/formal/security_service.htm`.

[Object Management Group, b] Object Management Group. CORBA/IIOP Specification. `http://www.omg.org/technology/documents/formal/corbaiiop.htm`.

[Oh and Park, 2000] Oh, S. and Park, S. (2000). An Integration of Role-Based Access Control and Activity-Based Acces Control Using Task. In *Proceedings of the 14th Annual IFIP WG 11.3 Working Conference on Database Security*, pages 557–569.

[Sandhu et al., 1996] Sandhu, R. S., Coyne, E. J., Feinstein, H. L., and Youman, C. E. (1996). Role-Based Addess Control Method. *IEEE Computer*, 29.

[Thomas, 1997] Thomas, R. K. (1997). Team-based Access Control (TMAC): A Primitive for Applying Role-based Access Controls in Collaborative Environments. In *Proceedings of the Second ACM Role-Based Access Control Workshop*, pages 13–19.

[Vossen and Weske, 1999] Vossen, G. and Weske, M. (1999). The WASA2 Object-Oriented Workflow Management System. In *SIGMOD 1999, Proceedings ACM SIGMOD International Conference on Management of Data, June 1-3, 1999, Philadephia, Pennsylvania, USA*, pages 587–589.

IV

INFORMATION WARFARE AND INTRUSION DETECTION

REORGANIZATION OF THE DATABASE LOG FOR INFORMATION WARFARE DATA RECOVERY

Rumman Sobhan and Brajendra Panda
Computer Science Department, University of North Dakota

Abstract: Using traditional logs that contain only before and after images of data items and record neither any of the read operations nor actual mathematical or logical operations associated with an update, a complete damage assessment and repair of the database is not possible in the post Information Warfare scenario. In this research, a new logging protocol is proposed which records all appropriate information required for the complete repair of a database that was updated by committed but affected transactions. This information includes various predicates and statements used in the transaction. An algorithm to incorporate these in the log is offered. Based on this new log, a method to perform damage assessment and recovery is presented.

1. INTRODUCTION

The process of information sharing has gathered pace with the advent of high-speed networks and Internet technologies. The Internet has made every organization, government or industry, virtually connected to the entire world. This connectivity has created opportunities for intruders to access and possibly damage sensitive information. In many cases, the system cannot distinguish between a hacker and a legitimate user, and makes the malicious updates permanent in the database.

Existing intrusion detection methods cannot always successfully detect an attack immediately [12]. An attack can therefore go unnoticed for several days even months in some situations. In the mean time, valid transactions can read the damaged data and update other items, thus, spreading the damage in the database. This can have a cascading effect over time.

Therefore, during damage assessment and recovery, it is crucial to detect all affected transactions and undo their effects along with the attacking transaction's updates, then, re-execute these affected transactions.

The scope of all conventional recovery protocols, ([2], [3], [5], [8], [11]), for example, are confined only to recovery from system and hardware failures. These mechanisms depend heavily on traditional logs. Traditional logs record only the before and after images of updates, and none of the read operations. The log is also purged from the system from time to time. For recovery in a post information warfare scenario, identities of all read items are required to determine the "read-from" relationships for complete damage assessment [7]. In addition, for complete repair of the database, all affected transactions must be re-executed to reach a final consistent state, which would have been achieved if there were no attack [9]. Therefore, for re-execution purposes, all operations of all transactions need to be recorded in the log. Furthermore, the log must be available to the recovery module in its entirety - no part of it can be purged at any time.

Some researchers have proposed new models and novel recovery techniques to handle electronic attacks on databases. Among them, [1] followed a transaction dependency approach. Panda and Giordano [13] adopted a data dependency approach to recover from malicious attacks. Patnaik and Panda [14] developed a log clustering method to make the recovery process efficient. However, these models are based on the assumption that the log maintains detailed information about transaction operations, which are crucial for carrying out UNDO and REDO activities of committed transactions. On the contrary, no such log model exists as yet.

In this paper, we have presented a model to restructuring the logging protocol. This protocol facilitates storage of all information necessary for complete damage assessment and recovery of an affected database in a convenient and efficient manner. Based on this new approach, we have developed a method to identify damaged transactions and recover the database to a consistent state, which would have been there had there been no attack. The next section outlines our model. Section 3 presents the logging protocol. Damage Assessment and Recovery algorithms are provided in section 4. Section 5 offers the conclusion of the paper.

2. THE MODEL

2.1 Transaction Model

This model agrees with that presented in [4]. In our model, a transaction is visualized as a program. For each transaction, the information will include one or more conditions, statement(s) associated with each condition, and before and after images of any data item that is updated by the transaction. The model formalizes the transaction program in terms of predicates and statements. A predicate is a precondition that must be evaluated to be true for the statements associated with it to be executed.

Traditionally, a predicate is attached to or followed by a set of statements. The set can be a singleton or otherwise. The statements are, in general, semantically related in some way and are organized to achieve a goal or part of a goal in a unified fashion. The proposed model defines the cluster of one such predicate and its following statement(s) as a *Predicate Statement Block.* A Predicate Statement Block is representative of a "branch" in a multi-branch IF – ELSE IF – ELSE structure where the branch contains a predicate (the condition) and the statements that are associated with it. In any IF – ELSE IF – ELSE structure, multiple Predicate Statement Blocks can be connected to each other in an exclusive conditional fashion. Our model defines such a collection of Predicate Statement Blocks as a *Predicate Block.* A transaction can comprise of one or more Predicate Blocks. It must be noted that an IF block can have one or more nested IF blocks. The proposed model requires that such nested blocks are simplified to a basic multi-branch IF – ELSE IF – ELSE structure by the database system. The model also requires that a LOOP structure in a transaction be decomposed into a combination of IF structure (to check the loop condition) and GOTO statement (to continue looping).

A Predicate Block can be of two kinds: *conditional* or *unconditional.* In a conditional Predicate Block, each of the branches has a predicate. The boolean value of the predicate must be evaluated before the associated statements can be executed. If the value is true then the statements are executed. Otherwise, the predicate of the next branch is evaluated. However, in an unconditional Predicate Block, there is always only one Predicate Statement Block and an explicit predicate is absent. Here, the database system assumes a virtual predicate and it always evaluates to true. Due to the constant true value of the predicate, in an unconditional Predicate block, the statements are always executed, unless, the transaction is aborted before their execution. These concepts are explained in the example 1 below. This example shows a typical transaction, say, T_1 with two Predicate Blocks. Start and end of the blocks are indicated in the example. Block 1 is a conditional Predicate Block. It comprises of three Predicate Statement Blocks. Each Predicate Statement Block has its own predicate. It must be noted that the third Predicate Statement Block of Predicate Block 1 has an implicit predicate of $(x > 5)$. The model requires that it be generated by the system by complementing the other predicates of the target Predicate Block. Predicate Block 2 in the above example is an instance of an unconditional Predicate Block. There is only one Predicate Statement Block, and it does not have an explicit predicate. Here, a true predicate is assumed and therefore, the statements are always executed.

```
Example 1: T1 : /* Start of Predicate Block 1 */
    If (x < 5) then { a = a + 1; b = b + 1; }
    Else If (x = = 5) then { a = a - 1; b = b - 1; }
    Else { a = 0; b = 0; } /* Implicit predicate (x > 5) */
    /* End of Predicate Block 1 */
    /* Start of Predicate Block 2 (unconditional) */
    { p = p − 1; q = 100; r = p + q; }
    /* End of Predicate Block 2 */
```

The proposed model requires that each transaction is broken into one or more predicate blocks. Then identifiers are assigned to the corresponding predicates and statements. Here, the predicate and the statement IDs require some explanation. A transaction may have multiple Predicate Blocks. Each block can contain multiple Predicate Statement Blocks. Each of these Predicate Statement Blocks has one predicate (implicit or explicit), and one or more statements. In the rest of the paper, T_i represents the i-th transaction, $T_i.P_{j.k}$ denotes the k-th predicate in the j-th Predicate Block of transaction T_i, and $T_i.P_{j.k}.S_l$ represents l-th statement of predicate k, of j-th Predicate Block, which belongs to transaction T_i. Moreover, $T_i.P_j$ represents Predicate Block j of transaction T_i. The identification scheme is shown with the help of the following example.

```
Example 2  T2 : If ((x > 5) AND (y < 15)) then
    { u = t + u + 1; v = t + v − 1; }
    If (a < 10) Then {w = w * 25;}
    Else w = w / 25; /* implicit predicate (a >= 10) */
```

The transaction in Example 2 has two Predicate Blocks. Each of the blocks has only one Predicate Statement Block. The identifier of the transaction is T_2. The identifiers of the predicates and statements are shown in Table 1. It must be noted that the predicate ($a >= 10$) is generated by the system by complementing the predicate (a < 10). The model defines the terms "Read_Set" and "Write_Set", and provides them with special usage. The Read_Set refers to the set of data items that are read in the execution of a statement. Similarly, the Write_Set refers to the set of data items that are updated in a statement. When used with an argument, these terms can be used as functions. In Example 2, Read_Set($T_2.P_{1.1}$) represents the set $\{x, y\}$ and Read_Set($T_2.P_{1.1}.S_1$) represents the set $\{t, u\}$. The Write_Set($T_2.P_{1.1}.S_1$) refers to the set $\{u\}$. It must be noted that the Read_Set defined in this research is applicable to a predicate or a statement, and not a transaction. The Write_Set applies to only a statement. Naturally, a Read_Set can contain multiple members, while a Write_Set is always a singleton.

A Predicate Statement Block mostly consists of update type statements each of which is basically an assignment statement where zero or more number of data items are read and only one data item is written. It has the general form $x = f(I)$, i.e., the values of the data items in set I are used in calculating the new value of x. Based on the semantic content of the right side of a statement, there can be two cases:

Case I : $I = \phi$. This means that no data items were read to calculate the value of x. That is, the statement is of the form: $x = c$, where c is a numeric or string constant. We define it as a direct update. A simple example is $x = 5$.

Case II : $I \neq \phi$. This means that one or more data items were read to calculate the new value of x. The data item x may or may not belong to the Read_Set of that statement. We define it as a calculated update. An example would be $x = x + y - 10$.

Table 1. Demonstration of the Identifier Scheme

Predicate/Statement	ID
Predicate: $((x > 5)$ AND $(y < 15))$	$T_2.P_{1.1}$
Statement: $u = t + u + 1;$	$T_2.P_{1.1}.S_1$
Statement: $v = t + v - 1;$	$T_2.P_{1.1}.S_2$
Predicate: $(a < 10)$	$T_2.P_{2.1}$
Statement: $w = w * 25;$	$T_2.P_{2.1}.S_1$
Predicate: $(a >= 10)$	$T_2.P_{2.2}$
Statement: $w = w / 25;$	$T_2.P_{2.2}.S_1$

2.2 Database Model

In this research, the database system model presented in [2] is followed. The logging, damage assessment, and recovery models proposed require that the functionality of the transaction manager and recovery manager be enhanced to some degree. Our model requires that the transaction manager accepts the operations, the predicates, and the statements from transaction programs. It is also expected that in addition to delegating identifiers for transactions, the database system issues identifiers for Predicate Statement Blocks and statements as well. In the traditional database model, the transaction manager sends each operation tagged with the transaction identifier to the scheduler. The scheduler either directly sends it to the data manager for immediate execution, delays its execution by putting it on a queue, or rejects it. The recovery manager accepts an operation from the scheduler and records it in the log. The proposed model requires that the predicates and statements, along with their identifiers be sent from the transaction manager, through the scheduler, to the recovery manager.

2.3 Assumptions

Our model uses a log sequence number (LSN) for each log record and follows the write-ahead-logging protocol as described in [10]. The model also assumes that the system follows the STEAL/NO FORCE protocol [6]. As a result, it keeps both Undo and Redo type log records. It also requires that the checkpoint activities are performed periodically and are recorded in the log. We assume the use of cache consistent checkpointing [2] for our proposed model as this does not impose delay on transaction execution and it reduces and simplifies restart activities better than any of the other checkpoint methods. Some other basic assumptions made regarding the operations of the database system are: (1) the scheduler produces rigourous serializable history [3], (2) the log is not modifiable by users, (3) no part of the log can be purged at any time, (4) nested transactions are not allowed, and (5) a transaction writes a data item to the stable database only once. The next section presents the proposed logging protocol.

3. THE LOGGING PROTOCOL

An integral part of our logging method is the different kinds of information that need to be recorded in the log. The proposed protocol requires the recording of the following entries:

1. [Start_Transaction, T_i]: Denotes that transaction T_i started execution.
2. [Record_Predicate $T_i.P_{j.k}$, *Predicate_String*] : Predicate k of Predicate Block j of transaction T_i is being recorded. *Predicate_String* represents the actual predicate.
3. [Record_Statement, $T_i.P_{j.k}.S_l$, *Statement_String*] : Statement l of predicate $j.k$ belonging to transaction T_i is being recorded. *Statement_String* represents the actual statement.
4. [Read_Item, T_i, x] : Records that T_i read the value of database item x.
5. [Write_Item, $T_i.P_{j.k}.S_l$, x, *old_value*, *new_value*] : Records that transaction T_i has updated the value of the data item x of Statement $T_i.P_{j.k}.S_l$. Both before image (*old_value*) and after image (*new_value*) of the data item are recorded.
6. [Undo, $T_i.P_{j.k}.S_l$, x, *undo_value*] : Transaction T_i has aborted (due to transaction failure or system crash) and the data item x of statement $T_i.P_{j.k}.S_l$ was flushed to the stable database. The data item must be reset to the *old_value* of the write operation log record it is attempting to undo. The *undo_value* represents the *old_value*.
7. [Redo, $T_i.P_{j.k}.S_l$, x, *redo_value*] : The system has crashed after Transaction T_i has committed, but the data item x of statement $T_i.P_{j.k}.S_l$

was not flushed to the stable database. The data item must be changed to the *new_value* of the write operation log record it is attempting to redo. The *redo_value* represents the *new_value*.

8. [Flush, x, LastUpdatePtr] : Records that the cache slot containing data item x is flushed to the stable database. The LastUpdatePtr represents the LSN of the log record that last updated x. It is the only log record that the cache manager communicates to the recovery manager.
9. [Commit, T_i] : Records that T_i has completed successfully, and affirms that its effect can be committed (recorded permanently) to the database.
10. [Abort, T_i] : Records that transaction T_i has been aborted.

It must be noted that the Undo and Redo log entries in this protocol do not hold the traditional connotation of log entries of "update" activity of data items described in [6]. Instead, the Undo and Redo log entries in this protocol refer to actual undo and redo operations that follow a transaction failure or a restart after a system failure. The main goal of the logging protocol is to record all scheduled operations in the log. Obviously, the different operations include start of a transaction, read and write operations on data items, undo and redo operations on updates, flushing of pages to the stable database, commit, and abort operations of transactions. The recovery manager, which is responsible for maintaining the logging protocol must methodically identify each operation and write a log entry for it. If the activity is a start, flush, redo, undo, commit or abort operation of a transaction, then the recovery manager will write Start_Transaction, Flush, Redo, Undo, Commit, or Abort type log record respectively. In addition, one of the principal parts of the logging mechanism is to record a Predicate Block in terms of its predicates and statements. This is performed at the arrival of the first read or write operation of a Predicate Block. A Predicate Block can be recorded in only three specific cases. All these three cases represent the first operation from that Predicate Block.

Case 1: The current operation is a "read" and the data item belongs to a predicate.

Case 2: The current operation is a "read" and the data item belongs to a statement. The Predicate Block is unconditional.

Case 3: The current operation is a "write". The operation represents a direct update from an unconditional Predicate Block.

Whenever a read or write operation is scheduled it must be checked whether the Predicate Block has already been recorded. If not, it is recorded in the log in terms of its predicates and statements. The read or write record is written after that. Next, we present the logging algorithm based on the above-proposed protocol.

3.1 Logging Algorithm

1. If (Operation = = Start transaction T_i) then
   1.1 Write the record [Start_Transaction, T_i] in the log
2. Else If (Operation = = Read the data item x of transaction T_i) then
   2.1 If ($x \in$ Read_Set(Predicate $T_i.P_{j.k}$)) then
   2.1.1 If the Predicate Block j has not yet been recorded then
   2.1.1.1 Repeat until all Predicate Statement Blocks of Predicate Block $T_i.P_j$ have been processed
   2.1.1.1.1 Write the record [Record_Predicate, $T_i.P_{j.k}$, *Predicate_String*] in the log
   2.1.1.1.2 Record each statement associated with predicate $T_i.P_{j.k}$ in the form [Record_Statement, $T_i.P_{j.k}.S_l$, *Statement_String*]
   2.2 If ($x \in$ Read_Set (Statement $T_i.P_{j.k}.S_l$)) then
   2.2.1 If the Predicate Block j has not yet been recorded then
   2.2.1.1 Record each statement associated with Predicate Block j in the form [Record_Statement, $T_i.P_{j.k}.S_l$, *Statement_String*]
   2.3 Write the record [Read_Item, T_i, x]
3. Else If (Operation = = Write the data item x of statement $T_i.P_{j.k}.S_l$) then
   3.1 Perform Step 2.2.1
   3.2 Write the record [Write_Item, $T_i.P_{j.k}.S_l$, x, *old_value*, *new_value*]
4. Else If (Operation = = Undo the update of data item x of statement $T_i.P_{j.k}.S_l$) then
   4.1 Write the record [Undo, $T_i.P_{j.k}.S_l$, x, *undo_value*]
5. Else If (Operation = = Redo the update of data item x of statement $T_i.P_{j.k}.S_l$) then
   5.1 Write the record [Redo, $T_i.P_{j.k}.S_l$, x, *redo_value*]
6. Else If (Operation = = Flush the cache slot containing data item x) then
   6.1 From x's cache slot, obtain the LSN of the log record that last updated data item x
   6.2 Write the record [Flush, x, LastUpdatePtr]
7. Else If (Operation = = Commit the transaction T_i) then
   7.1 Write the record [Commit, T_i]
8. Else If (Operation = = Abort the transaction T_i) then
   8.1 Write the record [Abort, T_i]

4. DAMAGE ASSESSMENT AND RECOVERY

In this section, we propose a method to perform damage assessment and recovery using the new log model. This method scans the log from the point of attack until the end. To provide this direct access an index on each transaction's start operation could be maintained. While scanning, the mechanism determines the spread of damage and re-executes parts of transactions to repair the database.

4.1 Damage Assessment and Recovery Procedure

When a new affected data item is found, it is added to the list of affected items. However, if the Read_Set of a statement does not contain any bad data, an affected data item is changed to an undamaged item. From that point in the history, the particular data item becomes "fixed". Therefore, it is removed from the list of affected items. Thus the list can "shrink" with the on-going process of recovery. The unit of processing is one log record at a time, and the unit of recovery is one Predicate Block at a time. It checks up on one Predicate Block, determines whether it has accessed any damaged data items, and re-executes that block or part of that block to fix the affected data items. Malicious transactions are never re-executed. While re-executing affected Predicate Blocks, all parts of it may not be executed. There may be one or more statements that did not read or write any damaged data. These statements are not re-executed. When a Predicate Block or part of it is re-executed, some damaged data items are recalculated to new correct values, and they are updated in the damaged item list. When the recovery process is continuing, the data items are not corrected in the stable database. If the database were updated every time an affected item received a new correct value, it would involve a large number of disk access operations. Instead of doing that, the data items and their correct values are simply kept in the list and flushed to the hard disk at the end of the recovery process.

The recovery mechanism declares a Predicate Block affected if it has accessed any damaged data. As mentioned earlier, these affected Predicate Blocks are re-executed for recovery purposes. Based on the source of the bad data, there can be two scenarios.

Scenario 1: The affected data item (one or more) comes *only* from the statement(s) of the Predicate Block. Since only the statement data items are found damaged, it means that the data items in the predicates that were evaluated for the execution of the corresponding statements are all unaffected. Here, the recovery process is relatively simple. Since the data items in the predicates are all "good", there is no need to re-evaluate the predicates. During repair, the same set of statements that executed previously, need to be re-executed. Furthermore, there is no need to undo the data items corresponding to the statements, since the same data items would be updated during re-execution. Based on the semantic content of a statement, there can be two cases. First, the Read_Set of the statement contains one or more damaged data items. Here, first it is checked whether the data item is already in the affected item list. If it is in there, its value is updated to the newly calculated value. If the data item is not in the list, then it is added to the list with the new value. Secondly, the Read_Set of the statement does not contain any damaged data item. It means that either the statement represents a direct update, or the read data items are all unaffected. Therefore, with the execution of this statement, the affected data item became unaffected. In this case, the statement is not re-executed, and the data item is simply removed from the affected item list, if it is already there.

Scenario 2: The affected data item(s) comes from the predicates or from both statements and predicates of the affected Predicate Block. Since the predicate data item (could be more than one) is affected, during recovery, a completely different Predicate Statement Block may get executed. Therefore, theoretically, the data items that were updated in the first run of this Predicate Block need to be undone. But for all practical purposes, this is not needed at all. The affected item list keeps track of all affected items and their current, correct values. Therefore, during recovery of such a Predicate Block, the values are not updated in the affected item list, since the list already contains good values. If an updated data item is not in the affected item list, it needs to be added in with the before image of the update. For recovery, the Predicate Block is re-executed. Any data item that gets updated by this is first checked if it is in the affected item list. If it is there, its value is updated with the newly calculated value. Otherwise, the data item is added to the list with the newly calculated value.

In both *Scenarios 1* and *2*, for recovery purposes, the current correct value of some of the data items may be required. If the data item is in the affected item list, then its current correct value can be easily obtained from there. But if the data item is not in the list, it means that the item was unaffected at that particular point in history. Its value cannot be obtained from the database because a latter transaction may have updated it. So using the database value would be incorrect. To get its value for that point of time, the log must be searched in the forward direction to find the next update of that data item. The before image (*old_value*) of that update record will reflect the correct value. If such an update is not found, then the stable database is accessed.

4.2 Implementation

The following damage assessment and recovery algorithm uses several data structures to accomplish its tasks. The first such structure is *Malicious Transaction List* (*Malicious_TL*). This list contains the transaction identifiers of all malicious transactions, in the order they committed. The second structure *Affected Item List* (*Affected_IL*) is basically a collection of data item records that were damaged or affected directly or transitively by the attacking transaction(s). It has two fields, Data_Item and Fresh_Value. The Data_Item field represents the identifier of the data item (e.g., x) and the Fresh_Value field contains the correct value of the data item. The value of the Fresh_Value field for a data item can change as repair continues. The last structure *Affected_Predicate_Block_*T_i (*Affected_PBT*$_i$), contains the identifiers of Predicate Blocks of transaction T_i that have been affected directly or transitively by a malicious transaction. Each entry of this list has two fields, ID and Source. The ID field contains the Identifier of the Predicate Block. The Source field value can be "P", or "S", or "PS" depending on whether a damaged data item is found in the predicate block, or the statement, or both predicate block and statement respectively. The developed algorithm is presented below.

4.3 Damage Assessment and Recovery Algorithm

1. Create *Affected_IL* and initialize it to null, i.e., *Affected_IL* = { }
2. Get the first entry of the *Malicious_TL*, say T_{Mi}
3. Find the log record [Start_Transaction, T_{Mi}] in the log
4. Scan the log until the end. For every committed transaction,

   4.1 If ((Log Record = = [Start_Transaction, T_i]) AND ($T_i \notin$ *Malicious_TL*)) then

   4.1.1 Create *Affected_PBT*$_i$ list and initialize it to null

   4.2 If (Log Record = = [Read_Item, $T_i.P_{j.k}$, x]) then

   4.2.1 If (($T_i \notin$ *Malicious_TL*) AND ($x \in$ *Affected_IL.Data_Item*)) then

   4.2.1.1 If ($T_i.P_j \notin$ *Affected_PBT*$_i$*.ID*) then

   Set *Affected_PBT*$_i$ = *Affected_PBT*$_i$ $\cup$ [$T_i.P_j$, P]

   4.3 Else If (Log Record = = [Read_Item, $T_i.P_{j.k}.S_l$, x]) then

   4.3.1 If (($T_i \notin$ *Malicious_TL*) AND ($x \in$ *Affected_IL.Data_Item*)) then

   4.3.1.1 If ($T_i.P_j \in$ *Affected_PBT*$_i$*.ID*) then

   4.3.1.1.1 If the corresponding item is [$T_i.P_j$, P] then

   Substitute it with [$T_i.P_j$, PS]

   4.3.1.2 If ($T_i.P_j \notin$ *Affected_PBT*$_i$*.ID*) then

   Set *Affected_PBT*$_i$ = *Affected_PBT*$_i$ $\cup$ [$T_i.P_j$, S]

   4.4 Else If (Log Record = = [Write_Item, $T_i.P_{j.k}.S_l$, x, *old_value*, *new_value*]) then

   4.4.1 If ($T_i \in$ *Malicious_TL*) then

   4.4.1.1 If ($x \notin$ *Affected_IL.Data_Item*) then

   Set *Affected_IL* = *Affected_IL* $\cup$ [x, *old_value*]

   4.4.2 If (($T_i \notin$ *Malicious_TL*) AND ($T_i.P_j \notin$ *Affected_PBT*$_i$*.ID*)) then

   4.4.2.1 If ($x \in$ *Affected_IL.Data_Item*) then

   Remove the entry for x from the *Affected_IL*,

4.4.2.2 Else Do nothing
4.4.3 If (($T_i \notin$ *Malicious_TL*) AND ($T_i.P_j \in$ *Affected_PBT$_i$.ID*)) then
4.4.3.1 If the Source field of the entry for $T_i.P_j$ in the *Affected_PBT$_i$* list contains only "S" then
Call Procedure Check_ReExecute($T_i.P_{j.k}.S_l$)
4.4.3.2 Else // Source field of $T_i.P_j$ contains "P" or "PS"
4.4.3.2.1 If ($x \notin$ *Affected_IL.Data_Item*) then
Add an item to the *Affected_IL*
4.4.3.2.2 If the currently scanned update log record is the last update by the Predicate Statement Block k, then
Call Procedure ReExecute_PB($T_i.P_j$)
4.5 Else If (Log Record = = [Commit, T_i]) then
4.5.1 If there exists any *Affected_PBT$_i$* list
4.5.1.1 Delete *Affected_PBT$_i$* list

5. For each data item in the *Affected_IL*,
   5.1 Bring the data item into the cache from the stable database
   5.2 Update its value to the Fresh_Value of the entry
6. Start and end a checkpoint to flush the updated data items to the stable database
7. Delete *Affected_IL*

Procedure Read_Item (Data_Item : *p*)
{ 1. If ($p \in$ *Affected_IL.Data_Item*) then
1.1 Read its current correct value from the Fresh_Value field of the corresponding entry
2. Else // ($p \notin$ *Affected_IL.Data_Item*)
2.1 Scan forward to find the next update record that modified data item p and obtain the *old_value* from the log record.
2.2 If forward scan is unsuccessful, retrieve the value directly from the database }

Procedure Update_AIL (Data_Item : *q*; Data_Value : *new_value*)
{ 1. If ($q \in$ *Affected_IL.Data_Item*) then
1.1 Substitute the Fresh_Value field of the entry in *Affected_IL* with the newly calculated value (*new_value*)
2. Else // ($q \notin$ *Affected_Item_List.Data_Item*)
2.1 Add a new entry for q in the *Affected_IL* with the newly calculated value }

Procedure Check_ReExecute (Statement Identifier : $T_i.P_{j.k}.S_l$)
{1. Use $T_i.P_{j.k}.S_l$ as a pointer to locate the "Record_Statement" log record for S_l of Predicate Statement Block k of Predicate Block j
2. Read the log record into a buffer

3. If ((Read_Set(S_l) $\cap$ *Affected_IL.Data_Item*) == $\emptyset$) then
   3.1 For the data item q that is updated by S_l
   3.1.1 If ($q \in$ *Affected_IL.Data_Item*) then
   3.1.1.1 Remove the entry q from the *Affected_IL*
4. Else // Read_Set(S_l) contains one or more affected data items
   Re-Execute S_l
   4.1 For every data item P that needs to be read for re-execution,
   4.1.1 Call Procedure Read_Item (p)
   4.2 For the data item Q that gets updated upon re-execution of S_l
   4.2.1 Call Procedure Update_AIL(q, *new_value*), where *new_value* represents the newly calculated value of q }

Procedure ReExecute_PB (Predicate Block Identifier : $T_i.P_j$)

{1. Use $T_i.P_j$ as a pointer and locate the beginning of Predicate Block j in the log.
2. From the log reconstruct the entire string for Predicate Block j in a buffer
3. Re-execute the Predicate Block j
   3.1 For every data item P that needs to be read for re-execution
   3.1.1 Call Procedure Read_Item (p)
   3.2 For every data item q that gets updated due to re-execution,
   3.2.1 Call Procedure Update_AIL(q, *new_value*), where *new_value* represents the newly calculated value of q }

5. CONCLUSION

In case a malicious transaction damages a database and the attack is detected, it is necessary to carry out prompt recovery. All damage assessment and recovery algorithms developed so far require more semantic information about transaction operations than what is available in the log. In this research, a new logging protocol is proposed which records all appropriate information regarding transactions. This information includes various predicates and statements whether they have been executed or not. This helps in accurate damage assessment and fast recovery. We have discussed, in detail, requirements of damage assessment and recovery process and have presented a suitable algorithm. The algorithm performs damage assessment and recovery concurrently. A procedure for recovery from system failures is also described.

ACKNOWLEDGMENT

We are thankful to Dr. Robert L. Herklotz and Capt. Alex Kilpatrick for their support, which made this work possible. This work was partially funded by AFOSR grant F49620-99-1-0235.

REFERENCES

[1] P. Amman, S. Jajodia, C. D. McCollum, and B. Blaustein, Surviving Information Warfare Attacks on Databases, Proceedings of the 1997 IEEE Symposium on Security and Privacy, May 1997.

[2] P. A. Bernstein, V. Hadzilacos, and N. Goodman, Concurrency Control and Recovery in Database Systems, Addison-Wesley, Reading, MA, 1987.

[3] R. Elmasri, and S. B. Navathe, Fundamentals of Database Systems, Third Edition, Addison-Wesley, Menlo Park, CA, 2000.

[4] K. P. Eswaran, J. N. Gray, R. A. Lorie, and I. L. Traiger, The Notions of Consistency and Predicate Locks in a Database System, CACM, 19(11), November 1976.

[5] J. Gray and A. Reuter, Transaction Processing : Concepts and Techniques, Morgan Kauffmann, San Mateo, CA, 1993.

[6] T. Haerder and A. Reuter, Principles of Transaction-Oriented Database Recovery, Computing Surveys, 15(4), December 1983.

[7] S. Jajodia, C. D. McCollum, and P. Amman, Trusted Recovery, Communications of the ACM, 42(7), pp. 71-75, July 1999.

[8] H. F. Korth and A. Silberschatz, Database System Concepts, Second Edition, McGraw-Hill, New York City, NY, 1991.

[9] P. Liu, P. Ammann, and S. Jajodia, Rewriting Histories: Recovering from Malicious Transactions, Distributed and Parallel Databases, 8(1), pp. 7-40, January 2000.

[10] C. Mohan et. al, ARIES: A Transaction Recovery Method Supporting Fine-granularity Locking and Partial Rollbacks Using Write-Ahead Logging, ACM Transactions on Database Systems, 17(1), March 1982.

[11] M. T. Ozsu and P. Valduriez, Principles of Distributed Database Systems, Second Edition, Prentice-Hall, Upper Saddle River, NJ, 1999.

[12] B. Panda and J. Giordano, Defensive Information Warfare, CACM, July 1999.

[13] B. Panda and J. Giordano, Reconstructing the Database After Electronic Attacks, Database Security XII: Status and Prospects, S. Jajodia (editor), Kluwer Academic Publishers, 1999.

[14] S. Patnaik and B. Panda, Dependency Based Logging for Database Survivability from Hostile Transactions, Proceedings of the 12th International Conference on Computer Applications in Industry and Engineering, November 1999.

RANDOMLY ROVING AGENTS FOR INTRUSION DETECTION

Ira S. Moskowitz
Information Technology Division, Mail Code 5540
Center for High Assurance Computer Systems
Naval Research Laboratory, Washington, D.C. 20375
moskowitz@itd.nrl.navy.mil

Myong H. Kang
Mitretek Systems, 7525 Colshire Dr., McLean, VA 22102

LiWu Chang
Information Technology Division, Mail Code 5540
Center for High Assurance Computer Systems
Naval Research Laboratory, Washington, D.C. 20375

Garth E. Longdon
ITT Industries, Mail Code 5540
Center for High Assurance Computer Systems
Naval Research Laboratory, Washington, D.C. 20375

Abstract Agent based intrusion detection systems (IDS) have advantages such as scalability, reconfigurability, and survivability. In this paper, we introduce a mobile-agent based IDS, called ABIDE (Agent Based Intrusion Detection Environment). ABIDE is comprised of various types of agents, all of which are mobile, lightweight, and specialized. The most common form of agent is the DMA (Data Mining Agent), which randomly moves around the network and collects information. The DMA then relays the information it has gathered to a DFA (Data Fusion Agent) which assesses the likelihood of intrusion. As we show in this paper, there is a quantifiable relationship between the number of DMA and the probability of detecting an intrusion. We study this relationship and its implications.

1. INTRODUCTION

An intrusion to a computer system may be indicated by abnormal network traffic, anomalous user activity, or application misbehavior. Intrusion detection systems (IDS)* which focus on detecting abnormal network activity are called *network-based* IDS, whereas intrusion detection systems that focus on detecting abnormal host activity are called *host-based* IDS. In addition, some "hybrid" IDS have sensors which collect both host and network data.

Traditional IDS which use a monolithic architecture (i.e., a centralized architecture of data collection and analysis) have a variety of problems. These problems include introducing a single point of failure (which is bad for survivability), lack of scalability, and in addition traditional IDS may be difficult to reconfigure. To overcome these shortcomings, agent based IDS which are distributed, scalable, and re-configurable have become popular [1],[2]. To take advantage of this agent based IDS idea, the US Naval Research Laboratory is designing a host-based intrusion detection system called *ABIDE (agent based intrusion detection environment)*,†. that uses mobile agent technology. ABIDE differs from other agent-based IDS, which usually introduce some level of coordinated communications among IDS components, in the following way:

> To avoid a targeted attack to disable the IDS, all agents randomly move around monitoring hosts. There is no fixed infrastructure, except that each host needs to be monitored, and has an agent-platform that can host agents when they decide to move in. There is neither a central site for analysis, nor a scheduler for agents in ABIDE. Also, to make the agent lightweight (i.e., using a small amount of code, which reduces network overhead associated with agent movement), tasks are split among different kinds of agents that perform different functions.

In ABIDE, there are four different kinds of agents. These agents have an implied hierarchy for the purpose of data and command flow.

1 A data mining agent (DMA) roams around (i.e., randomly chooses hosts and moves to the hosts) and acquires environmental information. It is small, lightweight, and specialized. For example, a DMA may be tasked to verify a checksum on an import system binary such as the Unix PS binary. If the agent finds suspicious data, it will acquire it for further analysis.

2 A data fusion agent (DFA) roams around and randomly interacts with the various DMA. It receives the DMA data payload and builds a larger picture of events from this data. As the DFA collects data, it can apply classic IDS techniques to determine whether an intrusion is taking place. Of course, when the DMA and DFA meet up is a function of time and the size of the network.

*A detailed version of this paper is available as NRL CHACS Tech. Report TM/002/003. Abbreviations can be taken as either singular or plural depending upon the context.

†The ABIDE idea grew out of the work of Michael Reed while he was at NRL [3, 4]

3 A probe agent (PA) is dispatched by a DFA to perform a test to confirm intrusion.

4 Once the DFA has decided that a system has been compromised, a corrective agent (CA) can be dispatched to take actions. The CA is the only agent empowered to change system state on the host systems.

In this paper, we focus on the first two types of agents about which ABIDE is concerned. We study the probabilistic behavior of the DMA reporting to a DFA. Specifically, we are concerned with two questions:

- Q1 — Given a network of a fixed number of hosts and a fixed number of DMA, what is the probability of detecting an intrusion?
- Q2 — Given a network of a fixed number of hosts, if we want to detect an intrusion with a certain confidence, how many DMA have to be deployed?

2. SPECIAL CASE

In this section, we consider the situation of K DMA randomly visiting nodes of a network to discover various pieces of information and report this information back to one DFA. Each individual piece of information that a DMA obtains may not be in itself, enough to alert the DFA to an intrusion; however an aggregate of the individual pieces of information collected by the DMA may alert the DFA to an intrusion. It is this threshold criteria with which we are concerned. Once this threshold is reached, the DFA deploys a PA. Our analysis stops at the decision to deploy a PA. We refer to each host which a DMA visits as a node $\mu_i, i = 1, \ldots, M$. We assume that, as each DMA randomly travels from node to node, it picks up a unique atom of information α_i at each node μ_i. In our special case, a DMA never visits the same node twice. (In reality, a DMA may visit the same node more than once, due to the randomness of its travels, but it must visit a given fixed number of unique nodes during its sojourn. We examine the simple case, which is equivalent.) For simplicity, we assume that, at a specific time, the DMA transfers its atoms to the DFA. (In reality both the DMA and the DFA randomly travel the network. When a DMA meets up with a DFA, it then transfers its atoms to the DFA.) For simplicity, we assume that there is only one DFA. If the DFA has sufficient atoms, it declares that the intrusion threshold Θ has been reached and therefore it deploys a PA.

This is similar to the threshold schemes discussed in [5], in that below the threshold level of Θ, one can assume no knowledge, but at or above Θ, the game is up. In this paper we do not discuss how Θ is determined, nor do we discuss the case where, below Θ, the DFA has no knowledge of an intrusion. In addition, we have made further simplifying assumptions and will discuss the general situation in future work. What is salient about our work in this paper is that even with the assumptions made for simplification, the mathematics are quite difficult to derive and computationally quite expensive to perform. We are presently investigating approximations to the formulas presented in this paper to speed up the computation and to develop "rules of thumb."

2.1. Formalism

We will now formally present our problem.

- The network is made up of M nodes μ_i , $i = 1, \ldots, M$.
- There are K DMA A_k, $k = 1, \ldots, K$.
- Each A_k visits n and only n nodes, and each node is distinct. A_k obtains a unique atom from each node. Every DMA that visits the same node μ_i receives the same atom α_i.
- After A_k has visited n nodes, it gives the n (unique) atoms α_{k_i}, $i = 1, \ldots, n$ to (the single) DFA.

Note that even though A_k has n unique atoms, $A_{k'}$ might have some of the same atoms as A_k. Therefore, when all of the A_k have reported to the DFA, we can then view the DFA as a bag of atoms, i.e., an atom might be in DFA more than once. We are only interested in the unique number of atoms in the DFA. Note that since visiting the node μ_i is equivalent to obtaining the atom α_i, so we will sometimes blur the distinction.

Let $P_K(M, n : T)$ be the probability that the DFA contains exactly T unique atoms, given that K agents have searched through M nodes, picking n (distinct) nodes per agent. Keep in mind the actual probabilistic term of interest, when a threshold Θ is given, is the more complicated $\sum_{T \geq \Theta} P_K(M, n : T)$. This allows us to answer Q1 in this special case.

Calculating the probabilistic terms $P_K(M, n : T)$ quickly becomes quite complicated. Therefore we present a closed form solution. Each agent is considered a draw. Without any restrictions there are $\binom{M}{n}$ ways for a DMA to pick n nodes out of the total of M nodes. Let us start with $K = 2$. The total number of draws, *without restriction*, are $\binom{M}{n}^2$, which is the number of elements in the sample space. Now let us consider the event under question — this is where the combined number of distinct nodes picked by both agents is T. A_1 has no restriction so there are $\binom{M}{n}$ ways for A_1 to pick n nodes. Now A_2 has to pick nodes so that there are exactly T distinct nodes between the two nodes. Since A_1 has chosen n distinct nodes $M - n$ nodes are left unchosen. Thus, A_2 must pick $T - n$ nodes from the $M - n$. A_2 still has $n - (T - n) = 2n - T$ nodes to pick from the n that A_1 has chosen. Therefore there are $\binom{M-n}{T-n}\binom{n}{2n-T}$ ways for A_2 to choose. Combining this with the $\binom{M}{n}$ ways for A_1 to pick, we see that $P_2(M,n:T) = \frac{\binom{M}{n}\binom{M-n}{T-n}\binom{n}{2n-T}}{\binom{M}{n}^2} = \frac{\binom{M-n}{T-n}\binom{n}{2n-T}}{\binom{M}{n}}$. Of course for things to make sense we must have that $n \le T \le \min(M, 2n)$. Therefore we have that

$$P_2(M,n:T) = \begin{cases} \binom{M}{n}^{-1}\binom{M-n}{T-n}\binom{n}{2n-T} & n \le T \le \min(M,2n)\,, \\ 0 & \text{otherwise.} \end{cases}$$

To simplify terminology we use the extended definition of the binomial coefficient $\binom{a}{b}$ as:

$$\binom{a}{b} = \begin{cases} \frac{a!}{(a-b)!b!} & a \ge b \ge 0,\ a \text{ and } b \text{ are integers} \\ 0 & \text{otherwise.} \end{cases}$$

So we see that

$$P_2(M,n:T) = \binom{M}{n}^{-1}\binom{M-n}{T-n}\binom{n}{2n-T} \tag{1}$$

Similarly $P_3(M,n:T) =$

$$\binom{M}{n}^{-2}\sum_{n_2=0}^{n}\left\{\binom{n}{n_2}\binom{M-n}{n-n_2}\binom{2n-n_2}{3n-T-n_2}\binom{M-2n+n_2}{T-2n+n_2}\right\}. \tag{2}$$

Of course this will only result in non-zero values for $n \le T \le \min(M, 3n)$.

Similarly for 4 agents we can derive the following formula for $P_4(M,n:T)$.

$$P_4(M,n:T) =$$
$$\binom{M}{n}^{-3}\sum_{n_2,n_3=0}^{n}\left\{\binom{n}{n_2}\binom{M-n}{n-n_2}\binom{2n-n_2}{n_3}\binom{M-2n+n_2}{n-n_3}\right.$$
$$\left.\cdot\binom{3n-n_2-n_3}{4n-T-n_2-n_3}\binom{M-3n+n_2+n_3}{T-3n+n_2+n_3}\right\}.$$

In general, for K picks of n distinct things from a total out of M the probability of picking T unique items is:

$$P_K(M,n:T) =$$

$$\binom{M}{n}^{-(K-1)}\sum_{n_2,\ldots,n_{K-1}=0}^{n}\left\{\binom{n}{n_2}\binom{M-n}{n-n_2}\binom{2n-n_2}{n_3}\binom{M-2n+n_2}{n-n_3}\cdots\right.$$

$$\cdot\binom{(K-2)n-n_2-\ldots-n_{K-2}}{n_{K-1}}\binom{M-(K-2)n+n_2+\ldots+n_{K-2}}{n-n_{K-1}}$$

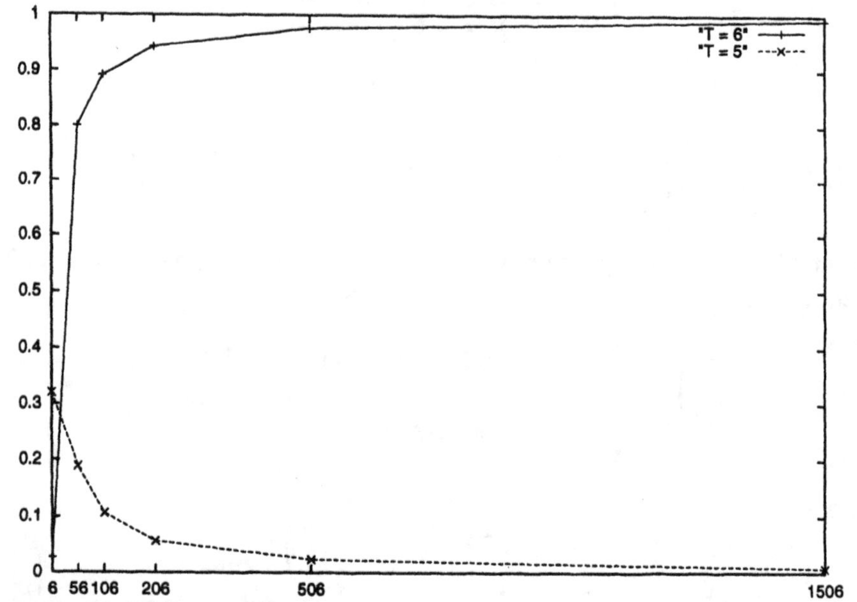

Figure 1: Limiting behavior, as M grows, of $P_3(M, 2:5)$ and $P_3(M, 2:6)$

$$\cdot \binom{(K-1)n - n_2 - \ldots - n_{K-1}}{Kn - T - n_2 - \ldots - n_{K-1}} \binom{M - (K-1)n + n_2 + \ldots + n_{K-1}}{T - (K-1)n + n_2 + \ldots + n_{K-1}} \Bigg\},$$

$$K \geq 4. \tag{3}$$

Thus Eqs. (1), (2), and (3) give us $P_K(M, n : T)$ for all $K > 1$. As discussed before, concentrating solely upon the probability $P_K(M, n : T)$ is not sufficient. $P_K(M, n : T)$ is the probability of getting exactly T unique atoms of information. If the information that the agents are attempting to retrieve is revealed when $T = C$, then the correct probabilistic term of interest (as previously discussed with respect to the threshold) is defined as:

$$P_K(M, n : C^+) \stackrel{\text{def}}{=} \sum_{T \geq C} P_K(M, n : T) \,.$$

This is the probability of K DMA obtaining at least C unique atoms.

Let us consider $P_K(M, n : T)$ and its limiting behavior for some small values of M, n, and K. The only non-zero probabilities are $P_K(M, n : T)$, for $n \leq T \leq \min(M, K \cdot n)$. Now let us consider how $P_K(M, n : T)$ behaves as $M \to \infty$. This is the situation when the agents are searching over a large network.

Let M be very large with respect to Kn. The larger M is the smaller the chance of intersection between nodes picked by different agents. In Figure 1 we see a plot of the probability $P_3(M, 2 : 6)$ (approaches 1) and $P_3(M, 2 : 5)$

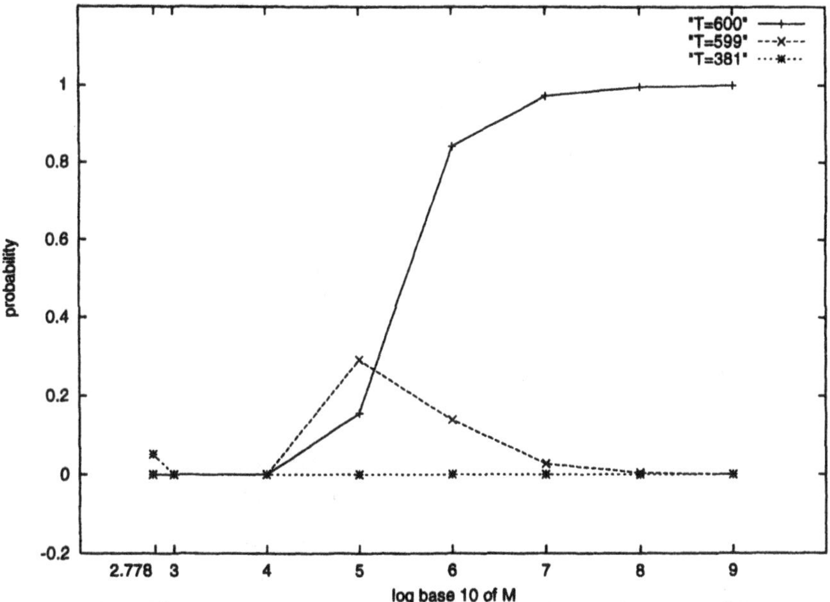

Figure 2: Simulated 1000 times limiting behavior, as M grows, of $P_{30}(M, 20 : 381)$, $P_{30}(M, 20 : 599)$ and $P_{30}(M, 20 : 600)$

(approaches 0) against M. Of course Figure 1 is only dealing with a very few picks of a small number of nodes. The total number of nodes M must be several orders of magnitude larger that Kn before the limiting behavior becomes apparent. We will return to limiting behavior in the next subsection.

2.2. Some Simulation Results

In this subsection we study the behavior of $P_{30}(M, 20 : T)$. Simulations are used since the time to run the closed form solution is on the order of n^K, and thus closed form calculations are only feasible for very small values of the various terms. Simulations of 1000 were sufficient for Figure 2 (in later plots we use much larger simulations). Of course one should keep in mind that theoretically $P_K(M, n : T)$ is never 0, for $M \leq T \leq Kn$, and that $P_K(M, n : T)$ is never 1, for $M \leq T \leq Kn$. The simulations might have a value of 0 or 1, but this is because in reality the probability is either extremely small, or large, respectively. Thus we will often say that a probability is "essentially" 0 or "essentially" 1.

In Figure 2 we see what happens when $K = 30$ and $n = 20$. Figure 2 shows the plots of $P_{30}(M, 20 : 381)$, $P_{30}(M, 20 : 599)$, and $P_{30}(M, 20 : 600)$ for $M = 600, 1000, 10000, 10^5, 10^6, 10^7, 10^8, 10^9$. For the $P_{30}(M, 20 : T)$ case, M must be at 10^9 before we start seriously approaching the limiting probabilities.

We see that the distribution of the T values indexed by M, $\mathbf{T}_M(T)$ (index over M and let T run through its values in $P_K(M, n : T)$ with K, n fixed.) behaves like $I_{Kn}(T)$, which is the distribution that has probability 1 when $T = Kn$ and is zero elsewhere, as M grows. To be precise:

Given $\epsilon > 0$ and for any value of T, there exists a Ψ such that
$|\mathbf{T}_M(T) - I_{Kn}(T)| < \epsilon$, for all $M > \Psi$.

We need not discuss the various types of probabilistic convergence for our needs. It suffices that $\mathbf{T}_M(T)$ behave like $I_{Kn}(T)$ for large m. We can also heuristically state this as

$$P_K(\infty, n : T) = \begin{cases} 1 & T = Kn \\ 0 & \text{otherwise} \end{cases} \tag{4}$$

The limiting behavior of $P_K(M, n : T)$ determines the limiting behavior of $P_K(M, n : C^+)$ which we may also state this heuristically as

$$P_K(\infty, n : C^+) = \begin{cases} 1 & C \leq Kn \\ 0 & \text{otherwise} \end{cases} \tag{5}$$

Let us continue to use $P_{30}(M, 20 : T)$ as an example. Above we have shown that for M large the only value of T of interest is the limiting value of $600 = 30 \cdot 20$. This agrees with our intuition. If the "universe" of the network is essentially infinite, then the different DMA do not have to be concerned with visiting the same nodes — probabilistically, it will not happen. Therefore, $T = Kn$ is the only non-zero probability, and it is of course 1. Now let us look at M values near the minimum limiting value of $M = 20$. The smallest M can be, and for the problem to still make sense, is that M is bounded from below by n. Of course, when $M = n$ the probability collapses to

$$P_K(n, n : T) = \begin{cases} 1 & T = n \\ 0 & \text{otherwise} \end{cases}$$

$M = n$ is the smallest that M can be. What happens when M is small, but not at its minimum value of n. Here we have 30 DMA, and each DMA randomly travels through a network of M nodes, and each DMA selects 20 distinct nodes from the network, and then transfers the atoms of information to the DFA.

We wish to investigate how $P_K(M, n : T)$ behaves as $M \to n^+$. Figure 3 shows the results of simulations, run 100000 times each, of $P_{30}(M, 20 : T)$ for $M = 20, 21, \ldots, 45$. We see that, for small M, we have

For M"near and greater than" n,

$$P_K(M, n : T) = \begin{cases} \text{essentially } 1 & T = M \\ \text{essentially } 0 & \text{otherwise} \end{cases}$$

This is because the universe is so small when M is small that, with probability

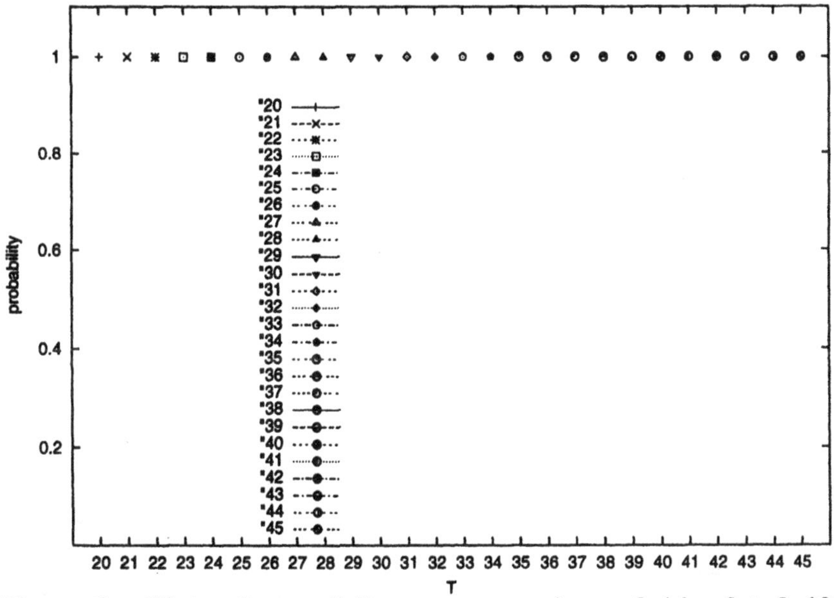

Figure 3: Plots of essentially non-zero values of (simulated 100000 times/M) of $P_{30}(M, 20 : T)$, for $M = 20, 21, \ldots, 45$. Note the simulated distributions have all their mass at $T = M$.

very close to 1, all of the nodes are chosen by the 30 DMA. The question is how "near" is "near." In our example, the above property holds approximately for $M \leq 2n$, however, it does not hold much beyond. In Figure 4 we see what happens as M increase from 45 to 165 in steps of 10. For $M = 55$, $P_K(M, n : T)$ has two essentially non-zero values. We stay with two values in the simulations until $M = 85$. As M increases the number of essentially non-zero probabilities increase, and by hooking the values up with a curve they start to slide into a bell shape. The bell shape is very obvious in Figure 5, where we are investigating M in the intermediate range of 200 to 1000, in increments of 100. As M increases greatly, as shown in Figure 6, the bell shape slowly "hits the wall" at $T = 600$ and finally we have the limiting behavior as discussed with respect to Eq. 4. From this analysis we see that $P_K(M, n : T)$ behaves like a uni-valued distribution for M small — $P_K(\text{small } M, n : T)$.

$$\text{For } P_K(\text{small } M, n : T) = \begin{cases} \text{essentially 1} & T = M \\ \text{essentially 0} & \text{otherwise} \end{cases}$$

and it is essentially uni-valued for M large as given by Eq. 4. In the intermediate range the graph of $P_K(M, n : T)$ slides into a bell shape from the right as M increases, then behaves like as a bell shape (normal distribution), and then slides into a uni-valued distribution from the left as $M \to \infty$.

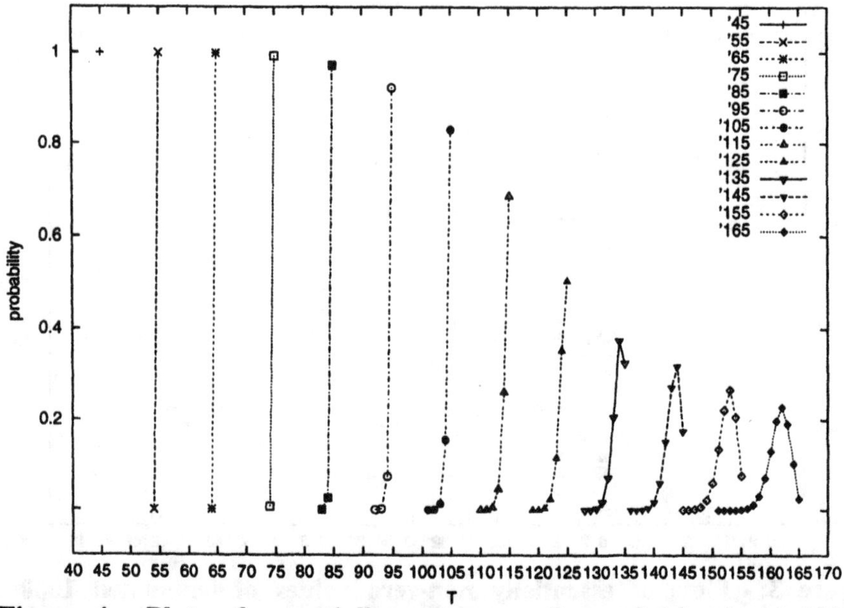

Figure 4: Plots of essentially non-zero values of (simulated 100000 times/M) $P_{30}(M, 20 : T)$ for $M = 45, 55, \ldots 165$.

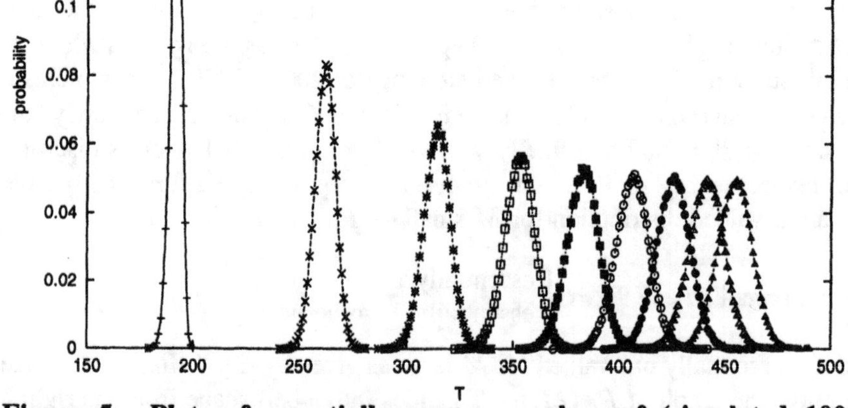

Figure 5: Plots of essentially non-zero values of (simulated 100000 times/M) of $P_{30}(M, 20 : T)$, as M grows.

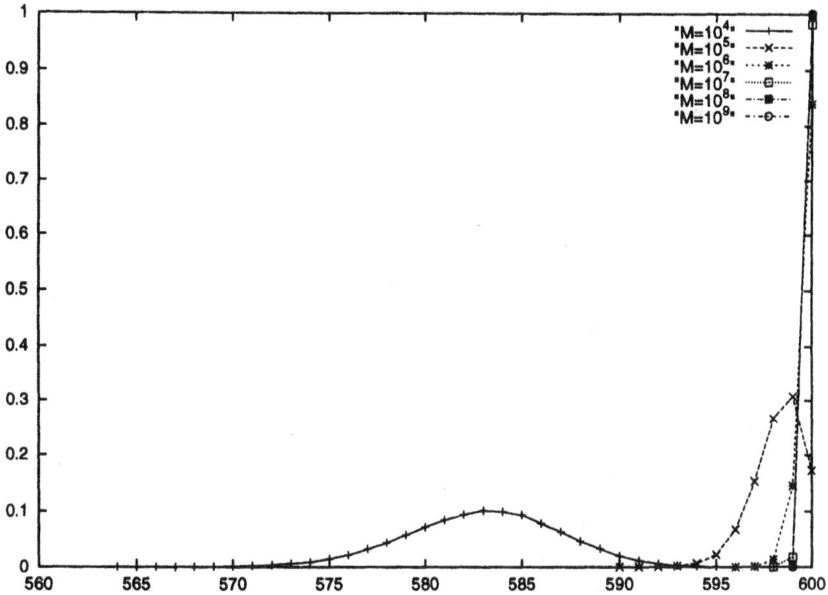

Figure 6: Plots of essentially non-zero values of (simulated 100000 times/M) of $P_{30}(M, 20 : T)$ for $M = 10^4, 10^5, \ldots, 10^9$.

2.3. Cumulative Distributions from the Simulations

Recall that the actual term of interest is $P_K(M, n : C^+)$. We could of course just sum the results from the simulations for the T values that are greater than or equal to C. However we wish to exploit the bell shape of the distribution for M in the intermediate range.

We do not know why the distribution has a bell shape. (We hypothesize that it is related to the normal approximation to the binomial distribution.) We are presently investigating it and we hope to discuss it with the workshop participants. With knowledge of the mean of T, μ and variance of T, σ^2 we could easily compute the probability, for intermediate M, by

$$P_K(M, n : C^+) = \sum_{T \geq C} P_K(M, n : T) \approx \frac{1}{\sqrt{2\pi\sigma^2}} \int_C^{\infty} e^{-\frac{(x-\mu)^2}{2\sigma^2}} dx \qquad (6)$$

We are viewing , with M, n, K fixed, $P_K(M, n : T)$ as a random variable T. Of course this approximation introduces error by approximating a discrete mass function by a continuous density function. If $C = \mu$ then we have, independent of the value of the variance σ^2, that

$$P_K(M, n : \mu^+) \approx \frac{1}{\sqrt{2\pi\sigma^2}} \int_{\mu}^{\infty} e^{-\frac{(x-\mu)^2}{2\sigma^2}} dx = 1/2$$

Note that this only holds in the intermediate range of M values, which is a relative term with respect to the size of K and n. We cannot determine how to get a computable term for the mean T value from the closed form Eqs. (1),(2), and (3). However, we are able to theoretically determine an approximation to the mean. In fact, when we compare it with our simulations it seems to be better than an approximation! The problem is that the same approach does not work for the variance. In our problem a DMA must pick n unique nodes. There is nothing probabilistic about the number n, it is a hard constraint. However, if we pick one particular node and ask "What is the probability that a particular DMA picked this node (given no other information)?" one would answer n/M. In our problem knowledge of certain nodes being picked affects the conditional probability. For example if we know that a particular DMA did not pick any of the first $M - n$ nodes it picks node μ_{M-n+1} with probability 1. In other words we cannot assume independence. Now we perform our approximation, *assuming* independence. For a given node, we say that a DMA has a probability of picking that node equal to n/M, and all of the nodes are independent. (We see that on the average, independence does not matter. We note though that the variances derived assuming independence are larger than sample simulation variances.) Therefore the probability that a node is not picked by a DMA is $1 - (n/M)$. Hence, the probability that no DMA picks a particular node is $(1 - (n/M))^K$. So the probability that at least one DMA picks the node is $1 - (1 - (n/M))^K$. Now we are in the situation of a binomial random variable, with M trials, where the probability of a success is $1-(1 - (n/M))^K$. Therefore the mean is $M \cdot \left(1 - (1 - (n/M))^K\right)$. Hence, we use this for our approximation of the mean T value, we call the approximation F, thus $F \approx$ mean of T, where

$$F = M \cdot \left(1 - (1 - (n/M))^K\right) \tag{7}$$

Table 1. mean values

distribution	*# simulation*	*sample mean*	*F*
$P_{42}(500, 17 : T)$	10^4	383	383
$P_{42}(1000, 17 : T)$	10^4	513	513
$P_{30}(600, 20 : T)$	10^5	383	383
$P_{30}(950, 20 : T)$	10^5	448	448
$P_{30}(1000, 20 : T)$	10^5	455	455
$P_{30}(10^4, 20 : T)$	10^5	583	583
$P_{30}(10^5, 20 : T)$	10^5	598	598
$P_{30}(10^6, 20 : T)$	10^5	600	600

Based on Table 1, and other data we have obtained, it seems that the approximation might actually be an equality, but we cannot prove it. There are slight differences between the F values and the sample means derived from our simulations. Of course, simulation sample means are only approximations themselves. Unfortunately, since the closed form for $P_K(M, n : T)$ is so computationally expensive, we cannot use it to compare F to the actual mean μ of $P_K(M, n : T)$. We note in Table 1, that Eq. 7 agrees with the limiting value of the distributions, as M grows, and the distributions collapse to a single non-trivial value. This is because $(1 - (n/M))^K = (1 - (K\frac{n}{M}/K))^K$. Since $e^x = \lim_{K\to\infty}\left(1 + \frac{x}{K}\right)^K$ we have for large K that $(1 - (K\frac{n}{M}/K))^K \approx e^{\frac{-Kn}{M}}$. Therefore, for large K, $F \approx M \cdot \left(1 - e^{\frac{-Kn}{M}}\right)$. By using the Taylor series for e^x we have for very large M that $F \approx Kn$.

The usefulness of F is that it gives us a way of determining if the probability associated with a given threshold is more or less than 50%. Of course, if we find a way of approximating the variance we could use any probability, not just 1/2.

In Figure 7 we see the plot of F against different K values (only the integers make sense) for $M = 1000$ and $n = 20$. If the threshold value is above (below) F, then there is less (greater) than a 50% chance of detecting the intrusion.

Hence, we have developed a useful rule of thumb, for intermediate M, that is easily calculated from only knowing M, n, and K. Of course, one should keep in mind that M being in the intermediate range is relative to the sizes of K and n. For very large M, with moderate n, one would need to deploy a large amount of DMA to use the cut-off regions. For non-intermediate M values we can use the our previous limiting results to handle the case where M is either very small or very large. Thus we have some handle on the probabilistic behavior of $P_K(M, m : C^+)$.

Let us go through a specific example using F, Figure 7, and Table 1. Consider a network of size $M = 1000$, $K = 30$ DMA, and each DMA visits $n = 20$ nodes, and we assume that an intrusion is detected as soon as the DFA has $\Theta = 400$ atoms of information. Since $400 < F = 455$, the probability of detecting the intrusion is greater than 1/2. If we use a different Θ that is less than 400, the probability of detecting the intrusion is even greater. On the other hand if $\Theta = 500$, we have less than a 50% chance of detecting the intrusion.

3. MORE GENERAL SCENARIOS

We have seen in the previous section that even for the simple scenario put forward we can derive a closed form solution for the probability, but it is not computationally feasible. Then why did we derive it? Intellectual integrity demands that we attempt to solve the problem. We do not have the tools to simplify the closed form but we are working on it. The terms making up the

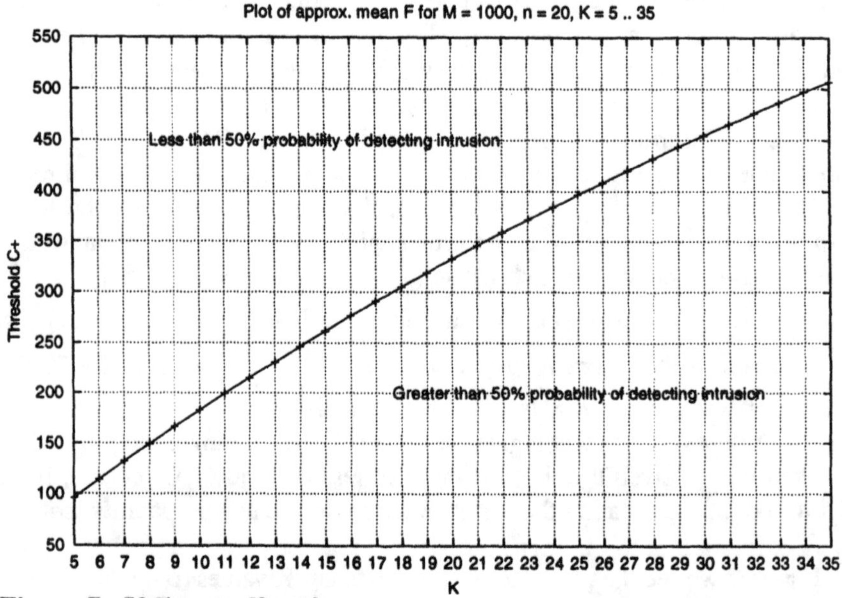

Figure 7: 50% cut-off regions

closed form are special functions and one can do approximations with them. We have also used the closed form to verify our simulations in simple cases. Another important reason that we presented the closed form solution was to show that if the solution is so computationally complex, even in the simple scenario put forward, how can we expect to derive and use a closed form solution in more complex scenarios? With this in mind, until we can approximate the special functions in $P_K(M, n : T)$, we suggest only simulations for the more general scenarios.

4. CONCLUSION

We have presented a model for a mobile-agent based IDS, called ABIDE. Using ABIDE as a framework we have analyzed a probabilistic scenario for determining if an intrusion alarm should be sounded. We have presented the closed form solution and detailed simulation results for a simple scenario. A rule of thumb has been obtained for determining certain probabilistic regions of interest. We have also discussed how our results can be used and extended to more complex scenarios.

5. ACKNOWLEDGEMENTS

We appreciate helpful suggestions from Allen Miller and the anonymous referees.

References

[1] D. J. Ingram, H. S. Kremer, & N. C. Rowe: *Distributed Intrusion Detection for Computer Systems Using Communicating Agents,* The 2000 Command and Control Research and Technology Symposium (CCRTS), 2000.

[2] E. H. Spafford & D. Zamboni: *Intrusion Detection Using Autonomous Agents,* Computer Networks, 34(4): 547-570, October 2000.

[3] M. Reed: *Agent Based Intrusion Detection Environment Architecture,* NRL Technical Report 5540/TM/117, 18 July, 2000.

[4] M. Reed: *ABIDE: Scalability,* NRL Technical Report 5540/TM/118, 6 September, 2000.

[5] A. Shamir: *How to Share a Secret,* Communications of the ACM, 22(11): 612-613, November 1979.

PUBLIC TELEPHONE NETWORK VULNERABILITIES

G. Lorenz, J. Keller, G. Manes, J. Hale, S. Shenoi

Abstract The convergence of public telephone networks (PTNs), wireless networks and the Internet makes it possible to disrupt vital information and communications systems from afar with software. PTN vulnerabilities are also growing due to system complexity, deregulation, increasing numbers of highly-skilled attackers, and the automation of attacks. This paper analyzes PTNs vulnerabilities, and presents an attack taxonomy. The taxonomy considers security threats posed by in-band attacks, out-of-band attacks, wireless attacks and Internet attacks.

Keywords: Public telephone networks, converged networks, vulnerabilities, attack taxonomy

1. INTRODUCTION

Public telephone network (PTN) fraud originated in 1961, when *Blue Boxes* were used to make free long-distance calls [4]. In the 1970s, "phone phreaking" drew attention: whistles packaged in *Cap'n Crunch* cereal boxes were used by "phreakers" to generate control tones, enabling them to modify telephone service at will [4]. The explosion of global communications has increased the scope and magnitude of fraud [4,14,19]. In 1997, a fifteen-year-old breached telephone systems at a high tech company to make free calls, access voice mail and eavesdrop on company business [4]. In 1998, a company lost $700,000 in two days from PBX attacks [4]. Worldwide losses – due to toll fraud, insider misuse, cell phone cloning and slamming – now exceed $30 billion a year [4].

But new dangers are posed by insidious penetrations into PTN networks [19,22]. Most penetrations are by thrill-seeking hackers and novices using "kiddie scripts." However, criminals, terrorists and foreign governments are also systematically probing PTNs, potentially monitoring communications and searching for vulnerabilities [22].

Public telephone networks are massive heterogeneous networks comprising a backbone, wireless networks and the Internet. The PTN backbone, driven by the Signaling System 7 (SS7) protocol suite [1,2,18] has significant vulnerabilities [10,17]. Originally designed for a closed industry, SS7 incorporates weak authentication facilities. However, deregulation requires phone companies to provide SS7 connections to any entity [19]. Increased PTN access, coupled with Internet-PTN convergence (e.g., xDSL, Dial-Up and ISDN connections) [8,23], make it easier for attackers to enter and then exploit poorly secured SS7 networks [10].

Wireless networks, an explosive growth area [6,9], also pose serious risks. Wireless communications are inherently vulnerable. Moreover, the rapid evolution of wireless technologies, the lack of standards and the pervasive use of legacy systems give attackers opportunities to wreak havoc on a massive scale [10,19,22].

Accentuating the problem is the lack of sustained research and development efforts focused on PTN security [22]. Very few systems exist for securing PTNs [20,21]. Published research and prototypes for defending PTNs against attacks are virtually non-existent.

This paper focuses on the problem of securing PTNs. The PTN backbone, wireless networks and the Internet-PTN convergence are described in detail. Vulnerabilities are analyzed to obtain a taxonomy of attacks on PTNs. The taxonomy considers security threats posed by four separate PTN attack modes: in-band attacks, out-of-band attacks, wireless attacks and Internet attacks. The taxonomy provides an opportunity for the systematic development of mitigative and preventive strategies, and the identification and classification of emerging threats.

2. PTN OVERVIEW

Public telephone networks (PTNs) are massive heterogeneous networks comprising three overlapping sub-networks: a PTN backbone, the Internet and wireless networks (Figure 1). The PTN backbone primarily uses the SS7 protocol [1,2,18], the Internet employs the TCP/IP prototol suite [5,12], and wireless networks use the CDMA, TDMA or GSM protocols [6,9,16]. The PTN backbone is connected to the Internet and wireless networks via IP and wireless gateways, respectively. In addition, the PTN backbone maintains various connections to entities ranging from individual users to large organizations. For example, individuals may use xDSL, Dial-Up and ISDN connections to access the PTN (and Internet). Large organizations employ analog trunks to connect private branch exchanges (PBXs) to the PTN.

Attackers have numerous points of entry due to network convergence [8,19, 23]. Indeed, every point of attachment between the sub-networks represents an opening to potential attackers.

The Internet (attack point 1 in Figure 1) is a convenient platform for launching attacks on the PTN. Numerous hacker exploits can be used to compromise or seize control of Internet hosts connected to PTN elements. The threats are increased as convergence technologies, e.g., xDSL, dial-up and ISDN, propa-

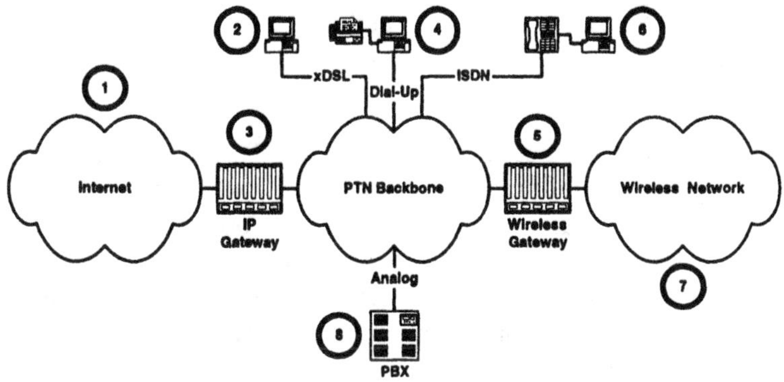

Figure 1. PTN overview (with attack points numbered).

gate (attack points 2, 4 and 6). The concern is that while they provide increased access to PTN services, convergence technologies are intrinsically insecure.

PTN gateways (points 3 and 5) are highly vulnerable. These gateways authenticate users before providing access. However, attackers who circumvent the authentication procedures have free reign over PTN assets.

Wireless networks (attack point 7) open new vulnerabilities. Especially problematic are services providing wireless access to the Internet.

PBXs often use legacy technologies (in-band signaling) which are known to have serious vulnerabilities (colored box attacks [7,10,19]; attack point 8). Indeed, PBXs – because they use many connections to the PTN backbone – are often used as bounce points for attacks [17].

Thus, the PTN backbone is completely surrounded by expanding networks, each with significant vulnerabilities that provide attractive entry points for attackers. At the same time, the PTN backbone is the central and most important component of the global communications network. A significant portion of the Internet uses leased telephone lines and wireless communications are routinely routed through land lines. If the PTN backbone fails, everything else will fail.

3. PTN BACKBONE VULNERABILITIES

The U.S. PTN incorporates four regional Bell operating companies (RBOCs) (Verizon, SBC, BellSouth and Qwest) and numerous independent phone companies, all connected by long-distance providers. Figure 2 shows an RBOC supporting telephone customers as well as small companies (CLECs) that use X.25/SS7 data lines. Each RBOC is connected to other RBOCs via long distance companies (possibly themselves).

The PTN backbone uses signaling, transmission and operations equipment (Figure 2) [18]. Signaling equipment sets up and tears down calls, and includes databases and processors for number translation and call routing. Transmission equipment carries telephone conversations. Operations equipment, including the operations support system (OSS), performs management, inventory, engineering and repair functions.

Signaling

PTNs use in-band or out-of-band signaling. The older in-band technique combined signaling and transmission over copper wires, but it was inefficient and did not support advanced services [2]. Modern out-of-band communication between PTN central-office switches occurs via dedicated (private and public) X.25 data networks using the SS7 protocol for setting up and tearing down calls, establishing billing and returning busy signals [18]. These dedicated networks prevent in-band fraud and conserve resources. However, modern telecommunications systems still use in-band signaling because it is more easily deployed.

In-band signaling uses multi frequencies (MF) and dual tone multi frequencies (DTMFs) – tones generated using telephone touchpads – to send control signals [2]. MFs send control signals directly to telephone trunks and switches. DTMFs are used for number dialing, ringbacks, busy signals, dial tones; they also activate and deactivate services, e.g., call-forwarding (*72/*73) and call-return (*66/*69).

Out-of-band signaling using SS7 has largely replaced in-band DTMF for the U.S. PTN [2,19]. An international standard, SS7 governs network architecture and configuration, and message transport [1,18]. The architecture includes: (i) service switching points (SSPs), the switches that handle base communications; (ii) signal transfer points (STPs), the switches that handle routing; and (iii) service control points (SCPs) that provide database access for routing and advanced PTN services, e.g., caller ID, call forwarding and toll-free calls. To increase reliability, SS7 elements are deployed in redundant mated pairs. The SS7 protocol reflects the OSI model, splitting the message transport layer (MTP) into three levels (MTP 1-3: the physical, data link and network equivalents to the OSI), and call management (ISUP, TUP) and advanced services (SCCP, TCAP), which are built on top of the MTP layer [1,18].

Transmission

The U.S. PTN was originally designed to carry analog signals. Currently, transmission initiates with analog signals being sent to a central office where they are converted to digital to facilitate switching and routing within the PTN [1]. Digital signals are converted back to analog via pulse code modulation (PCM) sampling before their presentation at the destination. Using time division multiplexing (TDM), the PCM is transmitted over a physical connection for the call duration. Voice transmission typically employs channelized T1 (1.544Mbps) circuits. (Each T1 line has 24 64kbps trunk circuits over two copper pairs; each call uses one circuit.) Synchronous TDM is inefficient be-

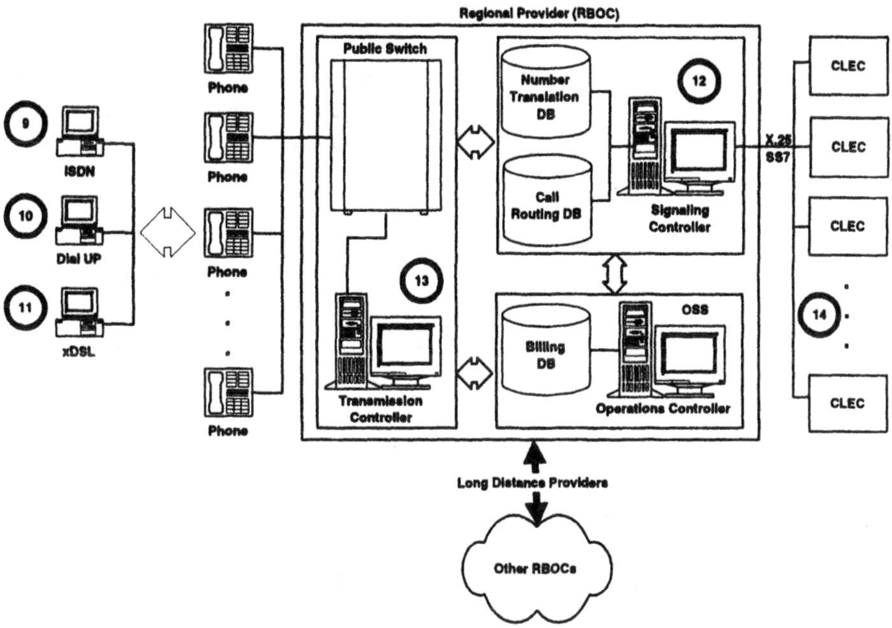

Figure 2. PTN backbone (with attack points numbered).

cause each time slot is dedicated to the user for the call duration, even when nothing is transmitted. Modern transmission systems address this inefficiency by integrating heterogeneous technologies, e.g., voice over IP (VoIP).

Operations

Operations support systems (OSSs) are the remote maintenance centers of PTNs [1,18,19]. They perform management, inventory, engineering, planning and repair functions. Originally, OSSs were mainframe systems that supported business operations. Modern OSSs support these operations, but also manage network systems and advanced customer services. OSSs comprise several computer systems and databases (service control points (SCPs) described above) that handle ordering, inventory, activation and customer information services throughout PTNs via digital interfaces. The systems are also responsible for updating, maintaining and monitoring all SCP databases. A service management system (SMS) consisting of a command set and several GUIs provides a standard interface to SCP databases. SMS also maintains SCP integrity: it acts as a central point to update SCP databases, which then propagate throughout the SS7 backbone.

Vulnerabilities

The PTN backbone is susceptible to numerous threats. The replacement of in-band signaling with out-of-band (SS7) signaling largely eliminated the well-known colored box attacks [1,7,10,19]. However, the SS7 architecture and protocol are vulnerable because they possess limited authentication mechanisms (SS7 was originally designed for a closed community) [17,18,19]. Moreover, deregulation coupled with the proliferation of VoIP and other integrated services (attack points 9, 10 and 11 in Figure 2) significantly increase the vulnerability to fraud, eavesdropping and denial of service attacks [14,19,22].

Major PTN vulnerabilities stem from the SS7 signaling system [19]; thus, SS7 components (points 12 and 14) are prone to numerous exploits. PTN databases or service control points (SCPs) – such as number translation, call routing and billing databases – are particularly vulnerable. Attackers can wreak havoc by modifying important information maintained in these databases. During a terrorist bombing incident, an attacker can modify entries in a call forwarding database to re-route all phone calls to emergency services (e.g., 911), disrupting them and increasing the number of casualties.

Transmission systems, especially central office switches, are also prime targets (attack point 13). These switches are vital to PTN operation, but they are vulnerable to a range of denial of service attacks.

4. WIRELESS NETWORK VULNERABILITIES

Wireless networks are the largest growth sector for voice communications, and are used increasingly for data transmission [6]. A typical network is shown in Figure 3. It comprises a cellular system linked to a base station subsystem via tower/transceivers. The base station subsystem is connected to a network subsystem and ultimately to the PTN backbone using SS7 (X.25) data lines.

The cellular system is a network of towers that define cells. Radio signals received by a tower in the originating cell are routed to the corresponding base station subsystem. This subsystem comprises a base transceiver station (BTS) and a base station controller (BSC). The BTS is responsible for radio transmission and reception in one or more cells within a service area. It contains radio transceivers that define cells and handle the radio-link protocols with handsets (mobile stations). The BSC manages radio resources for one or more BTSs, handling radio-channel setup, frequency hopping and handovers. It also connects the mobile stations to the network subsytem.

Wireless network subsystems are essentially "mini" PTN regional providers (RBOCs), i.e., they use SS7 signaling, circuit switching and operations support systems. As shown in Figure 3, a wireless network subsystem comprises a mobile switching center (MSC), equipment identity register (EIR), authentication center (AuC), home location register (HLR), and a visitor location register (VLR). The MSC provides circuit switched network access, database access and connections to the PTN backbone. The MSC, in conjunction with other network subsystem entities, also handles registration, authentication, location updating, handovers and call routing to mobile subscribers.

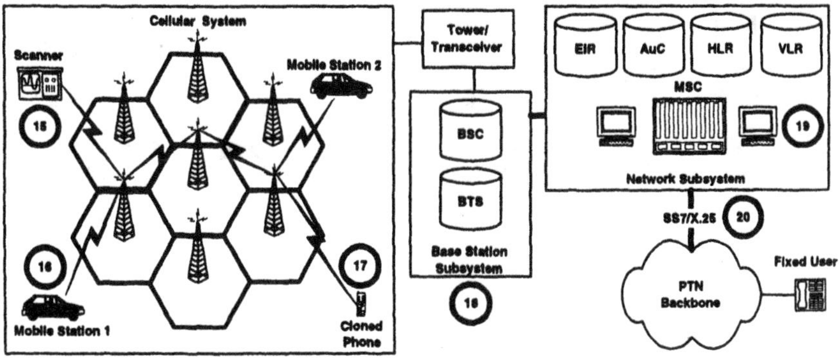

Figure 3. Typical wireless network (with attack points numbered).

The EIR database contains lists of valid mobile devices, allowing providers to deny service and track stolen/cloned equipment. The AuC database stores secret keys corresponding to subscriber identification modules (SIMs) and electronic serial numbers (ESNs) used for authentication and encryption. HLR and VLR (and MSC), provide call-routing and roaming capabilities. HLR and VLR contain all administrative information pertaining to registered subscribers and their locations. VLR works in conjunction with HLR to locate roaming users. When a mobile station enters a new network cell, data are entered into the VLR so that it can be located. Wireless networks provide excellent mobility, but they are very complex and are not yet standardized.

Wireless communication has inherent risks because radio signals are readily intercepted and exploited [16]. Eavesdropping is widespread. All that is needed is a scanner tuned to the right frequency (point 15).

Phreakers perform cloning [4,16] by stealing the security codes (e.g., electronic serial numbers (ESNs)) of legitimate mobile stations (Figure 3). Typically, ESNs are gleaned using scanning devices. Cellular phones are reprogrammed with stolen ESNs to create cloned phones (point 17). A cellular cache box automates this process [7]. It captures an ESN, uses it once, purges it from memory, and then repeats the cycle. Some protocols, e.g., CDMA, scramble data using psuedo-random noise codes, effectively eliminating scanner-based eavesdropping and cloning [16]. However, this technology is limited and expensive. Meanwhile, phreaking techniques are continuously improving, e.g., using frequency-hopping scanners [7].

Denial of service attacks are increasingly directed at wireless networks. Attackers masquerading as legitimate mobile stations have flooded radio towers, denying service to thousands of users (point 16) [4,19]. The *Timofonica* virus of June 2000 was designed to flood cell phones that had text capabilities, posing a serious threat to millions of handheld computers, pagers and phones [3].

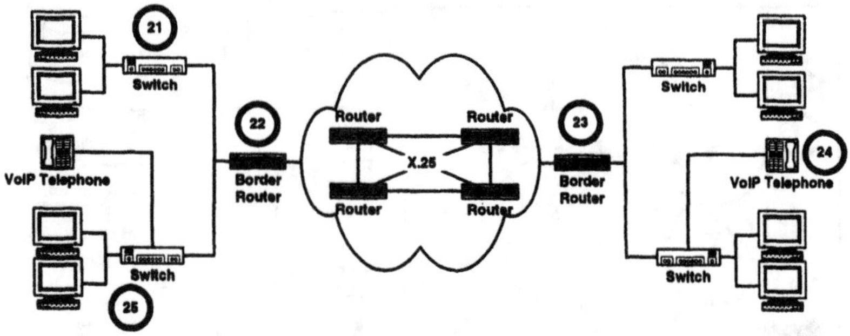

Figure 4. Internet backbone (with attack points numbered).

Radio signals received by a cellular tower are routed to a base station subsystem before being sent to the network subsystem (Figure 3). The base station subsystem thus interfaces radio signals to the hard line. It is an attractive target (point 18) because it is a single point of failure for an entire sector of wireless cells.

Wireless network subsystems, like RBOCs in the PTN backbone, use the SS7 architecture and protocol. Thus, the vulnerabilities described in Section 3 apply here (point 19). Specialized databases are also vulnerable. For example, each sector of cells maintains VLR and HLR databases with the ESNs of all mobile stations in the proximity. Attackers can tap into these databases and steal ESNs. Conversely, they can perpetrate large-scale denial of service attacks by modifying, erasing or shutting down these vital databases.

Cellular networks rely on connections to the PTN backbone. Attackers can seize control of a wireless network subsystem and then utilize its PTN connections to launch a slew of attacks (point 20).

5. INTERNET VULNERABILITIES

Originally developed for data transmission, the Internet is increasingly carrying voice transmissions [5]. The Internet backbone is primarily a collection of routers linked by X.25 data lines leased from PTNs (Figure 4). Individual networks use border routers to connect to this backbone.

Internet (VoIP) telephony is more efficient than PTN voice transmission (using TDM), but the quality of service (QoS) is not as good. Nevertheless, the attraction of free long-distance has significantly increased VoIP applications, blurring the PTN-Internet distinction.

The increasing interdependence and interconnectivity between the Internet and the PTN backbone makes Internet vulnerabilities (e.g., CVE and ICAT databases [11,13]) particularly relevant [19,22]. Large portions of the Internet use leased phone lines. Conversely, PTN components are networked using Internet technologies, and often, the Internet itself. Thus, Internet vulnerabilities affect the PTN backbone.

Packet sniffing is a major concern. Sniffers attached to Internet switching devices can intercept email, e-commerce transactions, as well as user names and passwords passed as plaintext (attack point 21). VoIP telephony enables attackers to eavesdrop on voice communications as they traverse the Internet (point 24). Furthermore, attackers who compromise Internet routers can direct traffic to compromised switches (points 22 and 23). Such routing attacks give sniffers access to much broader areas, particularly if core routers (point 23) are compromised.

Internet vulnerabilities can be exploited from any host (point 25). Therefore, attacks can be launched remotely at any system within the PTN backbone, within wireless networks or within the Internet itself. Note that since Internet hosts are routinely infiltrated, they will become the primary attack points in the converged PTN-Internet environment.

6. PTN ATTACK TAXONOMY

A PTN attack taxonomy provides an opportunity for the systematic development of mitigative and preventive strategies, and the identification and classification of emerging threats. The taxonomy presented in Figure 5 and discussed in this section considers the four main security threats: modification, interception, interruption and fabrication [15]. Four separate attack modes are examined: in-band attacks, out-of-band attacks, wireless attacks and Internet attacks.

6.1. PTN In-Band Attacks

In-band (colored box) attacks have been largely eliminated by SS7-based out-of-band signaling [18]. However, private branch exchanges (PBXs) used by large enterprises commonly rely on in-band signaling, and are therefore vulnerable to colored box attacks [10]. Moreover, certain advanced services engage in-band signaling [2]. E.g., caller ID requires that the caller's telephone number and the date/time of the call be sent in ASCII format within the first 4-second silent interval in the ringing cycle. This protocol can be easily spoofed or disrupted.

In-band modification attacks mainly involved unauthorized alteration of central office switches to commit toll fraud. Modification attacks, and the three other attack types, were also perpetrated by tampering with switches using colored boxes [7,10], e.g., a chartreuse box that facilitated the theft of electricity from phone lines [7].

Interception was historically performed using wire taps. However, it was simplified by special colored boxes, e.g., brown and dayglo, designed for eavesdropping [7]. In addition, copper and blotto boxes facilitated sabotage by enabling service interruption without the need to physically cut lines [7].

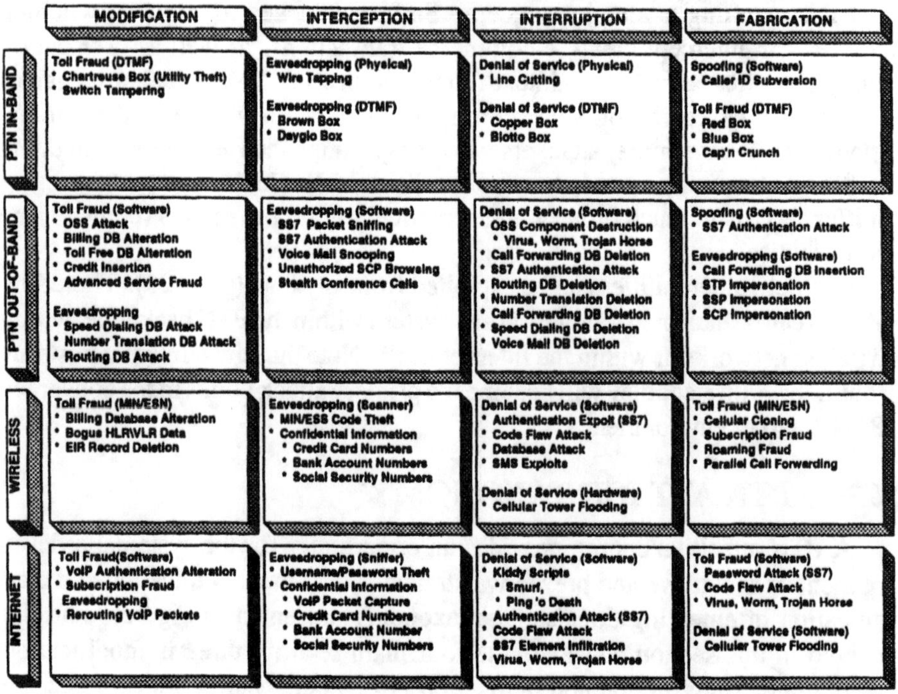

Figure 5. PTN attack taxonomy.

Colored box attacks utilized fabricated tones to gain unauthorized access to PTN components [4,7]. For example, a red box simulated coin (quarter) tones required by the automated coin toll system (ACTS), permitting free calls from pay phones. The legendary "Cap'n Crunch" whistles and blue boxes produced 2600 Hz tones for seizing control of switches [4]. In fact, a veritable rainbow of colored boxes [7] was available for in-band attacks (Figure 6).

6.2. PTN Out-of-Band Attacks

Out-of-band attacks primarily abuse the SS7 protocol. SS7 was designed for a closed industry and, therefore, incorporates weak authentication facilities [18,19]. However, deregulation now requires phone companies to provide SS7 connections to any entity for a $10,000 fee [19]. This, coupled with the Internet-PTN convergence, makes it easier for attackers to enter and then exploit poorly secured SS7 networks.

Once entry is gained, attackers could target network databases with critical information. For example, call forwarding, speed dialing, number translation or routing databases can be modified to re-route calls and intercept or interrupt transmissions. Attackers could also erase billing records, modify toll free num-

- **Black** - Allows the calling party not to be billed for calls
- **Blue** - Emulates an operator by seizing a trunk with a 2600hz tone
- **Brown** - Creates a party line from two phone lines
- **Chartreuse** - Uses the electricity from a phone line
- **Dark** - Re-routes outgoing or incoming calls to another phone
- **Green** - Emulates the coin collect, coin return, and callback (DTMF) tones
- **Pearl** - Generates tones
- **Red** - Generates quarter tones allowing free phone calls from pay phones
- **Silver** - Generates tones for ABCD keys
- **Violet** - Keeps a payphone from hanging up
- **White** - Acts as a portable DTMF keypad

Figure 6. Common PTN colored-boxes.

bers, insert credit and update subscribed services records. They could obtain unlimited free calls, as well as call waiting, caller ID and conference calling, by simply altering the appropriate customer records.

Interception can be accomplished in numerous ways, especially by voice mail snooping and SS7 packet sniffing. SS7 communications are transmitted in plaintext. This enables attackers to obtain confidential user information without having to access PTN databases (SCPs).

PTN interruptions can be accomplished by deleting data maintained by SS7 network components (particularly SCPs). Data deletion can completely disrupt a network, yet this is very easy to do once access is gained to an SS7 network, especially its operations support system (OSS). The deletion of records from call forwarding, speed dialing and voice mail databases produces relatively minor service interruptions. However, deleting information maintained in routing and number translation databases can cause large-scale outages.

PTN computer systems are vulnerable to trojans, viruses and worms. Also, fabricating credentials – or spoofing – is facilitated by weak SS7 authentication and expanding network connections. Attackers masquerading as legitimate SS7 entities can wreak havoc throughout the PTN.

6.3. Wireless Attacks

Wireless communications are most vulnerable to toll fraud, eavesdropping and denial of service. Attacks are relatively easy because wireless technology is inherently insecure [3,16].

Unauthorized modification of wireless network databases is a serious threat to wireless communications and to the operation of the PTN backbone. E.g., inserting bogus home location register (HLR) and visitor location register (VLR) data allows attackers to activate and use phones free of charge. Such falsified data allows attackers to fool networks into believing that fraudulent wireless devices are legitimate. Since wireless phone calls eventually travel through the PTN backbone, this type of fraud affects the entire PTN. Likewise, modification attacks could target equipment identity register (EIR) databases to increase the fraudulent use of illegal or cloned equipment.

Interception attacks are facilitated by the nature of wireless transmissions and the availability of inexpensive scanners. Attackers have been known to scan transmissions and steal electronic serial numbers (ESNs) to create cloned wireless devices. In addition, sensitive information, e.g., credit cards, social security numbers and bank account information, can be intercepted by scanning wireless communications.

Wireless interruptions can be accomplished in a variety of ways. Since databases are vital to call processing, denying access to them cripples a network. E.g., slowing or interrupting HLR and VLR database accesses will stifle call processing as call routing cannot proceed. A denial of service attack could be launched by broadcasting numerous short message service (SMS) messages. Alternatively, a brute force attack could simply flood reserved wireless transmission frequencies.

Fabrication attacks (cellular cloning) are a major concern for wireless communications providers. Indeed, this type of fraud costs providers several billion dollars a year [4].

6.4. Internet Attacks

Internet attacks are well documented [11,13]. The focus here is on attacks that can affect PTN systems and operations.

Modification attacks are typically aimed at VoIP toll fraud and eavesdropping. E.g., altering VoIP authentication data allows attackers to circumvent billing and call verification. Likewise, modifying Internet routing tables (by compromising routers) gives attackers the ability to re-route and intercept VoIP communications.

Interception, e.g., eavesdropping on conversations and data, is simplified by IP packet sniffers. In fact, the proliferation of sophisticated sniffing software is a huge concern as the Internet and PTNs converge.

Interruption attacks, like those regularly perpetrated on the Internet, will become increasingly common. Given that networked computers control most PTN services, hackers and script kiddies can launch significant denial of service attacks. Attackers could also deploy viruses and trojans to target key PTN components, creating widespread service outages.

Internet-based fabrication attacks will be significant in converged environments. E.g., attackers could use spoofing software to bypass authentication procedures, gain unauthorized access to PTN components, and perpetrate attacks ranging from toll fraud to service disruption.

7. CONCLUSIONS

PTN vulnerabilities are growing due to system complexity, deregulation, increasing numbers of highly-skilled attackers, and the automation of attacks. Unfortunately, relatively little research has specifically addressed PTN vulnerabilities.

The attack taxonomy described in this paper considers in-band attacks, out-of-band attacks, wireless attacks and Internet attacks. It provides an opportunity for the systematic development of mitigative and preventive strategies, and the identification and classification of emerging threats. We hope that this work will stimulate further studies of PTN vulnerabilities and the development of sophisticated systems for safeguarding vital telecommunications networks

References

[1] Black, U. (1997) *ISDN and SS7: Architectures for Digital Signaling Networks*. Prentice Hall, Upper Saddle River, New Jersey.

[2] Bosse, J. (1997) *Signaling in Telecommunication Networks*. Wiley, New York.

[3] Cable News Network (June 12, 2000) Palm antivirus protection in the works (www.cnn.com).

[4] Denning, D. (1999) *Information Warfare and Security*. Addison Wesley, Reading, Massachusetts.

[5] Faynberg, I. *et al.* (2000) *Converged Networks and Services: Internetworking IP and the PSTN*. Wiley, New York.

[6] Glisic, S. *et al.* (1997) *Wireless Communications: TDMA v.CDMA*. Kluwer, Boston.

[7] *Hacker Quarterly* (2001) (www.2600.com).

[8] Kuhn, P. *et al.* (1999) *Broadband Communications: Convergence of Network Technologies*. Kluwer, Boston, Massachusetts.

[9] Lin, Y. *et al.* (2000) *Wireless and Mobile Network Architectures*. Wiley, New York.

[10] Lorenz, G. *et al.* (2000) Characterization of attacks on public telephone networks, *Proceedings of the SPIE Conference on Technology on Law Enforcement*. Boston, Massachusetts.

[11] MITRE Corporation (2001) *Common Vulnerabilities and Exposures (CVE)* (cve.mitre.org).

[12] Muller, N. (1999) *IP Convergence: The Next Revolution in Telecommunications*. Artech, Norwood, Massachusetts.

[13] National Institute of Standards and Technology (2001) *I-CAT Database* (csrc.nist.gov/icat).

[14] Network Reliability and Interoperability Council (1997) *Final Report of the Network Reliability and Interoperability Council*. Federal Communications Commission, Washington, D.C.

[15] Pfleeger, C. (1997) *Security in Computing*. Prentice Hall, Upper Saddle River, New Jersey.

[16] Rhee, M. *et al.* (1998) *CDMA Cellular Mobile Communications and Network Security*. Prentice Hall, Upper Saddle River, New Jersey.

[17] Rozenblit, M. (2000) *Security for Network Telecommunications Management*. IEEE Press, Piscataway, New Jersey.

[18] Russell, T. (2000) *Signaling System #7*. McGraw-Hill, New York.

[19] Schneider F. (Ed.) (1999) *Trust in Cyberspace*. National Academy Press, Washington, D.C.

[20] SecureLogix Corporation (2001) San Antonio, Texas (www.securelogix.com).

[21] Sevis Systems (2001) San Antonio, Texas (www.sevis.com).

[22] Wadlow, T. (2000) *The Process of Network Security*. Addison-Wesley, New York.

[23] The White House (2000) *Defending America's Cyberspace: National Plan for Information Systems Protection*, Washington, D.C.

V

RELATIONAL DATABASES

FLEXIBLE SECURITY POLICIES IN SQL

Steve Barker
Cavendish School of Computer Science,
University of Westminster, London, UK
barkers@westminster.ac.uk

Arnon Rosenthal
The MITRE Corporation,
202 Burlington Road, Bedford, MA, USA
arnie@mitre.org

Abstract We show how a wide variety of role-based access control policies may be formally specified in the stratified subset of clause form logic. We then show how these formal specifications may be automatically translated into a small subset of SQL to be used to seamlessly protect an SQL database from unauthorized read and update requests made by authenticated users. We demonstrate the power of our approach by showing how a variety of access control policies can be represented.

Keywords: Role-Based Access Control, Stratified Logic, SQL.

Introduction

In the SQL2 standard [6], the security-specific language features are restricted to simple GRANT and REVOKE statements (albeit views may also be used to provide security). Unfortunately, the GRANT-REVOKE model enables a *security administrator (SA)* to represent only a small subset of the access control policies that are needed in practice.

While RDBMS products and the SQL3 standard include some support for roles as well as GRANT and REVOKE, there are still many important policies that existing products and SQL cannot express. To get more expressive power, application programs are typically used. However, this approach complicates the maintenance of an access control policy and makes it difficult for SAs to reason about their behavior. We therefore envisage making use of a high-level policy specification language which enables a range of access control policies to be formulated, and which can be translated into an implementation of the policy using SQL views and triggers. Furthermore, we aim for the translation from specification to implementation to be automated.

In our proposal, function-free, *stratified clause logic* [10] is used by a SA to formulate RBAC policies that define the set of authorized actions that can be performed on a database.* We believe that most realistic access control policies may be expressed in the high-level language of stratified logic by using a small number of clauses which have a simple declarative and operational meaning that makes it relatively easy for SAs to reason about the consequences of a specification of an access policy. Representing access policies directly in SQL and reasoning about their effects is much harder. Stratified logic and SQL share a well-defined and uncontroversial model-theoretic semantics (the *perfect model semantics* [12]), stratified logic has a simple equivalence preserving translation into SQL [1], and this translation may be automated.

There are certainly other computational options to the one we propose, e.g., using a logic engine, a hybrid of SQL and logic, and even implementing high performance parts in C++. However, there are several reasons why the translation approach is worth investigating. It is natural to consider managing the authorization system for an SQL database by using SQL alone, it is attractive to execute only SQL, instead of adding a logic execution engine, it is attractive to provide security and transaction protection using the ordinary RDBMS facilities, and by avoiding extra software systems (beyond the translator), we avoid requiring experts to manage and maintain them. Moreover, there are a number of attractive technical results which are applicable to our approach.

The RBAC models that we specify in stratified logic are based on the family of models described in [14]. That is, we assume that an RBAC theory includes role and permission assignments ($RBAC_0$), and may additionally include specifications of either role hierarchies ($RBAC_1$) or constraints ($RBAC_2$). $RBAC_3$ includes role hierarchies and constraints.

The rest of this paper is organized thus. In Section 1, we provide a basic introduction to stratified logic, and we discuss some relevant notions from database and access control theory. In Section 2, we describe the formulation of a generic $RBAC_1$ model as a stratified theory, an $RBAC_1$ theory. In Section 3, we show how an $RBAC_1$ theory can be translated into SQL and used to control access to an SQL database. In Section 4, we demonstrate the power of our approach by showing how a range of access control policies may be represented in a small subset of SQL. In Section 5, we further extend our representation of $RBAC_1$ to include constraints on $RBAC_3$ theories, and we consider constraint

*A GUI may be used to help a SA formulate policies expressed using stratified clauses.

enforcement. In Section 6, some conclusions are drawn and suggestions for further work are made.

Henceforth, any references to SQL and databases should be, respectively, interpreted as referring to SQL2 (plus a WITH RECURSIVE construct and triggers) and SQL databases. In the sequel, we use upper case **bold type** for indicating reserved words of SQL and lower case *italic type* for user-supplied information in SQL statements.

1. PRELIMINARIES

In our proposal, RBAC theories are formally specified in a subset of function-free normal clause logic. A normal clause is an expression of the form: $H \leftarrow L1, L2, \ldots, Lm$ ($m \geq 0$). The *head* of the clause, *H*, is an *atom* and *L1,L2,...,Lm* is a conjunction of *literals* that constitutes the *body* of the clause. If *L1,L2,...,Lm* is true (proved) then *H* is true (proved). A literal is an atomic formula or its negation; in this paper negation is *negation by failure* [16], and the negation of the atom *A* is denoted by *not A*. A *normal theory* is a finite set of normal clauses. A clause with an empty body is an *assertion* or a *fact*. A clause with an empty head is a *denial*. A *definite clause* is a normal clause with no negative literal in its body; a *definite theory* is a finite set of definite clauses.

In the clause $H \leftarrow L1, L2, \ldots, Lm$, *H* is said to positively (negatively) *refer to* the literal *Li* ($i \in \{1,..,m\}$) if *Li* is a positive (negative) literal in the definition of *H*. A *dependency graph* [16] has an edge labeled + (−) if *H* refers to *Li* positively (negatively). A normal theory is *stratified* [16] iff its dependency graph contains no cycle with a negative edge. A stratified theory is a finite set of stratified clauses.

In this paper, the constants that appear in clauses are denoted by lower case symbols; variables are denoted by using symbols that appear in the upper case.

In the sequel we will relate the discussion of stratified logic and SQL to subsets of *SPCUD-algebra* [1]. The SPCUD-algebra is a language that includes the five primitive operators of relational algebra viz.: select, project, cartesian product, union and set difference. The *SPCU-algebra* is SPCUD-algebra without the set difference operator; *SPC-algebra* is SPCU-algebra without the union operator.

Since the RBAC theories that we consider are stratified, these theories have a unique *perfect model* [12]. The perfect model of an RBAC theory is the set of logical consequences of the theory and includes the set of authorized accesses defined by the theory. These authorizations will be defined by a predicate *permitted(U,P,O)* where *U* denotes a user of a database, *P* denotes a permission and *O* is an object. The permissions we consider include insert, delete, update and select (read). The objects to be protected are base tables, views and attributes in base tables.

Given an RBAC theory Σ and a request by U to perform a P operation on O, the approach adopted for access control involves deciding whether an instance of *permitted(U,P,O)* is authorized by Σ. Informally, the desired enforcement semantics are:

IF permitted(U,P,O) THEN execute the P action on O for U ELSE provide informative error message and abort

As we will see, the approach we adopt for evaluating access requests is based on *query modification* [15]. That is, security information is used to modify a user's query such that the revised form of the query satisfies access control restrictions.

2. REPRESENTING $RBAC_1$ AS A STRATIFIED THEORY

Any RBAC model provides means for creating associations between a role and (1) permissions to perform operations on database objects and (2) a set of users. These may be represented in clause form logic by defining *ura(U,R)* and *rpa(R,P,O)* predicates (see [3] for details).

In the *ura(U,R)* relation, the predicate name *ura* is shorthand for *user-role assignment*; definitions of *ura* are used to represent that user U is assigned to the role R. Similarly, *rpa(R,P,O)* stands for *role-permission assignment*; definitions of *rpa* are used to specify that role R is assigned the P permission on the object O.

An instance of an $RBAC_1$ role hierarchy may be represented using a set of *d-s* facts (where *d-s* is short for "directly senior to"); *d-s* is an irreflexive, intransitive and non-symmetric relation. The assertion *d-s*(r_i,r_j) records that the role r_i is directly senior to the role r_j in an $RBAC_1$ role hierarchy.

The clauses that follow define a *senior_to* relation as the reflexive-transitive closure of the *d-s* relation (where '_' is an anonymous variable):

senior_to(R1,R1) $\leftarrow$ *d-s(R1,_)*
senior_to(R1,R1) $\leftarrow$ *d-s(_,R1)*
senior_to(R1,R2) $\leftarrow$ *d-s(R1,R2)*
senior_to(R1,R2) $\leftarrow$ *d-s(R1,R3),senior_to(R3,R2)*

To define authorized access, the following clause may be used:

permitted(U,P,O) $\leftarrow$ *ura(U,R1),senior_to(R1,R2),rpa(R2,P,O)*

The *permitted* clause expresses that a user *U* has the *P* permission on an object *O* if *U* is assigned to a role *R1* that is senior to a role *R2* in an $RBAC_1$ role hierarchy and *R2* is assigned the *P* permission on *O*. That is, *U* has the *P* permission on *O* if *U* is assigned to a role that inherits the *P* permission on *O* via an $RBAC_1$ role hierarchy.

The definition of *permitted* implies that a *closed access policy* [5] is to be used to protect a database. That is, a user's permission to access information must be specifically authorized in an access control theory; users do not have access to information in the absence of a denial prohibiting the access (*an open policy* [5]). However, any number of access policies can be represented in our approach by making simple modifications to the definition of *permitted* and the specification of permissions.

To see how different policies may be represented, suppose that an open policy is required such that a user *U* has the *P* permission on an object *O* if *U* is not explicitly denied this permission. For this policy, definitions of a *d-rpa(R,P,O)* predicate are included in an $RBAC_1^-$ theory instead of *rpa*. Here, *d-rpa* is short for "denied role permission assignment" and $RBAC_1^-$ is $RBAC_1$ with denials of access expressed via *d-rpa* predicates. The *d-rpa(R,P,O)* clauses in an $RBAC_1^-$ theory are used to specify that role *R* is denied the *P* permission on *O*. The required open access policy may be represented by the following (stratified) clause:

permitted(U,P,O) ← *not denied(U,P,O)*

The definition of the auxiliary *denied* relation in $RBAC_1^-$ is as follows:[†]

denied(U,P,O) ← *ura(U,R1), senior_to(R2,R1), d-rpa(R2,P,O)*

The definition of *denied* specifies that negative permissions are inherited downwards in an $RBAC_1^-$ role hierarchy (an $RBAC_1^-$ role hierarchy is as defined in $RBAC_1$). That is, if *U* is assigned to the role *R1*, the role *R2* is senior to *R1* in an $RBAC_1$ role hierarchy, and *R2* is denied the *P* permission on *O* then *R1* and hence *U* is denied *P* access on *O*. An instance of *permitted(U,P,O)* will hold in an $RBAC_1^-$ theory iff there is no instance of *denied(U,P,O)* that overrides the default assumption that *permitted(U,P,O)* holds.

Any number of hybrid (open/closed) policies may be expressed using stratified clauses, and open and closed policies may be specified as coexisting in a single theory (with *various conflict resolution policies* [9] being represented to

[†]This definition assumes that every user is assigned to at least one role and that there is a single $RBAC_1$ role hierarchy defined in an $RBAC_1$ theory.

manage situations where an instance of a *(U,P,O)* triple is both permitted and denied).

Apart from the clauses that define *permitted* (or *denied*) all other clauses in an RBAC theory are application-specific. The fact that a small number of application non-specific clauses are required to express RBAC policies is important since it makes the representation of a policy, reasoning about the policy and the maintenance of the policy relatively simple. What is more, these clauses may be equivalently represented by using only a small number of SQL statements.

In RBAC, users are usually required to be active in appropriate roles when making access requests. In our representation of $RBAC_1$ as a stratified theory, *sessions* [14] may be modeled by using an *activate(U,R1)* predicate. A ground instance of *activate(U,R1)* is appended to the $RBAC_1$ theory if user *U* successfully activates role *R1*. Conversely, a ground instance of *activate(U,R1)* is removed from an $RBAC_1$ theory if *U* deactivates role *R1*. If *activate* predicates are included in an $RBAC_1$ theory then the definition of *permitted* is extended to include an *activate(U,R1)* condition to ensure that the user *U* is active in the role *R1* at the time at which *U* makes an access request.

3. $RBAC_1$ IN SQL

We represent user-role and permission-role assignments as logic predicates that have a one-to-one correspondence with SQL tables. There is a table for *d-s* and tables for the explicit assignments of users and permissions to roles. Intensional predicates define implicit accesses; these are translated into SQL views.

Since *permitted*, *senior_to* and *d-s* are specified using definite clauses and *ura* may reasonably be assumed to be defined by a set of ground assertions, it follows that if the definitions of *rpa* clauses in an $RBAC_1$ theory are expressed in definite clause logic then the $RBAC_1$ theory will be definite. It is well known that function-free, non-recursive definite clause form theories (i.e., non-recursive Datalog theories [16]) can be translated into an equivalent set of statements in *SPCU-algebra* [1]. Since SQL is sufficiently powerful to represent any expression in a *relationally complete* language [6], it follows that SQL is sufficiently powerful to enable any formula in *SPCU*-algebra to be expressed. From [1], *SPC-algebra* expressions can be equivalently represented in SQL using the **SELECT-FROM-WHERE** construct, and the **UNION** operator of SQL corresponds to the union operator of relational algebra. For representing the recursive definition of *senior_to* in SQL, the **WITH RECURSIVE** construct is sufficient since *senior_to* is defined by a set of *linear recursive* [2] and definite clauses. If *safe* [16], function-free and recursion-free stratified clauses are used to represent the *ura* and *rpa* clauses that appear in an $RBAC_1$ theory then the theory can be equivalently represented in *SPCUD*-algebra [1]. To represent the *n* negative literals that may appear in clauses in an $RBAC_1$ theory, SQL statements that include **NOT EXISTS** (or **NOT IN**) may be used [1].

3.1. $RBAC_1$ in SQL: Representational Issues

In this section we discuss the representation of $RBAC_1$ theories in SQL. Since we assume that *ura* is a set of ground atomic assertions, the set can be represented by a table. To represent, in SQL, a clause form definition of *rpa* with a non-empty set of literals in its body that protects a relation *r*, a **CREATE VIEW** definition is used to define the subset of *r* that members of a given role are permitted to access. A **CREATE TABLE** *rpa* statement is used to record the set of permissions users have on the views and base tables in the database. In the case of the binary *ura* relation, we will assume that the attribute names used in the **CREATE TABLE** statement are *U* and *R*, for user and role respectively. For the ternary relation *rpa*, we assume that the attribute names are *R*, *P* and *O* where *R* is for role, *P* is for permission and *O* is for object. A **CREATE TABLE** statement is also required to create a 2-attribute base table corresponding to the *d-s* relation.

A special role *public* may be used to specify public access on objects. For that, we may include a *d-s*(r_i,*public*) assertion in an $RBAC_1$ theory for each role $r_i \in$ *Role(X)* (where *Role(X)* is the set of roles appearing in an $RBAC_1$ theory) such that $\neg\exists r_j[r_i \rightarrow r_j]$ holds in an $RBAC_1$ role hierarchy (where $r_j \in$ *Role(X)*). The *public* role is the unique least element in the partial order of roles that comprises an $RBAC_1$ role hierarchy (i.e., $\forall r_k \in$ *Role(X)* *senior_to*(r_k,*public*)). Appropriate instances of *rpa(public,P,O)* are added to the access policy specification to record that the *P* permission on *O* is assigned to *public*.

The *senior_to* relation may be defined in terms of **WITH RECURSIVE**. In the ensuing discussion we will assume that *senior_to* includes the pair of attributes (*senior,junior*). Each tuple (r_i,r_j) in *senior_to* records that role r_i is senior to role r_j in an $RBAC_1$ role hierarchy.

Finally, to represent *permitted*, an SQL view is used to define the set of (*U,P,O*) triples such that the user *U* has the *P* permission on *O*. The required SQL is:

```
CREATE VIEW permitted(U,P,O) AS
SELECT ura.U, rpa.P, rpa.O
FROM ura, rpa, senior_to
WHERE ura.R=senior_to.senior AND senior_to.junior=rpa.R;
```

To implement our approach, *permitted* could be stored as a *materialized view* [1] that is recomputed (in an incremental way) whenever changes are made to the relations in terms of which *permitted* is defined. Similarly, *senior_to* is stored as a materialized relation to avoid its recomputation each time an access request is evaluated; *senior_to* is recomputed each time the set of *d-s* assertions is modified.

To represent *permitted* in SQL when *activate* assertions are included in an $RBAC_1$ theory, a **CREATE TABLE** statement is required to record the set of all pairs *(U,R1)* such that the user *U* has active the role *R1*. The only modification required to the view definition of *permitted* in SQL is for the following conjunctive condition to be added to the **WHERE** clause: **AND** *ura.U=activate.U* **AND** *ura.R=activate.R*.

3.2. $RBAC_1$ in SQL: Evaluating Access Requests

To ensure that only authorized access to an SQL database is allowed, **EXISTS** subqueries, which include security information, are added to the access requests a user *U* makes. For example, if *u* is the identifier for an authenticated user requesting to retrieve all information in a table *t1* (for which read permission is required) then the required SQL is:

```
SELECT *
FROM t1
WHERE EXISTS
(SELECT * FROM permitted WHERE permitted.U='u'
AND permitted.P='read' AND permitted.O='t1');
```

The above approach has the elegance of existing entirely within the representation of $RBAC_1$ as a stratified theory. By going beyond what is representable as a single logic clause, we can implement the desired semantics of Section 2 viz.:

IF *(appended predicate)* **THEN** *(query)* **ELSE** *(error message)*

The **IF-THEN** form has two pragmatic advantages. First, it lets users distinguish between denial and empty result; second, it will be efficient even with query processors that do not handle nested predicates efficiently. With either approach, we envisage security management tools being used to modify the request before submitting it to a DBMS. Alternatively, a DBMS would be extended to handle this modification itself.

The '*u*' value in the *permitted.U* condition is taken from user *u*'s login details which are provided as part of the authentication process; the *read* value in *permitted.P='read'* comes from the fact that a request to **SELECT** is made by *u*; and the *t1* value in the *permitted.O* condition is taken from the **FROM** clause in the SQL **SELECT** statement that *u* issues. A *permitted.O=ti* (*permitted.O=vi*) condition is required for each table *ti* (view *vi*) that appears in the **FROM** clause of a **SELECT** statement and which is read protected.

Example 1 *Consider the following relations from [6]: S(Sno, Sname, Status, City) for Suppliers, P(Pno, Pname, Color, Weight, City) for Parts, J(Jno, Jname, City) for Projects, and SPJQ(Pno, Sno, Jno, Quantity) (recording the quantity of parts suppliers supply to each project). Primary keys are underlined and Pno, Sno and Jno are foreign key attributes in SPJQ. Suppose that a query, to list all project numbers for projects supplied with red parts by suppliers located in London, is posed by the authenticated user Sue on a database, Θ, that includes the S, P, J and SPJQ relations (all of which are read protected). The secure form of the SQL query on Θ is:*

```
SELECT JNo
FROM SPJQ, S, P, J, permitted
WHERE J.JNo=SPJ.JNo AND SPJQ.PNo=P.PNo AND
P.Colour='red' AND SPJQ.SNo=S.SNo AND S.City='London' AND
EXISTS(SELECT * FROM permitted WHERE permitted.U='Sue'
AND permitted.P='read' AND permitted.O='SPJQ') AND
EXISTS(SELECT * FROM permitted WHERE permitted.U='Sue'
AND permitted.P='read' AND permitted.O='S') AND
EXISTS(SELECT * FROM permitted WHERE permitted.U='Sue'
AND permitted.P='read' AND permitted.O='P') AND
EXISTS(SELECT * FROM permitted WHERE permitted.U='Sue'
AND permitted.P='read' AND permitted.O='J');
```

That is, a JNo value may be disclosed to Sue iff it is true in Θ that a project with the JNo is supplied with red parts by a supplier located in London, and Sue is authorized to read the SPJQ, S, J and P relations that are required to be accessed in order for her to know that the JNo value is true in Θ.

◇

For protecting SQL databases from unauthorized modifications the same approach as that described above is used.

Example 2 *Suppose that Sue wishes to change the color of all red parts to yellow. For that, the secure SQL is:*

```
UPDATE P
SET Color='yellow'
WHERE Color='red' AND
```

```
EXISTS(SELECT * FROM permitted WHERE permitted.O='P'
AND permitted.P='update' AND permitted.U='Sue');
```

◇

In the examples of access control that we have given, the objects that have been referred to are base tables and views. However, it is also possible to protect the individual attributes appearing in a table. For example, a tuple *(r1,read,t.a)* may be included in *rpa* to record that role *r1* is assigned the read permission on the attribute *a* in the table *t*. The access control information on attributes may be used to rewrite user access requests in a secure way by using the approach we have described.

4. BEYOND $RBAC_1$

The $RBAC_1$ policy that we have described thus far is a simple one and could be represented in some existing RDBMSs. However, an attraction of our approach is that it can be extended to implement various access policies that cannot be represented in existing RDBMSs, and without requiring any language features beyond those included in SQL. Since access requirements are often application and organization-specific, the flexibility that our approach offers is important in practice.

To demonstrate the power of our approach, we consider the representation of a hybrid access control policy which allows positive permissions to be expressed using *rpa* definitions and denials to be expressed via *d-rpa* definitions. The denials may be used to override positive permissions (i.e., a *denials take precedence* conflict resolution policy is enforced [9]). The set of authorized accesses may be represented in stratified logic thus (where *permitted* and *denied* are as defined in Section 3):

access(U,P,O) ← permitted(U,P,O), not denied(U,P,O)

The *access* clause specifies that *U* has the *P* permission on *O* if *U* has been assigned the *P* permission on *O* and this (positive) permission is not overridden by a denial of *P* access on *O* to *U*.

The translation of *access* into SQL produces the following view definition (where *permitted* and *denied* are views defined in SQL):

```
CREATE VIEW access(U,P,O) AS
SELECT * FROM permitted
WHERE NOT EXISTS(SELECT * FROM denied);
```

The conditional form used in this case would be:

IF NOT *denied* **THEN** *(user query)* **ELSE** *(error message)*

A natural generalization is to allow the assignment of limited permissions. Instead of simply assigning a permission to a role (a pair, easily represented by a table), one may also attach a *limitation predicate* [13] to be evaluated before the permission can be used. In this case, the SQL will include the limitation predicate in the appended condition. Moreover, any number of access policies may be represented by using the approach we have described.‡

5. $RBAC_3$ IN SQL

In this section, we consider the representation of constraints and thus $RBAC_3$ policies in stratified logic and SQL. The high-level nature of stratified logic makes it easy for a SA to express constraints (albeit a GUI may be used to help a SA to formulate constraints). Moreover, the translation of constraints expressed in stratified logic into SQL can be easily and efficiently automated.

In our approach, constraints may be expressed in denial form viz: $\leftarrow L1,L2,....,Ln$ (where Li $(i=(1..n))$ is a literal and $n > 0$). The reading of this statement is that it is impossible for the conjunction of literals $L1 \wedge L2 \wedge \ldots \wedge Ln$ to evaluate to true (be satisfied) in a $RBAC_3$ theory. Since denials may be expressed using constants or variables, it is possible for a SA to make the constraints on an $RBAC_3$ theory as specific or as general as is required. However, we believe that constraints should be written in as general a form as is possible, and should be specialized at the time of checking by using application-specific assertions in an $RBAC_3$ theory. These assertions may be represented by using base tables in the SQL representation of an $RBAC_3$ theory, and enable Nicolas' Simplification Method [11] to be exploited when checking constraints.

Constraints expressed in denial form have a very straightforward representation as assertions in SQL. To see that, consider a *static separation of duty* constraint [14] expressed thus:

$$\leftarrow ura(U,R1),ura(U,R2),ssd(R1,R2)$$

This constraint specifies that: it is impossible for a user to be recorded in an $RBAC_3$ theory as being assigned to a pair $(R1,R2)$ of roles that are specified as being statically separated. A set of *ssd* assertions is used to record specific pairs of roles that are statically separated. To represent the set of *ssd* assertions in SQL, a **CREATE TABLE** $ssd(role\ T_i, excluded\ T_j)$ statement may be used (where T_i and T_j are the types associated with the attributes *role* and *excluded* (i.e., roles)). The *ssd* table is populated with tuples consisting of a pair of values

‡For example, the temporal authorization model described in [4].

(r_i,r_j) (where $r_i,r_j \in Role(X)$). Because of the symmetry of the *ssd* relation, the *ssd* table will additionally include the pair of roles (r_j,r_i) $(i \neq j)$.

Since a denial expresses negation and variables are universally quantified, $\leftarrow L1, L2, \ldots, Ln$ may be expressed by the universally closed sentence $\forall\neg(L1 \wedge L2 \wedge \ldots \wedge Ln)$ and thus the existentially closed sentence $\neg\exists(L1 \wedge L2 \wedge .. \wedge Ln)$. Hence, to express the *ssd* constraint in SQL the following statement may be used and is checked each time a tuple is inserted into *ura*:

```
CREATE ASSERTION ssd CHECK
NOT EXISTS
(SELECT subject, ssd.role, ssd.excluded
FROM ura U1, ura U2, ssd
WHERE U1.S=U2.S AND U1.R=ssd.role AND U2.R=ssd.excluded);
```

Unfortunately, the **ASSERTION** above involves some expensive join conditions. A more efficient approach is to use triggers.[§]

To formally specify triggers, *range form* formulae may be used [8]. A statement is in range form if it is an existentially quantified first order sentence. Constraints expressed in range form have a simple translation into an equivalent SQL form. Equivalence here means that if a change to an $RBAC_3$ theory does not violate a constraint *I* expressed in denial form or its equivalent range form then the change to the $RBAC_3$ theory expressed in SQL is not rejected by the representation of *I* as a trigger in SQL. The translation of constraints in range form into SQL can be easily and efficiently automated. Moreover, it is simple to enforce assertions *incrementally* by triggers whose logic exploits the fact that before the current update the constraint was satisfied.

As is usual in RDBMSs, we assume that two cached and user inaccessible relations *inserted* and *deleted* exist with *n* attributes corresponding to the degree of the table into which a tuple is to be inserted or deleted (in the sequel we will use the notation *r.i* to refer to the *i*-th argument of the tuple to be inserted/deleted from an arbitrary relation *r*). The *inserted* (*deleted*) relation is used to store the tuples to be inserted (deleted) in a change transaction on an $RBAC_3$ theory. The triggers that define the constraints on an $RBAC_3$ theory represented in SQL may be expressed in terms of violations of the constraint by specifying that a **ROLLBACK** action is to be performed if the constraint is violated.

For the *ssd* constraint, the required trigger is as follows (see [8] for details of the translation of range form into trigger form):

```
CREATE TRIGGER ON ura FOR INSERT
```

[§] Triggers are proposed for inclusion in the SQL3 standard and are already supported in commercial RDBMSs.

```
IF(EXISTS (SELECT * FROM inserted WHERE
EXISTS (SELECT * FROM ura u1, ssd
WHERE u1.user=inserted.1 AND inserted.2=ssd.role) AND
EXISTS (SELECT * FROM ura u2, ssd WHERE ssd.excluded=u2.role)))
ROLLBACK
```

The meaning of this SQL statement is as follows: if (u_i,r_j) is the pair of values in the *ura* tuple that is proposed for insertion into an $RBAC_3$ theory, u_i is also recorded as being assigned to a role r_k in *ura*, and (r_j,r_k) is a tuple in the table *ssd* that records pairs of roles that are statically separated then the insert request is rolled back since otherwise the *ssd* constraint on an $RBAC_3$ theory would be violated.

Any number of other types of (static) constraint on an $RBAC_3$ theory (e.g., cardinality constraints on roles) can be represented in essentially the same way that *ssd* is.

6. CONCLUSIONS AND FURTHER WORK

The great challenge for improving the formulation of access control policies is to provide practitioners with usable, high-level constructs which possess clear semantics. We have shown how that can be done. The approach that we have described enables a SA to specify a variety of access control policies using elements of RBAC that map directly into stratified logic. Moreover, we have demonstrated how these constructs can be implemented by using a small subset of SQL3.

The development of tools for the translation of RBAC theories into SQL is a matter for further work. We also intend to investigate how the proof procedures used in stratified logic may be exploited to help administrators to reason about the access control policies they specify.

References

[1] Abiteboul, S., Hull, R., and Vianu, V., *Foundations of Databases*, Addison Wesley, 1995.

[2] Bancilhon, F., Maier, D., Sagiv, Y., and Ullman, J., Magic Sets and Other Strange Ways to Implement Logic Programs, *Proc. ACM PODS*, 1-15, 1986.

[3] Barker, S., Data Protection by Logic Programming, *1st International Conf. on Computational Logic (CL2000)*, LNAI 1861, 1300-1313, Springer, 2000.

[4] Barker, S., and Rosenthal, A., Flexible Security Policies in SQL, *Proc. 15th IFIP Conf. on Database Security*, 2001. Also available at http://www.mitre.org/resources/centers/it/staffpages/arnie/

[5] Castano, S., Fugini, M., Martella, G., and Samarati, P., *Database Security*, Addison Wesley, 1995.

[6] Date, C., *An Introduction to Database Systems*, Addison Wesley, 2000.

[7] Date, C., and Darwen, A., *A Guide to the SQL Standard*, Addison Wesley, 1993.

[8] Decker, H., Soundcheck for SQL, *3rd International Symposium on Practical Applications of Declarative Languages (PADL'01)*, LNCS 1990, Springer, 214-228, 2001.

[9] Jajodia, S., Samarati, P., and Subrahmanian, V., A Logical Language for Expressing Authorizations, *IEEE Symp. on Security and Privacy*, 94-107, 1997.

[10] Lloyd, J., *Foundations of Logic Programming*, 2nd Ed., Springer, 1987.

[11] Nicolas, J., Logic for Improving Integrity Checking in Relational Databases, *Acta Informatica*, 18(3), 227-253, 1982.

[12] Przymusinski, T., Perfect Model Semantics, *Proc. 5th ICLP*, MIT Press, 1081-1096, 1988.

[13] Rosenthal, A., and Sciore, E., Extending SQL's Grant and Revoke Operations to Limit and Reactivate Privileges, *Proc. 14th IFIP Conf. on Database Security*, 2000.

[14] Sandhu, R., Coyne, E., Feinstein, H., and Youman, C., Role-Based Access Control Models, *IEEE Computer*, 29(2), 38-47, 1996.

[15] Stonebraker, M., Implementation of Integrity Constraints and Views by Query Modification, *Proc. SIGMOD Workshop on Management of Data*, 65-78, 1975.

[16] Ullman, J., *Principles of Database and Knowledge-Base Systems: Volume 1*, Computer Science Press, 1990.

THE INFERENCE PROBLEM AND UPDATES IN RELATIONAL DATABASES

Csilla Farkas
Department of Computer Science and Engineering
University of South Carolina, Columbia, SC 29208
farkas@cse.sc.edu

Tyrone S. Toland
Department of Computer Science and Engineering
University of South Carolina, Columbia, SC 29208
toland@cse.sc.edu

Caroline M. Eastman
Department of Computer Science and Engineering
University of South Carolina, Columbia, SC 29208
eastman@cse.sc.edu

Abstract In this paper, we extend the Disclosure Monitor (DiMon) security mechanism (Brodsky et al. [1]) to prevent illegal inferences via database constraints in dynamic databases. We study updates from two perspectives: 1) updates on tuples that were previously released to a user may cause that tuple to be "outdated", thus providing greater freedom for releasing new tuples; 2) observation of changes in released tuples may create cardinality based inferences, which are not indicated by database dependencies. We present a mechanism, called *Update Consolidator* (UpCon) that propagates updates to the user's history file to ensure that no query is rejected based on outdated data. We also propose a *Cardinality Inference Detection* (CID) module, that generates all data that can be disclosed via cardinality based attacks. We show that UpCon and CID, when integrated into the DiMon architecture, guarantee *confidentiality* (completeness property of the data-dependent disclosure inference algorithm) and maximal *availability* (soundness property of the data-dependent disclosure inference algorithm) even in the presence of updates.

Keywords: disclosure inference, confidentiality, availability, updates, access control.

1. INTRODUCTION

During the last couple of decades, our society became increasingly dependent on computerized information resources. Electronic databases contain information with sensitivity levels ranging from public (e.g., airline schedules, phone numbers, and addresses) to highly sensitive (e.g., financial and medical information, military research). The aim of information security policies is to protect the *confidentiality* (secrecy) and *integrity* of data, while ensuring data *availability*. Access control mechanisms, such as discretionary and mandatory access control, prevent unauthorized, direct accesses to data. However, they are unable to protect against indirect data accesses, when unauthorized information is obtained via inference channels.

Most of the inference channels in relational databases are created by combining *meta-data* (e.g., database constraints) with non-sensitive data to obtain sensitive information. Techniques to detect and remove inference channels can be organized into two categories. The first category includes techniques that detect inference channels during database design time [2, 3, 7, 8, 11, 14, 15, 17, 18, 20]. Inference channels are removed by modifying the database design and/or by increasing the classification levels of some of the data items. The techniques of the second category seek to eliminate inference channel violations during query processing time [5, 10, 12, 13, 16, 19]. If an inference channel is detected, the query is either refused or modified to avoid security violations. While, in general, database design time approaches are computationally less expensive and may provide better online performance than query processing time approaches, database design time approaches often result in over-classification of data items, thus reducing data availability. Query processing time approaches allow greater availability by analyzing the data released to the user to determine whether a security violation is present or not.

Updates in multilevel secure databases have been studied from the perspective of how to perform updates safely, creating the problem of polyinstantiation [6, 9]. The main problem is that users with different security levels see different versions of a multilevel secure database. Updates may create inconsistencies among these versions (e.g., inserting a new tuple with an existing but invisible primary key) or create downward signaling channels (e.g., rejection of an update because of the existence of a high security data item).

In this paper we study updates from a different perspective. Instead of addressing the problem of how to ensure secure updates, we focus on how updates can increase data availability due to outdated data. Our work extends the Disclosure Monitor (DiMon) model presented by Brodsky et al.[1]. DiMon detects and eliminates inference channels created by database constraints by using a Disclosure Inference Engine(DiIE) that generates all information that can be disclosed based on a user's previous queries (results), the current query (result) and a set of Horn-Clause constraints. The disclosure inference algorithms by the properties of *soundness* and *completeness*. Intuitively, soundness means that only existing disclosure inferences are generated by the algorithm (data availability); completeness means that all existing disclosure inferences are generated (secrecy).

However, Brodsky et al. do not consider dynamic databases where updates may lead to cardinality based inferences or may violate the soundness property of the data-dependent disclosure inference algorithm. The following two examples show a proper execution of DiMon (first example) and an execution that violates the soundness property (second example). Consider the original *Employee* relation in Table 1, containing information about the name, rank, salary, and department of employees. The relation satisfies the functional dependency (FD) $RANK \rightarrow SALARY$. The security requirement is that the employees' salaries should be kept confidential; that is, partial tuples over attributes *NAME* and *SALARY* can only be accessed by authorized users. However, to increase data availability, unauthorized users are allowed to access values for *NAME* and *SALARY* separately.

Suppose an unauthorized user submits the following two queries:

Query 1: "List the name and rank of the employees working in the Toy department." $(\Pi_{NAME,RANK}\sigma_{DEPARTMENT='Toy'})$

Query 2: "List the salaries of all clerks." $(\Pi_{SALARY}\sigma_{RANK='Clerk'})$

The answers to these queries are:

Query 1: $\{< John, Clerk >, < Mary, Secretary >\}$

Query 2: $\{< Clerk, 38,000 >\}$

Since the *Employee* relation satisfies the FD $RANK \rightarrow SALARY$, these answers reveal that John's salary is \$38,000. These kinds of inferences are correctly detected by DiIE.

Now, consider the following series of events when the *Employee* relation is updated between the queries. **Time 1**: User submits Query 1, **Time 2**: Salaries of all clerks are raised by 4%, **Time 3**: Employee John is promoted to the rank "Manager", and **Time 4**: User submits Query 2. The answers of the two queries are:

Query 1: $\{< John, Clerk >, < Mary, Secretary >\}$, (same as in the first scenario)

Query 2: $\{< Clerk, 39,520 >\}$

The second relation of Table 1 shows the updated *Employee* relation (Query 2). In this case, DiIE would indicate that subtuple $< John, 39,520 >$ is disclosed and, since it is confidential, Query 2 should be rejected. However, this subtuple is not contained in the updated relation and has never been present in any of the earlier versions. Therefore, the second query could be safely answered. The reason for this is that the FD was applied on data values that have been modified. We call inferences that were established on outdated (i.e., modified)

Table 1. *Employee* relation

ID	*NAME*	*RANK*	*SALARY*	*DEPT.*
1	John	Clerk	38,000	Toy
2	Mary	Secretary	28,000	Toy
3	Chris	Secretary	28,000	Marketing
4	Joe	Manager	45,000	Appliance
5	Sam	Clerk	38,000	Appliances
6	Eve	Manager	45,000	Marketing

Original

ID	*NAME*	*RANK*	*SALARY*	*DEPT*
1	John	Manager	45,000	Toy
2	Mary	Secretary	28,000	Toy
3	Chris	Secretary	28,000	Marketing
4	Joe	Manager	45,000	Appliances
5	Sam	Clerk	39,520	Appliances
6	Eve	Manager	45,000	Marketing

Updated

data values "wrong" inferences. We will permit queries that generate "wrong" inferences to increase availability.

In this paper we propose a conceptual framework, called Dynamic Disclosure Monitor (D^2Mon), that guarantees data confidentiality and maximal availability even in the presence of inferences and updates. Our work extends the DiMon [1] model by taking into consideration that the data items received by a user may have been updated and are not valid any longer. To the authors' best knowledge, this is the first work that considers updates from the perspective of increased data availability. We propose formal characterizations of the effects of updates. We also study the cardinality inference problem that is created by observing changes in query answers over a period of time. Our model addresses both inferences via generalized database dependencies (represented as Horn-Clause constraints) and cardinality based (statistical) inferences within the same framework.

We develop a security mechanism, called *Update Consolidator* (UpCon) that, given a user's history file, updates on the base relation, and the database constraints, generates a new history file that marks outdated data values and indicates only valid inferences. All updates on the base relation are recorded in an update log. The history file of a user contains all data that the user previously received or can be disclosed from the received answers. When a new query is submitted by a user, the history file is modified according to the updates that have happened since the history file was last created. Each modified data value in the history file is stamped with the new, modified value. Intuitively, a stamped value means that the value is no longer valid, and the new value, that is unknown to the user, is the stamp. Stamping will prevent the disclosure inference algorithm from indicating a disclosure based on outdated values (soundness) while maintaining maximal equalities among modified data values, thus allowing maximal dependency application (completeness). We show that with the use of UpCon the Data-Dependent Disclosure Inference Algorithm [1] is *sound* and *complete* even in the presence of updates.

Moreover, we recommend a *Cardinality Inference Detection* (CID) mechanism. This module can detect illegal inferences based on small query set size, query overlap, complementary attacks and aggregation based attacks. Since CID may detect a disclosure of a partial secret which, when combined with database dependencies, discloses a secret (DiIE) and vice verse; CID and DiIE work together until no more changes occur.

The paper is organized as follows. In the next section we describe our Dynamic Disclosure Monitor architecture. Section 3 contains the preliminaries and our notations. In Section 4 we present our Update Consolidator and Cardinality Inference Detection mechanisms. Finally, we conclude our research in Section 5 and recommend future extensions.

2. SECURITY ARCHITECTURE

2.1. Dynamic Disclosure Monitor

Our model is built upon the Disclosure Monitor (DiMon) security architecture, developed by Brodsky et al. [1], to protect data confidentiality against illegal inferences in Multilevel Secure (MLS) relational databases. However, DiMon addresses the inference problem in static databases, and thus may overprotect information due to some already modified data values (see the second example in the Introduction). Our extended architecture, called Dynamic Disclosure Monitor (D^2Mon), incorporates this liberating effect of updates, while still guaranteeing that no unauthorized disclosure is possible via data requests. Note, that we assume that updates are performed in a secure way, i.e., we do not consider covert channels created by updates. We propose two extensions to DiMon: 1) an Update Consolidator (UpCon) module that incorporates the effects of the updates on the history files maintained for each user; and 2) a Cardinality Inference Detection (CID) module that detects illegal inferences based on the cardinality of the released answers. The functionality of D^2Mon is shown in Figure 1. The shaded modules represent the components of DiMon. The actual algorithm of D^2Mon is given in Figure 2. The additional features of D^2Mon over DiMon are used when Disclosure Inference Engine (DiIE) works in data-dependent mode. Clearly, in data-independent mode when the actual data items received by a user are not known by DiIE, updates made on the base relation will not effect the processing of DiIE.

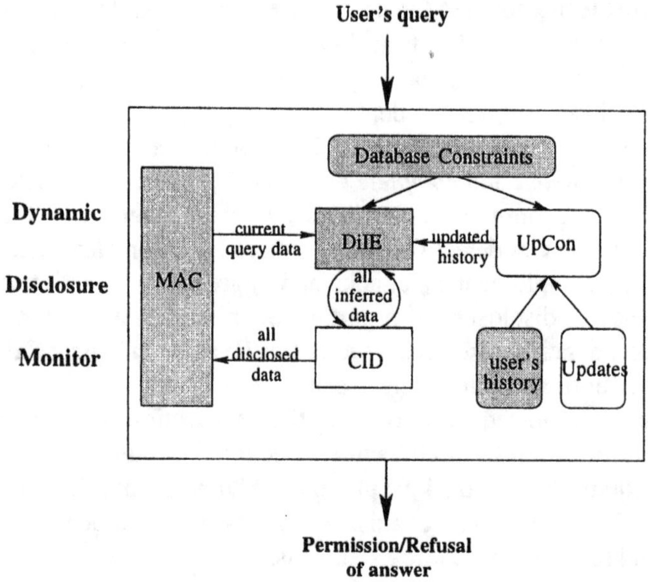

Figure 1. Dynamic Disclosure Monitor

3. PRELIMINARIES AND NOTATIONS

Before explaining the functionality of the *Update Consolidator* (UpCon) we need to modify the concept of data-dependent disclosure in dynamic databases and introduce some related concepts. We require that each tuple within the database has a unique tuple identifier ID that is maintained internally and not released to the user. Table 1 shows the original *Employee* relation with tuple identifiers. When a new record is added to the database, a unique ID is assigned to it. Modifications to the database are stored in the update log, which we will now define.

Definition 3.1 (Update)
Given a schema R and a relation r over R, an *update* UP on r is a 5-tuple of the form $(t, id, att, v_{old}, v_{new})$, where t is the time of the update, id is the identifier of the tuple in r that is being updated, att is the attribute name that is being updated such that $att \in R$, and v_{old}, v_{new} are the old and the new (updated) values of att, respectively such that $v_{old}, v_{new} \in dom(att) \cup \{-\}$. The special symbol $-$ is used to represent new values of the attributes when the update is a deletion.

Consider the examples presented in the Introduction. The updates at times t_2 and t_3 are recorded as follows: $\mathcal{UP} = (t_2, 1, SALARY, 38,000, 39,520)$, $(t_2, 5, SALARY, 38,000, 39,520)$, $(t_3, 1, RANK, Clerk, Manager)$,

Algorithm 1: Dynamic Disclosure Monitor (D^2Mon)
INPUT
1. User's query (object) Q_i 2. User's id U 3. Security classification $< \mathcal{O}, \mathcal{U}, \lambda >$ 4. User's history-file $U_{history}$: data which were previously retrieved by the user 5. $\mathcal{D}$, a set of database constraints
OUTPUT
Answer to Q_i and update of the user's history-file or refusal of Q_i
METHOD

MAC evaluates direct security violations:
IF direct security violation is detected **THEN** Q_i is rejected
(D^2Mon functions as the basic MAC mechanism)
ELSE (no direct security violation was detected)
BEGIN
1 Use *Update Consolidator* (UpCon) to modify $U_{history}$ according to the relevant updates to create $U_{updated-history}$
2 Let $U_{all-disclosed} = U_{updated-history} \cup Q_i(answers)$
begin
Repeat until no change occurs:
(a) Use *Disclosure Inference Engine* (DiIE) to generate all data that can be disclosed from the $U_{all-disclosed}$ and the *database constraints* $\mathcal{D}$
$U_{all-disclosed} = U_{all-disclosed} \cup U_{newly-disclosed}$
(b) Use *Cardinality Inference Detection* (CID) to find all data that can be disclosed by cardinality inferences
$U_{all-disclosed} = U_{all-disclosed} \cup U_{newly-disclosed}$
end
3 MAC reevaluates security violations in $U_{all-disclosed}$:
IF illegal disclosure is detected **THEN** reject Q_i and
$U_{history} = U_{updated-history}$
4 **ELSE** (security is not violated) answer Q_i and
$U_{history} = U_{all-disclosed}$
END

Figure 2. Algorithm for Dynamic Disclosure Monitoring

$(t_3, 1, SALARY, 39, 520, 45, 000)$. We represent updates on tuples which were previously released to a user by "stamping" these values with the new value. For this, we need the notion of a stamped attribute value.

Definition 3.2 (Stamped Attribute)
Let A be an attribute name and $dom(A) = a_1, \ldots, a_l$ the domain of A. A *stamped attribute* SA is an attribute such that its value sa is of the form

${a_i}^{a_j}$ $(i, j = 1, \ldots, l)$. We call a_i the value of SA and a_j is the stamp or updated value of the stamped attribute SA.

For example, assume that the user has received the tuple $< Clerk, 38,000 >$ over the attributes *RANK* and *SALARY*. If at a later time the salaries of the clerks are modified, e.g, increased to \$39,520, the corresponding tuples in the history file are stamped as follows $< Clerk, 38,000^{39,520} >$.

Definition 3.3 (Equalities of Stamped Attributes)
Given two stamped attributes $sa = {a_i}^{a_j}$ and $sb = {b_i}^{b_j}$, we say that $sa = sb$ *iff* $a_i = b_i$ and $a_j = b_j$. Given a stamped attribute $sa = {a_i}^{a_j}$ and a non-stamped attribute b, we say that $sa = b$ *iff* $a_i = b$ and $a_i = a_j$.

Next, we need the notion of projection facts and stamped projection facts which are manipulated by the DiIE.

Definition 3.4 (Projection Fact)
A *projection fact* (PF) of type $A_1, \ldots, A_k$, where $A_1, \ldots, A_k$ are attributes in R, is a mapping m from $\{A_1, \ldots, A_k\}$ to $\bigcup_{j=1}^{k} dom(A_j) \cup \bigcup_{j=1}^{k} dom(SA_j)$ such that $m(A_j) \in dom(A_j) \cup dom(SA_j)$ for all $j = 1, \ldots, k$. A projection fact is denoted by an expression of the form $R[A_1 = v_1, \ldots, A_k = v_k]$ where R is the relation name, and $v_1, \ldots, v_k$ are values of attributes $A_1, \ldots, A_k$, respectively.

A *stamped projection fact* (SPF) is a projection fact $R[A_1 = v_1, \ldots, A_k = v_k]$, where at least one of v_j $(j = 1, \ldots, k)$ is a stamped attribute.

A *non-stamped projection fact*, or simply a projection fact, is a projection fact $R[A_1 = v_1, \ldots, A_k = v_k]$, where all v_js are constants in $dom(A_j)$.

For example, $Employee[NAME = John, Rank = Clerk]$ is a projection fact, and $Employee[NAME = John, Rank = Clerk^{Manager}]$ is a stamped projection fact.

Definition 3.5 (Un-Stamping a Stamped Projection Fact)
Given a SPF of the form $R[A_1 = a_1^{b_1}, \ldots, A_k = a_k^{b_k}]$, where some of the b_i $(i = 1, \ldots, k)$ may not exist. The un-stamped projection fact PF is generated from SPF by simply removing the stamps of SPF, i.e., $PF = R[A_1 = a_1, \ldots, A_k = a_k]$

Definition 3.6 (Query-answer pair)
An *atomic query-answer pair* (QA-pair) is an expression of the form $(P, \Pi_Y \sigma_C)$, where P is a projection fact over Y that satisfies C or P is a stamped projection fact, such that the un-stamped projection fact generated from P satisfies C. A query-answer pair is either an atomic QA-pair or an expression of the form $(\mathcal{P}, \Pi_Y \sigma_C)$, where $\mathcal{P}$ is a set of (stamped) projection facts $\{P_1, \ldots, P_l\}$ such that every P_i, $(i = 1, \ldots, l)$ is over Y and satisfies C.

Definition 3.7 (Dynamic data-dependent disclosure)
Let $\mathcal{D}$ be a set of database constraints, $\mathcal{UP}=\{UP_1,\ldots,UP_m\}$ be a set of updates, $P_1,\ldots,P_n$ be sets of projection facts over attribute sets $X_1,\ldots,X_n$, PF be a projection fact over Y, and $t_1 \leq \ldots \leq t_n \leq t$ are times. We say that the set $\mathcal{P}=\{[(P_1,\Pi_{X_1}\sigma_{C_1}),t_1],\ldots,[(P_n,\Pi_{X_n}\sigma_{C_n}),t_n]\}$ *discloses* $[(PF,\Pi_Y\sigma_C),t]$ under database constraints $\mathcal{D}$ and in the presence of updates $\mathcal{UP}$, if
1) there is no update recorded on P_is ($i = 1,\ldots,n$) between t_n and t, and
2) for every $r_0, r_1,\ldots,r_n, r$ over R, that all satisfy $\mathcal{D}$, $P_i \subseteq \Pi_{X_i}\sigma_{C_i}(r_i)[t_i]$ ($i = 1,\ldots,n$) implies $PF \in \Pi_Y\sigma_C(r)[t]$, where r_0 is the original relation and r_i ($i = 1,\ldots,n$), r are the relations generated from r_0 by the updates in $\mathcal{UP}$, respectively. Dynamic data-dependent disclosure is denoted as $\mathcal{P}\models_{\mathcal{UP},\mathcal{D}}[(PF,\Pi_Y\sigma_C),t]$.

We denote by $[(PF,\Pi_Y\sigma_C),t_1] \models_{\mathcal{UP}} [(PF',\Pi_{Y'}\sigma_{C'}),t_2]$ the disclosure $\{[(PF,\Pi_Y\sigma_C),t_1]\} \models_{\mathcal{UP},\mathcal{D}} [(PF',\Pi_{Y'}\sigma_{C'}),t_2]$, where $\mathcal{D}$ is empty. In this case, we say that $[(PF,\Pi_Y\sigma_C),t_1]$ *dominates* $[(PF',\Pi_{Y'}\sigma_{C'}),t_2]$.

The above definition requires that all updates are performed according to the database constraints; that is, if a relation r satisfies the set of constraints $\mathcal{D}$ before an update, it will also satisfy $\mathcal{D}$ after the update. Furthermore, disclosure is established based on updated tuples rather than the originally released tuples. Intuitively, this may allow a user, who is unaware of the update, to generate a fact that may have never existed in the base relation or is not valid any longer. In either case, we allow such "wrong" inferences, since our goal is to prevent disclosure of valid sensitive data.

By extending the concepts of projection fact and query-answer pairs to incorporate stamped attributes, DiIE can operate on relations containing regular attribute values (constants), stamped attribute values, and null-values. In the following section we develop the Update Consolidator (UpCon) module that creates a new input history file for DiIE by stamping those attribute values that have been modified by an update operation.

4. UPDATE AND CARDINALITY INFERENCES

In this section we introduce our remaining extensions, the Update Consolidator (UpCon) and the Cardinality Inference Detection (CID) modules.

4.1. Update Consolidator

As we illustrated in the Introduction, in dynamic databases it may happen that answers received by a user may not be valid any longer after an update. Clearly, if we refuse a new request of the user based on some outdated data value we unnecessarily limit data access. Update Consolidator (UpCon) propagates updates that happened between the current and the last answered query to the user's history file. For this we require that every tuple of the relation has a unique

Table 2. The *User's* history file after Query 2

ID	*NAME*	*RANK*	*SALARY*	*DEPARTMENT*
1	John	$\text{Clerk}^{Manager}$	δ_1	Toy
2	Mary	Secretary	δ_2	Toy
5	δ_3	Clerk	39,520	Toy

identifier and all original answers (after the application of selection conditions on the answers) are kept permanently. Also, we keep track of the database dependencies D that were previously applied on the history-file. Figure 4 shows the algorithm of UpCon. Table 2 shows the stamped history file (tuples 1 and 2) and the incorporated answer of Query 2. Clearly, in this case the FD $RANK \rightarrow SALARY$ cannot be applied, since *Clerk*^{Manager} $\neq$*Clerk*.

Theorem 1 (Dynamic Data Decidability)
The following problem is decidable: Given a set $\mathcal{D}$ of database constraints, a set of updates $\mathcal{UP}$, and a set $\mathcal{P}$ of QA-pairs with the time when the QA-pairs have been generated, whether $\mathcal{P} \models_{\mathcal{UP},\mathcal{D}} S$ for a given set S of atomic QA-pairs.

Theorem 1 will be a corollary to Theorem 2 that states correctness (i.e., soundness and completeness) of DiIE in the presence of updates.

Proposition 4.1 *Given a set $D = d_1, \ldots, d_k$ dependencies that can be applied by DiIE on a set of projection facts S, i.e., projection facts without stamped attributes. Then at most $D = d_1, \ldots, d_k$ can be applied on S', a set of stamped projection facts generated from S by stamping some of the attribute values.*

Proofsketch 4.1 Assume by contradiction that a dependency d_m can be applied on S' but not on S and that $d_m \notin D$. Since a dependency can be applied only if we can find a valuation from the body of the dependency to the (stamped) projection facts, such valuation must exist from the body of d_m to S'. Since stamping cannot introduce new equalities (Definition 3.3) there must also exist a valuation from the body of d_m to S, thus d_m is applicable on S, which contradicts our original assumption.

Theorem 2 The data-dependent disclosure inference algorithm is *sound* and *complete* when used with UpCon.

Proofsketch 4.2 To prove Theorem 2 we use that the Data-Dependent Disclosure Algorithm is sound and complete in static databases. This is a special case of dynamic data-dependent disclosure (Definition 3.7), when $UP = \emptyset$, thus $r = r_1 = \ldots = r_n$. Then, we need only to show that stamping a released data value will not incorrectly modify a history file, i.e., all valid equalities

Algorithm 2: Update Consolidator (UpCon)
INPUT
1. Time of last query $time_{last}$ 2. Time of current query $time_{current}$ 3. Update log $\mathcal{UP}=\{up_1, up_2, \ldots, up_m\}$ 4. User's history-file $U_{history}$ 5. DA, a set of database constraints previously applied on $U_{history}$
OUTPUT
Updated history-file of the user $U_{updated-history}$
METHOD

Construct $TUP = \{up_1, up_2, \ldots, up_l\}$ (temporary update file) from $\mathcal{UP}$ such that
■ $time_{last} \leq up_i[t] \leq time_{current}$, where $up_i[t]$ is the time of the update, and
■ there exists a tuple t_j in $U_{history}$ such that $up_i[id] = t_j[id]$, $up_i[id]$ is the identifier of the tuple that has been updated and $t_j[id]$ is the identifier of the tuple t_j in $U_{history}$.
IF *TUP*$\neq \emptyset$ (i.e., updates occurred on the tuples of the base relations from which some of the released tuples originated) **THEN**
BEGIN
1 $U_{history} = U_{history} - \{t \; if \; t[id] ='' 999''$ (drop inferred tuples)
2 For every $up_i = (t, id, att, old, new) \in TUP$ **DO**
■ Find tuple t in $U_{history}$ such that $t_{id} = id$
■ Stamp value *old* of attribute *att* in t with value *new*
3 $U_{updated-history} = U_{history}$
4 Chase $U_{updated-history}$ with DA.
END

Figure 3. Update Consolidator

exploited by the inference algorithm to apply a database dependency remain intact (completeness) and only the valid equalities are present (soundness).

Since stamping an attribute value only reduces possible equalities, and therefore, possible application of the dependencies, the proof of preserving the soundness property is straight forward.

The proof of completeness is constructed as follows: assume by contradiction that a tuple t is correctly disclosed from the originally released tuples, the current query answer, the database dependencies and the updates but t was not generated by DiIE applied on the stamped history file. Since the Data-Dependent Inference Algorithm, used by DiIE is complete and t is disclosed, DiIE must generate a tuple that dominates t if the originally released tuples, the current query answer and the database dependencies are given as input. t

clearly cannot be one of the originally released tuples, because those are stored in the stamped history and stamps are only added according to the updates. But then, t must have been generated by a sequence of dependency applications $d_1, \ldots, d_l$. But since the updates satisfied the database dependencies and t is correctly disclosed based on valid inferences then $d_1, \ldots, d_l$ must be applicable on the stamped history file. But then, $d_1, \ldots, d_l$ would have been applicable on the stamped history file, and DiIE would have created a tuple that coincides with t on the non-stamped attributes. This is a contradiction of our original assumption.

4.2. Cardinality Inference Detection (CID)

In this section we present an additional module to detect inferences based on the cardinalities of the query answers. Similar inferences have been considered in statistical databases (see Denning [4] for an overview) and protection techniques have been recommended. CID protects against illegal inferences due to small query set size, query overlap, complementary inferences, and data aggregation. CID and DiIE share their output repeatedly, until all possible inferences are detected. Due to space limitations, CID is not described in details in this paper.

5. CONCLUSIONS AND FUTURE WORK

In this paper we present a Dynamic Disclosure Monitor architecture that guarantees data confidentiality and maximal data availability in the presence of inferences based on database constraint and updates. We propose two extensions of DiMon to incorporate the effects of updates in order to increase data availability and decrease the risk of cardinality inferences: 1) UpCon uses the user's existing history file, updates that occurred, and the database constraints to generate a new history file that does not contain any outdated data values; 2) CID checks for cardinality based inferences, such as small query set size, query overlap, complementary inferences, and data aggregation. CID and DiIE share their output repeatedly, until all possible inferences are detected. We show that using UpCon with DiIE will guarantee data secrecy (completeness property of inference algorithm) and data availability (soundness property of inference algorithm) in the presence of inferences via database constraints.

We conclude with suggestions for further work. Currently we are developing a prototype of DiMon and its extensions to D^2Mon. We use Java to express the security requirements and implement the disclosure inference algorithms. Completion of the prototype will allow us to provide experimental results in addition to theoretical evaluation of the model. In addition, we recommend the following improvements: Currently the model allows all "wrong" inferences, regardless of whether they reveal data items that had previously existed in the relation or not. However, in certain applications even outdated data might be sensitive, i.e., that John, as a clerk, earned $38,000. Our update-log based model can be extended to allow distinction of the different kind of inferences.

Also, this paper focuses on multiple attacks of a single user. However in a real-life situation, malicious users can share information, thus obtaining data for which they do not have the proper authorization. Users likely to share information could be grouped together to prevent security violations via collaborating users.

References

[1] A. Brodsky, C. Farkas, and S. Jajodia. Secure databases: Constraints, inference channels, and monitoring disclosure. *IEEE Trans. Knowledge and Data Eng.*, November, 2000.

[2] L.J. Buczkowski. Database inference controller. In D.L. Spooner and C. Landwehr, editors, *Database Security III: Status and Prospects*, pages 311–322. North-Holland, Amsterdam, 1990.

[3] S. Dawson, S.De Capitani di Vimercati, and P. Samarati. Specification and enforcement of classification and inference constraints. In *Proc. of the 20th IEEE Symposium on Security and Privacy, Oakland, CA*, May 9–12 1999.

[4] D.E. Denning. *Cryptography and Data Security*. Addison-Wesley, Mass., 1982.

[5] D.E. Denning. Commutative filters for reducing inference threats in multilevel database systems. In *Proc. IEEE Symp. on Security and Privacy*, pages 134–146, 1985.

[6] D.E. Denning and T.F. Lunt. A multilevel relational data model. In *Proc. IEEE Symp. on Security and Privacy*, pages 220–233, 1987.

[7] J.A. Goguen and J. Meseguer. Unwinding and inference control. In *Proc. IEEE Symp. on Security and Privacy*, pages 75–86, 1984.

[8] T.H. Hinke. Inference aggregation detection in database management systems. In *Proc. IEEE Symp. on Security and Privacy*, pages 96–106, 1988.

[9] S. Jajodia, R. Sandhu, and B. T. Blaustein. Solution to the polyinstantiation problem. In M. Abrams et al., editor, *Information Security: An Integrated Collection of Essays*. IEEE Computer Society Press, 1995.

[10] T. F. Keefe, M. B. Thuraisingham, and W. T. Tsai. Secure query-processing strategies. *IEEE Computer*, pages 63–70, March 1989.

[11] D.G. Marks. Inference in MLS database systems. *IEEE Trans. Knowledge and Data Eng.*, 8(1):46–55, February 1996.

[12] D.G. Marks, A. Motro, and S. Jajodia. Enhancing the controlled disclosure of sensitive information. In *Proc. European Symp. on Research in Computer Security*, Springer-Verlag Lecture Notes in Computer Science, Vol. 1146, pages 290–303, 1996.

[13] S. Mazumdar, D. Stemple, and T. Sheard. Resolving the tension between integrity and security using a theorem prover. In *Proc. ACM Int'l Conf. Management of Data*, pages 233–242, 1988.

[14] M. Morgenstern. Controlling logical inference in multilevel database systems. In *Proc. IEEE Symp. on Security and Privacy*, pages 245–255, 1988.

[15] G.W. Smith. Modeling security-relevant data semantics. In *Proc. IEEE Symp. Research in Security and Privacy*, pages 384–391, 1990.

[16] P.D. Stachour and B. Thuraisingham. Design of LDV: A multilevel secure relational database management system. *IEEE Trans. Knowledge and Data Eng.*, 2(2):190–209, June 1990.

[17] T. Su and G. Ozsoyoglu. Inference in MLS database systems. *IEEE Trans. Knowledge and Data Eng.*, 3(4):474–485, December 1991.

[18] T.H.Hinke, Harry S. Delugach, and Asha Chandrasekhar. A fast algorithm for detecting second paths in database inference analysis. *Jour. of Computer Security*, 3(2,3):147–168, 1995.

[19] B.M. Thuraisingham. Security checking in relational database management systems augmented with inference engines. *Computers and Security*, 6:479–492, 1987.

[20] R. W. Yip and K. N. Levitt. Data level inference detection in database systems. In *Proc. of the 11th IEEE Computer Security Foundation Workshop, Rockport, MA*, pages 179–189, June 1998.

MANAGING CLASSIFIED DOCUMENTS IN A RELATIONAL DATABASE

Adrian Spalka
Department of Computer Science III, University of Bonn
Roemerstrasse 164, D-53117 Bonn, Germany
adrian@cs.uni-bonn.de

Abstract: The handling of classified paper-based documents follows well established mandatory security policies and the mandatory access control model of Bell and LaPadula convincingly demonstrates how to implement these policies in operating systems. In view of the many difficulties encountered by SeaView's attempt to provide full support for these policies in relational databases, this work pursues the less ambitious aim to use a relational database only for the management of classified documents in concordance with mandatory security policies. In the first part we present the options for the conceptual design of the database, ie the database scheme and the adaptation of the data manipulation language. In the second part we address operational aspects related to the possible use of the database by untrustworthy programs. This investigation yields valuable hints to the solution of the more complex problem of constructing a complete multi-level relational database with sound static and dynamic semantics.

Key words: Databases, Security, Confidentiality, Integrity, Logic

1. INTRODUCTION

Most commercial companies, government agencies and the military possess classified documents. The term classified states that the content of the document and often also its existence are subject to confidentiality requirements. If a document is marked as classified, then only a specific group of persons is allowed to have access to it and it must be kept secret from all other persons.

Since not all classified documents should be kept secret from the same group of persons it is common practice to assign the persons and the documents to named groups and to establish a correspondence between the groups of persons and the groups of documents. If the document group D is in correspondence to the person group P, then the members of P are authorised to have access to the documents in D and, which is the main requirement of all mandatory security policies concerned with confidentiality, the documents in D should be kept secret from all persons not in P. The document groups express the documents' degree of sensitivity, often also denoted as degree or level of confidentiality; one says that document A has a higher sensitivity than document B if A should be kept secret from more persons than B and, accordingly, fewer persons are authorised to have access to A than to B. The person groups, on the other hand, express the persons' degree of trustworthiness, sometimes also denoted as clearance; one says that person X has a higher trustworthiness than person Y if X is authorised to have access to more documents that Y and, accordingly, fewer documents should be kept secret from X than from Y.

The handling of classified paper-based documents often follows well established mandatory security policies. In government institutions and the military the following two rules stated in [8] capture the essence of these policies:

> The dissemination of information of a particular security level (including sensitivity level and any compartments or caveats) to individuals lacking the appropriate clearances for that level is prohibited by law.

and:

> When a document is not in a safe, it is in the custody of some individual trusted not to distribute it improperly.

We prefer to speak of a mandatory confidentiality policy (MCP), if the main rules, as is the case here, refer only to confidentiality. We call the first rule the Primitive Mandatory Requirement (PMR) for it expresses the basic confidentiality requirement, which is the main concern of the policy. The second rule asserts that authorisations to have access to documents are granted in full compliance with the PMR; we call it the Trustworthiness Assumption (TWA).

The PMR has a purely declarative style. It states only that a classified document A should be kept secret from a person X, if X's clearance is insufficient with respect to A's sensitivity. It does not tell us how to enforce confidentiality of A in front of X and it does not tell us which actions disseminate information about A to X. The TWA has a purely declarative style, too. It takes that those authorised to have access to a document will keep it secret from others im compliance with the PMR and, by far more important, that they know how to do it.

This work has the following objective: Find a constructive interpretation of the PMR in the context of a relational database that manages only classified documents.

One can be tempted to say that this objective is not very challenging. However, we show that this database retains the sound semantics of relational databases and enforces confidentiality. In view of the troubles encountered by SeaView, it preserves the semantic properties of integrity constraints and never encounters 'polyinstantiation'. We also take a look at extensions to this database that are prone to polyinstantiation. We use the examination to show, however, that sound semantics can be preserved and confidentiality still enforced if we if allow the database not only to withhold data but also to return bogus data. We therefore believe that the findings of this paper provide valuable hints for the construction of a full relational database with the ability to enforce confidentiality – which, of course, by the definition of a relational database implies the preservation of integrity.

The subsequent section comments on some previous works. The main investigation is presented in section 3. Lastly, a conclusion summarises our results.

2. PREVIOUS AND RELATED WORK

Security-level-based mandatory controls of information dissemination were originally developed for information recorded on paper. Today the security model developed by Bell and La Padula ([1]) is generally accepted as the standard formalisation of the mandatory security policy. Since the establishment of this model's non-disclosure properties is attributed to a large extent to two of its rules (which are called properties), the Simple-Security-Property and the *-Property, these two rules are regarded as the core of Bell and La Padula's model. Originally, this model has been developed for operating systems. It protects a system's confidentiality from a wide range of untrustworthy Trojan Horse programs. But gradually the opinion has consolidated that the two core rules are also indispensable prerequisites for guaranteeing non-disclosure in any kind of multi-level database systems – an opinion that needs to be revised in view of the semantic problems that these databases still struggle with.

The success of Bell and La Padula's security model in operating systems encouraged attempts to construct a relational database with the ability to manage classified items with a more complex structure than those of documents. However, the enticing idea that such a database can be defined as the plain 'sum' of a relational database and the two rules from Bell and La Padula's security model soon turned out to lead to intricate semantic problems. The multi-level relational data model introduced in [3] and formalised in [4] is claimed to be an extended relational data model suitable for the enforcement of mandatory security. A multi-level relation scheme is defined as $R(A_1, C_1, ..., A_n, C_n)$. Each C_i defines a range of security levels for the attribute A_i. The reason for classifying single attributes, according to the authors' opinion, is that an attribute value represents a fact (which is in clear contradiction to the definition of a relational database). In addition to it, a security level is assigned to the whole relation scheme and a tuple's security level is computed from those of its attribute values'. The authors note that: 'Functional dependencies correspond to real-world constraints; that is, they are not just a property of a particular relation instance' and 'The requirements for consistency [at each access class] affect the integrity rules of the relational model, which are formulated as global constraints on an entire database.' Yet their approach to the handling of integrity in this database does not account for these facts. It relies on purely syntactical – obviously inadequate – adjustments instead. The name of the resulting self-made semantic havoc is 'polyinstantiation'.

An approach to a logic foundation of multi-level databases is presented in [16]. The author offers two views: the system-high world and the per-level world views. The author states that 'The system-high world method does not accommodate polyinstantiation ... since each piece of data is assigned only one level...'. In the per-level world, polyinstantiation is allowed, yet its operational treatment does not seem to rest on any fixed semantics. In conclusion, while correctly stressing the necessity of a formal basis for multi-level databases, no concrete advances in this direction are presented.

A similar idea is presented in [7], which regards a multi-level database as a collection of databases. The data of each database is represented as one logical theory of first-order logic. Promising though the authors' observations are, the approach has not been further developed.

3. CLASSIFIED DOCUMENTS IN RELATIONAL DATABASES

3.1 Preliminary considerations

The essence of mandatory confidentiality policies is the PMR, which specifies confidentiality demands in an informal manner. Its application to an environment involves two steps: a declarative definition of confidentiality and an operational translation for its enforcement. This is carefully done for operating systems managing classified documents by [1] and for general systems defined through a sequence of inputs and outputs by, eg, [6].

In a computer system, the common understanding of the confidentiality demand stated in the PMR is that a secret item is kept confidential if the user gets no information from the system on it. Translated to prohibitions, we must ensure that:

1. the user does not get the secret data itself or any part of it
2. the data the user gets from the system must not depend or be influenced by secret data

Point (1) prevents that a user gets any secret data directly. Point (2) expresses two concerns; it prevents that:

- the user learns of the secret data's existence
- the user gets secret data from a Trojan horse, ie an untrustworthy program

We can translate these prohibitions into the following positive requirements:

The result of an operation executed by the user

(P1) may comprise only data he is authorised to get and

(P2) may refer only to items he is authorised to get.

Our aim in this paper is the enforcement of confidentiality of classified documents stored in and managed by a relational database. We approach this task at the declarative level and the operational level. The declarative level defines data structures and operations on them; it has no notion of programs and, therefore, is not concerned with untrustworthy ones. The operational level deals with implementation details and the particularities of a computer; it is this level that can take untrustworthy programs into account.

A classified document consists of two parts, a name and content, with the following structure:

- document name: (security level, name)
- document content: (reference to a document name, content)

In a database the user can retrieve data with the select operation and he can modify data with the insert, delete and update operations. The select operation refers only to relations and its result is a, possibly empty, answer set. The modifying operations refer to relations and to integrity constraints. Their result is a yes/no-answer, which is dictated by the integrity constraints.

Therefore, the satisfaction of the PMR in our database has the following interpretation:

(P3) Confidentiality of the document parts is enforced, if the evaluation of a select command submitted by the user refers to and returns only data, ie document parts or results of functions applied to them, he is authorised to access (covers both the declarative and operational part of (P1)).

(P4) Confidentiality of the document's existence is enforced, if the computation of the answer to a modifying command submitted by the user refers only to document parts he is authorised to access (covers the declarative part of (P2)).
(P5) Given that the user has chosen a fixed security level for the current session, a Trojan horse cannot reveal secret data if a modifying command submitted by the user modifies only document names with the session's security level and document contents the referred names of which have the session's security level (covers the operational part of (P2)).

Thus, the procedure applied to a command submitted by the user comprises the following steps:

1. Tighten the conditions for selecting tuples so that only tuples he is authorised to access are selected for processing (applies to select, delete and update operations)
2. Ensure that integrity constraints need to evaluate only tuples he is authorised to access in order to yield the answer defined by their semantics (applies to modifying operations)

Note that point (2) implies that we do not tolerate a violation of integrity.

To construct our database we employ a preventive design. It prevents a loss or damage under the assumption that a user's clearance (and, consequently, the rights granted to him) reflects his actual trustworthiness and that the degree of sensitivity assigned to a document is based on its actual confidentiality. We do not address restorative support, which provides measures, by nature of the problem, to detect and, if possible, to restore a loss or damage resulting from misuse of granted rights by a corrupt user (an insider influenced by bribery or the like).

We assume that a set of security levels, *SL*, is given on which a partial order '≤' is defined. The SQL examples in the subsequent sections were tested on the MS SQL Server v7.

3.2 Approach 1: Grouped attributes

3.2.1 Database scheme

The database scheme needed to represent classified documents is fairly simple.

We have a relation to store document names, CDNames(SL, Name), such that SL is the security level component of the document name, Name is the name component of the document name, and if a tuple is in the extension of CDNames, then a classified document with the name (SL, Name) exists; otherwise such a document does not exist. Its semantic restrictions are: the domain of SL is the set of security levels SL, the domain of Name comprises suitable constants in the database language, eg character strings, and there is a primary key constraint on the pair (SL, Name), ie the combination of both attributes must be unique, which prevents the existence of two documents with identical names.

And we have a relation to store documents' content, CDContent(SL, Name, Content), such that the pair (SL, Name) is a reference to a document with this name, content is the content of the document with the referenced name, and if a tuple is in the extension of CDContent, then the classified document with the referenced name has the content of Content, otherwise the document has no such content. Its semantic restrictions are: the domains of SL and Name are inherited from CDNames, the domain of Content is any suitable data type, there is a foreign key constraint from CDContent(SL, Name) to CDNames(SL, Name), which prevents the existence of anonymous content, there is an (implicit) primary key constraint on all attributes, which prevents the existence of identical contents within a document and an (optional) primary key constraint on the pair (SL, Name), which can be used to ensure that a document has only one content; if defined, it overrides the preceding constraint.

Since the database must make some decisions based on the partial order of the security levels and the users' clearance, we can – as an option – store this information in the database as well. We therefore have three more relations. If a tuple is in the extension of the relation Levels(SL), then SL is an element of the set of security levels SL; otherwise SL has no such element. The partial order '≤' on SL can be represented by its transitive closure in the relation POL(GEL, LEL), such that GEL and LEL are references to security levels and if a tuple is in the extension of POL, then the security level referred to by GEL is greater than or equal to the security level referred to by LEL; otherwise these security levels are unrelated in '≤'. Lastly, we store the users and their clearances in the relation Users(Name, Clearance) with obvious semantics. We assume that the database obtains the identity of the user who submits a command to it from a source that previously authenticated the user and that all attributes are defined as NOT NULL.

All restrictions so far defined are semantic, ie they reflect only structural properties of classified documents and are not concerned with confidentiality. Modifications and restrictions needed to enforce the PMR, ie (P3), (P4) and (P5), in the database are examined in subsequent sections.

3.2.2 Enforcement of confidentiality during selection

As we will see, access restrictions are all we need to enforce the PMR during selection in a database with this scheme. Access restrictions can be expressed in two equivalent ways: by augmenting the user's select-statement with additional conditions (restrictions) or by defining views for the user. In this work we go the first way. We therefore consider a select-statement as it is submitted by a user and its modification that is actually executed.

We approach the general solution by first taking a look at some select-statements. Our user's name is U and we assume that the database knows the user's name.

In general, select-access to the relations Levels, POL and Users or a subset thereof can be granted or refused in concordance with an organisation's regulations. With respect to the PMR, the user may have select-access to the relations Levels and POL restricted to the subset indicated by his clearance, and in the relation Users select-access only to the tuple identifying himself.

(A) The user wants to retrieve the security levels:

Submitted statement: select SL from Levels

Executed statement in informal notation:

select SL from Levels, Users
where Users.Name = 'U' and Levels.SL <= Users.Clearance

Executed statement in SQL:

select SL from Levels, Users where Users.Name = 'U' and
  Levels.SL in (select LEL from POL where GEL = Users.Clearance)

(P3) and (P4) are not affected since the selection does not refer to any part of a classified document. However, the condition in the where clause shows that we can easily restrict the user's access to those security levels he is authorised to use.

We do not need to consider (P5) during selection since a Trojan Horse can only pass data in a modifying operation.

(B) The user wants to retrieve the names and content of classified documents

Submitted statement:

select * from CDNames, CDContent
where CDNames.ID = CDContent.Ref_ID

Executed statement in informal notation:

select CDNames.SL, CDNames.Name, CDContent.Content
from CDNames, CDContent, Users
  where CDNames.ID = CDContent.Ref_ID and
  Users.Name = 'U' and CDNames.SL <= Users.Clearance

We immediately see that both (P3) and (P4) are met. The condition in the where clause confines the reference to document names the user is authorised to access and, thus, the answer set comprises this set only or a subset of it.

(C) Conclusions

The satisfaction of the PMR for classified documents in a database is easily accomplished during selection.

Suppose that we want to admit document content parts with an individual security level. Then the select statements examined in C) and, in particular, in D) indicate that the security level of such a part should not be less than or incomparable to the security level attached to the document's existence. Due to (P3) and (P4) access to these parts is governed by the security level attached to the document's existence, which implicitly raises the security level of such a part to that of the document's existence.

3.2.3 Enforcement of confidentiality during insertion

All modifying operations modify a single relation only. However, they refer to the specified relation and to integrity constraints, which are affected by the intended modification. Semantic restrictions defined as integrity constraints are automatically evaluated by the database. We express further restrictions implied by the PMR as additional conditions in the where-clause or as triggers. We assume that the user has no modifying-access to the relations Levels, POL and Users.

The insert-statement does not comprise conditions for the insertion. Thus, it cannot be augmented and there is no distinction between the submitted statement and the executed one. If the insert-statement comprises a select-part, then the presented conditions on selection apply, too.

(A) The user wants to insert a document name

Submitted/executed statement:

insert into CDNames (SL, Name) VALUES (v1, v2)

Triggers: T1 Checks that the user specified a security level authorised for his clearance.

Informal notation:

```
if (not (Clearance of U >= v1)) then
  print 'Invalid security level. Insertion failed.'
    rollback transaction
  end if
```

SQL:

```
create trigger T1 on CDNames for insert as
declare @L varchar(20)
  select @L = SL from inserted
  if @L not in (select POL.LEL from POL, Users
     where Users.Name = 'U' and GEL = Users.Clearance)
  begin
     print ('Invalid security level. Insertion failed.')
```

```
      rollback transaction
   end
Affected integrity constraints:
Primary key on CDNames. This constraint performs the following check:
if (v1, v2) in (select SL, Name from CDNames) then
   print 'Primary key violation. Insertion failed.'
      rollback transaction
   end if
```

It can possibly violate (P4) since the select statement refers to all document names. But suppose that the trigger T1 executes before this constraint is checked. If T1 rolls the insertion back, then there is no need to check this constraint. If, on the other hand, T1 is successfully passed, then its check ensures that v1, the security level specified by the user, is authorised. And, hence, the check of the primary key constraint can be restricted to tuples with SL = v1. Without affecting the constraint's semantics, we can now rewrite its procedure as follows:

```
if v2 in (select Name from CDNames where SL = v1) then
   print 'Primary key violation. Insertion failed.'
      rollback transaction
   end if
```

If this check is passed, then the user gets the information that the specified document name does not exist. If it fails, then the user is notified of a name conflict the reason of which is a document he is authorised to access. In conclusion, this constraint meets (P4) if it T1 is executed first.

Foreign key to Levels: If passed, the trigger T1 ensures that this constraint never fails, ie, in effect, it is redundant for insert-operations.

Foreign key from CDContent: By definition, foreign key constraints never fail on insertions to the referenced relation.

Note that the satisfaction of (P4) depends on the order of execution: triggers must be evaluated before integrity constraints are checked. The MS SQL Server (used here to check the examples) first checks integrity constraints and then evaluates triggers. In this case another solution must be employed, eg, we can drop the integrity constraints from the table definition and insert their checks in our triggers.

To meet the operational requirements stated in (P5), we must assume that the insertion command is possibly submitted by a Trojan horse. To satisfy (P5) the database can either accept only the Name attribute in the insert command and supply the user's session security level for the SL attribute, or we modify the trigger T1 as follows:

```
if (not (session security level of U = v1)) then
   print 'Invalid security level. Insertion failed.'
```

```
    rollback transaction
  end if
```

(B) The user wants to insert a document content

This operation turns clumsy is we use surrogate-attributes and do not want the user to know their values. To insert the content of a document the user must also enter a reference to an existing document name. If we do not use surrogate-attributes, then the reference is the document name itself (which comprises both the security level and the name); if we use surrogate-attributes, then the reference is the surrogate value corresponding to the document name. Thus, if we want to allow the user to use the SQL insert-statement for performing this operation, then we must choose one of these options. From the viewpoint of semantics both options are equivalent: to insert the content of a document the user must know its name.

Submitted/executed statement:

```
insert into CDNames (Ref_ID, Content) VALUES (v1, v2)
```

Triggers. T2 Checks that the user specified a Ref_ID value corresponding to a document name he is authorised to select. Informal notation:

```
select SL from CDNames where ID = v1
if (not (Clearance of U >= SL)) then
    print 'Invalid reference ID. Insertion failed.'
    rollback transaction
  end if
```

Affected integrity constraints.

Foreign key to CDNames: It can possibly violate (P4) since it can check references to all document names. But, again, suppose that the trigger T2 executes before this constraint is checked. The check that the Ref_ID specified by the user corresponds to a document name he is authorised to access implies a check that the document name exists, which the foreign key constraint performs, too. Thus, if successfully passed, the trigger T2 ensures that this constraint never fails, ie, in effect, it is redundant for insert-operations, too.

Primary key on Ref_ID: This constraint performs the following check:

```
if v1 in (select Ref_ID from CDContent) then
  print 'Primary key violation. Insertion failed.'
    rollback transaction
  end if
```

It can possibly violate (P4) since the select statement refers to all document references. However, if T2 rolls the insertion back, then it is not executed. Suppose that T2 is passed. If the check of this constraint is also passed, then the user is notified that content for the referenced document does not exist, and if it fails, then the user is notified of a conflict the reason of which is a document he is authorised to access. In conclusion, this constraint meets (P4) if it T2 is executed first.

To satisfy (P5) we modify the trigger T2 as follows:

```
select SL from CDNames where ID = v1
if (not (session security level of U = SL)) then
      print 'Document name not found. Insertion failed.'
      rollback transaction
  end if
```

(C) Conclusions

The satisfaction of the PMR for classified documents in a database is also easily accomplished during insertion.

Suppose, again, that we want to admit document content parts with an individual security level. The insert statement examined in B) indicates that the security level of such a part should not be less than the security level attached to the document's existence. Due to (P3) and (P4) access to these parts is governed by the security level attached to the document's existence, ie the document name in our database, which implicitly raises the security level of such a part to that of the document's existence.

But can we assign to a document part a security level that is higher than that assigned to its existence? Suppose that such a part exists. Then the primary key constraint on Ref_ID fails if the user attempts to insert a part with a lower security level. This failure violates (P4) since the reason for it is data that should be kept secret from the user. But we can still admit parts with a higher security level if we find a way for the constraint to fail in concordance with (P4), ie without referring to this part. This can be accomplished with aliases the use of which is formally described, eg, in [15]. Basically, the insertion of a part with a higher security level must be accompanied by an insertion of a bogus part with a lower security level, which the user with a lower clearance cannot modify. His insertion will then fail on the account of the bogus part – it obviates a reference to secret data, ie complies with (P4), and preserves integrity. So the answer to our initial question is yes if allow the database not only to withhold data but also to return bogus data.

We omit the delete and update command from our paper for reasons of space.

3.3 Approach 2: Structured name-spaces

The approach presented in the preceding section uses two attributes to represent the composite name of a classified document. If we extend a relational database such that the value of an attribute can be a composite value, ie a tuple in the mathematical sense, then section 3.2 can be rewritten in a semantically cleaner fashion, but the results and findings are still the same.

The formal grounds for this approach, ie for a database with structured name-spaces, are given in [14] and can be used to elaborate the details in a straightforward manner. We omit it here for reasons of space and redundancy.

4. CONCLUSION

This little database is all we need to manage classified documents. Integrity constraints retain their standard meaning and are never violated. And the confidentiality demand stated in the PMR is enforced. We have followed some simple principles in this work:

- Do not use the special NULL value. It has no common meaning in open databases and, therefore, can make reasoning about confidentiality only more messy. Admittedly, this value is often used in practice, however, more for reasons of convenience than necessity. Most schemes can be designed in a way that avoids this value.
- Set the primary key on all identifying attributes and make sure that references to a relation (in both integrity constraints and select commands) use all of them.
- If the primary key constraint is defined on all attributes of a relation, then structured name-spaces can be used to enforce confidentiality in line with integrity.
- If the primary key constraint is defined on a proper subset of a relation's set of attributes, then aliases can be used to enforce confidentiality in line with integrity.
- The same methods can be used to enforce confidentiality in line with foreign key constraints.

Our database preserves the standard database semantics and enforces confidentiality with access restrictions only and a modelling of composite names. But we have also realised that a database with a more complex structure can also enforce confidentiality while preserving semantics if (carefully managed) bogus data are admitted. In view of some prominent problems of SeaView we never need to worry that a trusted user is confused ([17]), we do not have to guess about versions, degrees of interest or recency ([4]), nor do we have to deal with imprecise beliefs ([12]).

We intend to pursue this approach and soon present further results on sound databases with the ability to enforce confidentiality.

REFERENCES

[1] Bell, David Elliott, and Leonard J. La Padula. (1975) *Secure computer system: Unified exposition and multics interpretation.* MITRE Technical Report 2997. MITRE Corp, Bedford, MA.

[2] Bonyun, David A. (1980) 'The Secure Relational Database Management System Kernel: Three Years After'. *1980 IEEE Symposium on Security and Privacy.* IEEE Computer Society Press. pp 34-37.

[3] Denning, Dorothy E. *et al.* (1986) 'Views for Multilevel Database Security'. *1986 IEEE Symposium on Security and Privacy.* IEEE Computer Society Press. pp 156-172.

[4] Denning, Dorothy E., *et al.* (1987) 'A Multilevel Relational Data Model'. *1987 IEEE Symposium on Security and Privacy.* IEEE Computer Society Press. pp 220-234.

[5] Denning, Dorothy E., *et al.* (1988) 'The SeaView Security Model'. *1988 Symposium on Security and Privacy.* IEEE Computer Society Press. pp 218-233.

[6] Focardi, Ricardo. (1996) 'Comparing Two Information Flow Security Properties.' *9th IEEE Computer Security Foundations Workshop 1996.* IEEE Computer Society Press. pp 116-122.

[7] Garvey, Thomas D., Teresa F. Lunt, Xiaolei Qian and Mark E. Stickel. (1992) 'Toward a tool to detect and eliminate inference problems in the design of multilevel databases'. Ed Bhavani M. Thuraisingham and Carl E. Landwehr. *Database Security VI.* IFIP WG11.3 Workshop on Database Security 1992. Amsterdam: North-Holland, 1993. pp 149-167.

[8] Landwehr, Carl E. (1981) 'Formal Models for Computer Security'. *ACM Computing Surveys* 13.3:247-278.

[9] Lunt, Teresa F. (1988) 'SeaView'. Ed Teresa F. Lunt. *Research Directions in Database Security.* 1st RADC Database Security Invitational Workshop 1988. New York *et al*: Springer-Verlag, 1992. pp 13-32.

[10] Qian, Xiaolei, and Teresa F. Lunt. (1992) 'Tuple-level vs. element-level classification'. Ed Bhavani M. Thuraisingham and Carl E. Landwehr. *Database Security VI.* IFIP WG11.3 Workshop on Database Security 1993. Amsterdam: North-Holland, 1993. pp 301-315.

[11] Reiter, Raymond. (1984) 'Towards a Logical Reconstruction of Relational Database Theory'. Ed Michael L. Brodie, John Mylopoulos and Joachim W. Schmidt. *On Conceptual Modeling.* New York: Springer-Verlag. pp 191-238.

[12] Smith, Kenneth, and Marianne Winslett. (1992) 'Entity Modeling in the MLS Relational Data Model'. *18th VLDB Conference.* pp 199-210.

[13] Spalka, Adrian. (1996) 'The Non-Primitiveness of the Simple-Security Property and its Non-Applicability to Relational and Logic-Based Databases'. *9th IEEE Computer Security Foundations Workshop 1996.* IEEE Computer Society Press. pp 146-155.

[14] Spalka, Adrian, and Armin B. Cremers. (1997) 'Structured name-spaces in secure databases'. Ed T. Y. Lin and Shelly Qian. *Database Security XI.* IFIP TC11 WG11.3 Conference on Database Security. London *et al*: Chapman & Hall, 1998. pp 291-306.

[15] Spalka, Adrian, and Armin B. Cremers. (1999) 'The effect of confidentiality on the structure of databases'. Ed Vijay Atluri and John Hale. *Research Advances in Database and Information Systems Security.* IFIP TC11 WG11.3 13th Conference on Database Security. Boston *et al*: Kluwer Academic Publishers. pp 253-268.

[16] Thuraisingham, Bhavani M. (1988) 'Foundations of Multilevel Databases'. Ed Teresa F. Lunt. *Research Directions in Database Security.* 1st RADC Database Security Invitational Workshop 1988. New York *et al*: Springer-Verlag, 1992. pp 199-226.

[17] Wiseman, Simon. (1989) 'On the Problem of Security in Databases'. Ed David L. Spooner and Carl. E. Landwehr. *Database Security III.* IFIP WG 11.3 Workshop on Database Security 1989. Amsterdam: North-Holland, 1990. pp 301-310.

VI

IMPLEMENTATION ISSUES

A COMPARISON BETWEEN ConSA AND CURRENT LINUX SECURITY IMPLEMENTATIONS

Alexandre Hardy
Computer Science, Rand Afrikaans University
PO Box 524, Auckland Park, Johannesburg, South Africa
ah@adam.rau.ac.za

Martin S Olivier
molivier@rkw.rau.ac.za
Computer Science, Rand Afrikaans University
PO Box 524, Auckland Park, Johannesburg, South Africa

Abstract There are many extensions to the Linux security model that are available. ConSA [1] aims to provide a configurable architecture, and should allow many security systems to be implemented. A prototype ConSA system has been implemented in Linux. This paper will examine how ConSA relates to currently available Linux security extensions.

Keywords: Access Control, Security, Security Model

1. INTRODUCTION

Linux is a popular operating system based on Unix [17]. It therefore uses the same security model that Unix uses. The Unix model is well-known and has been thoroughly tested and investigated. Unfortunately a single, fixed security model does not fulfil everyone's needs. This is evidenced by the large number of security models that have been proposed and even implemented for Linux [6, 7, 8, 9, 10, 11, 13, 14, 15, 16]. ConSA [1] is a model that addresses the requirements posed by diverse security needs by providing a high degree of configurability.

The purpose of this paper is to compare ConSA to the diverse range of Linux security implementations to show that ConSA does indeed provide the flexibility that is required as illustrated by these implementations. By comparing ConSA to these implementations, the paper also gives an insightful overview of the security projects that are currently underway in the Linux environment.

This paper is structured as follows: Section 2 gives a basic overview of the ConSA model. Sections 3 to 7 discuss these Linux security implementations and how they relate to ConSA.

2. THE CONFIGURABLE SECURITY ARCHITECTURE

The Configurable Security Architecture provides a framework for the implementation and use of a security system. The architecture is illustrated in figure 1. Several modules are identified for implementation:

- Entity Labels — Entity Labels encode the security attributes for a resource in the system.
- Subject Labels — Subject Labels encode the security attributes of a subject or user of the system.
- Information Flow Manager — Information Flow concerns are implemented by this module.
- Authorization Control Module — This module determines the initial rights subjects have to newly created resources.
- Subject Management Module — The Subject Management Module maintains subject information and translates externally presented identifiers into Subject Labels.
- Message Dispatcher — This component is responsible for passing messages to the destination object, and enforcing the security model on those messages. This component is provided by ConSA.
- Protect Table — The Protect Table associates Entity Labels with resources. These resources are protected by the Entity Labels associated with them. This module is also provided by ConSA.

It is clear that the Subject Management Module (SMM), Authorization Control Module (ACM), Information Flow Manager (IFM), Subject Label and Entity Label implement the security model. The other modules will not be considered in the following discussion. These modules are implemented as objects, and each object must implement specific methods. The operation of ConSA as an access control mechanism is as follows:

- The Subject logs onto the system.

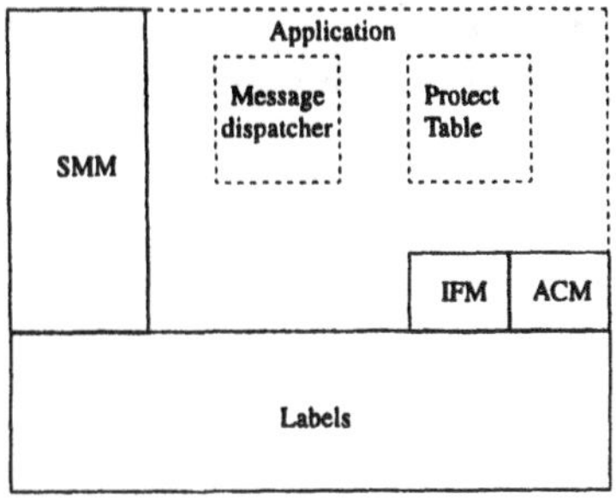

Figure 1. Configurable Security Architecture (from [1])

- A SubjectLabel is assigned to the subject by the Subject Management Module.

- If a subject wishes to access an entity, then the EntityLabel that protects that entity is determined by consulting the Protect Table. The EntityLabel determines if the SubjectLabel of the subject is allowed to access the object. The Information Flow Manager is consulted to make sure that this is a valid information flow. If these checks are passed, then the subject is granted access.

- If a subject creates a new entity, the Authorization Control Module creates an EntityLabel to protect the entity, and associates the EntityLabel with the entity in the ProtectTable. The EntityLabel is initialized to enforce the security policy on that entity.

- The subject logs off the system.

[1] provides a thorough discussion of the methods and requirements of each module. Here we briefly describe a few of these methods to facilitate the following discussion. Note that the definitions here are slightly different to [1].

2.1. `EntityLabel`

- `NoAccess()` — Remove all access from all subjects

- `GrantAccess(SubjectLabel` L_s`)` — Grant access to any subject that may use the label L_s.

- `RevokeAccess(SubjectLabel` L_s`)` — Revoke Access for subjects presenting this label. Subjects may still be able to gain access through other labels.

- `RevokeAccess*(SubjectLabel` L_s`)` — Revoke Access for subjects presenting this label. The subjects from whom access is revoked will not be able to access the entity with any label.

- `CheckAccess(SubjectLabel` L_s`)` — A test to determine if the subject presenting L_s may access the entity protected by this label.

2.2. `InformationFlowManager`

- `ActivateFlow(EntityLabel` L_e`, SubjectLabel` L_s`,` $Parameters$`)` — This method determines if access is allowed to entity *e* by subject s if s invokes a method of *e*. $Parameters$ specifies whether parameters are passed or not.

- `ReturnFlow(EntityLabel` L_e`, SubjectLabel` L_s`,` $ReturnVal$`)` — This method determines if access is allowed to entity *e* by subject s if *e* returns from a method invocation by s. $ReturnVal$ specifies whether information is returned or not. For languages such as C++ these methods may be evaluated before method invocation.

2.3. `AuthorizationControlModule`

- `EntityCreated()` — This method is invoked if an entity is created to provide an entity label that will protect the entity.

The following sections will analyse other security models, and determine if ConSA can achieve the same results. We begin with the standard Linux security model, since most of the extensions are further restrictions over and above the Linux security model.

3. STANDARD LINUX SECURITY

This section will focus on how the Linux security model may be implemented in ConSA. The Linux security system has no information flow control, and so a ConSA implementation of the Information Flow Manager will allow all operations. The implementation of the Subject Label and Entity Label will also illustrate that the security system is correctly implemented. Next we consider the implementation of each of the Subject Label and Entity Label methods.

3.1. Subject Label

The Subject Label stores the `uid` of the subject, this `uid` is used to obtain access to entities. Method implementations are as follows:

- `InitSubject` — This method will only need one parameter, the `uid` of the subject, which will be stored. For a Subject Label L_s the `uid` will be denoted as $L_s.uid$.

3.2. Entity Label

The entity label for this discussion will protect files. This discussion may be extended for other resources. The Entity Label stores a `uid` (the owner of the file) and a `gid` (the group owner of the file) as well as an ACL (Access Control List) in the form of a bit vector `rwxrwxrwx`. The first `rwx` refers to read, write and execute permissions for the user. The second `rwx` refers to permissions for the group, and the last `rwx` refers to the permissions of all other users. For an Entity Label L_e, $L_e.uid$ denotes the owner of the file, $L_e.gid$ denotes the group that owns the file. The user `rwx` bits will be denoted by $L_e.uid_r$, $L_e.uid_w$, and $L_e.uid_x$ (with values 0 or 1). A similar notation will be used for group bits `rwx`. Lastly, the protection bits for all other users in the system (`rwx`) will be denoted by $L_e.other_r$, $L_e.other_w$, and $L_e.other_x$. $invalid$ will denote some invalid identifier, that will not match any identifier in the system. The methods of the Entity Label class can now be implemented as follows:

- `NoAccess()`

$$\begin{aligned} L_e.uid &:= invalid \\ L_e.gid &:= invalid \\ L_e.uid_r &:= 0 \\ L_e.uid_w &:= 0 \\ L_e.uid_x &:= 0 \\ L_e.gid_r &:= 0 \\ L_e.other_r &:= 0 \end{aligned} \tag{1}$$

  Invalid identifiers ensure that the other bit vector is used for access checks, some of the initialization has been omitted due to space constraints.

- `GrantAccess(SubjectLabel` L_s`)`
  `GrantAccess` will be restrictive and may fail, to ensure Linux access semantics. A typical implementation may be as follows:

  - If there is no valid user that owns the file, or $L_s.uid = L_e.uid$ then set the `uid` to that of the Subject Label, and set $L_e.uid_r$, $L_e.uid_w$, and $L_e.uid_x$ according to the supplied mode parameter. Access should be granted by this parameter, and not revoked.
  - Otherwise, if there is no valid group or $L_s.uid \in G(L_e.gid)$ then follow a similar process for group assignment. A group should

be selected according to $L_e.uid$. Usually each user has a group associated with it such that `uid=gid`, and this `gid` may then be used. First set the `uid` rights and then the `gid` rights.

- Lastly, if neither of the above hold then adjust the access to $L_e.other$.

Granting access for mode *mode* (r,w or x) to category c (uid, gid or $other$) is achieved by

$$L_e.c_{mode} := 1$$

- `RevokeAccess(SubjectLabel` L_s`)`
This method is similar to GrantAccess, and will not be discussed due to space constraints.

- `RevokeAccess*(SubjectLabel` L_s`)`
This method is similar to GrantAccess, and will not be discussed due to space constraints.

- `CheckAccess(SubjectLabel` L_s`)`
This method simply consults the bit vectors according to the mode of access. Only read access will be considered. `CheckAccess` returns true for read access if

```
if (uid = 0) then
     return (true);
else if (Le.uid = Ls.uid) then
     return (Le.uid_r = 1);
else if (Ls.uid ∈ G(Le.gid)) then
     return (Le.gid_r = 1);
else return (Le.other_r = 1);
```

Note that the subject must have access to each of the parent directories that a file resides in to have access to that file.

The labels demonstrate that a non standard interpretation can be used, and the process still appears to be logical for the intended security model. The interpretation is inherently different due to the nature of the ACL implemented in Linux. Note also, that if the group can be modified, then users may be added to the ACL as necessary, however all users would have the same access rights. For example, to grant access to a file with gid gid to a subject with uid uid, simply set $G(gid) := G(gid) \cup uid$. The user with uid uid inherits the rights the rest of the group have. Another option to support more complex operations and perhaps to simplify implementation of command such as `chgrp`, is to implement an entity that provides access to labels, with the necessary security precautions. An entity may also be constructed to modify the group database. It should be clear that ConSA implements a superset of the Linux security model.

The Authorization Control Module must first grant access to the user creating the file, and then to a suitable group. A label must also be constructed to control who may grant or revoke access to the file. Naturally the super user is granted access by this label, and so is the owner of the file. Note that grant or revoke may be considered as another mode of access, and the algorithm for granting or revoking access will be different for these modes (since the concept of `uid` and `gid` no longer apply to this type of entity, namely labels). The Authentication Module may easily be written to authenticate users from the `/etc/passwd` file. The Subject Management Module also uses `/etc/passwd` to translate a user name to a uid.

4. LINUX TRUSTEES (ACL) PROJECT

The Linux Trustees(ACL) Project [14] extends the protection bit vector associated with files in Linux, and increases the flexibility of the algorithm used to determine if access is granted or not. The protection bit vector has been extended to the following:

Symbol	Meaning
R	Read files
W	Write files and directories
B	Browse (like UNIX execute for directories)
E	Read directories
X	Execute files
U	Use standard UNIX permissions
Modifiers	
C	Clear permissions instead of setting them
D	Deny access (instead of grant)
!	Complement of subject set (applies to all except user or group)
O	One level (does not apply to subdirectories)

This scheme extends the control over permissions, furthermore directories and files inherit the protection from directories higher up in the file tree, unless explicitly changed. The modified protection bit vector is known as a trustee object.

A ConSA implementation of the Linux Trustees system requires special attention — the inheritance of rights from a parent directory can be difficult to implement. The extension of the Entity Label representation (permission bit vector) is easily extended to include the extra permissions. Now there are a few factors to take into consideration:

- Multiple trustee objects — Multiple trustees can be handled in the same way that multiple ACL entries were handled in the ACL section.
- EntityLabel:CheckAccess — This method needs special attention, it may be implemented as specified in the first section. This includes the building

of the mask. Entity Labels would probably implement other methods for direct communication between Entity Labels.

5. LOW WATER-MARK MANDATORY ACCESS CONTROL (LOMAC)

This project assists in the protection of the integrity of processes and data, by enforcing Low Water-mark Mandatory Access Control policies. This project differs from the previous projects not only because of the policy implemented, but also because the implementation is in the form of a loadable kernel module. This means that the kernel need not be recompiled. The aforementioned projects do require recompilation of the Linux kernel. LOMAC extends the Unix security system, and does not replace it.
A LOMAC policy is made up of a series of levels or classifications $a_1, ..., a_n$ with $a_i \in \mathbf{N_0}$. Each object is assigned a level or classification at the time of creation. Objects include files, pipes, sockets, and semaphores. If an object with level a_i is considered to have lower integrity than an object with level a_j then $a_i < a_j$. Once an object has been assigned a level, that level is never changed. The primary goal of LOMAC is to prevent data from flowing from low level objects to high level objects. In particular viral data should not be allowed to flow from low level to high level objects. Each subject in the system is also assigned a level. The assignment takes place at creation of the subject, but could be altered at any time. The level selected can be fixed to a_k, or can be selected according to the perceived integrity of the subject. A subject's level may change over time. If a subject at level $a_s(t)$ accesses an object with level $a_o < a_s(t)$ then $a_s(t+1) := a_o$, for a time t. In other words, the subject is demoted to the level of the object it reads from. Subjects may not write to objects with a level higher ($a_s < a_o$) than their own. This is not strictly information flow since the data that is read is not tracked. However, data that is read from a low integrity source cannot be written to a high integrity source. Low integrity data may include data received from the network. LOMAC also prevents subjects of low level from interfering with subjects of higher level, and only allows subjects of sufficient level to access certain critical system functions, for example the reboot system call. In LOMAC a subject is a process group. Subjects are prevented from interfering with higher level subjects, by preventing signals from being sent from the lower level subjects to higher level subjects.

5.1. LOMAC in ConSA

To implement LOMAC only the Information Flow Manager need be implemented while using the ConSA implementation of the Linux security system. The following changes are necessary:

- SubjectLabel — The Subject Label needs to store the level of the subject a_s. This parameter will be set by the Subject Management Module.
- EntityLabel — The Entity Label has a new attribute a_o indicating the level of the object to be accessed. `GrantAccess` and `RevokeAccess` may be modified so as to alter the level of the entity associated with the label. Due to the static nature of the assignments, the configuration file technique of LOMAC is preferred.
- Information Flow Manager — Two methods need implementation namely `ActivateFlow` and `ReturnFlow`.
  - `ActivateFlow(EntityLabel` L_e`, SubjectLabel` L_s`,` $Parameters$`)`
    This method will be activated when an object is written to. `ActivateFlow` will return true exclusively if:
    $$L_s.a_s >= L_e.a_o \tag{2}$$
  - `ReturnFlow(EntityLabel` L_e`, SubjectLabel` L_s`,` $ReturnVal$`)`
    This method will be activated when an object is read from. The implementation is trivial:
    $$L_s.a_s := \min(L_s.a_s, L_e.a_o) \tag{3}$$
    and always returns true.

Domain and Type Enforcement (discussed in the next section) implements a similar policy, and can be generally more secure. It also resolves some problems that LOMAC has. Please refer to [16] for more details.

6. DOMAIN AND TYPE ENFORCEMENT (DTE)

Domain and Type Enforcement uses the "least privilege" concept, a subject is granted the least privileges necessary for that subject to complete the authorized task requested of it. To achieve this, mandatory access controls are enforced on all subjects, even the super user. The system is viewed as a collection of active entities (subjects) and passive entities (objects). Now an access control attribute, called the *domain*, is associated with each subject. The domain of a subject does not change. Each object has an attribute associated with it, known as the *type* of the object. A Domain Definition Table (DDT) is maintained that represents the access domains have to types. This table can be viewed as a mapping:

$$DDT(d,t) : D \times T \rightarrow \{true, false\}, d \in D, t \in T \tag{4}$$

where D is the set of domains, and T is the set of types. The mapping normally also represents the type of access, so that the range of the DDT mapping is not a boolean value, but a representation of the allowed access modes such as read or execute. Furthermore there is a table, the Domain Interaction Table (DIT) which lists, for each domain, the access subjects in that domain have to subjects in other domains. Once again this can be represented by a mapping:

$$DIT(d_1, d_2) : D \times D \rightarrow \{true, false\}, d_1, d_2 \in D \qquad (5)$$

and usually represents several interactions including signals. A subject is usually a process. The first process started in the system, usually the init process, begins in a specified domain. Applications (executables) are assigned domains according to the roles they must perform. Files and other objects in the system are assigned types. Implicit typing is used, whereby a file inherits the type of the directory in which it is found, unless stated otherwise explicitly. This technique reduces the overhead involved in managing security information in a system with a large number of objects. (ConSA can also implement implicit protection; the Authorization Control may assign one Entity Label to many objects, taking the resource hierarchy into account). Now programs must execute in the correct domain. To allow programs to remain unaltered DTE supports auto domain switching. Programs are started by making use of the `exec()` family of system calls. DTE will determine which domain the program, or entry point, must execute in and will change the domain of that process. DTE also supports new system calls that may be used to query various DTE attributes and may request domain changes. DTE is implemented over and above conventional UNIX security. One of the strengths of the DTE system is the high level configuration files that are used to configure DTE [7]. The reader may refer to [6, 7, 8, 9, 10] for more details of DTE and applications of the system.

6.1. DTE in ConSA

The implementation of DTE in the ConSA system is very similar to that of the LOMAC implementation. New entities may be created to access special DTE services, and possibly for use of the `exec` call. The `exec` call can be easily protected by the ConSA system. The changes to the Linux implementation are as follows:

- SubjectLabel — The Subject Label needs to store the domain of the subject s_d.
- EntityLabel — The Entity Label has a new attribute e_t indicating the type of the object. If the entity refers to a signal or other domain interaction, the attribute s_d will refer to the domain of the target subject. As in LOMAC, `GrantAccess` and `RevokeAccess` and associated methods may be used to modify the DDT and DIT.

- Information Flow Manager—Two methods need implementation namely `ActivateFlow` and `ReturnFlow`.

    - `ActivateFlow(EntityLabel` L_e, `SubjectLabel` L_s, *Parameters*)
    This method will be activated when an object is written to. The mode of access selected is important; however illustration with the boolean mapping of the DDT and DIT is sufficient to demonstrate the implementation. `ActivateFlow` returns true if

$$DDT(L_s.s_d, L_e.e_t) = true \quad (6)$$

    for entities that refer to objects and

$$DIT(L_s.s_d, L_e.s_d) = true \quad (7)$$

    for entities that refer to domains

    - `ReturnFlow(EntityLabel` L_e, `SubjectLabel` L_s, *ReturnVal*)
    This method will be activated when an object is read from. No distinction is made between the flow types, so the mode is used to determine access types. `ReturnFlow` can therefore be implemented exactly as `ActivateFlow`.

LOMAC and DTE are very simple policies that are extremely configurable and can assist in the security of a system considerably. In particular, they help to control the extent to which a system is system is compromised if compromise occurs as a result of application error.

7. RULE SET BASED ACCESS CONTROL (RSBAC)

Rule Set Based Access Control is an implementation of the Generalized Framework for Access Control [11]. The Generalized Framework for Access Control divides access decisions into four components:

- Access Control Information (ACI)
The Access Control Information are the security attributes of subjects and objects within the system. This may include, the sensitivity level of files, or the level of trust of a subject.

- Access Control Context (ACC)
Context is information about the system unrelated to the objects and subjects. For example time, or which subjects are the members of a certain group.

- Access Control Rules (ACR)
  These are the rules that determine if access is granted or not, and define the security policy that is implemented.

- Authorization (ACA)
  The authorization component implements the physical access control mechanism.

RSBAC has two main components to enforce access control:

- Access Enforcement Facility (AEF)
  This component enforces access control on all attempts to access an object. This is implemented by intercepting system calls (by modifying Linux kernel source). This component will then make use of the next component to implement the security model.

- Access Decision Facility (ADF)
  The Access Decision Component implements the decision making process, by consulting the ACC, ACI and ACR. The component consults the rule base, and relays the necessary subject and object attributes as well as the context. This may result in a change of attributes and/or context.

Several models have been implemented, and may work in conjunction, using a *logical and* function to determine the decision. These models include:

- Bell-LaPadula Mandatory Access Control
  The traditional Mandatory Access Control model.

- Functional Control
  A simple role based model, restricting access to security information to security officers, and access to system information to system administrators.

- Role Compatibility
  This model is similar to the DTE model, but it is implemented at subject level. So a subject has a role, and may access certain objects according to that role. The role does not change if a new process is started.

Please Consult [11] for further details.

7.1. RSBAC and ConSA

RSBAC and ConSA have similar goals, to provide a flexible system that may be used to implement several security policies. ConSA may be implemented in RSBAC with suitable access control information, by implementing a component that consults the Information Flow Manager and Entity Label to determine if access is granted. For ConSA to implement RSBAC, the necessary security attributes must be stored in the Subject Label and Entity Label. The Information Flow Manager should then have enough information to invoke the ADF to implement the access control decision. The AEF component is already implemented by intercepting system calls. RSBAC has the following deficiencies:

- Although RSBAC is a modular security system, the current implementation needs direct modification to support new security models. There is no interface for components to be automatically inserted into the system.
- RSBAC can implement many access control mechanisms, but the framework does not assist in the construction of a security model. The ADF component simply queries the supplied modules, and bases the decision on these components.
- Security Attributes are stored in a common ACI structure, this structure does not have support for arbitrary security attributes. The attributes are selected according to the implemented security models. Subject Labels and Entity Labels perform the same role in ConSA and are determined by the security system implementor. A generic ACI system is available through the modular implementation of these labels.

8. CONCLUSION

This paper has demonstrated theoretically that ConSA can implement a wide variety of existing security models, and that the architecture supports the implementation of security models.

References

[1] M. S. Olivier, *Towards a Configurable Security Architecture*, Data & Knowledge Engineering, To appear.

[2] D. E. Bell and L. J. LaPadula, "Secure computer system: unified exposition and Multics interpretation", *Rep. ESD-TR-75-306*, March 1976, MITRE Corporation

[3] *The Linux-PAM System Administrators' Guide*, Andrew G. Morgan, 1998

[4] *Inside Unix*, Chris Hare, Emmett Dunlaney, George Eckel, Steven Lee, Lee Ray, New Riders Publishing, 1994

[5] *The Linux Kernel book*, Remy Card, Eric Dumas, Frank Mevel, Wiley, 1997

[6] *Confining Root Programs with Domain and Type Enforcement*, USENIX UNIX Security Symposium, 1996

[7] *Practical Domain and Type Enforcement for UNIX*, L. Badger, D. F. Sterne, D. L. Sherman, K. M. Walker, S. A. Haghighat, IEEE Symposium on Security and Privacy, 1995

[8] *A Domain and Type Enforcement UNIX Prototype*, IEEE Symposium on Security and Privacy, 5th USENIX UNIX Security Symposium

[9] *Controlling Network Communication with Domain and Type Enforcement* , L. Badger, D. F. Sterne, D. L. Sherman, K. M. Walker, S. A. Haghighat, S. L. Murphy, Proceedings of the 1995 National Information Systems Security conference.

[10] *The Controlled Application Set Paradigm for Trusted Systems*, D. F. Sterne, Glenn S. Benson, Proceedings of the 1995 National Information Systems Security conference.

[11] *Rule Set Based Access Control as proposed in the 'Generalized Framework for Access Control'*, Amon Ott, Masters Thesis, 1997

[12] *From a Formal Privacy Model to its Implementation*, Simone Fischer-Hübner, Amon Ott, National Information Systems Security Conference, 1998

[13] *Design Specification: An Implementation of Access Control Lists for Linux*, http://students.dwc.edu/frival/acl/acldesign.html

[14] *The Linux Trustees Project*, http://www.braysystems.com/linux/trustees.html

[15] *Group ACL for ext2 in LiVE*, http://aerobee.informatik.uni-bremen.de/acl_eng.html

[16] *LOMAC - Low Water-Mark Mandatory Access Control User's Manual v0.2*, Tim Fraser, NAI Labs, 1999

[17] *The Single UNIXR Specification, Version 2*, The Open Group, 1997, *www.opengroup.org*

A NOVEL APPROACH TO CERTIFICATE REVOCATION MANAGEMENT

Ravi Mukkamala and Sushil Jajodia

Abstract: With the ever-increasing growth in electronic messaging and electronic commerce, the need for an infrastructure to provide confidentiality, security, and confidence for such exchanges to take place is quite evident [2]. Here, public keys and certificates are issued to users for authorization purposes. One of the primary concerns in these systems is the handling of certificate revocation prior to the expiration date. In this paper, we propose a new approach for managing certificate revocation. All existing schemes require that the information about revoked certificates be sent only periodically to the directories used for verification. This gives rise to the problem of obsolescence. To overcome this problem, we have introduced a new layer in the traditional architecture. Using a preliminary analysis, we show the impact of the new scheme on the up-to-datedness, robustness, load distribution, and response time of the system. Similarly, we show the additional costs incurred in terms of communication cost, processing cost, and hardware costs.

Keywords: Certification revocation list (CRL), public-key infrastructure (PKI)

1. INTRODUCTION

With the ever-increasing growth in electronic messaging and electronic commerce, the need for an infrastructure to provide confidentiality, security, and confidence for such exchanges to take place is quite evident [2]. Public-Key Infrastructure (PKI) is one such mechanism [2, 5, 8, 10]. Here, public keys are issued to users. In addition, certificates are issued to certify that a given public key does indeed belong to a user.

A certificate attests to the validity of a public key of an individual or other entity and is normally issued by a *Certification Authority* (CA). The purpose of a digital certificate is to allow verification of the claim that a specific public key does in fact belong to a particular entity or individual. Each certificate contains information such as the certificate version number, serial number, name of the issuer (i.e., the CA) and the subject (i.e., the person or entity to whom the certificate relates), a validity period (i.e., not valid before, and not valid after, specific dates/times), a public key, the CA's signature, and the signature algorithm used [2].

Once a Certification Authority (CA) issues a certificate, it is assumed that the certificate will be in use for its entire validity period. However, various circumstances such as compromise or suspected compromise of the private key may cause a certificate to become invalid or untrustworthy prior to its expiration date. Under such circumstances, the CA needs to revoke the certificate [16,18].

Several schemes have been proposed for maintaining and propagating the certificate revocation information. A certificate revocation list (CRL) is one such mechanism [3, 4, 6, 9, 11, 16]. Each CRL is a digitally certified list that identifies revoked certificates with its serial number and the date of revocation. This list could be significantly large depending on the number of certificates revoked by a CA prior to their expiration.

When a certificate is used, a check should be made (say, by a service-provider) on the certificate's signature and validity. The recipient of a certificate from an unknown or untrusted source can check the validity and trustworthiness of the certificate and the public key that it contains by verifying the signature contained in the certificate and checking if the certificate has been revoked or not. For this purpose, the service-provider seeks the services of a "directory" entity. CAs provide the information to the directories to offer such a verification service. When CRLs are used, the directory provides the service-provider with the latest CRL. The service-provider, in turn, can check whether or not the given certificate serial number is in the received CRL. The key question that the service-provider may have about the verification process is: "How much can I rely on the information provided by the directory service?" We refer to this as an issue of confidence that the service-provider is offered by the rest of the system. The answer to this question depends on the "currency" or "up-to-datedness" of the revocation information stored at a directory.

In this paper, we suggest a novel scheme to improve the confidence in the certification verification checking system. This is achieved by introducing a new layer in the multi-tier architecture. The entities at this layer are referred to as CADs (or CA-directories). The proposed architecture also improves the robustness of the certification verification system. In addition, it improves the system performance by transferring some of the CA's load on to its CADs (as explained later). This is shown using a preliminary analysis.

The paper is organized as follows. Section 2 briefly summarizes existing schemes to assemble and propagate revocation information. Section 3 describes the proposed architecture for disseminating the revocation information. Section 4 analyzes the proposed architecture in terms of its currency of information, robustness, and cost. Finally, Section 5 summarizes the paper and discusses possible future extensions to this work.

2. CURRENT SCHEMES FOR CERTIFICATE REVOCATION AND CHECKING

Several schemes have been proposed in the last few years for certificate revocation and dissemination of revocation information. The traditional method is the certification revocation lists (CRL), which are time-stamped, digitally signed lists containing the certificate serial numbers and the revocation dates of all revoked certificates within a CA. A CA typically publishes them periodically and sends them to the directories. The CRL scheme is included as part of the X.509 standard. CRLs are criticized for not providing adequate service and being too costly [14, 17]. However, at present CRLs are in wide use.

The Delta CRL scheme is a mechanism that addresses the size of the CRLs [7]. A Delta CRL is a digitally signed list of incremental changes that took place since the last posting of a full CRL. Delta CRLs are generally significantly smaller than full CRLs, and hence can be posted more frequently. Delta CRLs reduce the network load but may increase the processing load at a directory when it needs to service a verification request from a service-provider.

One of the major problems with CRLs having the same expiration date is that all service-providers may find that their CRLs have expired within a short time. This implies that a directory (or a repository) may suddenly be overloaded with such requests for CRLs. This is rectified by over-issued CRL policy where a CA issues CRLs with different expiration times. This means that depending on the time that a service-provider gets a CRL from its directory, the expiration date may be different. This distributes the request load at the directories. This is referred to as an over-issued CRL method [6, 7].

An alternate scheme to improve performance is the indirect CRL method [1]. Here, a different entity besides a CA can issue a CRL. In addition, a CRL can contain information from multiple CAs. This reduces the number of CRLs that need to be transmitted over the network. It is, however, assumed that the entity issuing the CRLs is trusted.

Certificate Revocation Status (CRS) directory was an early suggestion for reducing the large communication overhead in disseminating the CRLs [14]. In this scheme, a CA generates a 100-bit value for each unexpired certificate. The value would be different for a valid one and a revoked one. The CA periodically updates the directory with the 100-bit values as well as a list of all certificate serial numbers that have not expired. This scheme drastically reduces the communication load.

Other variations of the basic CRL scheme are the Certificate Revocation Trees (CRT) [16], and the On-line Certificate Status protocol (OCSP) [15].

In the rest of the paper, for simplicity, we assume the basic CRL protocol. The discussion and the analysis, however, are independent of the actual protocol and hence applicable for other schemes also.

3. PROPOSED SCHEME FOR CERTIFICATE REVOCATION AND CHECKING

One of the deficiencies of the current schemes (both CRL and CRS) [6, 14] is that the certification authorities only send periodic updates of revocation to the directories. In addition, the service-providers can only contact a directory (and no one else) for revocation status of a certificate. Thus, the up-to-datedness of the service offered by a directory to service-providers depends on the periodicity with which a CA updates the revocation information at the directory. Since there may be hundreds of CAs and thousands of directories [2] in a PKI system, the cost of keeping directories in sync with the CAs would be astronomical. On the other hand, keeping them out of sync reduces the confidence that the service-providers have about the PKI system. We propose an architecture that has a means to improve the service-providers' confidence.

Figure 1 illustrates the five-level PKI architecture. At level 1 are the users who submit requests for services to the service-providers. Along with a request for service, they also provide a public key and a certificate. The service-providers are at level 2. When a service-provider receives a request accompanied by a certificate from a user, it locally checks for the validity of the digital signature. Occasionally, it may contact a directory (at level 3) to check whether or not the certificate presented has been revoked prior to its expiration date. Since a directory itself is only updated with the revocation information periodically (and not as and when the revocation takes place), the service-provider has the option of contacting a CA-directory (CAD) at level 4 to verify the latest status of a certificate. In other words, a service

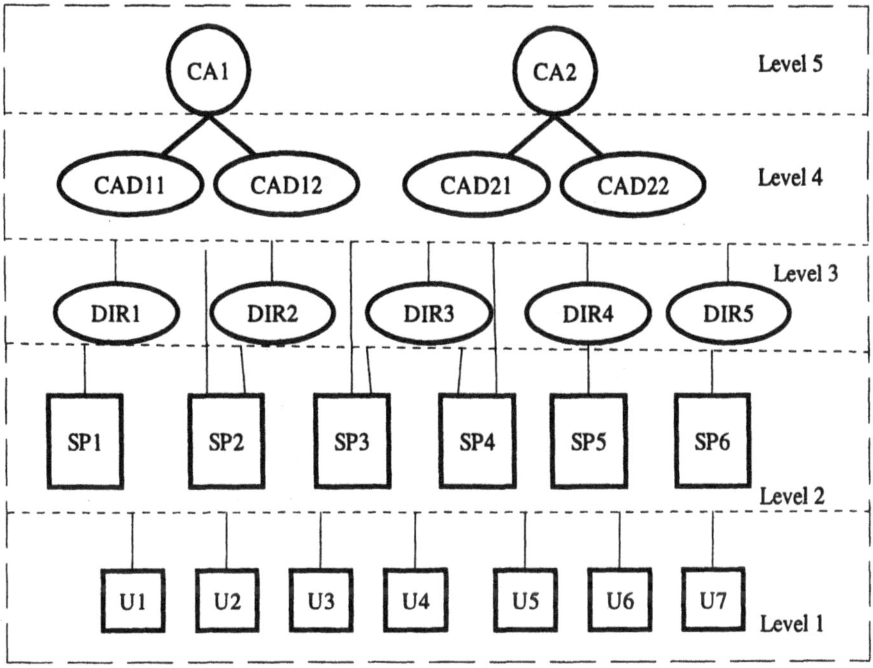

Figure 1. Proposed Architecture for Certificate Revocation and Checking

provider has three choices when a certificate is presented to it---use local information, check with a directory, or check with a CAD.

At level 3, we have directories that are untrusted or less trusted entities. Each directory contains information about the status of certificates issued by all the CAs in the system. In the case of a CRL-based system, a directory would have one CRL per CA. Whenever a service-provider sends a revocation-check request, the directory simply returns the CRL corresponding to the CA that issued the certificate. In the case of CRS, however, the directory sends a certified status information related to that certificate.

At level 4, we have the CADs or CA-directories. This is the additional level introduced in this paper to improve the up-to-datedness of revocation information. A given CAD (such as CAD11 in Figure 1) is associated with a single CA (such as CA1 in Figure 1). Since a CA does not get involved in the verification of certificate status [6], a CAD acts as a proxy for a CA in this task. For this reason, it is a *trusted entity*. It also should be noted that unlike the directories that simply act as intermediaries in delivering the CA (or CAD) supplied CRL to the service providers, a CAD needs to construct the CRLs. This calls for a *trusted CAD* since an untrusted one can generate its own CRLs irrespective of the input from its CA. A CA treats its CADs as its own replicas and keeps them informed of the certificate revocations (and optionally, certificate issues) as and when they occur. Whether or not such an update between the CA and its CADs is done atomically is an implementation issue. But our architecture does not mandate such an atomic update. A CAD keeps information about its own CA. This model can, however, be extended so that it can also act like a directory for other CAs. In other words, a CAD may contain most up-to-date information about its own CA's certificates but contain only periodically updated information about certificates issued by other CAs. This is an implementation and performance issue. For simplicity, we assume that a CAD only contains information about its CA. A CAD is responsible for periodically sending the revocation information about its own CA to all the directories. (In traditional architectures, this was a CA's responsibility.)

Finally, at level 5 are the CAs. These are trusted entities that issue and revoke certificates. Users directly contact a CA for the issue and revocation of certificates. CAs update the information immediately at their CADs. Table 1 summarizes the tasks of the entities at each level of this architecture.

4. COST-BENEFIT ANALYSIS

In this section, we analyze the proposed architecture in terms of the cost incurred and the benefits reaped. The primary cost is the communication cost among the levels and the processing cost at each entity. In addition, cost of additional hardware is also to be considered. The benefits are measured in terms of up-to-datedness of the information, robustness, load distribution, and response-time. In the following discussion, we model the system under a steady state. Thus, we do not model the system behaviour under transient conditions.

C1. Communication cost: Let us now consider the cost of adding an additional level, the CAD level, into the conventional architecture [2, 6, 14]. The interaction between the CA and CADs is an addition to the original architecture.

Every time there is either a new certificate issued or a certificate is revoked, CA would send a message to its CADs. If the rate of certificate issue per CA is λ_{CI}, the length of a certificate is L_{CI}, and the number of CADs per CA is N_{cad}, then the rate of additional messages transmitted (per CA) due to certificate issue is $\lambda_{CI} * N_{cad}$. Similarly, the rate additional bytes transmitted (per CA) is given by $\lambda_{CI} * N_{cad} * L_{CI}$.

Every time there is a certificate revocation, CA would send a message to its CADs. If the rate of certificate revocation per CA is λ_{CR}, and the length of certificate revocation information is L_{CR}, the rate of additional messages transmitted due to certificate revocation is $\lambda_{CR} * N_{cad}$. Similarly, the rate of additional bytes transmitted is given by $\lambda_{CR} * N_{cad} * L_{CR}$.

In summary, the rate of additional messages transmitted is $N_{cad}(\lambda_{CI}+\lambda_{CR})$ and the rate of additional bytes transmitted is $N_{cad}(\lambda_{CI}*L_{CI} + \lambda_{CR}*L_{CR})$. This does not include any messages that may be involved if a CA wants to carry out the updates in an atomic fashion. Since this depends on the specific implementation, we have not included it here.

C2. Processing cost. First, due to the transfer of the certificate status distribution functionality from a CA to its CADs, the processing load at a CA is significantly reduced. This improves the performance that it offers to users for certificate issues and certificate revocations. Additional processing, however, is introduced for updating the CADs as and when a CA issues or revokes certificates. This cost is reflected more in additional communication rather than in processing. Depending on the implementation, there could be a cost of synchronization between a CA and its CADs during such updates.

The processing at a CAD is, of course, an additional cost compared to the traditional architectures. A CAD participates in updating the status information with a CA---it updates the CRLs or CRSs, and distributes them to the directories periodically. In addition, it answers occasional queries from a service-provider regarding the status of a certificate. In summary, some of the processing cost is transferred from CAs and directories to the CADs. Since we assume them to run on independent processors, it would not overload any existing system. The actual impact depends on the implementation.

C3. Hardware and set-up cost. The CADs need additional hardware to run. Besides this cost, there would be no additional costs under this category.

B1. Up-to-date certificate information. In the traditional model, the CA sends the status information of its certificates to the directories periodically. So if the period of status update is T_{SU}, then the information at the directories may be out-of-date by as much as T_{SU}. Suppose the period is 1 week. Then a directory may be unaware of the revocation of a certificate for as long as a week. The cost of providing stale revocation information is borne by the service-providers. When the rate of certificate revocation is λ_{CR}, one may expect an average of $\lambda_{CR}*T_{SU}$ certificates to be revoked in the interval between two updates from CA.

The cost of obsolescence in revocation information can only be measured by its effect on a service-provider. Suppose the service provider assumes that the cost of obsolete information (i.e., providing service to a user whose certificate has been revoked) is C_{ex}. If a service-provider receives service requests at the rate of λ_{sr}, then a fraction of them may be submitting unexpired but revoked certificates. If we assume that a user with an unexpired but revoked certificate continues to behave as if it was never revoked, and if we assume that a service-provider does not keep track of the so called bad credit, then on the average $\lambda_{sr}* P_{rev}$ requests may be corresponding to revoked certificates. This may represent a loss of $C_{ex}*\lambda_{sr}* P_{rev}$ for the service-provider. To reduce this loss, a service-provider contacts the directory service to check the status of a certificate. However, there is a cost C_{cr} to confirm the status of a certificate. Hence, a service provider checks with a directory only with a probability P_{dir}. However, even with this cost, it cannot be completely confident about the status of a certificate.

In the proposed scheme, the service-provider has an option. If it wants to confirm the status of a certificate with 100% confidence, then it could send a verification request to the CAD. Since there are only a few CADs for each CA, the delay at a CAD is likely to be higher than the one at a directory. This could be considered as a cost. In addition, there will be a confirmation cost (similar to C_{cr} and probably higher). As a trade-off, a service- provider could send a fraction of requests to a directory and another fraction to a CAD. Clearly, a high-value request (e.g., high-value purchase) is to be sent to CAD and a medium-value request to a directory. In this way, the service-provider could reduce its losses due to revoked certificates. Of course, if a service-provider needs 100% confidence about a certificate prior to providing a service, then all status confirmations should be sent to CADs. If it prefers to have larger throughput than confidence in the status, then it may be satisfied with its own local validation. In general, it may divide its requests among the local validation, directory, and CAD.

In order to illustrate the effect of introducing CADs on the up-to-datedness of revoked information, we have simulated a system with thousands of generated certificates. Assuming the probability that a certificate is revoked during its lifetime is given, for a given lifetime (T_{LC}) of a certificate, we randomly determine the characteristics of a certificate---the generation time, whether or not it is revoked, and if so when it is revoked. We then vary the status update time (T_{SU}) as a fraction of T_{LC} and measure the impact of CADs. Figure 2 illustrates the results. We measure the impact of introducing CADs on the up-to-datedness in terms of the ratio of the number of unexpired certificates recoded in a CRL to the actual number of unexpired certificates. For example, if 1000 actual unexpired revoked certificates exist of which only 800 were included in the last CRL (for example), the measure of up-to-datedness is 800/1000 or 80%. This metric in some sense indicates the degree of up-to-datedness gained due to the introduction of CADs in the architecture. When Metric 1 is 80%, it indicates that 20% of the queries to a directory would be receiving incorrect answers. I.e., 20% of the time, even a revoked certificate would be reported as unrevoked by the directory. On the other hand, when a service-provider sends its request to a CAD, there would be no such errors.

While the basic definition of the metric is straightforward, the actual measuring process is not unique. One of the key questions that we encounter is the time at which this ratio be measured. In addition, suppose the measure is 70% during 100 units of time and 30% during 30 units, then should we take the time-weighted average as a representative value?

Since the answer was non-trivial, we decided to measure the up-to-datedness by two means. First, we measure it as a time-weighted average. This is referred to as Metric 1. To evaluate this metric, we identified three types of events in the system (i) CRL generation (ii) Certificate revocation, and (iii) Expiry of revoked certificate. At each of theses events, we measure the ratio defined above and then weight it with the time this ratio persists. The weighted average of these measures is represented as Metric 1. As an alternate, we measured the ratio at each instant of certificate revocation (i.e., event 2 of Metric 1), and averaged the ratio over all such events. This is represented as Metric 2.

In Figure 2, it is assumed that a certificate may be revoked at any given time during its lifetime with a probability of 0.1. In other words, 10% of unexpired certificates may be revoked [2, 14]. From the graph it is clear that as the ratio of TSU to TLC increases, the benefit of the proposed architecture increases. In other words, as the interval between CRL updates to directories increases, the up-to-datedness of CRL in directories in the traditional architecture decreases. This is, of course, avoided in the proposed architecture due to the presence of CADs. It may be noticed that the complex measure of Metric 1 as well as Metric 2 resulted in very close results. This may not be too surprising given that the transactions had random start time and revocation times (if revoked). The randomness in the transactions basically eliminated the time factor that we took into account in Metric 1.

Not surprisingly, the rate of arrival of transactions had negligible effect on metric 1 and metric 2. For example, when the rate of revoked transactions was doubled, then metric 1 changed from 76.8% to 77.1%. When it was tripled, it was still 77.1%. Similar behavior was observed of Metric 2. We are still investigating other properties of these metrics.

B2. Robustness: In the traditional architecture, there is a single CA responsible for the issue and revocation of certificates for a given group of users. In the proposed architecture, we have one or more CADs acting as proxies for the CA. Hence, temporary failure of a CA does not result in loss of revocation-checking service offered to the service-providers. If we assume that each service-provider first approaches its own CAD for revocation-checking, and in case of its unavailability seeks the services of other CADs, and ultimately, when all CADs are unavailable, seeks the CA itself, then the robustness offered for the revocation-checking service is given by the probability that at least one of CADs or CA is available. This may be expressed as $1-[(1-R_{CA})\Pi_{i=1,Ncad}(1-R_{CADi})]$, where R_{CA} is the probability that a CA is available, R_{CADi} is the probability that the ith CAD is available, and N_{cad} is the number of CADs per CA. Given the mean time between failures (MTBF) and the mean time to repair (MTTR) of a CA or CAD, the probability that a component is available can be computed as MTBF/(MTBF+MTTR). A CA or CAD may be unavailable either due to planned events such as backup or other maintenance functions, or due to unplanned events such as power failure, system crash, or communication failure.

Figure 3 illustrates the benefit of adding the new layer to the robustness of the system. The ratio MTBF/(MTBF+MTTR) represents the fraction of time that a CA or CAD is available. The benefit of CADs is clearly evident from this graph---as the number of CADs per CA is increased, the robustness is also increased. Of course, the incremental benefit beyond 2 CADs is not significant.

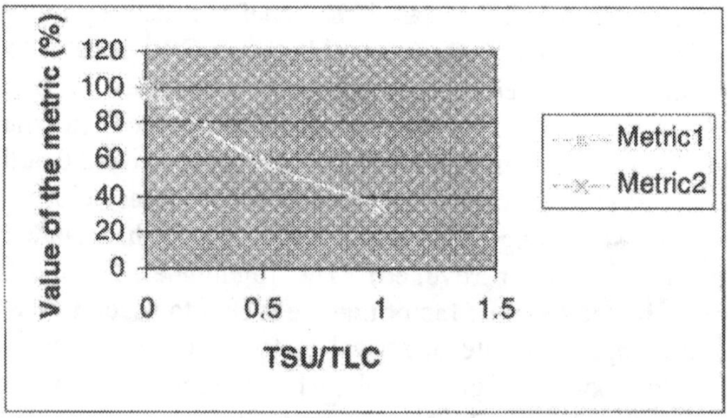

Figure 2. Impact on Up-to-datedness of revocation information

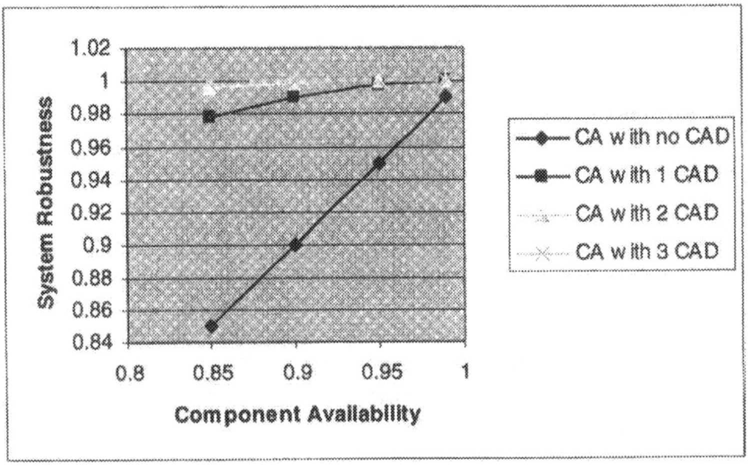

Figure 3. Robustness offered by the proposed architecture

B3. Load distribution: In the traditional architecture, in addition to the responsibility of issuing and revoking certificates, a CA is also responsible for distributing this information to the directories. In fact, this was of primary concern when the number of users and directories under a CA is large [6, 7]. In the proposed architectures, the latter responsibility of distributing the information to directories is delegated to the CADs. Typically, a CAD acts as a primary distributor of information for a specified set of directories. Only in the event that it is not available, either another CAD or the CA itself take up this responsibility. Accordingly, if the rate of periodic certificate status information to each of the N_{dir} directories is λ_{stat} and processing time to prepare and send a message is t_{stat}, then we have effectively eliminated a processing load of $N_{dir}*t_{stat}*\lambda_{stat}$ (per unit time) at the CA and distributed the same among the N_{cad}. Instead, the CA needs to inform each of its CADs whenever it issues or revokes a certificate. If processing time to send a revoke or issues information to a CAD is t_{ca}, the rate of revocation is λ_{CR} and the rate of certificate issue is λ_{CI}, then the additional rate of processing at a CA due to CADs is $t_{ca}*N_{dir}*(\lambda_{CI} + \lambda_{CR})$. This, of course, is a simplified model assuming that the time is proportional to the number of CADs. In general, it may be a more complex function. Thus, the net reduction in the rate of processing load is $(N_{dir}*t_{stat}*\lambda_{stat} - t_{ca}*Ndir*(\lambda_{CI} + \lambda_{CR}))$. This will be reflected in a change in the response time to the user's certificate issue and revocation requests at the CA.

B4. Response time. As mentioned earlier, the transfer of load from CA to CADs improves the response time offered by CAs for certificate issue and revocation requests. Similarly, since some status requests are now routed to CADs, the response at the directories will also be improved. Since CADs share the status query requests among themselves, and only a fraction of queries are received from the service-provider even they can provide a good response. In this paper, we did not quantify this benefit.

5. CONCLUSION

In this paper, we have proposed a new approach for managing certificate revocation in an electronic authorization scheme such as the public-key infrastructure. In all the existing schemes, the information about revoked certificates is only periodically sent to the directories that are used for verification. This gives rise to the problem of obsolescence. To overcome this problem, we have introduced a new layer in the traditional architecture. We refer to it as CAD or CA-directories layer. We then showed the impact of the new scheme on the up-to-datedness, robustness, load distribution, and response time of the system. The additional costs are measured in terms of communication cost, processing cost, and hardware costs. While the actual degrees of benefits depend on factors such as the frequency with which CRL updates are sent to directories and the percentage time a node is available, the benefits are visible over a wide range of these factors.

In the future, we propose to do a detailed simulation of the scheme and measure its other characteristics. In addition, we plan to study schemes under which more and more responsibilities are transferred from CA to CADs thereby improving CA's performance.

REFERENCES

[1] Adams, C., and S. Lloyd, Understanding Public-Key Infrastructure: Concepts, Standards, and Deployment Considerations, Macmillan Publishing, 1999.

[2] S. Berkovits, S. Chokhani, J. A. Furlong, J. A. Geiter, and J. C. Guild, "Public Key Infrastructure Study: Final Report," MITRE, McLean, Virginia, 1994.

[3] CertCo, Inc. White Paper by Richard C. Ankney: Certificate Revocation Mechanisms. Retrieved March 01, 2001 from the World Wide Web: http://www.certco.com./

[4] CertCo, Inc. White Paper by Richard Salz: The Transaction Instant: A Question of Validity. Retrieved March 01, 2001 from the World Wide Web: http://www.certco.com/b2b/OCSP_Salz.pdf

Level	Entity	Type	Functions
5	CA	Trusted	Responsible for issuing and revoking certificates. Inform CA-DIR about issues and revocations.
4	CAD	Trusted	Contains up-to-date information on the status of issued certificates. Responsible for verifying certificate status and periodically informing the directories about revocations.
3	Directory	Untrusted	Contains information that is periodically updated. Responsible for verifying certificate status.
2	Service-provider	Untrusted	Provides services after verifying the validity of users' certificates.
1	User	Untrusted	After obtaining certificates from CA, requests services from service-providers.

Table 1. Architectural entities and their functionality

[5] Chokhani, S., "Toward a National Public Key Infrastructure," IEEE Communications Magazine, September 1994, Vol. 32, Issue: 9, pp. 70-74.

[6] Cooper, D.A., "A model for certificate revocation," Proceedings of the 15th Annual Computer Security Applications Conference, pp. 256-264, December 1999.

[7] Cooper, D.A., "A more efficient use of Delta-CRLs," Proceedings of the 2000 IEEE Symposium on Security and Privacy, pp. 190-202, May 2000.

[8] Ellison, C. and B. Schneier, "Ten Risks of PKI: What You're not Being Told about Public Key Infrastructure." Computer Security Journal, v 16, n 1, 2000, pp. 1-7. [Magazine, selected stories on-line]. Retrieved March 01, 2001 from http://www.counterpane.com/pki-risks.html.

[9] Fox, B., and B. LaMacchia, "Certificate revocation: Mechanics and Meaning," URL: www.farcaster.com/papers/fc98/.

[10] Fratto, M., "Certificate Revocation: When not to trust," Network Computing, June 26, 2000 (URL: http://www.networkcomputing.com/1112/1112ws1.html)

[11] Housley, R., W. Ford,et al., "X.509 Internet Public Key Infrastructure Certificate and CRL Profile." The Internet Society,1999. Retrieved February 14, 2001 from ftp://ftp.isi.edu/in-notes/rfc2459.txt.

[12] McDaniel, P., "Windowed Certificate Revocation," Technical Report CSE-TR-413-99, Department of Electrical Engineering and Computer Science, University of Michigan, 1999 (URL: http://www.eecs.umich.edu/techreports/cse/1999/CSE-TR-413-99.pdf)

[14] Micali, S., "Efficient certificate revocation," Technical Memo MIT/LCS/TM-542b, Massachusetts Institute of Technology, Laboratory for Computer Science, 1996.

[15] Myers, M., R. Ankney, A. Malpani, S. Galperin, and C. Adams, X.509 Internet Public Key Infrastructure: On-line Certificate Status Protocol, IETF RFC 2560, June 1999.

[16] Naor, M., and K. Nissim, "Certificate revocation and certificate update," Proceedings of the 7th USENIX Security Symposium, 1998.

[17] Rivest, R.L., "Can we eliminate certificate revocation lists?" Proc. Financial Cryptogrpahy 1998, Springer-Verlag, Feb. 1998.

[18] Stubblebine, S., "Recent Secure Authentication: Enforcing Revocation in Distributed Systems," IEEE Symposium on Research in Security and Privacy, Oakland, May, 1995, pp. 224-234.

ODAR: AN ON-THE-FLY DAMAGE ASSESSMENT AND REPAIR SYSTEM FOR COMMERCIAL DATABASE APPLICATIONS

Pramote Luenam, Peng Liu
Dept. of Info. Systems, UMBC, Baltimore, MD

Abstract: This paper presents the design and implementation of an on-the-fly damage assessment and repair tool for intrusion tolerant commercial database applications, called ODAR. ODAR is a COTS-DBMS-specific implementation of a general on-the-fly damage assessment and repair approach developed by P. Ammann, S. Jajodia, and P. Liu in [8]. The general approach, given a set of malicious transactions reported by an intrusion detector, locates and repairs the damage caused by each malicious transaction on the database, along with the damage caused by any benign transaction that is affected, directly or indirectly, by a malicious transaction. The general approach locates and repairs damage on-the-fly without the need to periodically halt normal transaction processing. In this paper, the development of the first ODAR prototype, which is for Oracle Server 8.1.6, is discussed. ODAR uses triggers and transaction profiles to keep track of the read and write operations of transactions, locates damage by tracing the affecting relationships among transactions along the history, and repairs damage by composing and executing some specific UNDO transactions. ODAR is transparent to on-going user transactions and very general. In addition to Oracle, it can be easily adapted to support many other database application platforms such as Microsoft SQL Server, Sybase, and Informix. To our best knowledge, ODAR is the first tool that can do automatic on-the-fly damage assessment and repair for commercial database applications.

Key words: damage assessment, damage repair, database security, intrusion tolerance

1. INTRODUCTION

Database security concerns the confidentiality, integrity, and availability of data stored in a database. A broad span of research from authorization [3,4,5], to inference control [1], to multilevel secure databases [6,7], and to multilevel secure transaction processing [2], addresses primarily how to protect the security of a database. One critical step towards attack resilient database systems is *intrusion detection* (ID). ID protects systems by rejecting the future access of detected attackers. However, ID makes the system attack-aware but not attack-resilient, that is, ID itself cannot maintain the integrity and availability of the database in face of attacks.

To overcome the inherent limitation of ID, a broader perspective is introduced, saying that in addition to detecting attacks, countermeasures to these successful attacks should be planned and deployed in advance. In the literature, this is referred to as *survivability* or *intrusion tolerance*. In this paper, we will address a critical database intrusion tolerance problem beyond ID, namely *attack recovery*, and presents the design and implementation of an on-the-fly attack recovery tool, called *ODAR*. ODAR is a COTS-DBMS-specific implementation of a general on-the-fly damage assessment and repair approach developed by P. Ammann, S. Jajodia, and P. Liu in [8]. In this paper, the ODAR prototype, which is for Oracle Server 8.1.6, is discussed. ODAR is very general. It can be easily adapted to support many other DBMS. To our best knowledge, ODAR is the first tool that can do automatic on-the-fly damage assessment and repair for commercial database applications. We have tested ODAR using simulated data. The results show that ODAR causes very little performance penalty, is practical, and can be used to effectively help provide "data integrity" guarantees to arbitrary commercial database applications in face of attacks.

2. ON-THE-FLY ATTACK RECOVERY APPROACH

This section provides a simple introduction to our approach.

- Affecting Relationships among Transactions

In this approach, a *database* is a set of data items handled by *transactions*. A transaction is a partial order of *read* and *write* operations that either *commits* or *aborts*. The execution of a set of transactions is modelled by a structure called a *history*. In a history, a transaction T_i is dependency upon another transaction T_j if there exists a data item x such that T_i reads x after T_j updates it, and there is no transaction that updates x between the time T_j updates x and T_i reads x. The size of the intersection of T_j 's write set and

T_i 's read set is called the dependency degree of T_i upon T_j. The dependent upon relation indicates the path along which damage spreads. In particular, if a transaction which updates x is dependent upon a malicious transaction which updates y, we say the damage on y spreads to x, and we say x is damaged. Moreover, a transaction T_u affects T_v if the ordered pair (T_v, T_u) is in the transitive closure of the dependent upon relation. If malicious transaction B_i affects an innocent transaction G_j, the damage on B_i's write set will spread to G_j 's write set. If an innocent transaction G_j is not affected by a malicious transaction, G_j's write set is not damaged. Therefore, the damage will be repaired if we back out every malicious or affected transaction.

To illustrate, consider the history as follows. B_1 affects G_2 but does not affect G_1. x and y are damaged but z is not. So if B_1 is malicious then backing out B_1 and G_2 can repair the damage caused on x and y.

H: (B_1 reads x) (B_1 writes x) (B_1 commits) (G_1 reads z) (G_2 reads x) (G_1 writes z) (G_2 reads y) (G_1 commits) (G_2 writes y) (G_2 commits)

- The Algorithm

The approach, given a set of malicious transactions (denoted **B**) and a log that records every read and write operation, scans the log to identify every innocent transaction that is affected by **B**. When a malicious transaction is scanned, its write set will be marked *dirty*. When a committed innocent transaction is scanned, if it reads a *dirty* item, then its write set will be marked *dirty* and a specific UNDO transaction will be composed and executed. When a data item is *cleaned* by an UNDO transaction, it will not be marked dirty anymore. For every item that is updated by a transaction to be undone, if the item is not cleaned by any previous UNDO transaction, then a write operation that restores the item to the value before it was damaged will be added to the UNDO transaction.

- Termination Detection

Since the algorithm allows users to continuously execute new transactions as the damaged items are identified and cleaned, new transactions can spread damage if they read a damaged but still unidentified item. So we face two critical questions: (1) Will the repair process terminate? (2) If the repair process terminates, can we detect the terminations? The general approach clearly answers these two questions. First, when the damage spreading speed is quicker than the damage repair speed, the repair process may never terminate. When the damage repair speed is quicker, the repair process will terminate. Second, under the following conditions we can ensure that the repair process will terminate: (1) every malicious transaction is repaired; (2) no item is marked dirty; (3) further scans will not identify any new damage.

3. ODAR

In this section, we will present the design of ODAR. ODAR consists of six major components: (1) The Triggers (2) The Intrusion Detector (3) The Mediator (4) The Read Log Generator (5) The Write Log Generator (6) The Repair Manager. In Figure 1 we illustrate the architecture of ODAR.

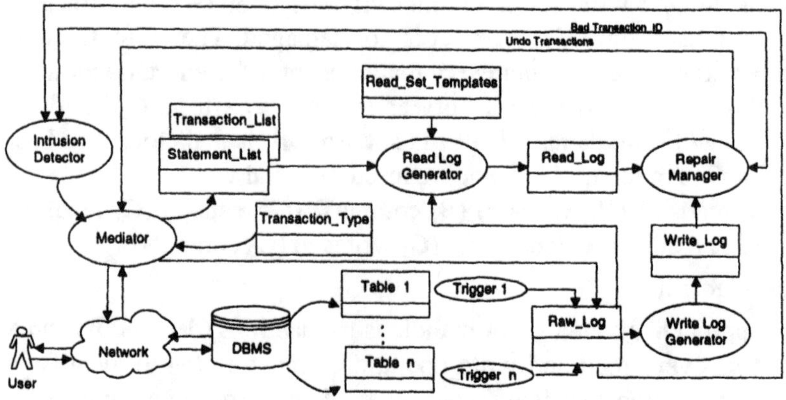

Figure 1. Design of ODAR

3.1 Triggers

We maintain read and write information by adding a trigger to each user table to collect the information about the write operations on that table. When a record is updated, deleted, or inserted, the corresponding trigger is executed and all the write operations are recorded into the Raw_Log table.

- Data Structure

– *Raw_Log*. This table keeps records of every write operation. Each record has 5 fields: (1) Transaction_ID that uniquely identifies a transaction; (2) Item_ID, a composite field, which consists of the Table_Name, Record_ID, and Field_Name; (3) Old_Value which keeps the item's value before it was modified; (4) New_Value which keeps the new item's value (5) Op_Type that indicates the categories of the command. The possible values include 'Insert', 'Update', 'Abort', and 'Commit'.

- An Example

To illustrate, we give an example to show how the trigger works. In this example, ODAR is applied to a banking application. Suppose we have a transaction for updating the customer account balance. The transaction contains 2 operations: an update and an insert. The update operation changes the customer account balance from $1,500.00 to $2000.00. Then, the insert operation records the user transaction into the Transactions table. In this example, writes information consists of the user transaction ID, Account_ID, Amount, Post_Date, and Teller_ID. This information is extracted from the transaction and inserted into the Raw_Log as shown in Figure 2.

Transaction_ID	Item_ID	New_Value	Old_Value	Op_Type
4.91.6240	Accounts.11746392.Acc_Balance	1500.00	2000.00	Update
4.91.6240	Transactions.2833.ID		2833	Insert
4.91.6240	Transactions.2833.Account_ID		11746392	Insert
4.91.6240	Transactions.2833.Amount		500.00	Insert
4.91.6240	Transactions.2833.Post_Date		21-Mar-00	Insert
4.91.6240	Transactions.2833.Teller_ID		Teller-1	Insert

Figure 2. Records in the Raw_Log generated by the trigger

3.2 Intrusion Detector

The Intrusion Detector has a responsibility to detect and report malicious transactions to the Repair Manager. It uses the trails kept in the Raw_Log and some other relevant proofs to identify bad transactions. If a bad transaction is active when being identified, the transaction will be aborted and any further malicious transactions submitted by the malicious user will be rejected. However, if a bad transaction is already committed when being identified, the bad transaction's identifier will be sent to the Repair Manager.

3.3 Mediator

The Mediator is responsible for maintaining read and write information. The main functions include: (1) Providing services to clients for accessing the database; (2) Capturing information about transactions' behavior. The information is then kept in the Statement_List and the Transaction_List; (3) Identifying the type of each in-coming transaction. This function provides support for capturing read operations. The Mediator identifies the type of a transaction by matching the transaction's statements with the transaction patterns kept in the Transaction_Type table.

- Data Structures

– *Transaction_List* table and *Transaction_Type* table. The transaction_list keeps some important information about transactions. The information includes the Transaction_ID, transaction status, and transaction type. The Mediator records log into the table when specific events occur in the transaction. The events include 'Start,' 'Commit,' and 'Abort.' The Transaction _Type keeps (1) transaction patterns that are used for matching operation and (2) the transaction type that is used to indicate the particular type of the transaction.

- *Statement_List*. This table records every client's SQL statement, which is sent to the database including the particular type and sequence.

- An Example

As described earlier, the Mediator is responsible for recording the read and write information into the Transaction_List and Statement_List (see Figure 4, 5). In addition, after a transaction is committed, the Mediator inserts a 'Commit' record into the Raw_Log (see Figures 6).

Pattern_Txt	Type	Compare_Len
SELECT Acc_balance FROM accounts WHERE Account_ID = :ID	A	50
SELECT Cust_name, Cust_addr FROM customers WHERE Cust_ID = :ID	B	50

Figure 3. Example of a record in the Transaction_Type

Transaction_ID	Session_No	Transaction_Status	Transaction_Type
4.91.6240	21253	Start	
4.91.6240	21253	Type	A
4.91.6240	21253	Commit	

Figure 4. Example of records in the Transaction_List maintained by the Mediator

Transaction_ID	SQL_Type	Statement_Text	Statement_Seq
4.91.6240	SELECT	SELECT Acc_balance FROM accounts WHERE Account_ID = 11746392	1
4.91.6240	UPDATE	UPDATE accounts SET Acc_balance = Acc_balance+500	2
4.91.6240	INSERT	INSERT INTO transaction (ID, Account_ID, Amount, Post_Date, Teller_ID) values (2833, 11746392, 500.00, '21-Mar-00', Teller-1')	3

Figure 5. Example of records in the Statement_List maintained by the Mediator

Transaction_ID	Item_ID	New_Value	Old_Value	Op_Type
4.91.6240	Accounts.11746392.Acc_Balance	1500.00	2000.00	Update
4.91.6240	Transactions.2833.ID		2833	Insert
4.91.6240	Transactions.2833.Account_ID		11746392	Insert
4.91.6240	Transactions.2833.Amount		500.00	Insert
4.91.6240	Transactions.2833.Post_Date		21-Mar-00	Insert
4.91.6240	Transactions.2833.Teller_ID		Teller-1	Insert
4.91.6240				Commit

Figure 6. Records in the Raw_Log after the 'Commit' operation is inserted

Suppose there are two types of transactions identified by 'A', and 'B' (see Figure 3) and the operation continues from the previous example in section 3.1. While the transaction is active, all SQL statements, including SELECT, UPDATE, and INSERT, will be recorded into the Statement_List (see Figure 5). In addition, the Mediator inserts three records about events of the transaction, 'Start', 'Commit' and the transaction type, into the Transaction_List table (see Figure 4). The transaction type is obtained by matching the first SQL statement of the transaction with the pattern stored in the Transaction_Type table. Before performing the pattern matching, the Mediator has to substitute the variable in the Pattern_Txt with the value extracted from the SQL statement. For example, the variable :ID will be substituted with '11746392' (Account_ID). After the Mediator successfully performs a matching, the transaction type will be searched out. In this example, the transaction type, obtained from the matching process, is 'A'.

3.4 Read Log Generator

The Read Log Generator maintains the Read_Log table to keep track of all the read operations. Once a 'Commit' operation is inserted into the Raw_Log table, the trigger on the Raw_Log will invoke the Read Log Generator. To capture read operations, First, the Mediator identifies the type of each in-coming transaction. This task can be done by matching each statement in a transaction with patterns kept in the Transaction_Type. Second, the Mediator records each SELECT statement and the relevant arguments in the Statement_List. The Mediator also keeps the type, status, and other information of the transaction in the Transaction_List. Third, the Read Log Generator uses the transaction type information and the arguments to materialize the relevant templates maintained in the Read_Set_Templates. Finally, the Read Log Generator retrieves read information from the Statement_List, and generates it into the Read_Log.

- Data Structures

- *Read_Log*. This table logs read operations of transactions. Each record has two fields: the Transaction_ID and the Item_ID.
- *Read_Set_Templates*. This table keeps the read operation patterns of transactions. Each record consists of: (1) Transaction_Type. The particular type of the transaction; (2) Statement_Seq. The sequence of the SELECT statements in the transaction; (3) Field_Seq. The sequence of fields in the SELECT statement; (4) Field_Name. The name of fields in the SELECT statement.

- An Example

Suppose this operation continues from the example in section 3.3. The Read Log Generator is invoked by the trigger on the Raw_Log, whenever a 'Commit' operation is inserted into the Raw_Log. The Transaction_ID ('4.91.6240') is passed to the Read Log Generator as an input parameter. By using the value, the Read Log Generator searches the *log serial number* (LSN) of the transaction from the Write_Log. However, the Write_Log is empty now. Therefore, the Read Log Generator has to generate the LSN itself. Suppose the generated value is 100. With the LSN = '100' and the Op_type = 'Start', the Read Log Generator inserts the first record into the Write_Log (see Figure 8).

In order to log the read operation, we need to know the value of the LSN, and the Item_ID. The Item_ID is composed of Table_Name, Record_ID, and Field_Name. The Table_Name and Record_ID can be extracted from the user SELECT statement while the Field_Name can be retrieved from the Read_Set_Templates by identifying the Transaction_Type and the Statement_Seq. The Transaction_Type can be obtained from the Transaction_List by searching with Transaction_ID = '4.91.6240' and Transaction_Status = 'Type'. As a result, the Transaction_Type = 'A' is returned (see Figure 4). For the Statement_Seq, we obtain the value from the Statement_Seq field in the Statement_List table. In this example, the Statement_Seq of the read operation = '1'. With the Transaction_Type = 'A' and Statement_Seq = '1', the Read Log Generator gets all field name specified in the read operation from the Read_Set_Templates (see Figure 7). Finally, the Read Log Generator inserts the read information into the Read_Log table as shown in Figure 9.

Transaction_Type	Statement_Seq	Field_Seq	Field_Name
A	1	1	Acc_Balance
B	1	1	Cust_Name
B	1	2	Cust_Addr

Figure 7. Example of records in the Read_Set_Templates

LSN	Transaction_ID	Item_ID	New_Value	Old_Value	Op_Type	Time_Stamp
100	4.91.6240				Start	21-Mar-00

Figure 8. Records in the Write_Log generated by the Read Log Generator

LSN	Transaction_ID	Item_ID	Time_Stamp
101	4.91.6240	Accounts.11746392.Acc Balance	21-Mar-00

Figure 9. Records in the Read_Log generated by the Read Log Generator

3.5 Write Log Generator

The Write Log Generator maintains the Write_Log table to capture write operations involved in an INSERT, UPDATE, or DELETE command. The Write Log Generator is invoked by the trigger associated with the Raw_Log table whenever a 'Commit' record is inserted into the Raw_Log table.

- Data Structure

– *Write_Log* Table. This table keeps records of every write operation. It has the same structure as the Raw_Log table except that it has the LSN column. The column keeps the LSN of a write record in a transaction.

3.6 Repair Manager

The Repair Manager has a responsibility to perform on-the-fly damage assessment and repair. To do the job, the Repair Manager receives a message from the Intrusion Detector. The message contains the Transaction_ID, which is used to specify records of the malicious and affected transactions. All corresponding records, which contain the Transaction_ID, are retrieved from the Write_Log and the Read_Log table. For each data item in those records, the following operations are performed:

1. Keep the data item that might be marked as dirty items later. The suspect data item will be added to the tmp_item_set, if it is found in the cleaned_item_set, and the LSN of the item is greater than the LSN of the last current record in the Write_Log table.
2. Determine if a transaction has to be undone. A data item will be added to the tmp_undo_list, if (1) the in-repair transaction has read any data items in the dirty_item_set, or the cleaned_item_set, and (2) the LSN of the last record in the Write_Log is greater than the LSN of the read record.
3. Undo all changes made by a malicious or affected transaction. To perform the operation, all write records within the transaction are retrieved from the Write_Log table. The 'Insert' operation can be undone by deleting the corresponding records from the application table. While the 'Update' operation can be undone by rollback the current value in the application table to the old value that is kept in the Write_Log table.
4. Maintain the submitted_item_set by recording some details of every data item that's undo operation has been submitted to the Mediator but the item still has not been cleaned.
5. Maintain the dirty_item_set to keep data items that are marked as dirty.

- Termination Conditions

On-the-fly repair operations are performed repeatedly until the following termination conditions are satisfied: (a) every bad transaction has been undone; and (b) the dirty_item_set and the tmp_undo_list are empty; and (c) the LSN of each item stored in the cleaned_item_set is not less than the LSN of the next Write_Log entry to scan.

- Data Structure

The Repair Manager uses the following major data structures:

- *tmp_item_set*, an array of records that is used to keep information about an item (i.e. Item_ID) that may have been damaged.
- *cleaned_item_set*, an array of records that is used to keep information about items that have been cleaned. Each record of the array has two

fields: (1) LSN that denotes log serial number of the bottom record of the log at the time when the item is cleaned; (2) Item_ID.
- *dirty_item_set*. This array keeps information of every data item that is marked as dirty. Each record of the array contains the Item_ID field.
- *tmp_undo_list*. This array keeps information about every in-repair transaction (i.e. Transaction_ID) that has read some data items in the dirty_item_set or satisfies others criteria which have been discussed in the previous section.

4. TESTING ODAR

In this section, we present the testing results of three experiments designed to examine the performance of ODAR. In each experiment, we measure the performance at two stages of databases -- busy and not busy. In busy status, the database was rarely idle. We simulated the busy status by running ten concurrent users. Each user continuously accessed the database at the same time. Each transaction made by a user is composed of several UPDATE and SELECT statements. However, these transactions only increase workload for database and do not generate any logs into our system.

For our testbed, we use Oracle 8.1.6 Server to be the underlying DBMS. The Oracle Server, the Mediator, and the Intrusion Detector are running on a DELL dual PIII 800Mhz PC with 512MB memory. The Repair Manager and the transaction simulator are running on a Gateway PC with a PIII 600Mhz and 128MB memory. These two PCs run Windows NT 4.0 and are connected by a 10/100Mbps switch LAN, however, the speed to the DELL Database Server is only 10Mbps. The current version of ODAR has around 20,000 lines of C++ and Oracle PL/SQL code. Each component of ODAR is implemented as a set of C++ objects that have a couple of CORBA calling interfaces through which other components can interact with the component and the reconfiguration can be done. We use ORBacus V4.0.3 as the ORB.

- **Experiment I: Average Repair Time vs. Dependency Degree**

The objective of this experiment is to study the effects of changing the value of dependency degree to the average delay for cleaning damaged items. In this test, we simulate a sequence of transactions with a specific probabilistic dependency degree. Each dependency degree number denotes size of the intersection of a transaction's write set and its previous adjacent transaction's read set.

- **Experiment I: in Not Busy Database**

Various *simulation parameters* are specified in this experiment. First, five concurrent users are simulated to launch the transactions. The database contains 10,000 records. Each record contains 140 bytes. Three types of transactions are simulated: large, medium, and small. A large size transaction is composed of 15 read operations and 10 write operations. A medium size transaction is composed of 8 read operations and 4 write operations. A small size transaction is composed of 5 read operations and 2 write operations.

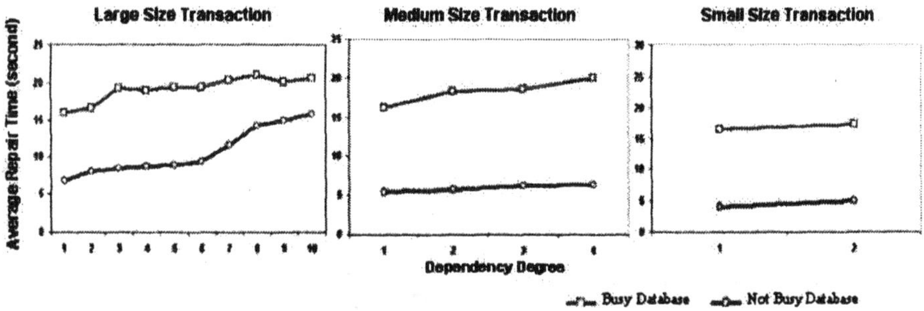

Figure 10. Average Repaired Time vs. Dependency Degree

The average values of the average repair time over dependency degree are plotted in graphs shown in Figure 10. Results show that the dependency degree affects system performance. For all three sizes of transactions, high dependency degree leads to high average repair time. The higher dependency degree increases the possibility of affected transactions. Consequently, the increase in the number of affected transactions increases the average repair time. Additionally, at the same dependency degree, performance suffers least when processing the small size transactions. Comparing the slope between three transaction sizes, the slope of the large size transaction is steepest. The reason is that more statements are needed to repair large size transactions. In addition, high average repair time for large size transactions may be due to data concurrency. Since we simulate this experiment with five concurrent users, there will be more chances for large size transactions when some records are simultaneously accessed by many transactions.

- **Experiment I: in Busy Database**

In this experiment, we measure the performance over dependency degree while the database is busy. Parameters used in this experiment are set to the same value as the previous one. Results are shown in Figure 10.

Compared to the previous experiment in the not busy database, the average repair time increases 70-150%, 130-160%, and 145-165% for the large size transactions, medium size transactions, and small size transactions respectively. From the results, the performance is affected most by the small size transactions. The slope of the large size transactions is steepest among three sizes of transactions. The results support the previous finding that the higher dependency degree increases the possibility of affected transactions in large size transactions than that in medium and small size transactions.

- **Experiment II: Average Repair Time vs. the Number of Transactions**

The objective of this experiment is to test the Repair Manager's performance by measuring the average of time used for cleaning damaged items regarding several numbers of transactions. We measure the performance in two statuses of databases – busy and not busy.

- **Experiment II: in not Busy Database**

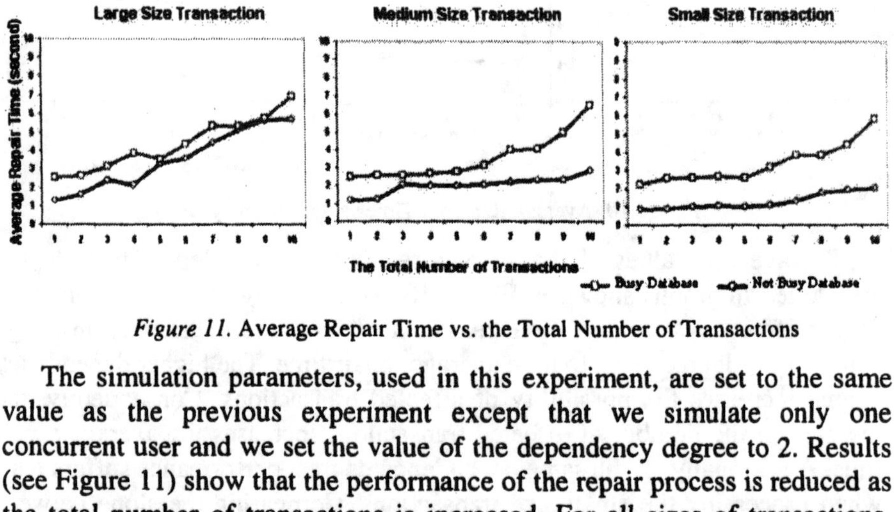

Figure 11. Average Repair Time vs. the Total Number of Transactions

The simulation parameters, used in this experiment, are set to the same value as the previous experiment except that we simulate only one concurrent user and we set the value of the dependency degree to 2. Results (see Figure 11) show that the performance of the repair process is reduced as the total number of transactions is increased. For all sizes of transactions, high total number of transactions leads to high average repair time. This is because higher numbers of transactions increase the workload of the Repair Manager since the number of statements to be processed is increased.

Additionally, at the same total number of transactions, performance suffers least when processing the small size transactions. When comparing the slope between three transaction sizes, we can see that the slope of large size transactions is steepest among the three sizes of transactions. The higher number of transactions increases the possibility of affected transactions in large size transactions than that in medium and small size transactions.

- **Experiment II: in Busy Database**

In this experiment, we measure the performance over the total number of transactions when the database is rarely idle. All parameters are set to the same value as the previous experiment. Results (see Figure 11) show that the repair process, in the busy database, takes more average repair time than the not busy database. Average repair time increases 2-95%, 25-130% and

120-190% for large size transactions, medium size transactions, and small size transactions respectively. From the results, the Repair Manager's performance is affected most for small size transactions.

– **Experiment III: Impact on Throughput**

The objective of this experiment is to evaluate the impact of ODAR on the throughput of transaction processing. This test is performed by comparing the average time used for executing a single transaction when ODAR is deployed with the average time when ODAR is not enforced. Note that the average time used for executing a transaction represents the throughput of a database server.

- **Throughput in not Busy Database**

In this experiment, we measure the average repair time while no other transactions are processed except the simulated transactions. We simulate two types of transactions – large and small. All parameters, except the dependency degree, are set to the same value as the previous experiment. The average values of the average repair time when ODAR is/is not deployed over dependency degree are shown in Figure 12.

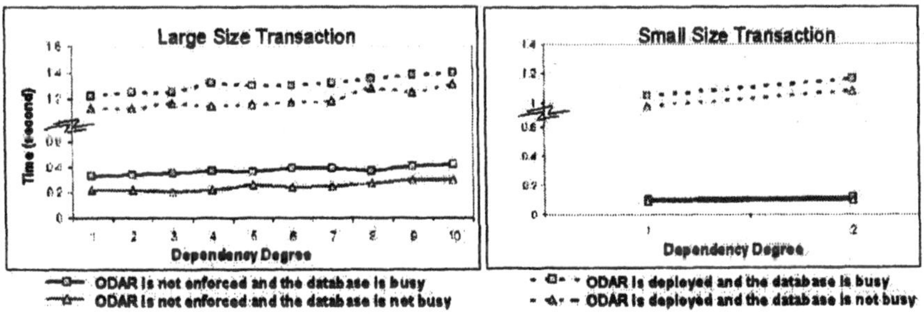

Figure 12. Impact on Throughput

Results indicate that ODAR affects performance of the system. The average time used for executing a transaction increases between 37-68% for large size transactions, and 11-20% for small size transactions. This is because large size transactions have much more read and write statements to be processed by the Mediator and the Repair Manager. Therefore, large size transactions have more performance penalty than small size transactions have. However, in real world applications where several read and write statements are usually combined into a single SQL statement, the response time delay should be much smaller than the results here.

- **Throughput in Busy Database**

In this experiment, we study the impact of ODAR on the average transaction execution time. Results are shown in Figure 12. Similar to the pervious experiment, performance drops when ODAR is deployed. Results show that, in the busy database, the average time used for creating a transaction increases for all sizes of transactions. It increases 30-50% for large size transactions and 10-30% for small size transactions. The results support the previous finding that large size transactions have more performance penalty than small size transactions have.

5. CONCLUSION

In this paper, we present the design and implementation of ODAR, an on-the-fly damage assessment and repair tool for intrusion tolerant commercial database applications. The first prototype of ODAR is tested using simulated data. The results show that the impact of ODAR on the performance of normal transaction processing is very small, which indicates that ODAR can be a practical solution towards providing "data integrity" guarantees to arbitrary commercial database applications in face of attacks.

ACKNOWLEDGEMENT

Luenam and Liu were supported by the Defense Advanced Research Projects Agency (DARPA) and Air Force Research Laboratory, Air Force Material Command, USAF, under agreement number F30602-00-2-0575.

REFERENCES

[1] M. R. Adam. Security-control methods for statistical database: A comparative study. ACM Computing Surveys, 21(4), 1989.

[2] V. Atluri, S. Jajodia, and B. George. Multilevel Secure Transaction Processing. Kluwer Academic Publishers, 1999.

[3] P. P. Griffiths and B. W. Wade. An authorization mechanism for a relational database system. ACM Transaction on Database Systems, 1(3):242-255, September 1976.

[4] S. Jajodia, P. Samarati, V. S. Subrahmanian, and E. Bertino. A unified framework for enforcing multiple access control policies. In Proceedings of ACM SIGMOD International Conference on Management of Data, pages 474-485, May 1997.

[5] F. Rabitti, E. Bertino, W. Kim, and D. Woelk. A model of authorization for next-generation database systems. ACM Transaction on Database Systems, 16(1):88-131, 1994.

[6] R. Sandhu and F. Chen. The multilevel relational (mlr) data model. ACM Transactions on Information and Systems Security, 1(1), 1998.

[7] M. Winslett, K. Smith, and X. Qian. Formal query languages for secure relational databases. ACM Transactions on Database Systems, 19(4):626-662, 1994.

[8] P. Ammann, S. Jajodia, and P. Liu. Recovery from malicious transactions. Technical report, George Mason University, Fairfax, VA. Under Review for Journal publication.

VII

MULTILEVEL SYSTEMS

AN EXTENDED TRANSACTION MODEL APPROACH FOR MULTILEVEL SECURE TRANSACTION PROCESSING

Vijayalakshmi Atluri

MSIS Department and CIMIC, Rutgers University, Newark, NJ 07102

atluri@andromeda.rutgers.edu

Ravi Mukkamala

Department of Computer Science Old Dominion University,Norfolk, VA 23529

mukka@cs.odu.edu

Abstract Multilevel secure transaction processing has been well explored in the past decade. Despite this research, the proposed secure concurrency control protocols are not completely satisfactory because of the stringent constraints imposed by multilevel security. In this paper, we argue that modeling a transaction as an extended transaction model could significantly reduce the performance penalty. We accomplish this by minimizing (1) the probability of restarting a high security level transaction; and (2) the portion of the transaction to be reexecuted, when a restart becomes inevitable. In particular, we exploit the non-flat nature of transactions by identifying dependencies among various components of a transaction and portraying a transaction as an advanced transaction model. We demonstrate, via formal proofs, that our approach preserves the semantics of the transaction, and our concurrency control algorithm guarantees serializability.

Keywords: Multilevel Security, Transaction Processing, Advanced Transaction Model

1. INTRODUCTION

Access control requirements on sensitive data can be broadly classified into two categories: (1) *discretionary access control* (DAC), in which users, at their discretion, are allowed to grant permissions on the data they own, and (2) *mandatory access control* (MAC), in which all data are labeled based on their level of sensitivity and all users are given clearances, where users are allowed to access data with a given label only if their level of clearance permits them. Although many commercial applications employ DAC, it is not adequate where more stringent security requirements are needed as they are vulnerable to sophisticated attacks, such as Trojan Horse Attacks. Such application domains call for multilevel secure (MLS) systems that enforce MAC.

The area of transaction processing in multilevel secure (MLS) database management systems (DBMSs) has substantially progressed in the past few years. The major emphasis of this progress can be seen in secure concurrency control, one of the essential components of secure transaction processing. Concurrency control aims at synchronizing the operations of concurrent transactions to ensure correct execution.

Despite the substantial research activity, the proposed secure concurrency control protocols are not completely satisfactory because of the stringent constraints imposed by multilevel security. Researchers have proposed transaction processing protocols, in particular, concurrency control protocols using locking, timestamping, hybrid (combination of locking and timestamping) techniques. Other solutions try to tackle this difficult problem by maintaining multiple versions of data. Unfortunately, these solutions do not meet all the requirements of a secure concurrency control protocol; they trade either performance or recency for achieving security.

More specifically, the problem with the secure transaction processing is that if a data conflict between a low security level transaction and a high security level transaction should occur, for security reasons, the conflict must *always* be resolved in favor of the low security level transaction. In other words, the low level transaction has the right of way, whereas the high level transaction is hindered or restarted.

In the cases where a transaction has to be restarted, some solutions require that all of the transaction's effects must be undone and then the transaction is reexecuted from the beginning [1]. Other solutions reexecute starting from the first low read operation [7, 4]. These approaches however, cause resource wastage and in some cases results in starvation of high security level transactions. Much of the prior research in this area has been limited to the traditional transaction concepts.

Motivated by the need for releasing the rigidity, traditional transaction models have been extended in various directions. The objective of this paper is to investigate how the properties of the extended transaction models can be utilized to yield better secure concurrency control solutions for MLS DBMSs.

We have recognized that modeling a transaction as an extended transaction model, in particular as a workflow model, could reap significant gains in performance. In our work, we explore mechanisms that are specifically tailored for reducing the performance penalty to be paid for restarts by designing protocols such that (1) the probability of restarting a high security level transaction is minimum; and (2) even when a restart becomes inevitable, the portion of the transaction to be reexecuted is minimum.

This paper is organized as follows. In section 2, we introduce the preliminaries of our extended transaction model and the security model. In section 3, we review the related work in this area. In section 4, we present an overview of our extended transaction model approach. In section 5, we present our secure concurrency control algorithm using the extended transaction model. Proofs of correctness that demonstrate that our redesign algorithm does indeed generate extended transactions that are equivalent to the original transactions, and the concurrency control algorithm guarantees (one-copy) serializability, have been omitted in this paper due to space limitations. Finally, in section 6, we summarize the results and discuss future work.

2. THE MODEL

In this section, we present our extended transaction model, and review the multilevel security model. Our approach assumes multiple versions of data and relies on the multiversion serializability theory reviewed in [7].

2.1. Extended Transaction Model

Driven by the needs of advanced application domains such as design, engineering, manufacturing and commerce, several extended transaction models have been proposed [6]. Many of these models recognize the fact that the transactions are not always flat. Some such extended models include nested transactions and workflow transactions. There has been an established model of nested transaction processing [3], which describes the way to ensure the correctness under the scenario where a transaction is split-up into various subtransactions. Splitting of a transaction into subtransactions based on semantic information is described in [2, 12]. Thus, in an extended transaction model, a transaction can be chopped into meaningful subtransactions, where there exist dependencies among them. In this paper, we recognize two types of dependencies among subtransactions within a transaction: data dependency and value dependency. In addition, we recognize another type of dependency between different transactions.

In the following, we develop the necessary formalism of the extended transaction model employed in this paper. Let T_i be a transaction. We use T_{ij} to represent the jth subtransaction of T_i.

Definition 1 We say that a data dependency $T_{ij} \rightarrow T_{ik}$ exists, if the results of the write operations in T_{ik} are dependent on the read operations of T_{ij}.

Definition 2 We say that a value dependency $T_{ij} \xrightarrow{exp} T_{ik}$ exists if T_{ik} has to be executed only if exp is true. Here, exp is an expression over the data items (accessed or modified) in T_{ij}.

The third type of dependencies that we present below are specified between either subtransactions of two *different* transactions, or between two transactions. We assume that every (sub)transaction is associated with a set of transaction management primitives that move the (sub)transaction from one state to the other. We assume for each transaction and subtransaction, the set of primitives and states as follows:

	primitives	states
transaction	{begin, precommit, commit, abort}	{initial, done, commit, abort}
subtransaction	{begin}	{initial, done}

Definition 3 A control-flow dependency $T_{ij} \stackrel{s_{ij},p_{kl}}{\longrightarrow} T_{kl}$ states that primitive p_{kl} of T_{kl} is invoked only if T_{ij} enters state s_{ij}.

Although several types of control-flow dependencies may be defined based on the above states and primitives [5], in this paper, we use the following two.

1. $T_{ij} \stackrel{bd}{\longrightarrow} T_{kl}$: This states that T_{kl} begins only if T_{ij} enters a "done" state.

2. $T_i \stackrel{t}{\longrightarrow} T_j$: This states that T_j terminates (either commit or abort) only if T_i terminates.

2.2. Multilevel Security Model

We assume the security structure to be a partially ordered set S of security levels with ordering relation $\leq$. A class $s_i \in S$ is said to be *dominated* by another class $s_j \in S$ if $s_i \leq s_j$.

Let D be the set of all data objects. Each data object $d \in D$ is associated with a security level. Every transaction T_i is associated with a security level. We assume that there is a function L that maps all data objects and tasks to security levels. That is, for every $d \in D$, $L(d) \in S$, and for every transaction $T_i \in W$, $L(T_i) \in S$. We require every transaction to obey the following two security properties — the simple security and the restricted $\star$-property.

1. A transaction T_i is allowed to read a data object d only if $L(d) \leq L(T_i)$
2. A transaction T_i is allowed to write to a data object d only if $L(d) = L(T_i)$.

In addition to these two restrictions, a *secure* system must prevent illegal information flows via covert channels.

3. RELATED WORK

Secure concurrency control with traditional transaction models has been well understood [8, 1, 7, 9, 10]. In the following, we only review the solutions that are closely relevant to our work. The protocol proposed by Keefe and Tsai [8] uses a priority queue where transactions are placed in the queue based on the security level of the transaction. A transaction is assigned a timestamp that is smaller than all active transactions executing at lower security levels.

As a result, a *high* transaction's read operation does not interfere with a *low* transaction's write operation since the *high* transaction is considered as an older transaction though it arrives later than the *low* transaction. Although this requires a trusted code for implementation, it ensures one-copy serializability (the usual notion of correctness when multiple versions are maintained in the database) without compromising security. Moreover, transactions are never subjected to starvation. However, high transactions are sometimes given stale versions of the low data.

The protocol proposed by Jajodia and Atluri [7] assigns timestamps to transactions as in a conventional timestamp ordering protocol. According to this protocol, transactions are sometimes made to wait for their commit. Whenever a *high* transaction reads *low* data, it is not allowed to commit until all *low* transactions with smaller timestamps than that of itself commit. This is because a *low* level transaction with a smaller timestamp can always invalidate the read operation of the *high* transaction by issuing a write. In such an event, the *high* transaction is reexecuted. This protocol guarantees one-copy serializability, is secure, and free of starvation. In addition, it can be implemented with completely untrusted code. Restarting a transaction may have significant impact on performance, especially if they are not short lived.

Researchers have proposed other solutions that compromise correctness for ensuring security. Jajodia and Atluri [7] have proposed three increasingly stricter notions of correctness for multiversion multilevel databases — *level-wise serializability, one-item read serializability* and *pairwise serializability* — that are weaker than one-copy serializability.

Bertino et al. [4] proposed a lock-based scheme for implementing transactions in a multilevel secure file storage system. Assuming the availability of a *trusted* lock manager and a *trusted* file manager, they implement a covert-channel-free MLS system. The main contribution of their work is the introduction of a "signal lock" along with the usual read lock and write lock in a 2PL scheme. They do assume a single version for each data item and use strict 2PL for concurrency control for transactions at the same security level. A high-level transaction intending to read a low-level data item obtains a signal-lock on the item. If the item is already write-locked by a low-level transaction, then the high-transaction has to wait until the write-lock is released. A low writer however does not need to wait when a data item is signal-locked by a high-level reader. In addition, they provide language primitives by which a high-level transaction can roll-back to a prespecified step when it receives a signal from the low-level indicating that the data item that it read has now been written. A transaction can then rollback to the state prior to the read statement. Similar strategy is also explained by Ray et al. in [11]. Both the approaches in [4, 11] incur the same penalty in performance as that in [7].

Our work deviates from prior work significantly. The novel part of our work is that we exploit the non-flat nature of transactions by identifying the dependencies among various components of a transaction. In other words, we redesign a transaction and model it as an advanced transaction model. As a result of this redesign, we can minimize the number of restarts or even unnecessary rollbacks to a prior save-state.

4. OVERVIEW OF THE EXTENDED TRANSACTION MODEL APPROACH

Our approach to achieve efficient execution of multilevel transactions relies on first recognizing the data dependencies among the various operations (sets of operations), and the non-flat nature of the transaction.

As mentioned in section 1, the goal of our approach is to reduce the amount of reexecution of the transaction when restart becomes inevitable. In the following, we describe three cases where such optimizations are possible. In the first case, a restart is necessary, however, the transaction need not have to be restarted in full. In the second case, a particular data modification by a low security level transaction does not necessitate any form of corrective action by a high security level transaction. In the third case, a data modification may require some corrective action, but the compensatory action is pre-specified and can be efficiently accomplished than by restarting the transaction. All these three techniques can also be used in conventional transaction processing systems. However, we expect that using them in the secure transaction processing scenario will significantly enhance the performance.

4.1. Exploiting non-flat nature of a transaction

Let us consider a transaction T_1 with subtransactions and dependencies as shown in Figure 1. As can be seen, the subtransaction T_{17} comprises of $read[x]$ where $L(x) < L(T_1)$. Suppose T_1 reads x. But, T_1 may have to be reexecuted due to a conflicting operation by a lower level transaction to ensure serializable execution. In such a scenario, not all parts of the transaction need to be reexecuted.

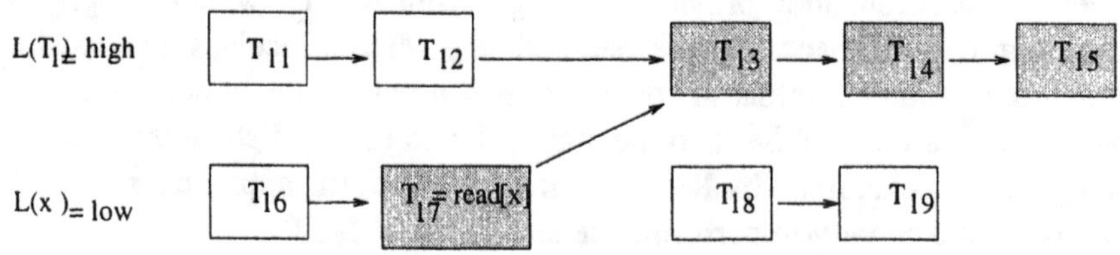

Figure 1. An example of partial reexecution

Our approach exploits the dependencies among subtransactions so that only those subtransactions which are effected by the modified low data item are reexecuted. For example, in Figure 1, subtransactions T_{11}, T_{12}, T_{16}, T_{18} and T_{19} are not required to be reexecuted for ensuring correctness since the change in the value of x does not affect those subtransactions.

4.2. Exploiting the value dependencies among subtransactions

Consider the scenario featured in Figure 2. Depending on the value of x, the transaction could follow either the execution sequence A (T_{18}, T_{19}) or the sequence B (T_{13}, T_{14}, T_{15}). Now assume that the value of x is 5 when the high level transaction begins its execution. Since the condition $x < 20$ is satisfied, the transaction follows the sequence A. Now if the value of x was changed to 6 at a later point of time due to a lower security level transaction, the transaction need not roll back since the condition $x < 20$ still holds. Therefore, by modeling this as a value dependency, one may evaluate the condition and thereby avoid reexecution entirely, and reexecute it only when it is necessary.

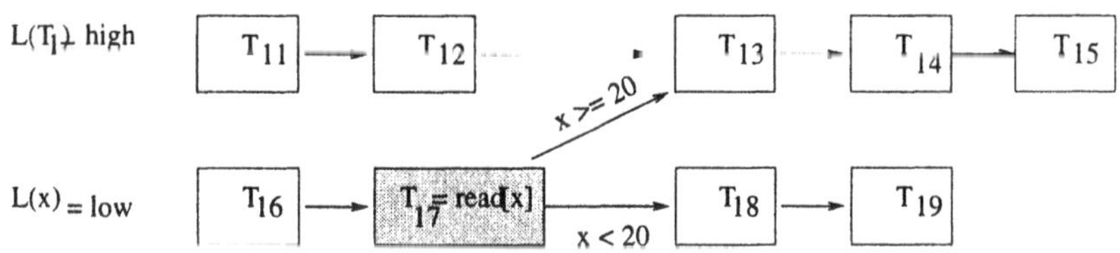

Figure 2. An example of value dependency approach

4.3. Employing compensating subtransactions

Now consider the case in Figure 3. In this case, the value of x changes from 6 to 10, while the transaction is executing. In a conventional scenario, this requires a transaction restart. However, the restart could be prevented here by executing a compensating module. We realize that devising a compensating action is much more difficult, and moreover, some subtransactions may not be compensatable. In this paper, we do not address this issue.

4.4. Example

In the following, we present an example where the dependencies introduced in section 2.1 exist among a real-world database scenario. Consider a corporate database that contains several types of information about its employees: social security number, name, address, rank, years of service, weekly pay (p), number of hours worked per week (h), number of overtime hours worked per week (o), hourly rate (r), additional compensation (c), yearly bonus, etc. The information

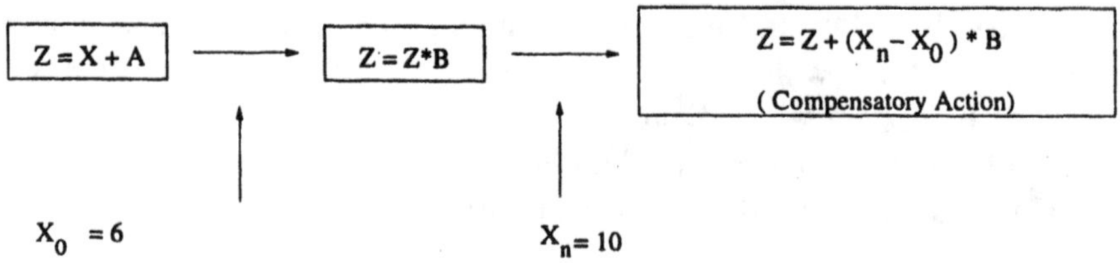

Figure 3. An example of compensation

such as weekly pay, hourly rate and additional compensation are considered sensitive, and are labeled *high*, while the rest of the information is classified *low*. Thus, $L(h) = L(o) = low$, and $L(p) = L(c) = L(r) = high$.

At the end of each week, the number of hours worked by an employee as well as the weekly pay of each employee is computed. The weekly pay of each employee is computed as follows:

Pay = ((number of regular hours + number of overtime hours)*hourly rate) + c, if overtime hours $\geq$ 20
= ((number of regular hours + number of overtime hours)*hourly rate), otherwise.

That is there will not be any additional compensation if an employee works less than 20 overtime hours per week. Since h and o are *low* data items, a *low* transaction (T_1) is initiated to enter h and o. A *high* transaction (T_2) is initiated to compute the weekly pay. They are as follows:

$T_1 =$ $write[h]\ write[o]$
$T_2 =$ $read[h]\ read[o]\ read[r]$
$read[c]\ [p = ((h + o) * r) + c]\ write[p]$, if $o \geq 20$
$[p = (h + o) * r]\ write[p]$, otherwise

Based on the semantics of the transaction, the dependencies as shown in Figure 4 can be seen among the operations within a transaction. Note that there exist both data dependencies as well as value dependencies.

5. PROPOSED CONCURRENCY CONTROL ALGORITHM

Algorithm 1 [The Scheduler]

1 There is a separate scheduler for each security level s.

2 Whenever a new transaction T_i arrives, the scheduler performs the following steps:

 (a) Assign a unique timestamp $ts(T_i)$. We assume that there is a shared hardware clock at system low which is used by each scheduler at

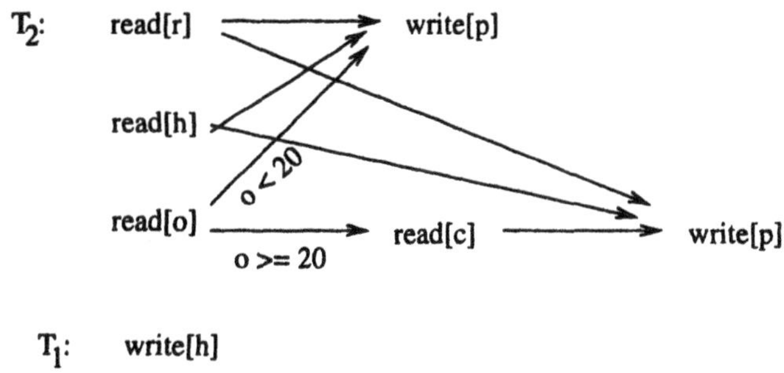

Figure 4. An extended transaction model for T_1 and T_2
write[o]

level s to assign a unique timestamp $ts(T_i)$ to every transaction T_i at its level.

(b) Each transaction T_i declares its write- and read-sets. The scheduler at level s maintains $W(T_i)$ and $R(T_i)$.

(c) If there exists a $read_i[x]$ such that $L(x) = s' < L(T_i)$,

i find every T_j such that $L(T_j) = s'$, $ts(T_j) < ts(T_i)$ and $W(T_j) \cap R(T_i)$. Add dependencies $write_j[x] \xrightarrow{bd} read_i[x]$ and $c_j \xrightarrow{t} c_i$.

ii Restructure T_i according to the restructuring algorithm.

3 Each version x_j of a data item x has a read timestamp $rts(x_j)$ and a write timestamp $wts(x_j)$ associated with it. We assume there is an initial transaction T_0 that writes into the database with $rts(x_0) = wts(x_0) = ts(T_0)$.

4 When a transaction T_i wants to read a data item x and if $L(T_i) = L(x)$, the scheduler selects a version x_k with the largest $wts(x_k)$ such that $wts(x_k) < ts(T_i)$, processes $read_i[x_k]$, and modifies $rts(x_k)$ as $rts(x_k)$ = maximum$\{ts(T_i), rts(x_k)\}$.

5 When a transaction T_i wants to write a data item x, scheduler selects a version x_k with the largest $wts(x_k)$ such that $wts(x_k) < ts(T_i)$. It rejects $w_i[x_i]$ if $rts(x_k) > ts(T_i)$; otherwise, it processes $write_i[x_i]$ and modifies the timestamps of the new version x_i as $rts(x_i) = wts(x_i) = ts(T_i)$.

6 Suppose a transaction T_i wants to read a data item x. If $L(T_i) > L(x)$, the scheduler at level $L(T_i)$ selects a version x_k with the largest $wts(x_k)$ such that $wts(x_k) < ts(T_i)$. Although the operation $read_i[x_k]$ is processed, the read timestamp $rts(x_k)$ is not modified for security reasons.

Algorithm 2 [Restructuring]

1 Add data dependencies between the operations of each transaction based on their semantics.

2 If there exist a value dependency $d_k = o_i[x] \stackrel{exp}{\longrightarrow} o_i[y]$, replace d_k with the following: $o_i[x] \stackrel{exp}{\longrightarrow} inc[counter_k] \stackrel{counter_k<2}{\longrightarrow} o_i[y]$.

Definition 4 We say that a transaction T is *semantically equivalent* to another transaction T', (i) if the set of data operations of both T and T' are equal, and (ii) if the values read by each read operation in both T and T' are the same, then the values written by each write operation in T and T' are the same.

Theorem 1 [Proof of Equivalence] Let T be a transaction. Let T' be the restructured transaction using algorithm 2. Then T' is semantically equivalent to T.

Theorem 2 [Proof of Correctness] Let H be a multiversion history produced by algorithm 1. Then H is one-copy serializable. In fact, H is equivalent to a one-serial history in which transactions are placed in a timestamp order.

5.1. Discussion

According to Step 2(c) of algorithm 1, the restructuring of a transaction is done only if a transaction reads from low. Otherwise, it is executed as a flat transaction. If it reads from low, the first step of algorithm 2 is to exploit the partial order of the operations and the data dependencies among them. In the second step of algorithm 2, we add counters to make sure that the operations are redone only if the condition has changed since the prior read. Let us consider various cases:

1. Suppose the schedule in the above example is

```
T2                read2[h]  read2[o]
T1 write1[h]                          write1[o]
```

Then the read2[o] operation is redone after write1[o] because of the "bd" dependency, as shown in Figure 5. Therefore this will result in a serializable schedule.

2. Suppose the schedule is

```
T2                read2[h]                 read2[o]
T1 write1[h]                   write1[o]
```

The above read2[o] is in fact the one triggered by write1[o]. This is also correct. So by adding these two dependencies, it makes sure that the write of low precedes the read of low if it hasn't already occurred in that order. That is, only the out-of-order read operation is redone but not all. This way, we are saving on the number of redoes. The dotted arrows indicate the added dependencies between transactions according to step 2(c)(i) of algorithm 1. Moreover, according to step 1 of algorithm 2, only parts of the transaction are to be redone, but not all.

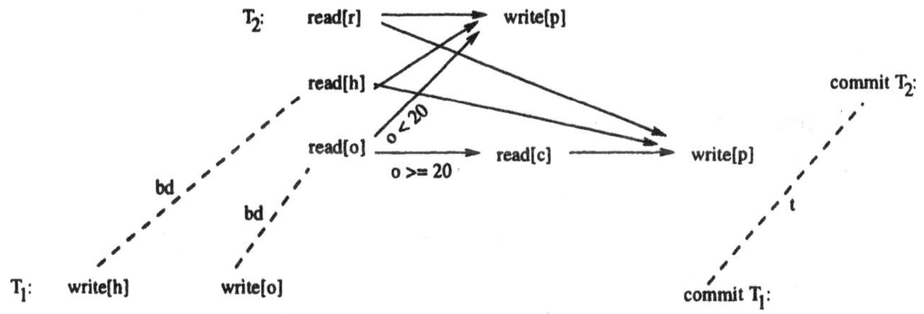

Figure 5. Dependencies added between T_1 and T_2 as in step 1 of algorithm 1

Now the idea of the second step of the restructure algorithm is to provide further optimization. The objective is to exploit the nature of the value dependency to avoid the redoing certain parts of the transaction by examining the value. For example, during the high transaction execution, the low value of "o" has changed. This does not have to necessarily trigger a redo. Consider the value read by read[o] is 10. Now it has changed to 15. This should not have any effect on the redoing part, and therefore, the write[p] operation (in Figure 6) does not have to redone. This is accomplished by incorporating counters in that path and incremented whenever transaction executes that part of the transaction.

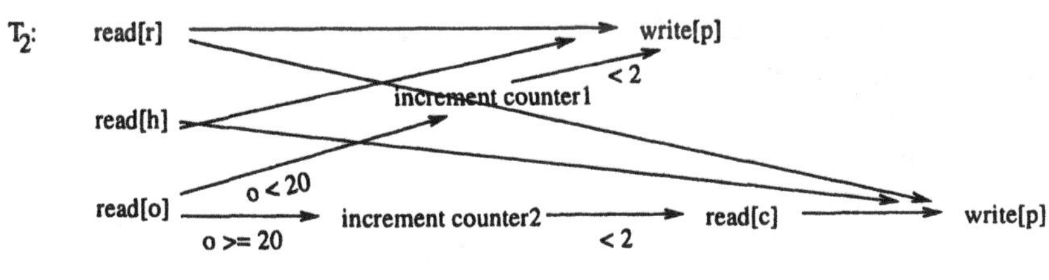

Figure 6. Exploiting the value dependencies in T_2

5.2. Implementation

The proposed system can be implemented in several ways. Here, we describe one such implementation. We assume that our system is implemented using the kernelized architecture. Thus, both the transaction manager (TM) and the Scheduler are untrusted. (We assume the functionalities of algorithms 1 and 2 are implemented in the TM and the scheduler. When a new transaction is received by the appropriate level TM, it assigns the transaction a unique timestamp by reading from a clock at system low. We assume that the granularity of the clock is high enough so that the timestamps are unique among the transactions at all the security levels.

A TM, upon receiving a transaction, invokes its redesign module. This module first identifies the low-level reads, and their dependencies with write operations at its own level. It builds both the value and data dependencies among the operations, as per algorithm 2. We refer to this as the dependency graph for a transaction. At this stage, however, there is no knowledge of the actual low-level transactions that the high-level transaction under consideration may be in conflict with. The TM, now, sends low-level read requests to the scheduler at its level. Since we assume a timestamp-based concurrency control, each read request is associated with a timestamp of the transaction that originated it. Accordingly, the scheduler selects the value of the latest version whose write timestamp is smaller than that of the transaction issuing the read request. Th read requests are then sent to the trusted OS to retrieve the data from the appropriate DB (as in a kernelized architecture). In addition to the data, the request also reads the active transaction log maintained by the scheduler, and determines the active transactions and their timestamps that conflict with its own read. (An active transaction is one that has started but not yet terminated.) Thus, the low-level read request returns the data value, its timestamp, and a set (possibly empty) of active low-level transactions that conflict with the high-level read.

The high-level TM, after receiving the transaction sets from the low-level read operations, saves them for use at the time of transaction commit. Actually, it is only concerned with low-level transactions with timestamps smaller than the high-level transaction and with read-write conflicts. Let us call this set the active-transaction set (ATS). At the time of transaction commit, the TM needs to determine the state of the transactions in the ATS. Accordingly, it sends "read-log" request to the low-level DBMS through the TCB. In return, it is presented with the current list of low-level active transactions. If none of the transactions in its ATS are still active, then it proceeds with the next step of examining the dependency graph. Otherwise, it waits and repeats the above two steps periodically. When all transactions in the active-set have terminated, the high-level TM resends all low-level read operations to the low-level scheduler. When the new values are returned, it checks with the dependency graph to determine the operations that need to be reexecuted. The reread values are used for both data and value dependencies.

In summary, our implementation uses untrusted TMs and schedulers at each security level, logs maintained by the schedulers indicating the current active transactions and their read- and write-sets, and multiple versions of data items.

6. SUMMARY AND FUTURE WORK

In this paper, we described an extended model for multilevel secure transaction processing. In a traditional MLS model, a high-level transaction is aborted and restarted whenever its low-level reads conflict with low-level transactions' writes. This is often a concern for high-level users in real systems. Here, we suggest a way to extend the rigid transaction model by using some of the workflow transaction redesign techniques. The proposed scheme uses timestamping as a means of concurrency control. In addition, it employs multiversion data. It employs value and data dependencies to identify the relationship between low-level read data and high-level writes within a transaction. This information is then used at the time of transaction commit. Depending on the conflicts during execution between a high-level transaction and low-level transactions, only some parts of a high-level transaction may need to be reexecuted. But what parts, if any, are to be reexecuted is determined by the data and value dependencies identified earlier and the actual conflicts and data values. We show the correctness of the proposed scheme by proving the serializability of the resulting transaction histories.

In the future, we plan to evaluate the performance of the proposed method in terms of thc throughput offered at higher security levels as well as the response time. We also plan to measure the additional protocol overhead imposed by the proposed system, especially the cost of maintaining additional versions of data, the list of active transactions, and the cost of active transaction enquiry and reread of low-level data. The costs and benefits will be compared with those of a traditional scheme where a high-level transaction is simply aborted when its low-read operation conflicts with a low-level write operation. In addition, we plan to compare the performance of our scheme with other schemes [11, 4] that have similar objectives.

Acknowledgments

The work of V. Atluri was supported in part by the National Science Foundation under grant IRI-9624222. We would like to acknowledge Binto George for taking part in the initial discussions on this work, while he was at Rutgers.

References

[1] Paul Ammann and Sushil Jajodia. A timestamp ordering algorithm for secure, single-version, multi-level databases. In Carl Landwehr and Sushil Jajodia, editors, *Database Security, II: Status and Prospects*, pages 23–25. North Holland, 1992.

[2] Paul Ammann, Sushil Jajodia, and Indrakshi Ray. A Semantic-Based Transaction Processing Model for Multilevel Transactions. *Journal of Computer Security*, 6(3), 1998.

[3] C. Beeri, P. Bernstein, and N. Goodman. A Model for Concurrency in Nested Transactions Systems. *Journal of ACM*, 36(2), 1989.

[4] Elisa Bertino, Sushil Jajodia, Luigi Mancini, and Indrajit Ray. Advanced transaction processing in multilevel secure file stores. *IEEE Transactions on Knowledge and Data Engineering*, 10(1):120–135, 1998.

[5] Panos K. Chrysanthis and Krithi Ramamritham. ACTA, A framework for specifying and reasoning about transaction structure and behavior. In *Proc. ACM SIGMOD Int'l. Conf. on Management of Data*, pages 194–203, June 1990.

[6] Ahmed K. Elmagarmid. *Database Transaction Models for Advanced Applications*. Morgan Kaufmann, San Mateo, California, 1992.

[7] Sushil Jajodia and Vijayalakshmi Atluri. Alternative Correctness Criteria for Concurrent Execution of Transactions in Multilevel Secure Databases. In *Proc. IEEE Symposium on Security and Privacy*, pages 216–224, Oakland, California, May 1992.

[8] T. F. Keefe and W. T. Tsai. Multiversion Concurrency Control for Multilevel Secure Database Systems. In *Proc. IEEE Symposium on Security and Privacy*, pages 369–383, Oakland, California, May 1990.

[9] William T. Maimone and Ira B. Greenberg. Single-level Multiversion Schedulers for Multilevel Secure Database Systems. In *Proc. 6th Annual Computer Security Applications Conf.*, pages 137–147, Tucson, Arizona, December 1990.

[10] John McDermott and Sushil Jajodia. Orange Locking: Channel-free Database Concurrency Control via Locking. In *Proc. of the 6th IFIP WG 11.3 Workshop on Database Security*, Vancouver, BC, August 1992.

[11] Indrajit Ray, Luigi V. Mancini, Sushil Jajodia, and Elisa Bertino. Asep: A secure and flexible commit protocol for mls distributed database systems. *IEEE Transactions on Knowledge and Data Engineering*, 12(6):880–899, 2000.

[12] Dennis Shasha, Eric Simon, and Patrick Valduriez. Simple Relational Guidance for Chopping Up Transactions. In *Proc. ACM SIGMOD Int'l. Conf. on Management of Data*, pages 298–307, San Diego, CA, June 1992.

MAINTAINING THE CONFIDENTIALITY OF INTEROPERABLE DATABASES WITH A MULTILEVEL FEDERATED SECURITY SYSTEM

Marta Oliva[1] and Fèlix Saltor[2]

[1]*Dept. Informàtica i Enginyeria Industrial, Universitat de Lleida, C. Jaume II, 69, E-25001 Lleida (Catalonia).*

[2]*Dept. Llenguatges i Sistemes Informàtics, Universitat Politècnica de Catalunya, Campus Nord-Mòdul C5, Jordi Girona Salgado, 1-3, E-08034 Barcelona (Catalonia).*

Abstract: When several databases with multilevel security policies are federated to form a tightly coupled federated database management system, heterogeneities such as different accreditation ranges must be overcome. This paper describes an extended methodology to integrate policies that use different lattices as accreditation ranges. A semi-automatic process obtains the federated accreditation range and needed translation functions among accreditation ranges in order to be validated by the security administrator.

1. INTRODUCTION

There is a growing need to interoperate several information sources, such as *DataBases* (DBs), to satisfy the demanding requirements of users. Technically, this is accomplished by superimposing a new system, a *Federated DB Management System* (FDBMS), as a layer of software upon the *Data Base Management Systems* (DBMSs) of each one of the pre-existing DBs, then called *Component DBs* (CDBs).

Security is a big concern in such an environment. Each CDB has its own security policy, enforced thru its own security mechanisms, to protect its data from unauthorized access. It joins the Federated system if its *autonomy* can be preserved, and wants to ensure that user queries coming from the FDBMS do not compromise the security of its data. These differences in security policies, models and mechanisms among the CDBs form the *security heterogeneity*, which comes in addition to the *system, syntactic* and *semantic heterogeneities* among them (see [SL90]), which are out of the scope of this paper.

A FDBMS can federate a number of CDBs using a *Discretionary Access Control* (DAC) security model –common in business data processing-, while other CDBs are required to use a more strict *Mandatory Access Control* (MAC) model, particularly in the form of *MultiLevel Security* (MLS, [BL75]).

In this environment, the CDBs that apply MLS systems would not easily accept to share information under the control of a DAC system, because those CDBs would want information flow under control. In addition, DAC systems are not powerful enough to avoid unauthorized logical inference and aggregation, and are subject to Trojan Horse attacks ([Per93]). Consequently, it is up to the FDBMS to have mechanisms to protect interoperation among several CDBs, using or not using MLS, at the highest level of security, i.e. in terms of MLS.

Our work is related to *tightly coupled* FDBMS, in the sense of [SL90]. In such systems, there is a federated administrator, and one or more federated schemas; they are of help in enforcing security. Among the subsystems forming the FDBMS, the one in charge of security will use, as explained above, MLS, and is called the *MultiLevel Federated Security System* (MLFSS).

Even for those CDBs based on the MAC and MLS mechanisms, there are lots of heterogeneities among them, particularly in their *accreditation ranges* ([MLTS92], [DJ94]). The number of classification levels will be different, as will be their names; the *dominance relation* among levels may be a total order or a partial order; frequently a lattice.

The objective of this work consists of extending our previous methodology to integrate multilevel security policies (using total ordered sets), to integrate multilevel security policies that use lattices as accreditation ranges. As a result of this work we are able to integrate any set of MLS DBs.

This paper is organized as follows. Our schema integration process is summarized in section 2, and an overview of our integration methodology, among multilevel security policies that use total ordered set as accreditation ranges, in section 3. Section 4, the core of the paper, presents the extended methodology to integrate multilevel security policies that use lattices as accreditation ranges. Section 5 includes related work and conclusions.

2. SCHEMA INTEGRATION PROCESS SUMMARY

When several DBs decide to share their data they can use several interoperation ways. Since we are interested in tightly coupled federations, we follow a building methodology like that presented by [SL90] by means of their 5-level schema architecture. In this case the integration process is based on our 7-level schema architecture ([ROSC97]), where one of the additional schemas (*Authorization Schema*) is related to security aspects. Another important aspect to note is that we use *BarceLona Object-Oriented Model* (BLOOM) as Canonical Data Model (CDM) of the federation.

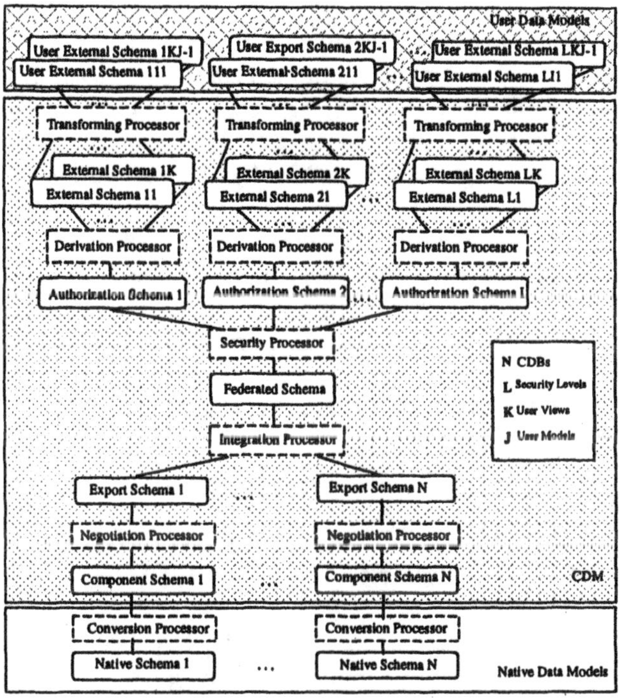

Figure 1. 7-level schema architecture

From the point of view of maintaining data confidentiality, it is necessary to extend several processors between schemas in our 7-level schema architecture (see figure 1). First of all, when the *Conversion Processors* convert schemas expressed in data models different from BLOOM into BLOOM schemas to obtain the *Component Schemas*, it is essential to maintain the classification of data, which depends on native accreditation ranges of security levels. Thus, it is also necessary to deduce the classification of the components obtained by the semantic enrichment process, to maintain the confidentiality of data and to prevent possible inferences. Through the negotiation process administrators decide which data of which confidentiality will be offered to the federation in the form of *Export Schemas*.

After that, the *Integration Processor* integrates the *Export Schemas* into a *Federated Schema*. The integration is performed in two phases: identifying semantically related objects in the detection phase, and integrating the CDBs BLOOM schemas after conforming them, by means of a discriminated form of generalization, in the resolution phase). Thus, the *Integration Processor* also has to solve heterogeneities (set of security levels and their semantics) among the *Component Accreditation Ranges* (CARs), obtaining the *Federated Accreditation Range* (FAR). Then, the translation functions between the FAR and each CAR could be deduced, and later the process will be able to classify each component of the *Federated Schema* in terms of the FAR (at the same time, solving differences of initial classification of equivalent components). Sections 3 and 4 of this paper focus on an integration methodology to be applied by the *Integration Processor* to integrate different CARs.

After that, the *Security Processor* creates as many *Authorization Schemas* as security levels the FAR has. Each *Authorization Schema* contains the subset of the *Federated Schema* that a federated user, with certain clearance level, can access (read-only). At the same time, *Authorization Schemas* allow changing the form of the *Federated Schema* in order to hide confidential data that could be inferred because of the semantics of BLOOM abstractions ([AOSS00]).

3. OUR METHODOLOGY TO INTEGRATE MULTILEVEL SECURITY POLICIES

Our proposed *semi-automatic* methodology, presented in [OS01], to integrate multilevel security policies and to solve their heterogeneities collaborates with the schema integration process summarized in the previous section. We use the term semi-automatic because this process needs to be validated by the *Security Administrator* of the federation.

The methodology was developed, at first stage, to integrate MLS CDBs that apply total ordered sets as accreditation ranges, for instance (S_1, $\leq_1$) and (S_2, $\leq_2$) (see figure 2.a).

To detect the relationships among security levels belonging to different ordered sets it uses the following information:

a) The confidentiality of data stored in the Export Schemas (see the classification of the components of each CDB schema in fig. 2.a).

b) The similarities between components of different Export Schemas, obtained by the schema integration process, these are more precisely, Equivalence Semantic Relationships (E-SRs) and Specialization Semantic Relationships (S-SRs) (see fig. 2.a).

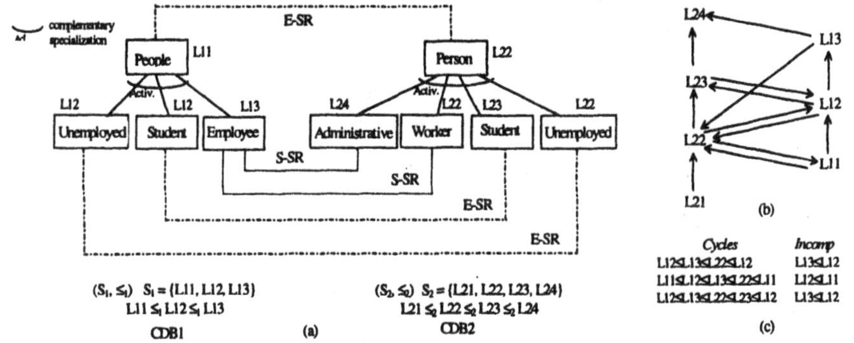

Figure 2. Multidigraph building and analysis example

The methodology is based on a multidigraph representation of the information described above (see an example in figure 2.b). The multidigraph is built from Hasse diagrams of ordered sets of the CDBs and a set of arcs representing possible dominance relations between security levels of different CARs. The first proposal of the set of dominance relations is obtained from the set of similarities between components of different Export Schemas (it is easy to think that similar concepts have similar confidentiality) without any analysis, so the greatest quantity of information is considered. For each E-SR (see fig. 2.a and 2.b) an arc is added to the multidigraph from the classification level of a class to the classification level of the class that is assumed the equivalent concept, and also the inverse arc. For S-SR (see fig. 2.a and 2.b) an arc is added to the multidigraph from the classification level of a class to the classification level of the class that is assumed to be the subclass concept.

Then, the multidigraph is analyzed to detect incompatible arcs. Two arcs are incompatible if their existence breaks the dominance relation between security levels of the initial ordered sets. A penalization approach is used to automatically solve incompatibilities losing the least number of arcs. The penalization approach is based on the detection of cycles with more than two participant vertices. An arc accumulates as many penalizations as the number of cycles it is involved in. For instance, in figure 2.b, the arc (L13, L22) is involved in 3 cycles and produces 3 incompatibilities (see fig. 2.c).

After that, the most penalized arc is removed and the penalization of the arcs are calculated again, repeating this process until the remaining arcs do not have any penalization. When there is no incompatibility, the resulting multidigraph is converted into an ordered set to be used as FAR, and at the same time translation functions are obtained. Note that in the final multidigraph, each cycle of only two participant vertices indicates that both security levels are the same. Finally, the components of the Federated Schema are classified taking the FAR and translation functions into account. The classification of classes that initially appears in Export Schemas are translated using appropriate translation functions, and new classes, built by means of the discriminant generalization, are classified at the least level of the set of classification levels belonging to their subclasses.

4. LATTICES INTEGRATION METHODOLOGY

As pointed out in the introduction of this paper, in MLS systems sometimes the dominance relation among security levels forms a partial ordered set or a lattice. The main characteristics of a lattice are that a greatest and a least element, among all elements forming the lattice, exist. Because of all ordered sets also have greatest and least elements they are lattices as well. Besides, as we can always include a fictitious greatest element as well as a fictitious least element into the set of elements forming a partial ordered set, then we can also work with partial ordered sets as they were lattices. So, a methodology that allows integrating lattices will also be able to integrate total and partial ordered sets.

Taking into account the integration methodology of multilevel security policies summarized in the previous section, the main difference between ordered set integration and lattice integration is the set of possible incompatibilities that can be obtained after building the corresponding multidigraph. In subsection 4.1 these possible incompatibilities are analyzed. After that, subsection 4.2 covers the penalization approach and the set of criteria used to solve the incompatibilities. Finally, three special cases that need a different automatic solution are treated in subsection 4.3.

4.1 Incompatibilities

From the point of view of possible incompatibilities, the difference between an ordered set and a lattice is the presence, in the latter, of no comparable elements. As a result, apart from incompatibilities originated by cycles produced by more than two vertices, another incompatibility is produced when the multidigraph contains a path between two incomparable security levels, belonging to the same lattice, which implies a dominance relation between them.

Figure 3.a shows an example where the set of dominance relations between lattices L_1 and L_2 produces a path. Because of this path relates two no comparable levels, belonging to the same lattice, it causes an incompatibility (see fig. 3.b).

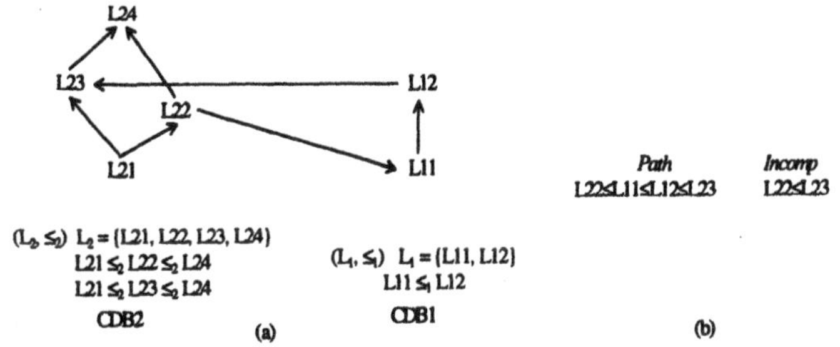

Figure 3 Example of a path between no comparable security levels

4.2 Penalization approach

Following the same penalization approach as in the methodology that integrates total ordered sets, each arc of the multidigraph (originated by the representation of the possible dominance relations between security levels of lattices) accumulates as many penalizations as the number of cycles and paths it is involved in.

After penalizing all arcs involved in cycles or in paths, the process uses the following criteria to decide which arc is the best to remove:

1. Look for the most penalized arc.
2. If there is more than one arc with the same greatest penalization, then the one that appears the least number of times is removed. Remember that we use a multidigraph because the same arc can be added several times, depending on the times that the schema integration process finds similarities that produce the same dominance relation between two security levels.
3. If it is possible to apply neither the first nor the second criterion, then the process chooses the arc that relates more confidential levels. Generally, it is easier to share less confidential than more confidential data.

Once an arc is removed, the penalization of the arcs are calculated again, and the previous process is repeated until all penalized arcs disappear.

Figures 4, 5 and 6 show an example of the application of the first, second and third criterion respectively using the lattices L_1 and L_2 previously depicted in figure 3. The part (a) of each figure contains the initial multidigraph, in the part (b) is depicted the resultant multidigraph after removing the arc. Finally, the part (c) shows the resultant FAR after integrating the initial lattices.

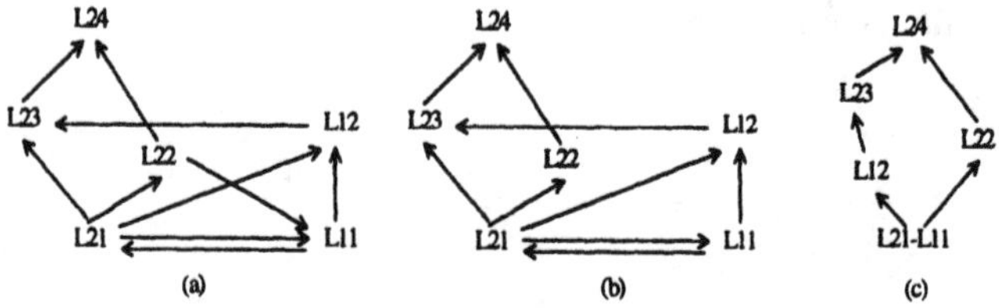

Figure 4. First criterion applicability example

Multidigraph in figure 4.a has the cycle L21-L22-L11-L21 and the path L22-L11-L12-L23, so the arc (L22, L11) is chosen for removing because it has 2 penalizations in front of the arcs (L11, L21) and (L12, L23) that only have a penalization. After removing the arc (L22, L11) no incompatibility remains (see fig. 4.b). Figure 4.c shows the resultant FAR where, as the cycle in figure 4.b points out, L21 and L11 are the same level, so the arcs (L11, L12) and (L21, L12) imply the same dominance relation, and the arc (L21, L23) disappears because is a redundant arc.

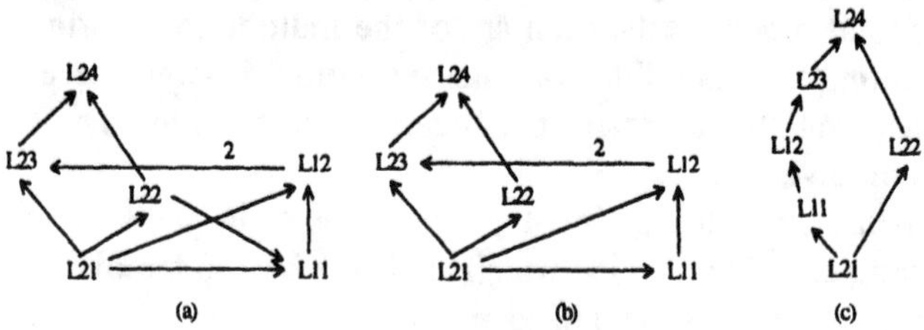

Figure 5. Second criterion applicability example

Multidigraph in figure 5.a only has the path L22-L11-L12-L23, so both arcs (L22, L11) and (L12, L23) has just a penalization. But as the arc (L12, L23) appears twice (see the number with which the arc (L12, L23) is tagged) then the arc (L22, L11) is chosen to be removed (see fig. 5.b). The resultant FAR depicted in figure 5.c is obtained in the same way that the FAR in figure 4.c.

Multidigraph in figure 6.a only has the path L22-L11-L12-L23, but this time the first and the second criterion are not applicable because both arcs have the same penalization and appear just the same number of times. Consequently, the arc (L12, L23), that relates more confidential levels than the arc (L22, L11), is removed (see fig. 6.b). The FAR in figure 6.c is obtained just as the previous ones, but this time we use a fictitious *Federated Top* (FT) security level in order to obtain a lattice.

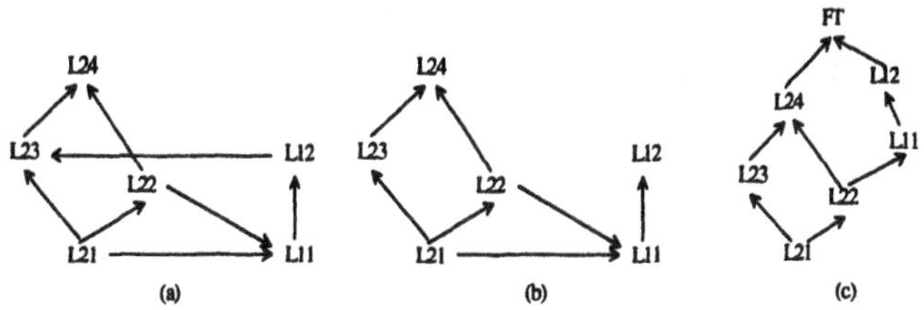

Figure 6. Third criterion applicability example

4.3 Special cases

In spite of the criteria described in previous section, there are three special cases that need a specific treatment. In all of these special cases there is at least a path between two no comparable levels, but it only passes through a unique level belonging to the other lattice. Although it is impossible to apply any of those criteria to solve the incompatibility, there is a different semi-automatic solution. Note that, in a MLS DB, the set of elements classified at one of the no comparable levels has nothing in common with the set of elements classified at the other one. So, it is possible to consider the set of elements classified at the level through which the path passes just as two different subsets. These subsets can be identified by means of the information about similar objects (E-SRs and S-SRs), obtained thru the schema integration process. Figures 7, 8 and 9 depict an example of each of these special cases. In the part (a) of each figure is depicted the multidigraph obtained thru the methodology summarized at section 3, while the part (b) of each figure shows the resultant FAR after applying the proper semi-automatic solution. In each figure, the part (c) includes a simple integration example of two CDBs. Each integration example depicts the CDBs Export Schemas with their classification and the similarities between objects. The classification, in terms of the FAR, of the resultant Federated Schema is shown as well. Consequently, you can see how applying our methodology to integrate security policies a secure interoperation without security breaches is obtained.

Multidigraph in figure 7.a shows the special case where there are two no comparable levels of the first lattice that are related with the same level of the second lattice. Thus, because the relation is an equivalent relation in both cases, it would imply that the L23 and L22 levels would be the same level (in this case L12). We avoid this by splitting L12 into L12a and L12b (because of the reason explained above), and including them, together with L12, in the resultant FAR (see figure 7.b). This is because each federated user only has to be assigned one clearance level, and at the same time, interoperation access using this clearance level has to comply with the autonomy and security principles of [GQ96]. In addition, FAR in figure 7.b includes a fictitious *Federated Bottom* (FB) security level, like the inclusion of FT in figure 6.c.

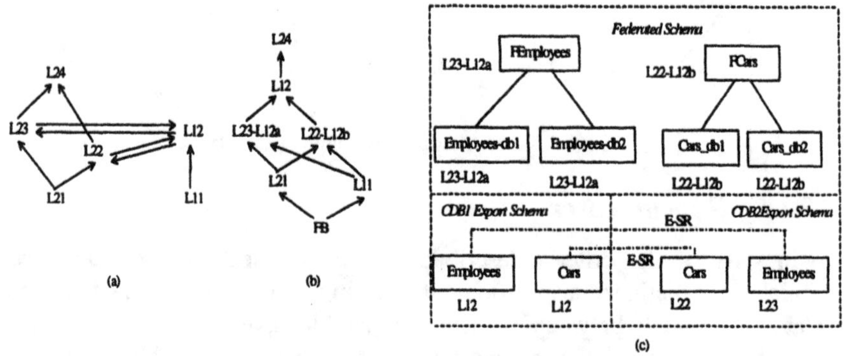

Figure 7. First special case example

Remember that the principle of autonomy and of security ([GQ96]) say, respectively, that any access permitted within an individual system must be also permitted under secure interoperation; and that any access not permitted within an individual system must be also denied under secure interoperation.

Table 1. Translation functions

f_2^F(L24)=L24	f_F^2(L24)=L24	f_F^1(L24)=L12
f_2^F(L23)=L23-L12a	f_F^2(L12)={L23, L22}	f_F^1(L12)=L12
f_2^F(L22)=L22-L12b	f_F^2(L23-L12a)=L23	f_F^1(L23-L12a)=part{L12}
f_2^F(L21)=L21	f_F^2(L22-L12b)=L22	f_F^1(L22-L12b)=part{L12}
	f_F^2(L21)=L21	f_F^1(L21)=∅
f_1^F(L12)=L12	f_F^2(L11)=∅	f_F^1(L11)=L11
f_1^F(L11)=L11	f_F^2(FB)=∅	f_F^1(FB)=∅

For better understanding, table 1 describes translation functions between each component lattice and the federated lattice, and translation functions between the federated lattice and each component lattice as well. The first functions are used to translate the component user clearance into the federated user clearance (f_i^F, where *i* is CDB_i). The last ones are used to translate a federated user clearance assigned to a query to the component user clearance (f_F^i), assigned to the corresponding component subqueries.

f_F^2(L12)={L23, L22} means that a query, belonging to a federated user with L12 clearance level, has to translate into two subqueries when the MLFSS passes the query to the CDB_2: first subquery tagged with the L23 clearance level, and second tagged with L22. Finally, the FDBMS has to consolidate the result of both subqueries. On the other hand, *f_F^1(L23-L12a)=part{L12}* means that a query belonging to a federated user with the

L23-L12a clearance level, has to be translated into a query tagged with L12 when it was passed to the CDB_1. After that the MLFSS will need to filter the result to return only part of elements classified at L12 security level.

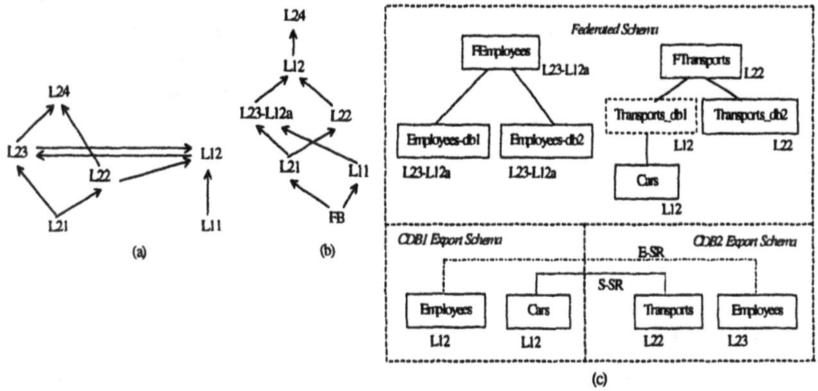

Figure 8. Second special case example

Figure 8 shows an example of the second special case. In this case, one of the two no comparable levels also has an equivalence relation with the security level of the other lattice, but the other one is dominated by the level of the other lattice (see fig. 8.a). As in the first special case, the solution consists of splitting the set of elements classified at level L12, but in this case it is enough to only take a subset into account, just the subset L12a (see fig. 8.b). Seeing the example of figure 8, note that the Federated Schema depicted in figure 8.c includes the class `Transports_db1` (not appearing in the CDB1 Export Schema) because it is originated thru the conformation of the CDB1 Export Schema during the schema integration process.

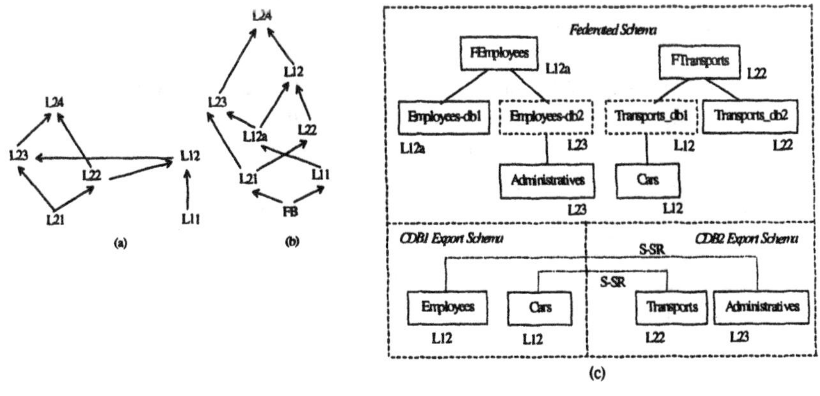

Figure 9. Third special case example

You can see an example of the third special case in figure 9. Both incomparable levels are not equivalent to the security level of the other lattice. Whereas L22 is dominated by L12, L23 dominates L12, so these dominance relations form a path (see fig. 9.a). As in the second special case, only considering the subset L12a is enough to solve the integration (see fig. 9.b). Translation functions between lattices and the FAR in examples in figures 8 and 9 can be obtained in the same way as those in example 7.

5. RELATED WORK AND CONCLUSIONS

Several papers in the literature are related to secure authorized accesses during interoperation among heterogeneous DBs. Some of them work in the context of FDBMSs and in particular in tightly coupled FDBMSs. [JD94], [JD96] and [DCdVS97] base their security systems on the DAC mechanisms; [Per93], [TF97] use canonical security systems, that support both the DAC and MAC mechanisms, and [Osb01] protects interoperable accesses by means of a *Role-Based Access Control* (RBAC) system. As far as we know, only [IGQ94] and [BSS96], apart from [DQS00] (that is related to loosely coupled using a mediator/wrapper approach), base the security system of the federation on a MLS system.
Particularly, [IGQ94] presents an integration methodology to solve confidentiality conflicts produced when a federation is built. The methodology is also based on a technique to create a global data schema, but the security systems of the CDBs use MLS systems with identical accreditation ranges. The problem is reduced to the resolution of the classification of each object belonging to the global data schema.

On the other hand, [BSS96] describes techniques (a logic programming approach and a graph-based approach) to obtain a unified accreditation range through a way of combining different accreditation ranges that preserves a set of interoperation security constraints. In this case, these techniques use a predefined set of interoperation security constraints, but the paper does not indicate how they are obtained.

Although [DQS00] is related to loosely coupled systems, there are some relevant aspects related to our work. The paper includes a way to check the correctness (consistency, nonambiguity and nonredundancy) of the specifications of mappings between levels of an external application and levels of the sources. They also analyze inconsistencies by means of cycles and paths among security levels of different accreditation ranges. But in this case, the analysis is not performed between CARs; it is performed among the accreditation range of an external application, defined manually by a human integrator/administrator, and the accreditation ranges of the sources. Mappings among accreditation ranges also are determined by the same human integrator/administrator and in case they are incorrect, the human integrator/administrator has to propose some changes in order to obtain a correct solution.

Finally, [GQ96] shows a study of the problem of secure interoperation among heterogeneous systems. This study insists on the detection and resolution of the security breaches caused by the interoperation but without specifying which security policy is applied. It starts from the assumption that mappings among security attributes and among distinct heterogeneous security systems have been previously solved (for example by the administrator of the FDBMS).

In this paper we extend our methodology to integrate multilevel security policies, presented at [OS01], that takes into account MLS CDBs that use total ordered sets as accreditation ranges, in order to integrate MLS CDBs that use lattices as accreditation ranges. The described methodology can also be used to integrate multilevel security policies using total or partial ordered sets. Using this methodology a semi-automatic process is obtained, and it only has to be supervised by the security administrator in order to validate it. As result, the accreditation range of the federation and translation functions between each CAR and the FAR are obtained.

REFERENCES

[AOSS00] A. Abelló, M. Oliva, J. Samos and F. Saltor. Information System Architecture for Data Warehousing from a Federation. In M. Roantree, W. Hasselbring and S. Conrad, editors, Engineering Federated Information System, (Proceedings of the 3rd Workshop EFIS 2000, June 19-21, 2000, Dublin (Ireland)), pages 33-40, infix, 2000.

[BSS96] P.A. Bonatti, M.L. Sapino and V.S. Subrahmanian. Merging Heterogeneous Security Orderings. In E. Bertino, G. Kurth, H. Martella and E. Montolivo, editors, Computer Security - ESORICS 96 (4th European Symposium on Research in Computer Security, Rome, Italy, September 25-27, 1996, Proceedings), volume 1146 of LNCS, pages 183-197, Springer-Verlag, 1996.

[BL75] D.E. Bell and L.J. LaPadula. Secure computer systems: Unified exposition and multics interpretation. Technical Report MTR-2997, (AY/W 020 445), The MITRE Corporation, Bedford, MA, Jul 1975.

[DJ94] K.R. Dittrich and D. Jonscher. Current Trends in Database Technology and Their Impact on Security Concepts. In J. Biskup, M. Mongersten and C.E. Landwehr (eds), Database Security VIII (A-60),. Elsevier Science B.V. (North Holland), pages 11-33, 1994.

[DCdVS97] S. De Capitani di Vimercanti and P. Samarati. Authorization Specification and Enforcement in Federated Database Systems. Journal of Computer Security, 5(2):155-188, 1997.

[DQS00] S. Dawson, S. Qian and P.Samarati. Providing Security and Interoperation of Heterogeneous Systems. Distributed and Parallel Databases, 8(1): 119-145, Jan 2000.

[GQ96] L. Gong and X. Qian. Computational Issues in Secure Interoperation. IEEE Transactions on Software Engineering, 22(1):43-51, January 1996.

[IGQ94] N.B. Idris, W.A. Gray and M.A. Qutaishat. Integration of Secrecy Features in a Federated Database Environment. In T.F. Keefe and C.E. Landwehr, editors, Database Security VII (A-47), pages 89-109. Elsevier Science B.V. (North-Holland), 1994.

[JD94] D. Jonscher and K.R. Dittrich. An Approach for Building Secure Database Federations. In Proccedings of the 20th VLDB Conference, pages 24-35, 1994.

[JD96] D. Jonscher and K.R. Dittrich. Argos – A Configurable Access Control System for Interoperable Environment. In T.C. Ting and D. Spooner, editors, Database Security IX: Status and Prospects. Chapman and Hall, 1996.

[MLTS92] M. Morgenstern, T. Lunt, B. Thuraisingham and D. Spooner. Security issues in federated database systems: panel contributions. In C.E. Landwehr and S. Jajodia, editors, Database Security V (A-6): Status and Prospects, pages 131-148. Elsevier Science B.V. (North Holland), 1992.

[OS01] M. Oliva and F. Saltor. Integrating Multilevel Security Policies in Multilevel Federated Database Systems. In B. Thuraisingham, R. van de Riet, K.R. Dittrich, Z. Tari, editors, Data and Applications Security: Developments and Directions. Kluwer Academic Publishers, 2001.

[Osb01] S. Osborn. Database Security Integration using Role-Based Access Control. In B. Thuraisingham, R. van de Riet, K.R. Dittrich, Z. Tari, editors, Data and Applications Security: Developments and Directions. Kluwer Academic Publishers, 2001.

[Per93] G. Pernul. Canonical Security Modeling for Federated Databases. In D.K. Hsiao, E.J. Neuhold, and R. Sacks-Davis, editors, Interoperable Database Systems (DS-5) (A-25), pages 207-222. Elsevier Science Publishers B.V. (North-holland), 1993

[ROSC97] M.E. Rodríguez, M. Oliva, F. Saltor and B. Campderrich. On Schema and Functional Architectures for Multilevel Secure and Multiuser Model Federated DB Systems. In S. Conrad, W. Hasselbring, A. Heuer, G. Saake, editors, Proceedings of the International CAiSE'97 Workshop on Engineering Federated Database Systems (EFDBS'97, Barcelona), Otto-von-Guericke-Universität Magdeburg, Fakultät für Informatik, preprint Nr. 6, pages 93-104, 1997.

[SL90] A.P. Sheth and J.A. Larson. Federated Database Systems for Managing Distributed, Heterogeneous, and Autonomous Databases. ACM Computing Surveys, 22(3):183-236, September 1990.

[TF97] Z. Tari and G. Fernandez. Security Enforcement in the DOK Federated Database System. In P. Samarati and R.S. Sandhu, editors, Database Security X: Status and Prospects, pages 23-42. Chapman and Hall, 1997

VIII

NEW APPLICATION AREAS

SECURITY PROCEDURES FOR CLASSIFICATION MINING ALGORITHMS

Tom Johnsten
Computer Science Department
Western Illinois University
T-Johnsten@wiu.edu

Vijay V. Raghavan
Center for Advanced Computer Studies
University of Louisiana Lafayette
raghavan@louisiana.edu

Abstract Classification mining algorithms can be used to discover protected values from non-protected data that are voluntarily released for mining purposes. We reported earlier on the development of an assessment algorithm, along with a set of security policies, for use in analyzing a protected data element's risk of disclosure with respect to decision-region based algorithms. This paper presents an extension of the previous work. Specifically, two algorithms, one for assessing a protected data element's risk of disclosure with respect to decision-region based algorithms and the other with respect to extended decision-region based algorithms, are developed. The former risk assessment algorithm has a relatively low execution time, but may not achieve an exact assessment of a protected data element's risk of disclosure. However, data collected from initial experiments indicate that the application of this particular assessment algorithm can lead to an exact assessment, under certain security policies.

Keywords: data mining, security, risk assessment, classification, database security.

Introduction

Nowadays companies and organizations frequently use data mining technology to analyze their stored data to discover valuable patterns or rules that can help them maintain their competitive edge. Recently, researchers within the information security community have begun to examine the impact of this technology on database security [1,2,3,4,5].

Our previous work focused on the disclosure of a protected data element through classification mining [5]. As part of that work, we identified a general category of classification mining algorithms, referred to as decision-region based, whose members possess a common set of properties related to the security risk assessment of a protected data element. Based on these properties, we developed a security risk assessment algorithm, along with a set of security policies, for use in analyzing decision-region based algorithms. We developed the risk assessment algorithm in the context of the relational data model. In the context of that model, we defined the terms protected attribute, non-protected attribute, and protected tuple. A *protected attribute* is the one that includes the protected data element (or attribute value) in its domain, a *non-protected attribute* contains no protected data elements in its domain, and a *protected tuple* contains a protected data element and at least one non-protected data element.

This paper introduces a broader category of classification mining algorithms, which we refer to as extended decision-region based, whose members possess a common set of properties that can be exploited during the assessment of the security risk of a protected data element. These algorithms, unlike those for decision-region based, are characterized as allowing for descriptions that are not entirely defined in terms of properties of the object. As a result, new assessment procedures must be developed with respect to this new category of classification algorithms. In this paper, we present an assessment algorithm, EXACT_OB2, designed specifically for use with extended decision-region based algorithms. We also present a new assessment algorithm, APPROX_EVAL, for use with decision-region based algorithms. The APPROX_EVAL algorithm is characterized has having a relatively low execution time, but may not achieve an exact assessment. However, data collected from initial experiments indicate that, in general, the application of the latter algorithm can lead to an exact assessment of the security risk associated with a protected data element, under certain security policies.

The rest of this paper is organized as follows. Section 1 presents an overview of our previous work, which we extend in this paper. Section 2 characterizes the extended decision-region based algorithms and presents an outline of the EXACT_OB2 algorithm. Section 3 presents an outline of the APPROX_EVAL algorithm; and, Section 4 describes the results of experiments that were conducted to assess the APPROX_EVAL's effectiveness. Finally, Section 5 presents the conclusions and discusses some future research projects.

1. OVERVIEW OF PREVIOUS WORK

We developed an algorithm, referred to as Orthogonal-Boundary (OB), that provides an exact assessment of the security risk of protected data elements with respect to decision-region based algorithms [5]. We define an *exact assessment* as one that guarantees the implementation of a security policy at the description space level. The notion of a description space level policy follows directly from the definition of a decision-region based classification algorithm.

A classification algorithm, A, is a *decision-region based* algorithm if and only if the following two conditions are satisfied:

- *Condition-1*: It is possible to identify a priori a finite set of descriptions, D, in terms of the attribute values present in an object O such that the particular description d used by A to classify O is an element of D.
- *Condition-2*: The "predicted accuracy" of assigning an object satisfying a description d ∈ D to a class c is dependent on the distribution of class label c relative to all other class labels among the objects that satisfy d in the training set.

These conditions lead to the property that the effective assessment of the security threat from decision-region based algorithms requires the construction of a class-accuracy set for each description d ∈ D. We define a *class-accuracy set* as a collection of ordered pairs (c_i, a_i), where c_i is the ith attribute value (class label) in the domain of the protected attribute and a_i is the predicted accuracy, according to the classification algorithm, of assigning to the protected tuple the class label c_i. Inference-based security policies may be applied at two levels. If it is known a priori that a particular description d ∈ D will be selected relative to the protected tuple, then we can apply a policy just to that description. We refer to this type of policy as being defined at the *description level*. A more desirable approach is to ensure that no matter which d ∈ D is chosen, the stated security policy is satisfied. We refer to this type of policy as being defined at the *description space level*. Given the above definitions and *Condition-1*, we concluded that inference-based security policies should be specified at the description space level, since description level policies require prior knowledge of which description will be chosen, which makes the results specific to a particular classification mining algorithm.

The OB algorithm has been designed for use with decision-region based algorithms that produce a specific type of description. In particular, those descriptions that are expressed as a logical conjunction of (attribute name, value) pairs and constructed from non-protected attribute values present in the protected tuple. The OB algorithm is, therefore, limited to decision-region based algorithms that divide the search space into hyper-rectangles. Those decision-region based algorithms that divide the search space into "tilted" regions, such as decision-tree algorithms that use an attribute selection criterion based on a weighted sum of attribute values, and k-nearest neighbor classifiers which are defined in terms of a similarity measure, are outside the scope of OB.

The hyper-rectangular regions associated with a protected tuple are the logical conjunctions formed from one or more non-protected (attribute name, value) pairs that appear within the tuple. We refer to this set of descriptions as the description space, D^*, of the protected tuple. It follows from *Condition-1* that the assignment of a class label to a protected tuple is a label associated with a description d $\in D^*$. There is no way to identify a priori the description d $\in D^*$ that will be chosen by a classifier without making explicit assumptions about its operation. Thus, in general, it is necessary to inspect all descriptions that belong to a tuple's description space.

The risk assessment algorithm implements the description level protected rank security policy [1, 1]. Given a class-accuracy set, a *protected rank policy* is *satisfied* if the ranked position of the protected data element is not within the non-secure range [L,U], where L and U are positive integers such that $1 \leq$ L $\leq$ U and L $\leq$ U $\leq |\{a_1, a_2, ..., a_n\}|$. To implement a protected rank policy it is necessary to compute a class-accuracy set for each individual description, d $\in D^*$. The class-accuracy sets are computed based on *Condition-2* as follows. Let c be a class label in the domain of a protected attribute. Given a description d $\in D^*$, the *predicted accuracy, a*, of assigning the protected tuple T the label c is the ratio of the number of tuples that are assigned label c and satisfy d to the number of tuples that satisfy d. This measure is equal to the classification accuracy measure defined in [6]. There are classification algorithms that satisfy *Condition-1*, but violate *Condition-2*. For instance, the CART decision-tree algorithm does not assume that the class labels are uniformly distributed, but instead computes predicted accuracy values using a weighted ratio based on prior probabilities [7].

A high-level outline of the OB algorithm, EXACT_OB1, is shown in Figure-1. The result of executing this algorithm is the implicit or explicit inspection of each description belonging to the protected tuple's description space, D^*. The inspection process ensures that all descriptions, d $\in D^*$, of a tuple's description space satisfy the stated description level security policy.

Unfortunately, the number of descriptions that belong to a protected tuple's description space is exponential in terms of the number of non-protected attributes. However, the recognition of a special type of description that we refer to as a *zero description* can significantly reduce the required number of inspections. The tuples that satisfy a zero description are characterized as having a class label that does not equal the protected data element. The occurrence of a zero description implies that there is no need to inspect any description that is a specialization since it will also be a zero description.

As shown in Figure-1, the EXACT_OB1 algorithm determines if a description, d $\in D^*$, is a zero description. If d is a zero description it is placed on a list so that it is not directly examined by the algorithm, otherwise the algorithm determines if the description is non-secure. A *non-secure* description, d, is a description that violates the stated description level security policy. Currently, a description, d, is considered non-secure if it violates the protected rank policy

```
EXACT_OB1 Algorithm
k = 1
while (exists descriptions to inspect)
  D = k-level descriptions requiring protection
      (excluding zero_description list)
  for each (description d in D)
    if (d == zero_description)
      append all specializations of d to zero_description list
    else if (d == non-secure description)
      append d to non-secure description list
  end_for
  transform non-secure descriptions to secure descriptions
  (by protecting subset of attribute values not belonging to
   protected tuple)
  k = k + 1
end_while
```

Figure 1. Orthogonal-Boundary Algorithm: EXACT_OB1.

$[1, 1]$. The transformation of a non-secure description into a secure description is performed by concealing a subset of attribute values from the domain of non-protected attributes that appear in the training set, but not in the protected tuple. The concealment of such values must decrease the number of tuples that satisfy the non-secure description with a class label equal to that of the protected data element, which can be repeated until there is no longer a violation of policy. This particular transformation has the following important property: *the implementation of a policy, P, at the description level implies the implementation of P at the description space level.* In the context of EXACT_OB1, this property ensures the implementation of the protected rank policy $[1, 1]$ at the description space level. It is important to note that EXACT_OB1 is only valid in the context of decision-region based algorithms. In the following section we present an algorithm that is designed for use with another category of classification algorithms, referred to as extended decision-region based.

2. EXTENDED DECISION-REGION BASED ALGORITHMS

We have generalized the EXACT_OB1 algorithm to provide an exact assessment of protected data elements with respect to extended decision-region based algorithms. A classification algorithm, A, is an *extended decision-region based* algorithm if and only if the following two conditions are satisfied:

- *Condition*-1*: It is possible to identify a priori a finite set of descriptions, D, in terms of the attribute values present in an object O, and the attribute values present in a finite set of objects O' derived from O, such that the particular description d used by A to classify O is an element of D.

- *Condition*-2*: The predicted accuracy of assigning an object satisfying a description d to a class c is dependent on the distribution of class label c relative to all other class labels among the objects that satisfy d in the training set.

In *Condition*-1*, an object O' is derived from another object O if it has at least one property in common with O. The difference between *Condition-1* and *Condition*-1* is that the latter condition allows for descriptions that are not entirely defined in terms of the properties of the target object. The second condition, *Condition*-2*, is identical to *Condition-2* defined for decision-region based algorithms. Thus, a decision-region based algorithm is also an extended decision-region based algorithm.

An example of an extended decision-region based algorithm is C4.5's consult interpreter when applied to protected tuples with missing non-protected attribute values [8]. To illustrate, consider the protected tuple, (*Cyl*=4; *Fuel*=null; *Tran*=manu; *Power*=med; *Mileage*=null) where *Mileage* is the protected attribute, and the following class-accuracy values, 0 (*low*), .62 (*med*) and .38 (*high*) produced by C4.5. These confidence values were obtained through the assessment of the descriptions shown in Figure-2. It follows from the descriptions that there are two relevant protected tuples, (*Cyl*=4; *Fuel*=efi; *Tran*=manu; *Power*=med; *Mileage*=null) and ($Cyl = 4; Fuel = 2-bbl; Tran = manu; Power = med; Mileage = null$). In general, there exists a relevant, or derived, protected tuple for each distinct value in the domain of a missing non-protected attribute. The total number of relevant tuples is equal to the product of the domain sizes of the various non-protected attributes to which the missing attributes values belong. For instance, in the above example there are two relevant protected tuples since there is one missing non-protected attribute, *Fuel*, and its domain size is two, $\{2-bbl, efi\}$. Similarly, if the protected tuple contains two missing non-protected attributes, *Fuel* and *Power*, the total number of relevant protected tuples is six since the domain size of *Fuel* is two and the domain size of *Power* is three, $\{low, med, high\}$. The description space of each relevant protected tuple must be inspected to determine if each description, d, satisfies the stated description level policy.

A high-level description of the EXACT_OB2 algorithm is shown in Figure-3. This algorithm is an extension of the EXACT_OB1 algorithm, and is designed for use with extended decision-region based algorithms. The EXACT_OB2 algorithm, like EXACT_OB1, has been developed in the context of descriptions that are represented by a logical conjunction of (attribute name, value) pairs. In

```
low = #(Cyl = 4 & Fuel = 2–bbl & Mileage = low) / #(Cyl = 4) +
      #(Fuel = efi & Cyl = 4) / #(Cyl = 4) *
      #(Cyl = 4 & Fuel = efi & Power = med & Mileage = low) /
      #(Cyl = 4 & Fuel = efi & Power = med)

Med = #(Cyl = 4 & Fuel = 2–bbl & Mileage = med) / #(Cyl = 4) +
      #(Fuel = efi & Cyl = 4) / #(Cyl = 4) *
      #(Cyl = 4 & Fuel = efi & Power = med & Mileage = med) /
      #(Cyl = 4 & Fuel = efi & Power = med )

High = #(Cyl = 4 & Fuel = 2–bbl & Mileage = high) / #(Cyl = 4) +
      #(Fuel = efi & Cyl = 4) / #(Cyl = 4) *
      #(Cyl = 4 & Fuel = efi & Power = med & Mileage = high) /
      #(Cyl = 4 & Fuel = efi & Power = med)
```

Figure 2. Example Descriptions.

```
EXACT_OB2 Algorithm
PT = generate all relevant protected tuples
for each (protected tuple in PT)
  apply EXACT_OB1
end_for
```

Figure 3. Orthogonal-Boundary Algorithm: Exact_OB2.

addition, we assume that the set of descriptions D is limited to those descriptions generated from the attribute values of the protected tuple as well as from values in the domain of the missing non-protected attributes of the protected tuple. Based on these restrictions, the result of executing the EXACT_OB2 algorithm is the inspection of the descriptions belonging to the description space of each relevant protected tuple. The structure of EXACT_OB2 is almost identical to the structure of EXACT_OB1. The only difference is that EXACT_OB2 inspects the description space of multiple protected tuples as opposed to a single protected tuple. The biggest limitation of EXACT_OB2, as well as EXACT_OB1, is the potentially high execution time. Specifically, the execution time of both algorithms is dependent upon the number of non-protected attributes and the occurrence of zero descriptions. As a result, we have developed an alternative assessment algorithm to approximate the exact assessment performed by EXACT_OB1.

3. APPROXIMATE ASSESSMENT ALGORITHM

In this section, we present an assessment algorithm, which we will refer to as APPROX_EVAL. It approximates the exact assessment performed by EXACT_OB1. The idea behind APPROX_EVAL is to decrease the required execution time by reducing the size of the description space. One way to reduce the size of a description space is to transform a non-secure description into a secure description by concealing one or more non-protected attribute values. For example, if (*Cyl*=4) is a non-secure description with respect to the protected tuple, (*Fuel*=efi; *Cyl*=4; *Tran*=manu; *Mileage*=null), then the concealment of the non-protected attribute value, *Cyl*=4, removes the description *Cyl*=4 from D^*. In other words, the description cannot be used by a decision-region based algorithm to assign a value to the protected attribute.

The concealed value also removes from D^* from the following descriptions, (*Fuel*=efi $\wedge$ *Cyl*=4), (*Cyl*=4 $\wedge$ *Tran*=manu), and (*Fuel*=efi $\wedge$ *Cyl*=4 $\wedge$ *Tran*=manu). As a result, there is no need to explicitly inspect any of these descriptions. However, as illustrated in the previous section, the concealment of non-protected attribute values may cause a classification algorithm, that normally adheres to the conditions of a decision-region based algorithm, to violate *Condition-1* [5]. The APPROX_EVAL algorithm must, therefore, determine if a concealed non-protected attribute value is likely to result in such a violation. A high-level outline of APPROX_EVAL is shown in Figure-4. If it is determined that a violation is unlikely then the protected tuple is evaluated using the APPROX_OB algorithm; otherwise, it is evaluated using the EXACT_OB1 algorithm described in the previous section. The difference between the two algorithms is that APPROX_OB, unlike EXACT_OB1, transforms a non-secure description into a secure description by concealing one or more attribute values from the domain of non-protected attributes that appear in the protected tuple. In general, the execution time of APPROX_OB will be less than that of EXACT_OB1 due to the concealment of non-protected attribute values, and will also maximize the amount of available data.

The APPROX_EVAL algorithm may not achieve an exact assessment since it must predict the impact of a concealed non-protected attribute value on a decision-region based algorithm. However, the results obtained from the experimental investigation suggest that the prediction is likely to be consistent with an exact assessment.

3.1. Predicted Accuracy Measure

We have developed a measure to compute a class-accuracy set to determine if a concealed non-protected attribute value is likely to result in a violation of *Condition-1*. In this context, the class-accuracy set is computed independently of any specific description belonging to the protected tuple's description

```
APPROX_EVAL Algorithm

prediction = predict impact of concealed non-protected attribute values
if (prediction == violation of Condition-1)
  apply EXACT_OB1 algorithm
else
  apply APPROX_OB algorithm
```

Figure 4. Approximate Evaluation Algorithm (High-Level).

space. Instead, the predicted accuracy value a, with respect to a class label c, is computed based upon the degree to which the protected tuple's non-protected attribute values predict the class c. The degree to which a non-protected attribute value predicts a protected attribute class depends upon the attribute value's relationship to the tuples that belong to the class as well as to the tuples that belong to other classes.

These relationships form the basis of our measure. Specifically, the proposed measure M, as shown in Figure-5, assigns a numerical value to a non-protected attribute value, a, that reflects the degree to which, a, predicts the protected attribute class b. The value N is equal to the number of tuples in the relation instance. The range of M is the interval $[-1, 1]$, where a value of positive (negative) one implies that the non-protected attribute value provides complete support (non-support) for the protected attribute class. The measure is comprised of two functions, *class(a,b)* and *nonclass(a,b)*. The function, *class(a,b)*, captures the degree to which an implication of the form $(b \rightarrow a')$ weakens an implication of the form $(a \rightarrow b)$. The quantity #(a,b) is the number of tuples in the relation instance with (attribute name, value) pairs A:a and B:b; and, the quantity #(a',b) is the number of tuples in the relation with (attribute name, value) pairs A:a' and B:b. The symbol a' represents an element belonging to the set $Dom(A) - a$. The other function, *nonclass(a,b)*, captures the degree to which an implication of the form $(b' \rightarrow a')$ weakens an implication of the form $(a \rightarrow b')$. The symbol b' represents an element belonging to the set $Dom(B) - b$. The quantity #(a,b_i) represents the number of tuples in the relation instance with (attribute name, value) pairs A:a and B:b_i, where b_i is an instance of B such that $b_i \neq b$; and, #(a', b_i) represents the number of tuples in the relation instance with (attribute name, value) pairs A:a' and B:b_i. Finally, the condition expressed as *cond-1* is satisfied if #(a,b_i) / #(a',b_i) $= 1$ and #(a,b_j) / #(a',b_j) < 1 for all j $\neq$ i where $b_i, b_j \in Dom(B) - b$. Intuitively, the function, *nonclass(a,b)*, computes the degree of predictability associated with the class, b', that the attribute value a predicts to the greatest extent.

$$M = \begin{cases} +1 & : \text{if } \#(a,b') = 0 \\ -1 & : \text{if } \#(a,b) = 0 \\ \log_2 ((\text{class}(a,b) / N + 1) / (\text{nonclass}(a,b) / N + 1)) & : \text{otherwise} \end{cases}$$

$$\text{class}(a,b) = \begin{cases} \#(a,b) - \#(a',b) & : \#(a,b) >= \#(a',b) \\ \#(a,b) / \#(a',b) & : \text{otherwise} \end{cases}$$

$$\text{nonclass}(a,b) = \begin{cases} 0 & : \text{if cond}-1 \\ \underset{i = \{B - b\}}{\text{Max}} \begin{cases} \#(a,b_i) - \#(a',b_i) : \text{if } \#(a,b_i) >= \#(a',b_i) \\ \#(a,b_i) / \#(a',b_i) \quad : \text{otherwise} \end{cases} & : \text{otherwise} \end{cases}$$

Figure 5. Predicted Accuracy Measure M.

The definitions of *class(a,b)* and *nonclass(a,b)* represent the concept of a non-protected attribute's relevance and non-relevance odds, respectively. This type of relevance relationship has been used previously in information retrieval systems to determine a document term's degree of importance in distinguishing relative and non-relative documents [9].

3.2. APPROX_EVAL Algorithm

The measure M is used to compute the class-accuracy set of a protected tuple. Specifically, the assigned weights that correspond to a class, c, are summed together to produce the corresponding predicted accuracy value. For example, suppose the application of M with respect to the protected tuple, (*Cyl*=6; *Fuel*=2-bbl; *Tran*=manu; *Power*=low; *Mileage*=null), produces the results shown in Figure-6. In this instance, the predicted class-accuracy set is {(low, -1.09), (med, -.255), (high, -.946)}. In general, a computed predicted accuracy value represents the degree to which the protected tuple predicts the corresponding protected data element.

The class-accuracy set is used in conjunction with the Protected Minimum Range (PMR) security policy to determine if there is a violation of *Condition-1*. The application of a PMR policy is dependent upon the rank position of the predicted accuracy value, a_i, of the protected data element relative to the other predicted accuracy values. If a_i is the maximum predicted accuracy value, then the *pmr* value is the difference between a_i and the next largest predicted accuracy value a_k; otherwise, it is the difference between a_i and and the maximum predicted accuracy value.

As shown in Figure-7, if *pmr* is greater than some established threshold, then the APPROX_EVAL algorithm evaluates the protected data element using

Low: {Cyl=6: .1699; Fuel=2–bbl: –.0458; Tran=manu: –.2157; Power=low: –1}

Med: {Cyl=6: –.1699; Fuel=2–bbl: –.0771, Tran=manu: 0; Power=low: –.0079}

High: {Cyl=6: –1; Fuel=2–bbl: .0458; Tran = manu: 0; Power=low: .0079}

Figure 6. Application of Measure M.

```
APPROX_EVAL Algorithm

compute measure M with respect to protected tuple
compute corresponding class–accuracy set
pmr = apply Protected Minimum Range policy to class–accuracy set
if (pmr >= threshold–value)
  apply EXACT_OB1 algorithm
else
  apply APPROX_OB algorithm
```

Figure 7. Approximate Evaluation Algorithm (Detail-Level).

the EXACT_OB1 algorithm; otherwise, the protected data element is evaluated using the APPROX_OB algorithm.

4. EXPERIMENTAL INVESTIGATION

Experiments were conducted to validate the use of the APPROX_EVAL algorithm in implementing the description space level protected rank policy [1,1]. In conducting our initial experiments, we restricted the evaluation to C4.5's decision-tree classifier and interpreter [8]. The experiments utilized ten distinct data sets, each of which contained at least ten non-protected attribute values and a single protected attribute with a domain size of five. All of the relations were constructed through the application of the Synthetic Classification Data Set (SCDS) program [10]. A total of fifty-one protected tuples were used in the investigation. Twenty-one of the protected tuples violated the description space level policy [1,1].

Figure-8 shows the *pmr* value computed for each of the fifty-one protected tuples. The APPROX_OB algorithm was applied to each protected tuple. The application of APPROX_OB resulted in the transformation of a protected tuple T into a protected tuple T' that, in general, contained one or more concealed non-protected attribute values. The transformed protected tuples, T', were

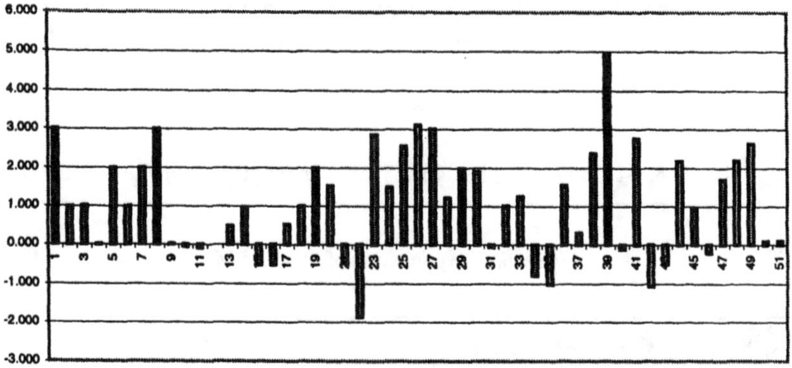

Figure 8. Computed *pmr* Values for Protected Tuples.

classified using C4.5's consult interpreter. In order to assess the generality of the APPROX_EVAL algorithm two distinct decision-tree models where generated for each relation instance. One model was constructed using the gain attribute selection criterion, while the other model was constructed using the gain ratio attribute selection criterion. We identified those protected tuples that violated the description space level protected rank policy [1,1]. There were a total of five such tuples, five with respect to the gain ratio criterion and one with respect to the gain criterion. These five tuples are shown as solid-filled columns in Figure-8.

The experimental results suggest that a *pmr* value greater than or equal to two identifies a potential violation of *Condition-1*. Unfortunately, such a *pmr* value may produce false positives. It appears that the occurrence of false positives may be related to the percentage of non-relevant attributes contained within a relation.

5. CONCLUSION AND FUTURE WORK

In this paper we identified a new category of classification mining algorithms, referred to as extended decision-region based, and presented a security risk assessment algorithm, EXACT_OB2, designed specifically for use with this category of algorithms. In addition, we proposed an alternative assessment algorithm, APPROX_EVAL, designed for use with decision-region based algorithms. This particular assessment algorithm is characterized as having a relatively low execution time, but may not achieve an exact assessment.

We have several additional research projects planned with respect to this challenging research area. Our immediate plans include further verification of experimental results using additional extended decision-region based algorithms and data sets, extending the security assessments to include continuously valued attributes, and the development of additional security assessments for other groups of mining algorithms.

References

[1] Chang, L. and Moskowitz, I. (1998). Parsimonious Downgrading and Decision Trees Applied to the Inference Problem. *Proceedings of New Security Paradigms*, pp. 82-89.

[2] Chang, L. and Moskowitz, I. (2000). An Integrated Framework for Database Privacy Protection. *Proceedings of the fourteenth Annual IFIP WG 11.3 Working Conference on Database Security.*

[3] Clifton, C. and Marks, D. (1996). Security and Privacy Implications of Data Mining. *1996 SIGMOD Workshop on Research Issues on Data Mining and Knowledge Discovery*, pp. 15-19.

[4] Clifton, C. (1999). Protecting Against Data Mining Through Samples. *Proceedings of the Thirteenth Annual IFIP WG 11.3 Working Conference on Database Security*, pp. 193-207.

[5] Johnsten, T. and Raghavan, V. (1999). Impact of Decision-Region Based Classification Mining Algorithms on Database Security. *Proceedings of the Thirteenth Annual IFIP WG 11.3 Working Conference on Database Security*, pp. 177-191.

[6] Holsheimer, M. and Siebes, A. (1994). Data Mining: The Search for Knowledge in Databases. *Report CS-R9406*. CWI. Amsterdam, The Netherlands.

[7] Steinberg, D. and Colla, P. (1997). CART User Manual. Salford Systems. San Diego, CA.

[8] Quinlan, J. (1993). C4.5: Programs For Machine Learning. Morgan Kaufmann, San Mateo, CA.

[9] Robertson, S. and Jones, K. (1976). Relevance Weighting for Search Terms. *Journal of the American Society for Information Science*, May-June, pp. 129-145.

[10] Synthetic Classification Data Sets, *http://fas.sfu.ca/cs/people/Grad Students/melli/SCDS/intro.html.*

REGULATING ACCESS TO XML DOCUMENTS

Alban Gabillon and Emmanuel Bruno

Alban Gabillon. gabillon@univ-pau.fr
LIUPPA/CSYSEC. Université de Pau. IUT Antenne de Mont de Marsan. 371 rue du Ruisseau BP 201, 40004 Mont de Marsan Cedex France.

Emmanuel Bruno. bruno@univ-tln.fr
SIS - Equipe Informatique. Université de Toulon et du Var. 83957 La Garde, France.

Abstract: In this paper, our objective is to define a security model for regulating access to XML documents. Our model offers a security policy with a great expressive power. An XML document is represented by a tree. Nodes of this tree are of different type (element, attribute, text, comment...etc). The smallest protection granularity of our model is the node, that is, authorisation rules granting or denying access to a single node can be defined. The authorisation rules related to a specific XML document are first defined on a separate Authorisation sheet. This Authorisation sheet is then translated into an XSLT sheet. If a user requests access to the XML document then the XSLT processor uses the XSLT sheet to provide the user with a view of the XML document which is compatible with his rights.

Key words: Security Model, Subject, Object, Authorisation Rule, Access Controls, XML, XPath, XSLT.

1. INTRODUCTION

XML is a mark-up language standardised by the World Wide Web Consortium (W3C) [1]. XML has become a standard for describing information distributed on Internet. Since Internet is a public network, internet applications need security mechanisms to protect sensitive data against unauthorised access. Standardisation activities for XML digital signature and element-wise encryption have already started [2]. However, a standardised authorisation mechanism for XML data still remains an open issue although some proposals have already been made [3][4][5].

In this paper, our objective is to define a security model for regulating access to XML documents. In [6], due to space limitations we only managed to present the basics of our model. In this paper we present the complete model. An XML document is represented by a tree. Nodes of this tree are of different type (element, attribute, text, comment...etc). The smallest protection granularity of our model is the node, that is, authorisation rules granting or denying access to a single node can be defined. The semantics of an authorisation rule is unique regardless of the node type. We show that our model allows us to define complex security policies including cover story management.

A prototype implementing our model is available online at `http://sis.univ-tln.fr/XML-secu`. Our prototype is based on XSLT [7]. The authorisation rules related to a specific XML document are first defined on a separate easy-to-read Authorisation sheet. This Authorisation sheet is then translated into an XSLT sheet. If a user requests access to the XML document then the XSLT processor uses the XSLT sheet to provide the user with a view of the XML document which is compatible with his rights.

Our model uses the XPath language. Therefore, section 2 of this paper briefly summarises the main characteristics of the XPath language. Section 3 presents our model. Section 4 sketches a straightforward implementation of our model using an XSLT processor. Section 5 discusses related work. Finally, section 6 concludes this paper.

2. XPATH

XPath [8] is a language for addressing parts of an XML document. XPath models an XML document as a tree of nodes. The following XML document represents a file of medical records which contains only one record. This XML document can be represented by the tree of Figure 1.

Nodes preceded by "/" are element nodes. Nodes preceded by "@" are attribute nodes and nodes preceded by "text()" are text nodes[1].

The following expressions are examples of *absolute* XPath *location paths* (see [8]):

- `/files/record`. This path addresses each record element which is a child of the files element.

[1] The XPath data model includes three other types of node namely namespace node, processing instruction node and comment node. For a concise presentation, we do not include such nodes in our example.

- `/files//text()`.This path addresses each text node which is a descendant of the `files` element.

```
<files>
 <record id="mrobert">
  <name>Martin Robert
  </name>
  <diagn osis>
    <item>Pneumonia</item>
  </diagnosis>
 </record>
</files>
```

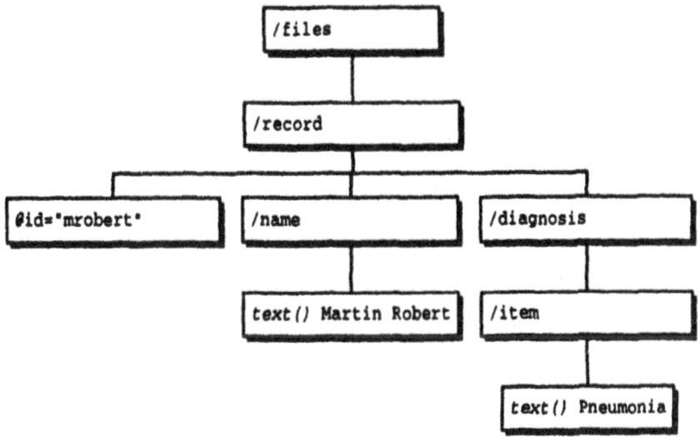

Figure 1 : Tree representation of an XML document

The following expressions are examples of *relative* `XPath` *location paths* (we assume the *context node* is the diagnosis element)(see [8]):

- `item/node()`.This path addresses all the child nodes (element or text node) of the `item` element.
- ../@*. This path addresses all the attribute nodes of the context node's parent element, that is, this path addresses all the attributes of the `record` element.

In addition to its use for addressing, `XPath` is also designed so that it has a natural subset that can be used for matching (testing whether or not a node matches a *pattern*). This use of `XPath` is made by `XSLT` [7]. A pattern specifies a set of conditions on a node. A node that satisfies the conditions matches the pattern. A node that does not satisfy the conditions does not match the pattern. Location paths that meet certain restrictions can be used as patterns (see [7]).

The following expressions are examples of patterns:

- `item`. Each `item` element matches this pattern.
- `item/text()`. Each text node of each `item` element matches this pattern.
- `record/@*`. Each attribute of each `record` element matches this pattern.
- `record[1]/node() | record[1]/@*`. Each child node and attribute of the first `record` element matches this pattern ("|" is the *union* operator).
- `item[contains(text(),'Cancer')]`. Each `item` element containing the string `'Cancer'` matches this pattern.

3. ACCESS CONTROL MODEL

The development of an access control system requires the definition of *subjects* and *objects* for which *authorisation rules* must be specified and access controls must be enforced.

3.1 Subjects

A subject is a user. Each user has an identifier which can be the login name. Each user is the member of one or several user groups. For the sake of simplicity we assume that groups are disjoint but they can be nested.

The subject hierarchy is described in a separate *XML Subject Sheet* (XSS). The document below shows a simple example of such a sheet.

```
<subjects>
    <users>
      <member id="dupont">
        <name>Pierre Dupont</name>
      </member>
      <member id="durand">
        <name>Jacqueline Durand</name>
      </member>
      <member id="frobert">
        <name>Francine Robert</name>
      </member>
      <member id="mrobert">
        <name>Martin Robert</name>
      </member>
      <member id="beaufort">
        <name>Colette Beaufort</name>
      </member>
    </users>
    <groups>
      <Staff>
         <Secretary>
            <member idref="beaufort"/>
         </Secretary>
         <Doctor>
            <member idref="dupont"/>
         </Doctor>
         <Nurse>
            <member idref="durand"/>
         </Nurse>
      </Staff>
         <Patient>
            <member idref="mrobert"/>
         </Patient>
      <Family>
         <Robert>
            <member idref="frobert"/>
            <member idref="mrobert"/>
         </Robert>
      </Family>
    </groups>
</subjects>
```

This XSS document describes a subject hierarchy with four users. In this example, each user is member of at least one group. There are three groups: *Staff*, *Patient* and *Family*. The *Staff* group is subdivided into three subgroups: *Doctor*, *Nurse*, *Secretary*. The *Family* group contains only the *Robert* family sub-group.

Users registered in this XSS sheet are selected with location paths relative to the subjects element. If a location path addresses a node *n* then we say that all users who are referenced in the sub-tree of which *n* is the root are selected. Examples of such a path are the followings:

- `users`. This path selects all users.
- `users/member[@id='mrobert']` . This path selects user Martin Robert.
- `groups//Secretary`. This path selects all secretaries
- `groups/*[name()!='Staff']`. This path selects all the users who are not staff members.

3.2 Objects

In section 3 we have seen that an XML document can be represented by an `XPath` tree. An object can be any node of an `XPath` tree.

3.3 Authorisation rules

An *authorisation rule* is a 4-tuple of the form,
<set-of-subjects, set-of-objects, access, priority>
We have seen in sections 3.1 and 3.2 that a subject is a user and an object is a node of an `XPath` tree. *set-of-objects* is expressed with a pattern. *set-of-subjects* is a location path relative to the element *subjects* of the `XSS` sheet (see section 3.1). The value of *access* is either *grant* or *deny*. *priority* is optional. It is used to fix the priority of the authorisation rule (see section 3.4 for more details). The default priority is 0.

In our model the semantics of an authorisation rule is unique regardless of the node type (element, attribute, text ...):

If access to node *n* is granted to user *u* then *u* is permitted to see the subtree of which *n* is the root.

If access to node *n* is denied to user *u* then *u* is forbidden to see the subtree of which *n* is the root.

The Security Administrator writes the authorisation rules on an *XML Authorisation Sheet* (XAS). The following XML document is an example of XAS sheet. This sheet contains the rules which apply to the document described in section 2 and refers to the XSS sheet defined in section 3.1.

```
<!-- D E F A U L T   H O S P I T A L   P O L I C Y -->
<!-- Rule 1 -->
<xas DefaultPolicy="open" DefaultSubjectsFile="subjects.xss">
<!-- Rule 2 -->
<rule access="deny"  object="record"
      subject="groups/*[name()!='Staff']"/>
<!-- Rule 3 -->
<rule access="deny"  object="diagnosis" subject="groups//Secretary"/>
<!-- Rule 4 -->
<rule access="grant" object="record[@id=$user]"
      subject="users/member[@id=$user]"/>
</xas>
```

The first element of an XAS sheet determines whether the default policy is *open* or *closed*[9]. If no authorisation rule is specified regarding a user *u* and a node *n* then *u* is permitted to access to *n* in case of the open policy and is forbidden to access to *n* in case of the closed policy. Rule 1 says that the default policy is open. Rule 2 says that non staff members are forbidden to see the records. Rule 3 says that secretaries are forbidden to see the diagnosis of a patient. Rule 4 says that a patient is permitted to see his personal medical record. `$user` is a variable which is instantiated with the *id* of the user accessing to the XML source document. Rule 4 overrides rules 2 when a user is accessing to his personal data. None of the authorisation rules of our example includes the *priority* attribute. Therefore, the priority of each rule is set by default to 0.

3.4 ComputeView Algorithm and Conflict Resolution Policy

If a user requests to see the XML source document then he has to be provided with the view of the document which is compatible with his rights. The aim of this section is to present the algorithm for computing such a view. Before presenting the algorithm itself we have to perform the following preliminary task in order to obtain an *easy-to-read* algorithm[2].

We replace each grant rule of the form,

```
<rule access="grant" object=n subject=u priority=p>,
```

by the following three consecutive grant rules:

```
<rule access="grant" object=n          subject=u priority=p>
<rule access="grant" object=n//node()  subject=u priority=p>
<rule access="grant" object=n//@*      subject=u priority=p>
```

The first rule is the same as the original rule. All the descendant nodes of[3] the node *n* match the object pattern of the second rule. All the attributes of *n* and the attributes of the descendant nodes of *n* match the object pattern of the third rule.

Note that this replacement does not change the security policy. Recall that granting access to node *n* to user *u* means that *u* is permitted to see the sub-tree of which *n* is the root (see previous section 3.3).

Finally, if the default policy is closed then we insert the following rule:

```
<rule access="deny" object="/" subject= "users" priority="-1">
```

and if the default policy is open then we insert the following rules:

```
<rule access="grant" object="/"        subject="users" priority="-1">
<rule access="grant" object="//node()" subject="users" priority="-1">
<rule access="grant" object="//@*"     subject="users" priority="-1">
```

The rules implementing the default policy all have a negative priority. Path, `users`, selects all the users registered in the XSS sheet.

Consequently, our previous example of XAS sheet can be interpreted as the following list of rules:

[2] We could define the conflict resolution policy and write the algorithm without performing this preliminary task. However the definition of both the conflict resolution policy and the algorithm would be less straightforward (although the complexity would be unchanged).

[3] or, of each node of the set *n*, if *n* is a set of nodes (cf section 3.3)

```
<!-- D E F A U L T   H O S P I T A L   P O L I C Y -->
<!-- Rules 1a, 1b and 1c -->
<rule access="grant"  object="/"         subject="users"  priority="-1">
<rule access="grant"  object="//node()"  subject="users"  priority="-1">
<rule access="grant"  object="//@*"      subject="users"  priority="-1">
<!-- Rule 2 -->
<rule   access  = "deny"        object   = "record"
        subject="groups/*[name()!='Staff']"    priority = "0"/>
<!-- Rule 3 -->
<rule   access  = "deny"        object   = "diagnosis"
        subject = "groups//Secretary"          priority = "0"/>
<!-- Rules 4a, 4b and 4c -->
<rule   access  = "grant"       object = "record[@id=$user]"
        subject = "users/member[@id=$user]"    priority = "0"/>
<rule   access  = "grant"       object="record[@id=$user]//node()"
        subject = "users/member[@id=$user]"    priority = "0"/>
<rule   access  = "grant"       object="record[@id=$user]//@*"
        subject = "users/member[@id=$user]"    priority = "0"/>
```

Rule 1 is replaced by three grant rules with a negative priority. The default policy has the lowest priority. Rule 4 is replaced by three grant rules.

There is a conflict between a deny rule and a grant rule for a node *n* and a user *u* if *n* matches the two *set-of-object* patterns and *u* is addressed by the two *set-of-subjects*.

In our example, Rule 2 conflicts with Rule 1b for each `record` element and each user who is not a staff member. Rule 3 conflicts with Rule 1b for each `diagnosis` element and each secretary. Rule 4a conflicts with Rule 2 for the current user's `record` element (in case the user is a patient).

The conflict resolution policy of our model is very simple:

1. If, for a node *n* and a user *u*, there is a conflict between a set of rules then the rules with the highest priority are selected.
2. If the selected rules are more than one then the last rule in the XAS sheet is elected.

Step 2 explains why Rule 4a of our example overrides Rules 2 in the conflicting cases. Considering this policy, we can now present our algorithm for computing the views:

```
ComputeView Algorithm
Let U be the user for which the view has to be computed
Let L be an empty list of nodes
Insert the root element into L
Let R be an empty list of nodes
While L is not empty Do
    N ← the first node of L
    Select all the rules such as N matches the object pattern and U is
    selected by the subject path
    Apply the conflict resolution policy defined above
    If the elected rule is a deny rule then
            Remove N from L
    Else
            Append N to R
            Replace N into L by the attributes and child nodes of N
```

After the algorithm finishes R contains the pre-order list of the nodes which belong to the view. Using this algorithm we can easily compute the view for each user

View for P. Dupont (Doctor) and J. Durand (Nurse) and M. Robert (Patient)

```
<files>
   <record id="mrobert">
     <name>Martin Robert</name>
     <diagnosis>
          <item>Pneumonia</item>
     </diagnosis>
   </record>
</files>
```

Pierre Dupont and Jacqueline Durand are permitted to see everything. Martin Robert is permitted to see everything because the file contains only one record: his own record.

View for C. Beaufort (Secretary)

```
<files>
   <record id="mrobert">
     <name>Martin Robert</name>
   </record>
</files>
```

Colette Beaufort is forbidden to see the diagnosis element.

View for F. Robert (Robert Family)

```
<files/>
```

The default hospital policy says that non staff members are forbidden to see the medical records. This rule applies to family members. Therefore, *Francine Robert* is forbidden to see the medical records, including Robert's record.

As we have seen above, the conflict resolution policy of our model is based on priorities (whether they are implicit or explicit). Conflict resolution policies based on priorities are usually considered as difficult to manage and understand. We agree that in some cases it might be difficult for a human to figure out the output of conflicting rules. However, we have decided to use priorities for the following two reasons:

1. We do not see what are the advantages of using conflict resolution policies based on principles like "the most specific object takes precedence" or "the most specific subject takes precedence" (see [3] for instance). These policies which were first used in Object-Oriented environments are not well adapted to XML. Indeed, in many cases it is impossible for a human to predict which XPath expression is going to be the most specific. As a matter of facts let us consider the following two rules:

```
<rule  access="deny"
       object="diagnosis[item='Cancer' or item='Pneumonia']
       subject="groups//Nurse"/>
<rule  access="grant"
       object="diagnosis[item='Pneumonia' or item='Ulcer']
       subject="groups//Nurse"/>
```

The first rule says that nurses are forbidden to see the trees the root of which is a diagnosis element which includes an item equal to Cancer or Pneumonia.
The second rule says that nurses are permitted to see the trees the root of which is a diagnosis element which includes an item equal to Ulcer or Pneumonia.
Clearly none of the `XPath` expressions for the `object` attribute is more specific than the other making difficult to predict what is going to happen if a nurse asks for an access to a diagnosis element which includes an item equal to Pneumonia.
We could show many examples like this where a human cannot possibly predict which rule is going to preempt the others.

2. Our prototype of security processor is based on `XSLT` (see section 4). The conflict resolution policy of `XSLT` processors mainly uses priorities and has been proved to be efficient.

In any case, whatever the conflict resolution policy is, we think that the Security Administrator has to be provided with some graphical policy debugging tools. Indeed defining and debugging security policies for tree data structures is not an easy task.

3.5 Highly Expressive Security Policy

The example that we used in the previous section is very simple and does not completely show the power of our model. The aim of this section is to show that our model allows us to express complex security policies easily. In particular we can define security policies supporting the concept of exception, the definition of content-based authorisation rules and the insertion of cover stories in the source document.

Consider our previous source document into which a new record has been inserted:

```
...
<record id="pfranck">
    <name>Patricia Frank</name>
    <diagnosis>
        <item>Cancer</item>
        <item coverstory="yes">Ulcer</item>
        <comments>life expectancy is limited to two years</comments>
    </diagnosis>
</record>
...
```

Patricia Franck is a new patient. She has a cancer. Her life expectancy is limited to two years. The item saying that she has an ulcer is a cover story. A cover story is a lie inserted in the source document in order to hide the existence of a sensitive information. Attribute `coverstory="yes"` informs users who are permitted to see everything that `ulcer` is a lie (see [10] for more information about cover stories and cover story management).

The XSS subject sheet is extended as follows:

```
...
  <users>
     ...
     <member id="pfranck"><name>Patricia Franck</name></member>
     <member id="gfranck"><name>Georges Franck</name></member>
     ...
  </users>
...
    <Patient>
        <member idref="pfranck"/>
        <member idref="mrobert"/>
    </Patient>
    <Family>
        ...
        <Franck>
           <member idref="gfranck"/>
           <member idref="pfranck"/>
        </Franck>
    </Family>
...
```

Patricia Franck and Georges Franck are new users. The *Franck* family is a new group. The XAS sheet is extended as follows:

```
...
<!-- P O L I C Y   F O R   P A T R I C I A   F R A N C K -->
<!-- Rule 5 -->
<rule  access  = "grant"    object = "record[@id='pfranck']"
       subject = "groups/Family/Franck"   />
<!-- Rule 6 -->
<rule  access  = "deny"     object = "record[@id='pfranck']//comments"
       subject = "groups/Family/Franck"      />
<!-- Rule 7 -->
<rule  access  = "deny"
       object="record[@id='pfranck']//comments/text()"
       subject = "groups//*[name()='Nurse']" />
<!-- Rule 8 -->
<rule  access  = "deny"     object = "item[contains(text(),'Cancer')]"
       subject = "users/member[@id='pfranck']" />
<!-- Rule 9 -->
<rule  access  = "grant"    object = "item[@coverstory='yes']"
       subject = "users/member[@id='pfranck']" />
<!-- Rule 10 -->
<rule  access  = "deny"     object = "item/@coverstory"
       subject = "users/member[@id='pfranck']" />
</xas>
```

Rule 5 says that the Franck family is permitted to see the data of Patricia Franck. Rule 6 says that the Franck family (including Patricia) is forbidden to see the `comments` element of Patricia Franck's medical record. Rule 7 says that nurses are forbidden to see the text of the `comments` element of

Patricia Franck's medical record. Note that rule 6 addresses the `comments` element itself. This means that the sub-tree of which the `comments` element is the root is protected. Rule 7 only protects the text of the `comments` elements. Rule 8 says that P. Franck is forbidden to see the `item` which says that she has a cancer. Rule 8 is a perfect example of a *content-based* authorisation rule. Rule 9 says that P. Franck is permitted to see the `item` which is a cover story ... but Rule 10 says that P. Franck is forbidden to know that the `item` is a cover story.

Rules 5 to 10 show that P. Franck is not considered as a standard patient. The default hospital policy does not apply to her. Doctors consider that for some psychological reasons, Patricia Franck must not know that she has a cancer. Therefore, doctors have decided to lie to Patricia Franck and to tell her that she has an ulcer. The family are told about this lie and are granted the permission to see the personal data of P. Franck. However the element saying that the life expectancy of P Franck is limited to two years must remain strictly confidential. Even nurses are forbidden to know this fact. The views for some of the users are listed below:

View for J. Durand (Nurse)

```
<files>
<record id="pfranck">
    <name>Patricia Frank</name>
    <diagnosis>
        <item>Cancer</item>
        <item
coverstory="yes">Ulcer</item>
        <comments/>
    </diagnosis>
</record>
<record id="mrobert">
    <name>Martin Robert</name>
    <diagnosis>
        <item>Pneumonia</item>
    </diagnosis>
</record>
</files>
```

Jacqueline Durand is a nurse. She can see everything except the content of the `comments` element.

View for G. Franck (Franck Family)

```
<files>
<record id="pfranck">
    <name>Patricia Frank</name>
    <diagnosis>
        <item>Cancer</item>
        <item
coverstory="yes">Ulcer</item>
    </diagnosis>
</record>
</files>
```

Georges Franck has access to the medical file of Patricia Franck. He knows that doctors have decided to tell Patricia Franck a lie regarding her illness. He is not aware of the existence of the `comments` element.

View for P. Franck (Patient)

```
<files>
<record id="pfranck">
    <name>Patricia Frank</name>
    <diagnosis>
        <item>Ulcer</item>
    </diagnosis>
</record>
</files>
```

Patricia Franck believes that she has an ulcer.

This example has shown us that we have the possibility of defining default security policies which can be overridden by specific policies for some particular cases.

Finally note that, in [3], authors define the concept of *instance level* and *DTD level* authorisation sheet. An instance level authorisation sheet only applies to a specific XML document. A DTD level authorisation sheet applies to a set of documents which conform to a specific DTD. Our model allows us to define such a *DTD level* authorisation sheet. If both a DTD level XAS sheet and an instance level XAS sheet apply to a specific XML document then the instance level authorisation rules are appended to the DTD level authorisation rules in a *global* XAS sheet. In other words, the global XAS sheet contains the authorisation rules expressed at the DTD level followed by the rules expressed at the instance level. The global XAS sheet is then used to compute the different views. We can mention that choosing relevant priority levels allows us to define both DTD rules which can be overridden (low priority) at the instance level and mandatory DTD rules which cannot be overridden (high priority).

4. SKETCH OF IMPLEMENTATION

We have developed an XSLT-based prototype of a security processor which implements our model. Our prototype is available online at `http://sis.univ-tln.fr/XML-secu`. Figure 2 describes the prototype.

Our prototype is integrated into the framework of an Apache Web server[4] which uses Tomcat[5] as a server for Java Servlets. Views of a source document are dynamically computed by using the Cocoon[6] publishing framework for XML data. In figure 2, the document to be protected is `Doc.XML`. `Doc.XAS` is the global XAS sheet. `Subjects.XSS` describes the subjects.

[4] http://www.apache.org

[5] http://jakarta.apache.org/tomcat/index.html

[6] http://xml.apache.org/cocoon/index.html

1. Easy-to-read authorisation rules expressed in `Doc.XAS` are translated into `XSLT` rules (*templates*) producing an XSL sheet (`Doc.XSL`). This translation is performed by the `XSLT` processor by applying `xas2xsl.XSL`. This translation is performed *once*. After this operation, the `XAS` sheet is no longer used unless it is updated (in this case, it is automatically retranslated). `Doc.XSL` is saved into the cache.

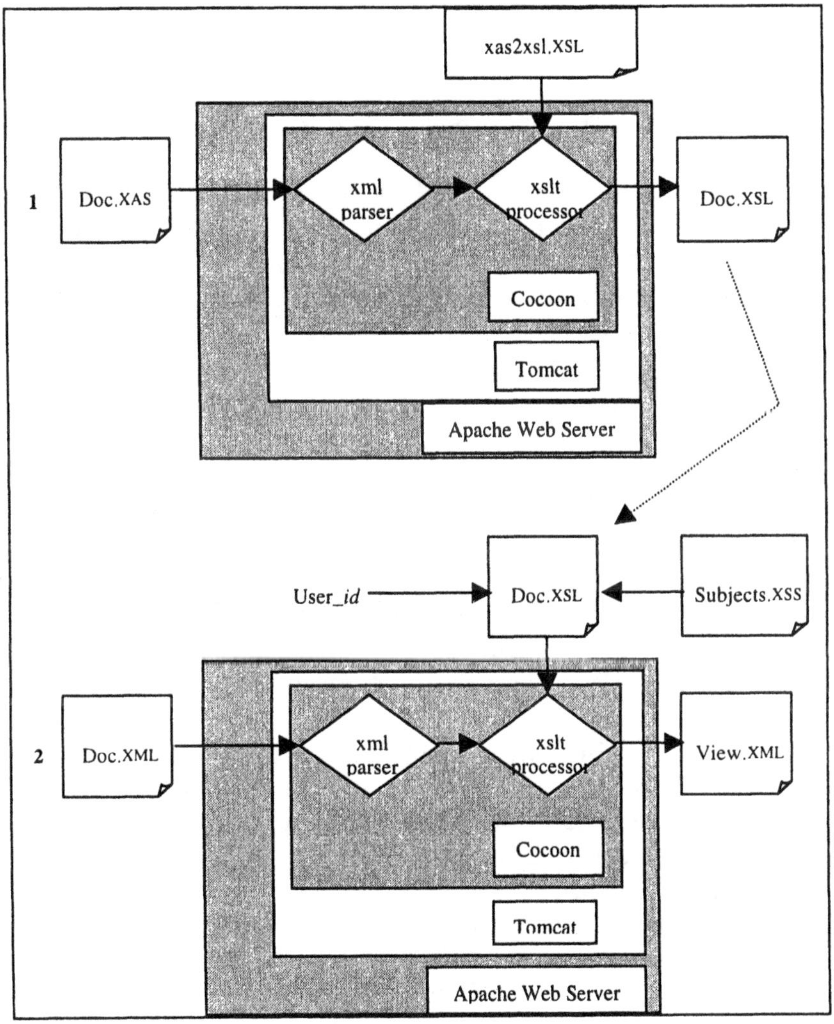

Figure 2: Prototype

2. If a user requests access to `Doc.XML` then he is provided with a view of the document which is compatible with his rights. This view is produced by the `XSLT` processor by applying `Doc.XSL`. Templates contained in

Doc.XSL are used by the XSLT processor to compute the view according to the algorithm defined in section 3.4. Doc.XSL requires, as parameters, the user *id* (transmitted as a parameter by the Web server after the user has been authenticated) and Subjects.XSS. The view is also saved into the cache.

5. RELATED WORK

Compared with other models, our model offers several advantages. Our model allows us to write security policies with a high expressive power since any node from an XML document can be independently protected (element, attribute, text ...). The semantics of an authorisation rule is unique and precisely defined. Our conflict resolution policy is simple, efficient and adapted to an XSLT processor. Our model offers the possibility of defining content-based authorisation rules. Our proposal fully respects the W3C recommendation since we use the XPath language to address XML fragments and the XSLT language to compute the views. In [3], the semantics of an authorisation varies. An authorisation can be local (in this case it applies to an element and its attributes) or it can be recursive (in this case, it applies also to the sub-elements). The expressive power is limited since nodes like text nodes cannot be independently protected. Moreover, the conflict resolution policy is quite complex. In [4] the semantics of an authorisation is defined as *polymorphic*, that is, it varies according to the protected object. The model does not include the possibility of protecting all kinds of nodes. In [5], the model does not offer the possibility of protecting attribute or text nodes independently. None of these three models fully exploits the XPath language.

Our prototype also offers many advantages compared with other prototypes. We use a standard XSLT processor to compute the views. Therefore, we can choose among existing XSLT processors (Apache[7], Oracle[8], IBM) the one with the best performances. If there is a new W3C recommendation for the XML, XPath, and XSLT languages, then the only thing we have to do is to replace the XML parser and the XSLT processor with an XML parser and an XSLT processor which conform to the new recommendation. Integration of our prototype into the framework of an existing Web Server is also straightforward. In prototypes [11][12][13] which implement the models defined in [3][4][5], the views are produced by proprietary processors written in Java. These processors do not have the

[7] http://xml.apache.org/xalan

[8] http://technet.oracle.com/tech/xml/

power and the performances of an XSLT processor. Moreover these processors need to be reprogrammed each time there is a new W3C recommendation.

6. CONCLUSION

In this paper, we have defined a model for regulating access to XML documents. We plan to extend this model in several directions:

- We are exploring the possibility of defining *provisional* authorisations. In [5] a provisional authorisation rule is defined as a rule which tells the user that his request will be authorised provided he or the system takes certain security actions.
- In the model described in this paper we implicitly assumed that users do not have access to the DTDs. Further versions of our model will include the possibility of protecting portions of DTDs or XML schemas.
- In this paper, we restricted ourselves to the *read* privilege. Indeed, the read privilege is the most important privilege to consider regarding documents which are published on the WEB. However, we plan to extend our model (and our prototype) with the *write* privilege.

REFERENCES

[1] T. Bray et al. "Extensible Markup Language (XML) 1.0". World Wide Web Consortium (W3C). http://www.w3c.org/TR/REC-xml (October 2000).

[2] M. Bartel et al. "XML-Signature Syntax and Processing". W3C Candidate Recommendation. http://www.w3c.org/TR/xmldsig-core (October-2000).

[3] E. Damiani, S. De Capitani di Vimercati, S. Paraboschi, P. Samarati, "Securing XML Documents," in Proc. of the 2000 International Conference on Extending Database Technology (EDBT2000), Konstanz, Germany, March 27-31, 2000.

[4] E. Bertino, S. Castano, E. Ferrari and M. Mesiti. "Specifying and Enforcing Access Control Policies for XML Document Sources". World Wide Web Journal, vol. 3, n. 3, Baltzer Science Publishers.

[5] M. Kudo and S. Hada. "XML Document Security based on Provisional Authorisation". Proceedings of the 7th ACM conference on Computer and communications security. November, 2000, Athens Greece.

[6] A. Gabillon, E. Bruno. "A Filtering Model for XML documents". WWW10 Conference Workshop on Information Filtering. Hong Kong, May 2001.

[7] J. Clark. "XSL Transformations (XSLT) Version 1.0". World Wide Web Consortium (W3C). http://www.w3c.org/TR/xslt (November 1999).

[8] J. Clark et al.. "XML Path Language (XPath) Version 1.0". World Wide Web Consortium (W3C). http://www.w3c.org/TR/xpath (November 1999).

[9] S. Jajodia, P. Samarati, V. Subrahmanian and E. Bertino. A Unified Framework for Enforcing Multiple Access Control Policies. Proc. of the 1997 ACM International SIGMOD Conference on Management of Data, Tucson, May 1997.

[10] F. Cuppens, A. Gabillon. "Cover Story Management". Data and Knowledge Engineering Vol 37/2, 2001, pp 177-201.

[11] E. Damiani, S. De Capitani di Vimercati, S. Paraboschi, P. Samarati "XML Access Control Systems: A Component-Based Approach" in Proc. IFIP WG11.3 Working Conference on Database Security, Schoorl, The Netherlands, August 21-23, 2000.

[12] E. Bertino, M. Braun, S. Castano, E. Ferrari, M. Mesiti. "AuthorX: A Java-Based System for XML Data Protection". In Proc. of the 14th Annual IFIP WG 11.3 Working Conference on Database Security, Schoorl, The Netherlands, August 2000.

[13] AlphaWorks. XML Security Suite (xss4j). http://www.alphaWorks.ibm.com/tech/xmlsecuritysuite.

IX

PANEL AND DISCUSSION

PANEL ON XML AND SECURITY

Sylvia Osborn
The University of Western Ontario, London, Canada
sylvia@csd.uwo.ca

Bhavani Thuraisingham
Mitre Corporation, USA
thura@mitre.org

Pierangela Samarati
Dip. di Tecnologie dell'Informazione — Università di Milano, 20163 Crema, Italy
samarati@dti.unimi.it

1. INTRODUCTION BY SYLVIA OSBORN

The panelists were asked to address the question: "XML security: are all the problems solved?" As we can see from the following sections, a large number of issues are being addressed by the www community as well as by the database security community related to XML and security. Both contributers indicate that there is a great deal of interesting research still to be done in this area.

2. POSITION BY B. THURAISINGHAM

Recently there has been increasing interest in developing access control models for XML documents. Since XML is becoming the standard document representation for the web, and XML extensions are being proposed for all types of documents including multimedia documents, it is critical that these documents are secure.

There are various aspects to securing XML documents. These include encryption, access control, and authentication. In providing access control for XML documents, one of the major challenges is the level of granularity. Should entire XML documents be protected or should access be granted depending on the content of the document, or to portions of the document? For example if John cannot have access to say information represented by a node in an XML document, then should John be denied access to all information emanating from that node? How can access be granted based on content of the document? What is the access control policy for XML documents? How should XML documents be updated? Is there an update policy for XML documents? How can inference threats be handled for XML documents? How can role-based access control policies be implemented?

Various standards groups are now working on securing XML documents. One question that arises often is what is the difference between securing XML documents and securing object models? In fact we can learn a lot from our experiences in developing access control for object database systems. We need to reuse the known techniques and models as much as possible if they make sense for XML documents. However XML also has its own features including XML and document type definitions. Therefore we need to ensure that appropriate security mechanisms are developed for XML documents.

Closely related to XML security is security for RDF (Resource Description Framework) and the Semantic Web. The World Wide Web consortium is actively involved in coming up with RDF specifications and providing the directions for the semantic web. XML security is just the first step toward securing the semantic web. We need to examine security for RDF, agents and many other technologies before we can develop security policies for the semantic web. It is critical that we examine security for the semantic web while various specifications are being developed.

3. POSITION BY PIERANGELA SAMARATI

Several works have recently addressed the topics of XML and security. With reference to authorization-based approaches, the relationships between the two topics can be distinguished as:

- protecting XML documents;
- protecting XML-based services;
- XML as a security specification language.

Protecting XML documents

Recent years have witnessed a tremendous growth in Web publishing and Web-based applications. At the early stage, Web publishing was associated with the release of information to be made publicly available. The subsequent increased use of the Web as a data communication medium introduced the need for selective publishing where documents and portions of them needed to be made accessible only to specific requestors. However, the variety of the format of documents to be published and the lack of a structure for them limited the specification of access restrictions: documents were simply viewed as files and their protection enforced by the operating system. For instance, the Apache server (www.apache.org) allows the specifications of access control lists via a configuration file containing the list of users, hosts (IP addresses) or host/user pairs, that must be allowed or forbidden connection to the server. The consideration of both positive and negative authorizations, together with a user-specified priority order for resolving conflicts among them and establishing a default policy ("allow, deny" vs "deny, allow"), introduce some flexibility in the specification of protection requirements [10]. However, the coarse granularity at which authorizations are supported does not addresses real protection needs, as a single document may indeed contain data with different protection requirements and enforcing them would require splitting the document in different files, possibly organized in different directories, each subject to its own security specifications. While this solution can reach the intended result, it is quite awkward and difficult to administer in practice. An attempt to provide a finer grained access control was proposed in [9] allowing the specification of authorizations with reference to specific portions of HTML documents (delimited by properly defined tags). However, conventional HTML tagging is aimed at defining page rendering and is seldom, if ever, related to information granulation. In fact HTML provides no clean separation between the structure and the layout of the document. Moreover, site designers often prepare HTML pages according to the needs of a particular browser. Therefore HTML markup has generally little to do with data semantics. The introduction and wide diffusion of XML (eXtensible Markup Language), maintaining formatting and rendering capabilities while providing semantics-aware markup techniques, represented the opportunity to overcome the limitation of free formatting in expressing access control restrictions. The attention of access control research therefore shifted to specification and enforcement of authorizations for XML documents.

XML provides several advantages. First, it allows reference to specific elements and attributes within the documents, thus permitting the specification and enforcement of different access restrictions within each document. Such capability is further made more advantageous by the ability of exploiting languages (such as XPath) to identify elements and attributes within a document in an expressive way. By exploiting such languages, not only authorizations can be referred to specific elements/attributes within a document, but the elements/attributes to which an authorization refers can be specified based on properties they satisfy (content-dependent authorizations). For instance, an authorization could specify that all employees could access the details (results and funding) of internal research on the web library, where whether research is considered 'internal' is specified as a value of some element in the documents. A further advantage of exploiting XML for access control is given by the hierarchical relationship [7] between document instances and the related DTD/schema, that allows the support of authorizations for single documents as well as sets of them. Several proposals have therefore been studied which joined current trends in providing flexibility in authorizations [10] with the fine-granularity and expressiveness advantages of XML and related query languages.

The definition of an access control model for XML documents pointed out several issues to be addressed, including:

- The identification of different *semantics for authorizations related to different propagation options*, such as in the case of element-level authorizations which may need to be supported with a recursive or local semantics (depending on whether authorizations on an element propagate on its sub-elements).
- The identification of different *resolution policies for solving conflicts* between authorizations. Among the policies to be supported, the one based on the most specific relationship among authorization objects (e.g., a document is more specific than its schema, and an attribute is more specific than the element in which it is defined) like in traditional hierarchical systems [7]. Since no single solution can fit all the needs, a way of subverting the predefined policy should be supported [2] together with alternative solutions [1, 6, 7].
- The identification of *processing techniques for enforcing authorizations and determining the view to be returned to requestors*. Among the issues to be addresses in this respect is how to deal with cases where an element should not be returned while part of its content should. In fact, authorization enforcement could lead to the result that a document's element (e.g., an article) should not be released to a requestor but one of its sub-element (e.g., the article's abstract) should be (e.g., because of a more specific positive authorization overriding the negative authorization on the element). What should the system do? At least three different approaches could be identified: *1)* return the sub-element but completely hide the element; *2)* return the sub-element and the tag for the element, to preserve the document's structure; *3)* hide the element together with its whole content (including the sub-element which could instead be released). The first solution, while strictly enforcing the requirements, has the drawback of loosing the document's structure and therefore the semantics of the data returned. Based on this argument, the second solution was adopted in [2] returning the start and end tag of elements with undefined or negative authorizations that have a descendant with a positive authorization. The third approach was instead proposed in the context of SOAP call filtering [4] (cf. next section).
- The identification of where *authorizations are stored*. Two different approaches could be taken in this respect. The first solution consists in

attaching authorizations directly to the elements on which they are specified. This is, for instance, what happens today where specific pairs user-password are associated with portions of HTML web-pages. It is also the solution adopted for the specification of fine-grained encryption [5]. The main drawback of such an approach is that it does not obey the principle of separation between data (and data model) and security specification [10]. An alternative approach attaches to each document/schema an authorization sheet [2].

- The definition of the *authorization's format and syntax*. Exploiting XML's own capability, several proposals have adopted recursive approaches, where *authorizations are expressed in XML*. These approaches have started the line of efforts on the definition of an XML-based authorization language.

Several points still remains to be fully investigated. Among them:

- *Balancing expressiveness and performance*. Enforcing access control requires the evaluation of the path expressions in the authorizations and the computation of the view to be returned to requestors based on authorizations applicable to the different elements/attributes. Performance issues become particularly critical, since XPath is a rich programming language that permits the definition of search expressions requiring exponential time for their evaluation. However, several works identify restrictions on XPath that reduce its complexity characteristics, keeping a level of expressibility adequate for most situations [2]. Another issue to be considered with reference to performance is how to actually compute the document view. For instance, [2] uses an approach based on the use of the Document Object Model (DOM), computing and uploading the DOM for the document for authorization enforcement.

- *Extending actions*. Although modification actions (write and update) have been considered by recent work for XML document protection [2], no consensus has emerged up to now in the research community on a model for XML updates. As research progresses there, access controls for update operations can be refined accordingly.

- *Query-based access control*. All approaches consider access control on a document basis (assuming each request refers to a specific document). In several applications, requests may be submitted as queries spanning several documents or portions of them. Access control should therefore be extended to the consideration of such requests.

Securing XML-based e-services

XML-based approaches have been proposed for lightweight network protocols and distributed applications, such as XML-RPC (www.xmlrpc.com) and SOAP (www.w3.org/2000/xp). For instance, SOAP defines a mechanism to pass commands and parameters between HTTP clients and servers and uses XML for data encoding and is therefore independent from the operating system, programming language, or object model used on either the server or the client side. Leveraging the XML encoding used by SOAP for both service invocations and responses, Damiani et al. [4] proposed an approach for protecting SOAP-based e-services. The approach extended and refined the author's proposal for protecting XML documents. Every SOAP invocation and its response are intercepted by the access control module that evaluates them against the specified restrictions to service accessibility. Depending on the restrictions to be enforced the request may: be rejected; be allowed as is; be filtered or executed in a modified form, where filtering of a request may involve elimination of some of its parameters that the current invoker is not allowed to specify. Service requestors are characterized by custom headers included in SOAP calls which accommodate for specifying the subjects identity, their roles, and possible digital certificates they can present. The specification of security restrictions directly on invocations and their responses provided a way of avoiding firewall dependence for the enforcement of security restrictions and of supporting fine-grained security constraints.

XML as a security specification language

Recent research in access control has been targeted to enriching the expressiveness and the flexibility of the authorization specification language. Most effective proposals are based on the use of logic languages (e.g., [7]). Logic-based proposals provide the needed flexibility and expressiveness; however they are not always easily accepted by end users. The wide accepted use of XML, its flexibility, expressiveness, and interoperability brought to efforts investigating the use of XML as a security specification language. The use of XML as an authorization specification language was already noticed within proposals for protecting XML documents, which recursively represented authorizations as XML documents [2, 8]. As another example, ContenGuard is developing an eXtensible Rights Markup Language (XrML) 2.0 (www.xrml.org) for fine-grained rights control on document-like content and on Web-based services.

OASIS (Organization for the Advancement of Structured Information Standards), a nonprofit international consortium that creates interoperable industry specifications based on public standards, has recently started a standardization effort on the use of XML-based languages to express and interchange access control policies. The effort is carried out by the OASIS eXtensible Access

Control Markup Language (XACML) technical committee whose goal is to define a standard core schema and corresponding namespace for the expression of authorization policies in XML against objects that can be themselves identified in XML. Exploiting the flexibility of XML, the committee is studying the definition of a schema that can represent existing authorization specification approaches and that can express different protection requirements. Moreover, the semi-structured feature of XML provides a powerful means for specifying authorizations whose validity depends on properties that requestors can satisfy (like enjoying a role, or belonging to a group).

Acknowledgments

Pierangela Samarati would like to thank Ernesto Damiani, Sabrina De Capitani di Vimercati, and Stefano Paraboschi: the observations reported here result from discussions and joint work with them.

References

[1] E. Bertino, S. Castano, and E. Ferrari Securing XML documents with author-x. *IEEE Internet Computing*, 5(3):21–31, May/June 2001.

[2] E. Damiani, S. De Capitani di Vimercati, S. Paraboschi, and P. Samarati. A fine-grained access control system for xml documents. *ACM Transactions on Information and System Security*, 2000. (to appear).

[3] E. Damiani, S. De Capitani di Vimercati, S. Paraboschi, and P. Samarati Securing XML Documents. *Proc. of EDBT 2000*, Volume 1777 of *Lecture Notes in Computer Science*, Konstanz, Germany, March 2000.

[4] E. Damiani, S. De Capitani di Vimercati, S. Paraboschi, and P. Samarati. Securing SOAP e-services. *International Journal of Information Security (IJIS)*, 2002. (to appear).

[5] D. Eastlake, J. Reagle, and D. Solo. *XML-Signature Syntax and Processing*, March 2001. ftp://ftp.rfc-editor.org/in-notes/rfc3075.txt.

[6] A. Gabillon and E. Bruno. Regulating access to XML documents. In *Proceedings of the Fifteenth Annual IFIP WG 11.3 Conference on Database Security*, Niagara on the Lake, Ontario, Canada, July 2001.

[7] S. Jajodia, P. Samarati, M.L. Sapino, and V.S. Subrahmanian. Flexible support for multiple access control policies. *ACM Transactions on Database Systems*, 26(2):214–260, June 2001.

[8] M. Kudoh and S. Hada. Xml document security based on provisional authorizations. In *ACM Computer and Communications Security Conference, (ACM CCS'2000)*, Athens, Greece, November 2000.

[9] P. Samarati, E. Bertino, and S. Jajodia. An authorization model for a distributed hypertext system. *IEEE Transactions on Knowledge and Data Engineering*, 8(4):555–562, August 1996.

[10] P. Samarati and S. De Capitani di Vimercati. Access control: Policies, models, and mechanisms. In R. Focardi and R. Gorrieri, editors, *Foundations of Security Analysis and Design*, LNCS 2171. Springer-Verlag, 2001.

SELECTED SUMMARY OF DISCUSSIONS

David L. Spooner and Martin S. Olivier

1. RECENT ADVANCES IN INFORMATION SYSTEMS SECURITY, *JAJODIA*

Rosenthal: Can you partition the world into objects requiring different types of access control policies?

Jajodia: The real world needs different types of policies. Currently this is often done within application systems. We would like to be able to do it in the operating system.

Rosenthal: Administration of access control policies may be the biggest impediment in the real world.

Rosenthal: Can you have different policies on the same objects?

Jajodia: You could do it, but it would be very complex.

Samarati: Using logic rules to represent policies, you can do it.

Rosenthal: Few database administrators would be able to handle the specification of such access control policies. An important research question is how can we make specification of access control policies easier.

Rosenthal: Are security rules with imperatives (e.g., add a proprietary notice to a returned document) a good idea? This could cause things to happen with the user unaware and which the user could consider undesirable.

Jajodia: The owner of an object must understand the policy being enforced for that object. This idea still needs some work.

2. ROLE-BASED ACCESS CONTROL ON THE WEB USING LDAP, *PARK*, *AHN*, AND *SANDHU*

Tan: Suppose the link between the Role Server and Web Server breaks. In the Server-Pull case, the user would not be able to access anything. What about in the User-Pull case?

Park: If the user gets his/her roles from the Role Server before the link breaks, then the user can still access the web. Therefore, the User-Pull case is less vulnerable to a single point of failure.

Audience: One can have redundant Role Servers to minimize this problem.

Ting: You must be careful in the User-Pull case that the user cannot modify the roles that he/she gets from the Role Server.

Gudes: You have a role hierarchy. How much of the hierarchy must be pulled to the user or the Web Server?

Sandhu: You must pull the entire relevant path in the hierarchy.

Rosenthal: What does the end-user need to know to use your system?

Park: In the User-Pull case, the user needs to know about the Role Server.

Rosenthal: Most users won't want to have to know about the Role Server.

3. CONSTRAINTS-BASED ACCESS CONTROL, *TAN*

Rosenthal: Doesn't the Turing completeness of the constraints make them hard to verify?

Tan: Yes, but subsets are verifiable.

Samarati: The predicates that you use in your rules don't appear to be predefined in your language. Therefore, how does this differ from previous work using logic rules?

Tan: We are working now to define a small set of predicates for the language.

Samarati: Do you keep a list of things that have been revoked?

Tan: Yes.

Rosenthal: There is a general problem of using a database of access control rules to control access to a database. Using logic rules is a good way to frame this problem. Is it better to use logic to implement the access controls or is it better to use the database system itself? The answer in general is not clear.

Gudes: This approach is useful for verifying the validity of an access request.

Rosenthal: You might use this approach to explore what happens when access polices are embedded in logic. Which is better, an efficient SQL-based system or a less efficient logic based system? Maybe security will be the killer application for logic databases.

Tan: We must figure out how to constrain the language so that it always works efficiently.

Jajodia: This is all fine as long as logic doesn't make the specification of policies harder.

Sandhu: This is yet another language that programmers will need to learn.

4. SUBJECT SWITCHING ALGORITHMS FOR ACCESS CONTROL IN FEDERATED DATABASES, *YANG*, *WIJESEKERA*, AND *JAJODIA*

Rosenthal: Do you see this as an interactive tool for use during schema design, a decision aid?

Wijesekera: Yes.

Rosenthal: There are some similarities here to work done on role comparisons and merging by Sylvia Osborn and her students.

5. EFFICIENT DAMAGE ASSESSMENT AND REPAIR IN RESILIENT DISTRIBUTED DATABASE SYSTEMS, *LIU* AND *HAO*

Jajodia: What happens when a site fails?

Liu: You cannot afford to wait for it to recover. One is forced to leave the damaged site damaged.

Jajodia: In this case, damage can spread.

Audience: How do you make sure that repairs to a database are faster than the transactions executing against the database?

Liu: One technique is to use priorities on transactions.

6. STATE-DEPENDENT SECURITY DECISIONS FOR DISTRIBUTED OBJECT-SYSTEMS, *BISKUP* AND *LEINEWEBER*

Audience: Can the final state from one decision be the same as the initial state for the next one?

Leineweber: Yes, but it is better to separate them to keep the definitions cleaner.

7. REORGANIZATION OF DATABASE LOG FOR INFORMATION WARFARE DATA RECOVERY, SOBHAN AND *PANDA*

Panda: We need the source code logic to implement redo in the log.

Rosenthal: It will be difficult to get people to use only languages that your system supports so that you can process the source code logic.

Liu: The logic is needed in this approach because it maintains the original order of the transactions.

Rosenthal: Source code logic may not be available for all transactions.

Jajodia: Maintaining the original serial order of the transaction requires much more work than other approaches.

Liu: Redo may kill some transactions since their preconditions are no longer met.

8. RANDOMLY ROVING AGENTS FOR INTRUSION DETECTION, *MOSKOWITZ*, *KANG*, *CHANG*, AND *LONGDON*

Jajodia: Can you give us an example of an attack that your agents will detect?

Kang: A checksum attach is an example.

9. PUBLIC TELEPHONE NETWORK (PTN) VULNERABILITIES, *LORENZ, KELLER, MANES, HALE AND SHENOI*

Reid: Do you have the differences between optical fiber and copper in mind?

Lorenz: Those are hardware issues. The taxonomy deals with software threats.

10. FLEXIBLE SECURITY POLICIES IN SQL, *BARKER* AND *ROSENTHAL*

Gudes: How does the translation algorithm work?

Rosenthal: Stage 1: translate to SQL (without materialization). Stage 2: decide what to materialize. Step 2 is based on guesses. One therefore needs experimental results upon which to base a decision for step 2.

11. THE INFERENCE PROBLEM AND UPDATES IN RELATIONAL DATABASES, *FARKAS*, *TOLAND*, AND *EASTMAN*

Rosenthal: A 2% improvement may not give much protection.

Farkas: Results are application-dependent.

Rosenthal: Have people tried to do this sort of thing in real systems?

Jajodia: No, the closest is statistical databases.

Rosenthal: It is likely that few organizations will be willing to pay the overhead.

Farkas: The approach can be made more efficient and then some companies might be willing to use it.

Rosenthal: The cost-benefit analysis may be weak in most cases.

Jajodia: It could be used for the web where you consider that you have a single user (i.e., the general public).

Rosenthal: I agree that we need to do inference analysis.

Spalka: Does requesting all information in one query circumvent security?

Farkas: No, related items will not be released together.

Audience: It appears that your approach cannot deal with an attack from multiple collaborating users.

Farkas: This is future work. One idea is to monitor groups of users as a single user.

Jajodia: We don't know how things will turn out in the future, so this sort of work could be important.

12. MANAGING CLASSIFIED DOCUMENTS IN A RELATIONAL DATABASE, *SPALKA*

Samarati: In your approach, when you lie, a high user must login as high to delete the high tuple, then logout, and finally login again at the low level to delete the lie. Polyinstantiation takes care of this automatically.

Spalka: A high user needs to remember lies and when to delete them. There is a trade-off between easy of use and level of confidentiality.

13. ODAM: AN ON-THE-FLY DAMAGE ASSESSMENT AND REPAIR SYSTEM FOR COMMERCIAL DATABASE APPLICATIONS, *LUENAM* AND *LIU*

Mukkamala: The approach doesn't appear to capture other types of dependencies such as semantic dependencies.

Jajodia: Semantic dependencies are difficult to capture.

Farkas: Cleaning transactions cause a significant performance penalty when there are lots of dependencies.

Liu: The use of a proxy is the biggest reason for this.

Farkas: Would it be better to stop the database and clean it periodically rather than continuously slowing it down?

Liu: Many applications do not want the database to be halted.

Ting: What do you do about users who get the wrong answer?

Liu: We are concerned about this, but we can't do much about it. There are problems at both the logical and the physical levels. We deal here with only the physical level.

14. PANEL: XML DATABASES – ARE ALL THE PROBLEMS SOLVED?

Osborn: XML is similar to the old hierarchical databases. Maybe we can leverage security concepts from old hierarchical database systems.

Rosenthal: As query languages improve for XML databases, we should be able to do more and more with the queries themselves.

Samarati: It is not clear how to make decisions when queries overlap. Negative authorizations can be a problem. It may be necessary to translate to finer grain objects to make decisions.

Thuraisingham: How similar are XML databases to object-oriented databases.

Samarati: There are similarities and differences.

Ting: XML is replacing the Electronic Data Interchange (EDI) format for electronic commerce. Certification and authentication of documents is a real problem.

Thuraisingham: eBXML is designed to handle electronic commerce applications.

Rosenthal: In many cases, required access controls should be the same regardless of the document type.

Samarati: You may want to encrypt or sign different parts of a document separately.

Gudes: XML isn't really a hierarchy but is more a graph. So you really need authorization based on path expressions.

Samarati: This would be true if you allow cross-links between documents that have different access control requirements. However, in practice you often don't allow cross-links in such cases.

Gudes: Does any research work consider these issues?

Samarati: The work of Samarati, Bertino and Jajodia ["An Authorization Model for a Distributed Hypertext System," *IEEE Transactions on Knowledge and Data Engineering*, August 1996, Vol. 8, No. 4, pp. 555-562.] considers this. You usually don't want propagation across links between documents.

Rosenthal: XML captures more of the real world complexity and we need to exploit this. It provides both elegance and simplicity. Using queries and views of XML documents may be one way to pull the concepts together into one framework.

Samarati: Views are not necessarily simpler and may be less powerful.

Rosenthal: These issues are worth exploration by the research community.

15. A COMPARISON BETWEEN CONSA AND CURRENT LINUX SECURITY IMPLEMENTATIONS, *HARDY* AND *OLIVIER*

Gudes: Do you view your work as a front-end to heterogeneous systems?

Hardy: That is one way to use it. It can also be used by applications to enforce application security.

Atluri: Do you assume that security levels are hierarchical in LOMAC?

Hardy: Yes.

Rosenthal: It should also work with a lattice of security classifications.

Hardy: It was originally intended for operating systems where a hierarchy is usually sufficient.

Olivier: The original paper shows that it can handle a lattice.

16. A NOVEL APPROACH TO CERTIFICATION REVOCATION MANAGEMENT, *MUKKAMALA* AND *JAJODIA*

Rosenthal: Managing CA's is extra overhead.

Rosenthal: This is similar to the web caching problem. Trusted replication is an interesting problem and is a general instance of this problem.

Audience: What is the communications overhead?

Jajodia: There is a cost going to a CAD and you may not always need the most up to date data. In this case, if you are not willing to pay the extra cost each time, you can use the CA.

Gudes: What happens if a CA is revoked?

Mukkamala: Users must go back and get new certificates.

17. AN EXTENDED TRANSACTION CONTROL MODEL APPROACH FOR MULTILEVEL SECURE TRANSACTION PROCESSING, *ATLURI AND MUKKAMALA*

Farkas: Have you compared your work to that of Ray and Jajodia?

Atluri: They do not make provision for value constraints.

18. REGULATING ACCESS TO XML DOCUMENTS, *GABILLON* AND *BRUNO*

Spalka: How do you know when you need a cover story?

Gabillon: It is not like cover stories in mandatory access control. You decide when you want to use a cover story; the system gives you no assistance.

Jajodia: There is a distinction between a provision and an obligation. A provision is an action that your security server takes. An obligation is part of the data received by the user.

Gudes: Can you compare your system to other systems?

Gabillon: The semantics are different. In some systems, nodes can't be independently protected. For example, text nodes can't be independently protected. We have no propagation policy. There are different conflict resolution policies. We use priorities. We use XSLT to build the system. Other prototypes use Java. As a result we had to do much less programming.

www.ingramcontent.com/pod-product-compliance
Lightning Source LLC
LaVergne TN
LVHW020056220926
848484LV00002BB/585

* 9 7 8 1 4 0 2 0 7 0 4 1 9 *